LAW, MODERNITY, POSTMODERNITY

In memory of my parents,
Patrick and Anne

Law, Modernity, Postmodernity

Legal change in the contracting state

BRENDAN EDGEWORTH
University of New South Wales, Australia

Routledge
Taylor & Francis Group
LONDON AND NEW YORK

First published 2003 by Ashgate Publishing

Reissued 2019 by Routledge
2 Park Square, Milton Park, Abingdon, Oxon, OX14 4RN
52 Vanderbilt Avenue, New York, NY 10017

Routledge is an imprint of the Taylor & Francis Group, an informa business

A Library of Congress record exists under LC control number:

ISBN 13: 978-1-138-74199-7 (hbk)
ISBN 13: 978-1-315-18258-2 (ebk)

Contents

Preface vi
Acknowledgements ix

1 Legal and Social Change 1

2 Cognitive Mapping 18

3 Modern Law and the Welfare State 64

4 Old Theories, New Paradigm 98

5 Legal Postmodernization 133

6 Critique and Reform 206

7 What Next? 263

Bibliography 279
Index 297

Preface

In a world that appears to be changing at a faster rate than at any other time, writing about fundamental social and legal change presents many problems. Inevitably, the exercise is dogged by an uneasy feeling that by the time the story is told, the conclusions have ceased to be relevant, and the message is already out of date. Where the subject-matter is the nature and extent of change in contemporary legal institutions, this sentiment is no less justified. So, from the time this book was first conceived as an argument about the appearance of a period of decisive historical transition in law and legal systems, an uneasiness has overshadowed it, insinuating that many new developments would outstrip the original evidence, so that by the time it was finished, the initial hypothesis would already be old news. But, in what can perhaps be considered a fluke, more and more empirical detail has appeared to support the original argument: that is, that the recent changes to the law of the modern interventionist welfare state are so profound that it is possible to talk of the appearance of a discernibly new legal order, no less historically and sociologically distinctive than its predecessor.

A large body of scholarship has examined the extent to which the law and legal structure of the welfare state represented a decisive historical break with *its* precursor, modern liberal law. Analyses in this genre have tended, of necessity, to be conducted on a large scale, identifying broad shifts in the sphere of law by reference to wider social change. In the eyes of many commentators the transformation of the liberal state and its economy in the direction of the welfare state fuelled a range of legal reforms that seemed to have changed forever fundamental elements of modern legality.

From a similarly broad perspective, I want to argue that contemporary social change is evidenced by a range of no less profound shifts that reconfigure, undo or overtake many of the innovations introduced earlier by welfare states. These transformations include the array of supranational developments conveniently, if cumbersomely, termed "globalization"; the dismantling of welfare safety nets; the greater reliance on markets to restructure regulatory frameworks; and the progressive withdrawal of states from former areas of responsibility. This book attempts to explore how far those changes *cumulatively combine* to produce an historically different type of legal order. In doing so, it is necessary to examine critically the adequacy of those earlier accounts of legal change.

An exercise even more problematic than writing about rapid social and legal change may be the deployment of the "p" word to comprehend recent developments. Any reference to the much-used, and more-abused, epithet "postmodern", especially at the present time given its clearly and understandably waning popularity, may provoke ennui, enraged antipathy, or a lunge for the holy water bottle. Ironically, despite the connotations of temporal sequence implied by the prefix "post", this body of scholarship generally ignores contemporary sociological developments, preferring to elaborate a sense of lugubrious disenchantment about many key elements of the modern world. One objective of this book is to review critically the adequacy of this work for the purposes of understanding law. Despite my generally negative assessment of its overall contribution, partly for its refusal to take seriously questions of contemporary social change, I nonetheless want to argue that there are strands of theoretical insight discernible within the mass of that literature – under-explored in legal commentary – that do offer insightful perspectives on this very question. Exemplified most conspicuously and compellingly by Zygmunt Bauman's analysis of the empirical features of "postmodernity", this line of theoretical inquiry suggests that recent transformations require us to see the present social landscape (law included, as I shall argue) as a uniquely novel sociological and historical constellation.

The claim that fundamental change is upon us is not intended to mean that a revolutionary break has occurred. Social change does not generally present itself in the form of sharp cleavages between one stage of development and another. The legal structures of contemporary advanced societies retain important continuities with their predecessors. Accordingly, rather than announcing the wholesale dismantling of the edifice of modern law, my argument proposes that a process of substantial renovation is in train. As in the case of some of those brutal modernist buildings that have been recently refurbished to let in more light, to allow more points of access, and to incorporate an array of distinctively non-modern embellishments, the resulting edifice is both uniquely old *and* new at the same time. Moreover, analogous legal developments are neither unidirectional, nor uniform in pace and in content; only a general, and unmistakable, trend of change is clear.

The shortcomings of an attempt to juggle so many balls are obvious. As Wolfgang Friedmann emphasized in his classic, wide-ranging study of legal change, "Every reader will find something missing" (1972: 13). Perhaps the point is even more relevant here, as I am trying to examine theoretical approaches as well as some of the empirical detail of social and legal change. There will clearly not be enough empirical evidence to convince those who wish to see the fine grain of historical change, and not enough theory to satisfy those who like theoretical arguments to be developed in depth. My reasons for not devoting further space to these themes are not merely because life is short, and trees are precious; but to take on this task would have unduly extended this work, and would have turned it into an undertaking altogether different from my present aim: to offer a large-scale conceptual map of contemporary legal change by reference to the forms of modern law that culminated in the particular legal order of the welfare state.

Acknowledgements

This book would not have been possible but for the support I have received on many levels from a group of people too numerous to name here. Special thanks go to my colleagues Mark Aronson, David Brown, Michael Chesterman, Arthur Glass, Martin Krygier, Christine Parker and Robert Shelly. Each has demonstrated great fortitude by wading through large portions of the book to offer valuable, critical comments. More broadly, I am very grateful to the colleagues in my workplace who collectively make it a particularly congenial environment for research. At various times I have also benefited from the wisdom and assistance of: Susan Armstrong, André-Jean Arnaud, Anne Barron, Colm Campbell, Jacques Faget, Simon Halliday, Owen Jessep, Jill McKeough, Jim Mooney and Colin Scott.

Many of the ideas in this book were developed on various occasions in the uniquely stimulating environment of the International Institute for the Sociology of Law at Oñati, in the Basque region of Spain. A workshop at the Institute under the Directorship of Johannes Feest in July 1997 did much to bring my sense of legal change to a clearer understanding. A faculty seminar in the law school of University College, Galway in October 1999, during my stay as visiting academic, provoked thoughtful questioning which clarified some of the ideas that appear in chapters 2 and 5, as did seminars at the Socio-Legal Research Centre of the Law School at Griffith University, Brisbane, and the Centre for Socio-Legal Studies, Wolfson College, Oxford University in 2002. Needless to say, errors and omissions are mine alone.

I have been given great assistance by a number of very able researchers: Ursula Armstrong, Janice Beavan, Roberto Buonamano, Lisa Di Ferrari, Rosalind Dixon, Catherine Hunter, Kamilla Johns, David Mitchell, James Paull, Sabina Pittrof and Katrina Sharman. I am very grateful to Alan Walker for the index. For other contributions, no less important, I should like to thank Jenny D'Arcy and Roger West, Doris and Kevin Duffy, Kevin and Elaine Edgeworth, Brian Quinn and Mairead Bourke, and Father Tony Smith.

The deepest debt of gratitude I owe is to my partner, Beverly, who has provided me with far more support, encouragement and reassurance than was reasonable to hope for when I embarked on this project. She also held the domestic fort – which includes our young sons Liam and Dominic – on more occasions than I dare to recall while I was absorbed with writing.

Sydney, September 2002

1 Legal and Social Change

> One of the birds lodging in the nicotined greenery outside his window seemed to have learnt how to imitate a car alarm: a looping lasso of sound. Various car alarms belonged to various types, various genres: the nagging, the hysterical, the scandalized. There was even a postmodern car alarm, which trilled out a fruity compendium of all other car alarms. This was the car alarm that all the birds of London would eventually know how to do (Amis, 1995: 464-465).

> Today legal practice privileges neither the conditional programs of bourgeois formal law nor the purposive programs of welfare law ... The opaque and inconsistent structure of such a legal order has thus stimulated the *search for a new paradigm* beyond the familiar alternatives (Habermas, 1996: 390; italics in original).

Introduction

The profound historical changes that have occurred over the last generation – social, economic, technological and political – confer on our age its particular distinctiveness. They reveal a world that appears to have broken from its past in a very decisive manner. Unsurprisingly, a transformation of such magnitude has been theorized in many, and contradictory, ways. One common method of measuring the novelty of the present is to focus on its historically unique features. Among many other descriptions, we are said to live in a "global age", a "digital age", or a "computerized society". A rather different way of defining our contemporary condition is by reference to its "pastness", or "*post*ness". On this view, where we now stand is best captured by means of charting how much history has been jettisoned or left behind. Typically, the relevant past is a *recent* past: the ideas and achievements of the preceding generation provide the yardstick. We are therefore "postsocialist", "postinterventionist", or "postwelfare".

This kind of retrospective thinking is also evident in theories that characterize the present by reference to more distant times. They make the more sweeping, macroscopic claim that our world has severed its links with a much larger tradition: the great edifice of modernity is seen to be transcended, its values questioned, and its promises open to unprecedented doubt. The various forms that this vision has taken in many spheres of contemporary culture and society are often (and still) denoted by the umbrella term *postmodern*. It has induced many influential commentators, whether in joyful celebration, melancholic lament or studied detachment, to suggest that we are now living in a postmodern age. As Agnes Heller and Ferenc Feher conclude: "those living the present as postmodern ... live in the present while at the same time, both temporally as well as spatially, they are *being after*" (1988: 1; italics in original).

The vast body of literature in this genre can be further subdivided into two basic categories. The first category – more firmly and widely established, and no less controversial – is concerned with the critical assessment of the values, ideologies and cognitive frameworks unique to modernity. It rejects as undesirable or unworkable those ways of seeing the world. The second category of theory that articulates the idea of "being after" in this larger sense examines the emergence of new or transformed social institutions. They are held to parallel the changed culture, and receive nourishment from it. The broad influence of this particular approach began with the claim that a distinctive practice of postmodern architecture had made an appearance (Jencks, 1977), to be followed by the identification of, among others, postmodern art (Taylor, 1988), postmodern film (Harvey, 1989: ch 13), postmodern fiction (McHale, 1987), the postmodern university, of course (Smith and Webster, 1997), and even the postmodern church (Newman, 1990). And not forgetting Amis' car alarm.

Yet to analyze the evidence of recent social change as in some way "post", and so to bring to the term a predominantly sociological and historical colouring, is very much a minor pursuit in the broad landscape of what is generally understood to be postmodern theory. Anthologies of writing in this genre routinely marginalize or ignore it. By contrast, for the purposes of the following chapters, by far the most valuable contribution to be gleaned from that vast body of work is its contribution to the analysis of social change. To the extent that social and legal change are inextricably intertwined it is also directly relevant to understanding the transformation of contemporary law. The focus of this book will be primarily on structural, systemic and doctrinal change *in law* as informed by this branch of theory, rather than postmodernist perspectives *on law*. And it will offer a critique of the latter in part by reference to the demands of the former.

My general argument is that law in the most developed societies has taken on a distinct postmodern identity, to no less a degree than modern law has reflected the character of modern societies. Mindful of the importance of not mistaking ephemeral and transitory trends for more fundamental social transformation, the conclusion I reach is that, taking a long view of historical development, there is more than enough evidence to suggest that, in Jürgen Habermas's terms above, "a new paradigm" of law has emerged. In particular, this paradigm is inextricably bound up with, and explained by, a restructured state apparatus (described in shorthand as a "contracting state"[1]), a transformed economy, and a reconfigured civil society. Briefly, my thesis is that as the modern interventionist welfare state gradually reduces the scope of its domestic functions, and the nation state declines in the face of supranational influences, many fundamental pillars of modern societies are weakened. In turn, law and legal institutions are subjected to historically unique changes in a wide variety of fields consistent with those broader developments. To understand those linkages, it is necessary to make use of what Zygmunt Bauman describes as a "sociology of postmodernity" (1988a). In this endeavour, the frameworks that have been deployed to understand *modern* society and its law in sociological and historical terms are not particularly helpful, nor will analogies with earlier times suffice. By way of an example, quips Bauman, "the present depression is not a later edition of the 1930s (one hears of the poor losing their jobs, but one does not hear of the rich jumping out of their windows)" (1988a: 235).

There are many who in the last decade or so have viewed law through a postmodern lens. In general, these analyses have tended to avoid sociological or historical perspectives in favour of a multidimensional critique of the various features of modern law. Notably scarce among these approaches is any consideration of how far the pattern of recent convulsive social transformation has affected law structurally and institutionally, and the extent to which legal change has marched in step with broader attitudinal and social change. In this respect legal scholarship stands in stark contrast to those studies of other social spheres that have analyzed changes within institutions in the context of a fundamentally changed social environment. In chapter 6 I will critically review some of the major themes in this body of legal scholarship. My conclusion is that its many weaknesses are partly traceable to an ingrained tendency to downplay or ignore wider institutional transformation; but those weaknesses also derive from the hyperbolic and dystopian claims pervasive in the critical predispositions of wider postmodern theory.

Before a survey of some of the key empirical changes in contemporary law can be examined, the term "postmodern" must be dissected, and to embark on this exercise demands a survey of its correlate, the "modern", in order to see more clearly what it is exactly that postmodernity is supposed to have surpassed or transcended. To the extent that there are major disagreements about the meaning of the terms here, and indeed there are many who believe alternatively that it is more accurate to refer to the condition as late modernity rather than postmodernity, or that all talk of being "post" is quite futile (eg Callinicos, 1989), or even that we are already post-postmodern (Frow, 1991), the definitional and theoretical question is a threshold one. Equally, insofar as these terms abound in contemporary theoretical analyses of law, and have appeared with growing intensity in recent years, a detailed examination of their various meanings, and the attendant perspectives they suggest for the analysis of law, is a preliminary focus of this study. Only after such an examination will it be possible to address my central argument: the extent to which many of the typically modern features of law have been eroded, reshaped and displaced by more recent developments.

The Problem of Postmodernity

The epithet "postmodern" has been current for almost half a century. From its humble beginnings in the works of the historian Arnold Toynbee (1963), and the sociologist C. Wright Mills (1959), a widespread obsession with evaluating, measuring and criticizing the "modern" has become one of the defining features of the contemporary intellectual landscape. This visibility is not only a feature of social and cultural theory; it has also become a vogue term of art, though more often abuse, all the way from popular to highly theoretical and philosophical social commentary. An important shift of perspective has surely appeared when journalists in popular newspapers commonly invoke the term, as in the identification of a present "postmodern monarchy" (Starkey, 1995), or claim that "if the Angelus could be taken off the airwaves, this would prove how post-modern and cool we all are now" (Kenny, 1999). At the other end of the spectrum of social analysis, it is hardly less significant that Margaret Thatcher can be described, if only ironically, "as the first genuinely 'postmodern' politician" (Habermas, 2001: 59).

Despite the tendency for the term to seep ever more widely into the collective consciousness, or perhaps because of it, a disquieting vagueness about its meaning persists. A label that can apply equally to buildings, novels, video clips and constitutional law, among many other social phenomena, has an understandably unsettling amount of inbuilt elasticity, and has, for that very reason at least, become "notoriously vertiginous" (Hebdige, 1988: 183). Therefore many who, like the fictional guest authors at the international literary theory conference in David Lodge's *Small World* (1985), disapprove of it as probable nonsense, dare not say why they do so, because they cannot – with considerable justification – fully comprehend all of its possible configurations. Practising lawyers and legal scholars in particular, with their ingrained proclivity for linguistic precision and who might be prepared, at a pinch, to tolerate the fuzziness of legal terms such as "reasonable foreseeability", "in good faith" and "just and equitable", are predictably suspicious of a notion of such indeterminate reference (Davies, 1994: ch 7).

By contrast, Raymond Williams has mounted a compelling argument against taking doubts of this nature too far (1976: 19). It would be a mistake to give up on any term purely on account of its many meanings, he concluded, for the reason that there is commonly a direct correlation between the number of shades and nuances of meaning that a word has acquired, and its centrality in historically important debates:

> In such a case, each group is speaking its native language, but its uses are significantly different, and especially when strong feelings or important ideas are in question ... What is really happening through these critical encounters, which may be very conscious or may be felt only as a certain strangeness and unease, is a process quite central to the development of language when, in certain words, tones and rhythms, meanings are offered, felt for, tested, confirmed, asserted, qualified, changed. In some situations this is a very slow process indeed ... In other situations the process ... can seem unusually rapid and conscious (1976: 11-12).

It follows that the many layers of meaning of postmodernity reflect not so much imprecise thinking, or even obscurantism – though there is a fair bit of both about – but *widespread* use which, in turn, suggests that it represents a cluster of ideas which significant numbers of people have felt crucial to analyze and debate. It is hardly surprising that where the ultimate focus of inquiry is on a phenomenon as vast and amorphous as modernity, and its manifestation in particular fields, the "post-" will exhibit a comparable measure of diversity. Inevitably, the various elements in this new theoretical concept will differ from user to user. What some may see as essential characteristics will appear to others as quite superficial, and the concept will be used in ways that reflect their respective idiosyncrasies. In time, and for postmodernity this is, in Williams' terms, a short time of "unusually rapid and conscious" development, it may come to bear little resemblance to its original meaning. Like the coat that has been wrapped around many shoulders, it eventually droops over all who come to wear it.

In this respect, terms such as postmodernity, or postmodernism, are no different from many of the concepts most frequently used in theoretical inquiry in any region of the humanities, as Williams made abundantly clear. "Liberalism", "positivism" and "totalitarianism", for instance, have undergone a similar measure of multiple and discrepant interpretation. But the fact of disagreement as to what the correct meaning is hardly justifies abandoning the term altogether; rather, the fact of disagreement points to the importance of the category as a descriptive and prescriptive marker. As it has extended ever wider it has acquired more meanings that, mushroom-like, generate even more debates. In consequence, Jean-François Lyotard, a leading theorist in the field, has concluded in his *The Postmodern Explained To Children*, "[t]he more the discussion develops internationally, the more complex the 'question of postmodernity' becomes" (1992: 29). Complex, yes, but it is no less important for that. A preliminary exercise in this study is a detailed analysis of the term's various meanings as advanced by the most influential theorists.

In order to begin analyzing what the postmodern is in detail, and justifying its use, it is necessary to offer some tentative, preliminary definitions. So, what is postmodernism, and how does it relate to the cognate terms, postmodernization and postmodernity?

Postmodernism, Postmodernization or Postmodernity?

Many theorists have advocated splitting analysis of the postmodern into at least "postmodernism" and "postmodernity". Even Terry Eagleton, a staunch, engagingly witty, and perceptive critic of most of the ideas embraced by postmodernism, has suggested this move in order to clarify discussion (1996: vii). I want to go one step further and propose three definitions: "postmodernism", "postmodernization" and "postmodernity". In doing so, I am foreshadowing the exercise of mapping the range of postmodern theories in the next chapter. But it may help at least to get a sense of the direction of my argument if I spell out in rough fashion general meanings for these terms, each of which appears in the wider literature. To be sure, some commentators define these concepts in ways at odds with my usage; but I want both to stipulate definitions of the terms as I use them, as well as to deploy them in ways that accord with most common practice. Unlike Eagleton who admits to sliding from use of the term "postmodernity" to "postmodernism" because the latter is of far wider currency (1996: viii), I will try to stick closely to my definitions, for the reason that my focus is a specific set of questions obscured by the all-embracing concept of postmodernism. In framing my definitions it may help to borrow from the parallel, "pre-Post-erous" (Hebdige, 1988: 205) definitions offered by Marshall Berman (1982) in relation to the term "modern".

To clarify his general study of modern society, Berman proposes definitions for the terms "modernization", "modernism", and "modernity" (1982: ch 1). The modern era can best be understood, Berman argues, by seeing it as the intersection of these three phenomena. First, modernization refers to the technological, economic and social processes introduced with the emergence of capitalism. Second, modernism is the cluster of visions and ideas that accompanied the rise of modern societies, which have been "nourished" by the "world-historical processes" of modernization. These ideas sought to give expression to the way in which those processes impact on the lives of those people caught up in them; they "aim to make men and women the subjects and objects of modernization, to give them the power to change the world that is changing them, to make their way through the maelstrom and make it their own" (1982: 16). Finally, modernity describes the "mode of vital experience" or the dramatically changed lives of those who inhabit this world. It operates as the umbrella concept to describe the interplay of the processes of modernization and the cognitive and normative features of modernism. As an historical and spatial category it locates when and where this dialectical interchange happens.

The postmodern can be similarly subdivided. Thus, "postmodern*ization*" refers to those processes of technological, economic and social change associated with the era of a later, transformed capitalism. Likewise, "postmodern*ism*" tends to refer to the cultural or critical perspectives on, or distinct sensibilities about, modern literature, the arts and society generally. Finally, "postmodern*ity*" is the time and place within which the dialectical processes of postmodernization and postmodern sensibilities are played out. Simplifying greatly, postmodernity, too, will function in this context as an umbrella term to capture the general interplay between structure and feeling, or between society and culture. It is this broader concept of postmodernity that I want to examine for the reason that it directs attention to the wide array of *empirical* changes both in society, and also in the nature and structure of law in its widest institutional sense – that is, the legal system, legal doctrine, and legal practices. This approach involves adopting Zygmunt Bauman's perspective of postmodernity as "a fully fledged, comprehensive and viable type of social system" replacing "classical modern, capitalist society and [it] needs to be theorized according to its own logic" (1988b: 811). Moreover, whatever the fate of postmodern*ism*, which may indeed be fading, and for some very good reasons,[2] this system, with its historically unique institutional features, is still with us, as we are with it.

But why attempt to see contemporary law as postmodern given the vast literature already on the subject of postmodernism, and the large body of work that has recently applied postmodern insights to law? The answer to this question lies in what I see to be five separate absences in the relevant literature. First, within general postmodern literature there is a relative paucity of studies of general social or structural developments of the kind to which Bauman refers: postmodern*ism*, rather than postmodern*ization* or postmodern*ity*, has attracted the vast bulk of scholarly interest. Postmodern*ist* accounts tend to be predominantly cultural, or critical, rather than historical or sociological. Second, even in the literature that does analyze such changes, there is negligible focus on law. Third, the many recent attempts to apply postmodern concepts to law have largely ignored these studies of social developments, focusing instead on critiques of law and legal institutions from the perspective of postmodern*ism*. Fourth, studies in the sociology of law and the relationship between law and social change have not yet been sufficiently reformulated to capture the breadth of contemporary legal transformations. Curiously, the array of more recent theory in the field of law and society which has focused on what might be called a post-welfare state legal paradigm, while providing valuable insights into changes in contemporary law and legal systems, has at best only touched on analyses of postmodernity. Fifth, the political and reform implications of the extant postmodern literature, particularly in the legal domain, are sufficiently problematic to require general critique and suggestions for alternative strategies. These very broad claims need to be developed in a little more detail.

Postmodern Theory and the Absence of Structure

The growing level of intellectual and theoretical interest in postmodernism in the last two decades has yielded an extraordinary range of diverse analyses, critiques and insights into various aspects of modern society, culture and philosophy. Yet these accounts largely ignore the material conditions of such attitudes, and the social environment in which they operate. Frederic Jameson, in a wide-ranging and insightful overview of postmodernism in art and contemporary culture, justifiably castigates mainstream postmodern theory for such refusal to look at structures or systems (1991: 332-336). As will be seen in the next chapter, in this guise postmodernism shades into "post*structural*ism". As against this style of postmodernism, it might be argued that, if there is a broad change in the *Zeitgeist*, it is to be expected that this will impact on the character of those structures and systems. Accordingly, postmodern visions and feelings will tend over time to influence, or even become, postmodern institutions. And similar pressures might operate in the other direction to *produce* postmodern attitudes. Anthony Giddens has addressed this theme, and concludes that much of the contemporary debate about modernity and postmodernity is unsatisfactory because it generally fails to address institutional questions. For him, an analysis of modern institutions must be absolutely central to any understanding both of the contemporary world and also the weaknesses of "established sociological positions" (1990: 3). He therefore rejects "poststructuralism-inspired" versions of postmodern theory (roughly akin to my definition of "postmodernism", as I will elaborate in chapter 2) for the reason that they fail to take such questions seriously by dwelling too much on questions of identity and epistemology, informed by a radical philosophical relativism.

This blind spot in postmodern theory is even evident in attempts to explain the appearance of postmodern*ism* because however apposite such a concept is to understand cultural or ideological questions, it is "singularly unfit to conceptualize the twin phenomena of the logic of historical succession and of the social embeddedness of ideas" (Bauman, 1992: 41). One particular weakness of such attempts lies in the rejection of the sociological practice of attempting to examine societies as "totalities", so that even if certain institutions are studied, the question of their inter-relationships with, and influences on, the broader society, are off the agenda. The narrowness of "postmodernism", therefore, has the effect of closing off examination of the inter-relationship between culture and society, and of the pace and extent of social change.

To a similar degree, traditional sociology seems unsuited to responding to recent change by virtue of an attachment to concepts that are more apt for understanding the main features of *modern* societies. With its central concepts "society" and "social order", it lacks the conceptual apparatus to uncover the present connections of a social world radically discontinuous with the model of modern capitalist, industrial societies. So, the notion of society has traditionally denoted bounded societies with an inner unity, roughly equivalent, or closely correlated, to nation states. Social order was similarly circumscribed within traditional sociological theory. Yet in an era of accelerating, and historically unique, globalization and fragmentation, which combine to produce profound changes in the form and functions of states, different forms of analysis are needed. These changes mean that the former dominant sociological understanding of modern institutions is more problematic than ever, and is in need of an overhaul.

As we shall see in the detailed analysis of the most influential forms of postmodernism in chapter 2, these various criticisms are well founded.

Postmodernity and Legal Change

Despite the great preponderance of analyses and exegeses of postmodernism, with its indifference to sociological and historical questions, the postmodern literature does contain a significant minority of works that examine the broader phenomenon of postmodernity. While studies of this nature may offer some insights for an understanding of postmodern law, they are very limited: it would be simplistic to assume that developments in one social subsystem such as architecture would be replicated or even paralleled in a straightforward way in another such as law. The analysis developed in this book is largely influenced by theorists who explore the general features of postmodernity and seek to deepen their arguments by reference to changes in specific social institutions. These theorists offer the study of law an array of novel analytical concepts. Among the most insightful of these is Zygmunt Bauman, who seeks to unbundle what he describes as a postmodernity with its own distinct "existential autonomy" (1992: 43). In a variety of domains, from contemporary art to sociology, he identifies key pointers to a postmodern present; but even in his account of the weakening of the nation state and welfare state, references to law are but fleeting and not pursued in any depth.

A related perspective is that of David Harvey who, in an overview of the "condition of postmodernity", ranges from art to film to industrial production and political and economic transformation, drawing connections between them in an innovative and insightful way, but without so much as a mention of law (Harvey, 1989). In a similar vein, Scott Lash and John Urry's insightful account of the dynamics of "disorganized capitalism" (1987) largely ignores law, while Agnes Heller and Ferenc Feher, in a work on political theory with a detailed examination of Max Weber's work, totally ignore the subject (1988). Finally, Stephen Crook, Jan Pakulski and Malcolm Waters' analyses of the most recent wave of structural social change under the label "postmodernization" (1992) extend to recent transformation in the shape and extent of state activity, and parallel shifts in social institutions; but their work also contains only scant treatment of law. The general absence of any attention on law is particularly notable in these works given that they purport to deal with postmodernity in all its manifestations. Yet these theorists do offer sufficiently broad analyses of contemporary social change to raise important questions about how law might be comparably affected by changes in its environment. A central focus of the argument that follows is to make connections between this body of theory and recent legal change.

Legal Postmodernism: the Absence of the Social

Within the discipline of law, too, there has been a dramatic increase in interest in the postmodern over the last few years. A bibliographic search by Litowitz identified over two hundred references to postmodern theorists in American law journal articles (1997: 182). And the books keep coming (eg Feldman, 2000; Stacy, 2001). The depth of interest is evident on two levels. First, a number of scholars have made use of some versions of postmodern*ism* to criticize various aspects of law and legal institutions (eg Carty, 1990; Douzinas et al, 1994). Second, the subject of "law and postmodernism" has attracted attention from the perspective of traditional legal theory. It has begun to appear in general anthologies of jurisprudence, for instance, as one of the more recent, critical, approaches to law (Davies, 1994; Freeman, 1994; Morrison, 1997). In both bodies of work, postmodern theory is overwhelmingly seen as confined to postmodern*ism* as defined above. For all the innovation in this work, there is still an absence of any real attempt to deploy the concept of the postmodern in an historical or sociological way. There appears to be a widespread assumption that while postmodern perspectives about law can be justified, the claim that somehow law itself has taken on a postmodern identity is not. Most of those who have examined postmodernism in relation to law have all but ignored this absence. One notable exception is Robert Post. But his final assessment of its relevance is in the negative: he concludes that law is one of those areas of social life unaffected by postmodernism:

> Postmodernism affects only certain segments of contemporary life. There is, for example, no postmodern physics, although there are postmodern histories of medicine. There is no postmodern law, although there are postmodern commentaries on law (1992: 396).

The basic reason for this limited influence, he adds, is that the practice of law, as a successful practice, involves the retention of a healthy respect for the authority of the relevant standards. As long as practising lawyers and judges willingly deploy standard interpretive techniques, and respect the traditional hierarchies of authority, postmodern assaults on interpretive coherence and the determinacy of meaning will remain forever outside of the law. On this view, postmodern critiques may exist, but the law goes on regardless. If legal practitioners were suddenly to start arguing in Derridean terms that there was no legislative *presence* in statutory texts, citations included, we could say a postmodern present had arrived; but that time seems to be a long way off. It follows that postmodernism in law has been deprived of any temporal or sociological function.

Yet this view holds only if it is conceived as an exclusively interpretive, or critical attitude: Post's assessment of the influence of postmodernism on legal practice is undoubtedly accurate if the narrower concept of postmodernism, as a set of critical sensibilities, is used. By contrast, in areas such as architecture, economics and literature the broader sociological concept of postmodernity has been used as an insightful analytical yardstick to determine how far the contemporary contours of the institutions justify commentators' claims that a modern past has been supplanted by postmodern present. Unlike law, they *are seen* to have become infected by these broader developments, and by implication, have been markedly less successful at retaining their "institutional policing mechanisms" to remain immune from changes in the environment (Post, 1992: 396). The highly acclaimed and influential overview given by Charles Jencks of contemporary architectural practice is a striking example. It examined not merely the recent changes in architectural styles and practices (that is, institutional questions which I refer to as postmodern*ization*), but also the changes in aesthetic and planning sensibilities that have accompanied and in some way explain these changes (postmodern*ism*) (1977). Thus Jencks operated with a notion of what I defined above as *postmodernity* which he used as an analytical yardstick to determine how far shifts in practice justified the conclusion that a modern past had been supplanted by postmodern present. In particular, he sought to show that postmodern architecture entailed a break with some of the guiding principles that underpinned the postwar (welfare state) planning philosophies. There is no comparable study of law and legal institutions.[3]

For these reasons I aim to take up Post's argument on two levels. First, I want to argue that though there may be no extant postmodern legal practice in the sense of a living, breathing interpretive nihilism or epistemological relativism (as we shall see, common meanings of postmodernism) there is more to the postmodern than this; and it is in this sense that it may be possible to talk about postmodern law. The emphasis here will be on postmodernization and postmodernity as defined above, rather than postmodernism. So, in the context of law, postmodernism is most commonly evidenced in philosophical debates about the nature of law and the judicial role, in professional ideology, and in various interpretive disputes about legal doctrine. Postmodernization and postmodernity, by contrast, raise questions about structural changes in the legal system, the legal profession, legal doctrine, transformations in the sources of legal norms, and shifts in the boundary between legal and non-legal control. And they do so in light of many dramatic, recent and convulsive changes marked by the decline of the nation and welfare state, the globalization of the economy, and corresponding reconfigurations of civil society.

The second point I want to make is that much contemporary legal change can be explained by reference to changes in attitudes or world-views that are best described as postmodern. In this way, too, the term postmodern takes on a broader meaning than the one Robert Post ascribes to it. To extend the term in this way offers significant insights into the structure of contemporary law.

Legal Sociology and Postmodernism

The absence in postmodernist legal scholarship of historical or sociological analysis is not addressed in general legal sociology either, despite the fact that there have been many exercises in the recent past – described by Gunther Teubner as "neo-evolutionist" (1983: 239) – that have sought to understand changes in law in the context of broader changes in culture and society. In particular, these studies have variously catalogued the manifold ways in which the law of the welfare state represents a decisive break from the law of classic liberal-capitalist societies. They include Philippe Nonet and Philip Selznick's identification of the emergence of "responsive law" (1978), Gunther Teubner's claims about the development of "reflexive law" (1983) or "autopoietic law" (1988), and Roberto Unger's analysis of what he describes as "postliberal society" (1976).

Viewed from the perspective of postmodernity, these influential analyses, each with their own powerful insights and strengths, are collectively impervious to the most recent convulsive changes affecting society on the one hand, and law, defined in its fullest sense as including the legal system, legal ideology, and legal doctrine, on the other. This is hardly surprising, because these changes have happened *since* the time those theories were written; so it would be unfair to criticize these works for some degree of scholarly failure in this regard. It is only in the last couple of decades that first, the postmodern has started to become established as a conceptual framework in its own right in the study of society and social institutions; and second, societies have undergone a range of dramatic structural changes. They encompass the following spheres: 1) the organization of production (postindustrial, post-Fordist, transnational, informational); 2) the *contracting* form of the state (post-welfare, post-interventionist, decentralized, weakened by globalization); and 3) the composition of classes and politics (identity- rather than class-based, social movement-driven rather than economically determined). Each of these elements, and other related factors, which will be examined in the next chapter, clearly differentiate present societies from those which formed the focus of attention of theorists of welfare states and their laws and legal systems.

I would argue, therefore, that in the same way that some (if only a small minority) of postmodern theorists have charted a divide between modernity and postmodernity, locating the welfare state as the high-water mark of the former (eg Bauman, 1997, 1992; Ingelhart, 1997; Crook, Pakulski and Waters, 1992; Harvey, 1989), there is much evidence to support the claim that corresponding structural transformations can be identified in the legal sphere, and are interconnected with broader social changes. It follows that the conclusions reached in these neo-evolutionary works, however valid in their own right, have been overtaken by recent events. To advance this argument, the emergence of postmodernity will be seen as coinciding with a series of reverses felt by welfare states which the legal sociological literature is ill-equipped to explain. In this regard, I want to make reference to a sociology of postmodernity that emphasizes "the novelty of the present situation" in contrast to a modern sociology which sees in contemporary social change only crises of the modern state (Bauman, 1992: 43). Employing sociological assumptions too modern in orientation, each of the above neo-evolutionist analyses of law in the welfare state not only theorize legal orders already far removed from the present, but also analyze it by reference to sociological concepts ill-suited to capturing the essential nature of contemporary social and legal change.

In those advanced societies that have shifted beyond the political aspirations and institutional arrangements that were central to the welfare state, a whole corpus of evidence has appeared to signal a break with the sorts of social structures that the neo-evolutionists described. Accordingly, chapter 3 will spell out in detail the nature of the changes that the welfare state introduced, and the convulsive transformations that have occurred in the last couple of decades that have both reversed and re-directed those earlier changes. The empirical evidence that points to an emerging new paradigm of legal postmodernization will be outlined in detail in chapter 5. In particular, it will traverse changes in the structure of law attendant on the decline of national sovereignty from above, and the increasing recognition of "private ordering" from below, heralding an historically unique legal pluralism. It will also look at those changes in legal doctrine that both undo and transform the welfare state developments that were either welcomed or criticized alternatively as "responsive", "postliberal" or "bureaucratic-administrative" law. Given constraints of space, and the other objects of analysis in the book, this evidence cannot be other than somewhat impressionistic and selective; but this fact alone ought not necessarily render it unreliable.

Furthermore, to use the concept of postmodernity in this way is to offer an argument which is at odds even with those (more recent) theories in the sphere of law and society which have sought to explain changes in the form and function of law in a contracting welfare/nation state. For example, Gunther Teubner's work on "reflexive law" (Teubner, 1983) in the context of domestic legal systems, and more recently his analysis of an emerging *lex mercatoria* (Teubner, 1997) in international law, uncovers only some of the elements of the structure of contemporary law in the context of tendencies toward de- and re-regulation and globalization. The broad sweep and acuity of Boaventura de Souza Santos's scholarship addresses this lacuna more than any other, but in its primary focus on epistemological and methodological questions, and in its development of an elaborate critique of contemporary law and legal systems, it is predominantly, to use Post's terms, a postmodern*ist* account. While it does offer many valuable insights into contemporary legal change, as discussed below in chapters 4 and 5, its focus is on only some very general and partial aspects of recent developments (1987; 1995).

A much wider array of empirical evidence suggests that a more dramatic transformation in the nature of contemporary law has occurred than these accounts claim. For instance, the current phenomenon of states "governing through contract" (Boston, 1995), and the emergence of global governance as reflected in the decline of the sovereign state (MacCormick, 1993), *in combination* profoundly transform domestic law and legal systems in ways that these neo-evolutionist theories do not describe. The changes cumulatively represent much more of a rupture with the past than do the transitory and ephemeral developments that characterize the normal life of legal systems. Chapter 4 will be concerned with offering a detailed critique of this body of work that either operates with concepts unsuited to analyze the emergence of a new paradigm, or misreads its extent and nature. But to note these changes, and to conclude that they mark out a postmodern present, is not the same as making the exaggerated claim that there is a completed transition to a new historical phase; rather, the more modest conclusion I will offer is that there is a quiet revolution at work where many of the central elements of legal modernity are being subjected to significant revision.

Equally, I want to emphasize the *relative* nature of the analysis here. The recent changes are appropriately "postmodern" only if a long view of the emergence of modern law is the reference point. If the lens is adjusted to see what has recently happened to the legal infrastructure of the welfare state, then the "post-welfare" paradigm becomes the appropriate conceptual inquiry. It is only because the present study attempts to examine the wider set of theoretical debates about the post*modern*, that modernity and its law are a central focus in the following chapters.

Some Problems of Postmodernism

It is not possible to deploy a large number of postmodern insights without self-contradiction, given the wide range of theorists who march under its banner offering widely divergent analyses. So, while I will be using some key perspectives from selective theories of postmodernity to examine contemporary law, I will reject others as undesirable or unworkable in order to avoid the (fleeting) temptation to do what John Frow suggests is eminently possible within postmodern discourse: that is,

> to denounce a reactionary or a subversive modernism in the name of a progressive or a conservative postmodernism, or vice versa; or to celebrate either one against the other, again with any political inflection; or to celebrate or denounce both modernism and postmodernism, from either side of the political fence (1991: 8).

A critical review of a range of postmodern concepts in the context of law will be developed in detail in chapter 6. A further reason for engaging in this exercise is to counter what I see to have been a narrowness of normative vision, from a legal reform and policy perspective (more than hinted at by Frow), of much of the writing that I will call "legal postmodernism". In particular, three leading thinkers considered to be exemplars of a postmodern approach, Michel Foucault, Jacques Derrida, and Jean-François Lyotard, advance theories that provide only limited guidance, both at the level of description and prescription, for examining the nature and extent of contemporary legal change. Some of their more influential epigones in legal theory will also be critically reviewed.

By contrast, in keeping with my primary focus on historical and sociological questions, I want to make use of the distinction between cultural theorizing and social theorizing in the context of what Nancy Fraser calls our "postsocialist condition" (1997: 5). Very broadly speaking, "cultural theorizing" closely resembles what I describe as postmodernism in both its general and specifically legal guises, while "social theorizing" parallels what is more of a central focus of the writers concerned with postmodernity or postmodernization. Social theorizing is both a descriptive examination of the social dimensions of postmodernity, as well as a normative one of attempting to re-activate some redistributive questions and their necessary institutional requirements. Too much of what I label postmodernism, particularly as developed in relation to law, seems exclusively cultural in orientation, at the expense of what Fraser describes as "the politics of redistribution" (1997: ch 1). Her assessment is powerful and timely, given that the factors she identifies are lamentably absent from most postmodernist accounts of law. In this respect my argument seeks to contribute to what Jürgen Habermas has described as the purpose behind developing paradigms of law:

> Legal paradigms make it possible to diagnose situations so as to guide action. They illuminate the horizon of a given society in view of the project of realizing the system of rights. To this extent, they primarily have a world-disclosive function. Paradigms open up interpretive perspectives from which the principles of the constitutional state (in a specific interpretation) can be related to the social context as a whole. They throw light on the restrictions and possibilities for realizing basic rights, which, as unsaturated principles, require further interpretation and elaboration (1996: 437).

A second dimension of postmodern theory which I will argue is less helpful for understanding recent legal change, again with roots in the writings of Foucault, Derrida and Lyotard, is the thesis that rejects all forms of grand social theory that aspire to present global or "totalizing" accounts of social reality. This line of argument emphasizes that social theorists should be less ambitious than their modern forebears, lower their sights to examine smaller, more discrete segments of social reality, and offer less grandiose prescriptions for reform. By contrast, the broader focus on postmodernity in general provides conceptual frameworks better suited to comprehend wider contemporary social change. Some may find the generality of the argument here unsatisfactory, attempting as it does to draw connections across a range of legal systems, doctrines and cultures. But if the project is seen more as an exercise in large-scale mapping (Santos, 1987), it can be readily acknowledged that it must necessarily omit certain "local" details. Large-scale maps can only provide an adequate perspective on their object of focus if they gloss over many of the details that other maps provide. This does not mean they are unhelpful; on the contrary, like maps of an entire continent, they reveal *more* because of what they leave out, and should not be rejected simply because they omit the topography of individual cities.

In analogous fashion, sociological overviews may nonetheless offer some useful large-scale generalizations about "definite episodes of historical transition" (Giddens, 1990: 6). Such generalizations can only be useful if, as in the case of maps, they avoid the pitfalls identified by C. Wright Mills in such theoretical exercises, namely, that highly general conceptual schemes be used with caution. In particular, they should be deployed in such a way that they make it possible to shuttle between different levels of conceptual and empirical abstraction (Mills, 1959: ch 2). This is not to suggest that, as far as the argument here is concerned, detailed empirical evidence will be offered for every claim; indeed, I am acutely aware of the sketchiness that constraints of space have imposed on this exercise. But as many examples as possible in a work of this kind will be provided, and the final chapter will propose possibly fruitful lines of future research that the theorizing here implies.

A further exercise attempted in this book is a critical review of the general postmodern theory that has informed many recent approaches to law. Of course, to open a gate onto what is an already well-ploughed field provokes much hesitancy. But despite the wide range of examples of this body of work in the area of legal inquiry, and the many excellent overviews of postmodern*ism* in law,[4] there is no comprehensive cartography of postmodern theory broad enough to embrace theories of postmodernity presently available in the legal literature. The question of surveying the range of the various theoretical approaches is therefore a necessary starting point for this study.

Notes

1 The term originates from Ian Harden's seminal study, *The Contracting State* (1992). See also, Freeman (2000a; 2000b). The heavily overworked concept "paradigm", as deployed in historical and sociological accounts, owes its popularity to Thomas Kuhn (1962). Try as I may, I cannot find a suitable replacement; but given that the term is used by many authors whose work I refer to throughout the book, it does not seem inappropriate to use it.

2 This point will be developed in chapter 6.

3 The absence explains why Alan Hunt, in his overview of postmodern approaches to law, considers together the two generally quite distinct concepts, deconstruction and postmodernism, while noting, with an understandable whiff of regret, that there has been no real attempt to deploy other aspects of postmodern theorizing, such as historical and sociological approaches, to the legal domain (1990: 516-517).

4 See, for example, Stacy (2001); Feldman (2000); Davies (1996); Patterson (1994).

2 Cognitive Mapping

> It begins to look as though the very engagement with the term [postmodernism] represents a trap: as though your words, whatever their content, have nothing to do but to roll through the clown's mouth into the groove waiting to receive them (Frow, 1991: 8).

> Indeed, the very enabling presence of the debate turns on an initial, strategic presupposition about our social system: to grant some historic originality to a postmodernist culture is also implicitly to affirm some radical structural difference between what is sometimes called consumer society and earlier moments of the capitalism from which it emerged (Jameson, 1991: 55).

Introduction

No account of postmodern theorizing can ignore its protean character. Yet its many meanings – Dick Hebdige, for instance, in a celebrated collection, lists over 40 (1988: 181-182) – basically reveal two distinct and parallel theoretical currents. In the same way that legal historians have described the development of the common law and equity, these currents cannot be seen as occupying completely different channels; rather, they move in the one stream, with water percolating from each to the other. They divide into analyses of "contemporary socioeconomic, cultural, political and technological transformations" on the one hand, and "parallel aesthetic, intellectual and epistemological developments" on the other (Smart, 1993: 62).[1] The analysis of social change is in the nature of an historical and sociological account, where "postmodern" refers to recent changes across a range of social institutions, from architecture to art to law, for instance. As in chapter 1, I will refer to this phenomenon as "postmodernization". Analysis of aesthetic and related developments describes a cultural or methodological position: postmodernism in this guise is a way of looking at the world, an intellectual, evaluative or attitudinal matter. Simplifying greatly, the sociological and historical account has originated in the Anglophonic world; the cultural or methodological approach, by contrast, is largely a creation of various French theorists.

A third category of theoretical inquiry has fitted various elements of both types of analysis together in a broader sociological framework. In this form "postmodern" refers equally to culture *and* society at the same time. In keeping with the threefold division of the concept of the postmodern elaborated in the previous chapter, I will describe this approach as concerned with the nature of *postmodernity*. This chapter will focus separately on some of the more significant positions in each of these categories of theory. Given the breadth and diversity of this work, it can only be sketched in outline. This exercise in "cognitive mapping" (Jameson, 1984: 89-92),[2] will reveal that the concepts provided by theories of postmodernization and postmodernity have much to offer the critical analysis of contemporary law. Moreover, this body of postmodern theory has been least utilized to date to examine and understand law and legal change.

Postmodernism: Its Origins as an Historical and Cultural Category

For the historian Arnold Toynbee, the "post-Modern age" began around 1875 and stretched to the mid-twentieth century. Writing in the 1940s, he saw it as a crisis-ridden successor to the comparatively peaceful bourgeois ascendancy of the "Modern Age" which stretched in his chronology from 1475 to 1875 (1963).[3] According to this view the progress and stability that characterized the Modern age had disintegrated into anarchy, nihilism and revolution by the latter part of the nineteenth century. History has not been kind to Toynbee in respect of this overview; hardly anyone has accepted the sweep of his vision. While there have been many historians and sociologists willing to see the 1870s as marking a distinct break with earlier forms of capitalism and colonialism on the one hand, and of cultural and political institutions on the other, no-one who would presently own up to being influenced by postmodernist approaches has subscribed either to Toynbee's definition or his periodization.

By contrast, the sociologist C. Wright Mills proposed in rudimentary terms that advanced industrialized societies by the 1950s were witnessing the twilight of "The Modern Age" which was "being succeeded by a post-modern period". This "Fourth Epoch" – Antiquity and the Oriental ascendancy being first and second – could not be satisfactorily described by the concepts of liberalism and socialism with their shared immanent and utopian linkage of reason and freedom. On the contrary, they had "virtually collapsed as adequate explanations of the world and of ourselves", so that it was now the case

> that too many of our standard categories of thought and of feeling as often disorient us as help to explain what is happening around us; that too many of our explanations are derived from the great historical transition from the Medieval to the Modern Age; and that when they are used today, they become unwieldy, irrelevant, not convincing (Mills, 1959: 166).

From Mills' vantage point, the prospect of liberation, progress and reform held to accompany the pursuit of reason since the time of the Enlightenment was misconceived. Rationality was at least as likely to enslave as liberate, as the collective experience of the twentieth century had painfully and compellingly demonstrated. With a sense of remorse, and an almost prescient invitation to the forms of theorizing that were to become prevalent within three decades of this assessment, he concluded that "Indeed, it is the fact of its unrecognized character, its lack of formulation, that is the most important feature of the contemporary problem of freedom and reason" (1959: 169). Sociology, on this view, had failed to develop the relevant postmodern theoretical concepts to make sense of these new changes. More accurately, Mills' argument places emphasis on "post-*modern*ism": it represented a call to reassess the legacy of modernity rather than a reference to the concept of modernism current in aesthetics. This plaintive perspective evokes in embryonic form some key ideas later typical of general postmodernism, and postmodernist accounts of law.

Mills' novel historical periodization was soon followed by analogous, critical accounts in the fields of art and literary theory. As Steven Best and Douglas Kellner note, a number of theorists such as Leslie Fiedler, Susan Sontag and Ihab Hassan from the late 1960s onward identified some novel currents in many regions of the arts (1991: ch 1). They assessed the contemporary turn in artistic production as evidencing a broadening loss of faith in the Enlightenment project of extending the light of reason to art. Where earlier movements emphasized the educative and illuminating function of aesthetics, reaching their high point in modernism, the postmodern turn revealed a new mood. So, Fiedler celebrated the new forms of artistic practice with their wholesale rejection of the distinction between high- and low-art, Sontag rejected the rationalist need for meaning and order, and Hassan identified the emergence of "anti-literature" which had as one of its themes a revulsion of Western civilization (Fiedler, 1971; Hassan, 1971; Sontag, 1966).

The development of a different style of aesthetic practice (post*modernism*) may appear to have little to do with historical analysis, and even less with law; but there are points of overlap with Mills' position. The new forms of art shared his critical attitude to modernity's intellectual obsession with reason. Also, their program was similar: they recommended innovative practice going *beyond* the modern. Importantly, there is no suggestion of a return to an Arcadian past that a heartless and brutal modernity swept away. Postmodernism should therefore be distinguished from antimodernism. Antimodernism expresses a lament for the passing of a noble past in the face of an ugly modern present. For these later theorists the agenda was for going onward; going back was out of the question.

Typical of this novel cultural sensibility, and the most thoroughgoing early application and development of the concept in relation to a particular sphere of social life, is the work of Charles Jencks. In his seminal *The Language of Postmodern Architecture* (1977) he traced the ways in which the emerging structures of feeling, and changes in contemporary architectural practice caused a break with many of the discipline's modern organizing principles. Jencks sought to suggest how architectural theory as well as its practice clearly demonstrated an epochal shift. For him, postmodernism, far from being the vague, amorphous and elusive concept of aesthetic theory, had made a clearly visible and unmistakably historical appearance: in St. Louis, Missouri, on July 15, 1972, at 3.32 pm "or thereabouts" (Jencks, 1977: 9). The Pruitt-Igoe public housing complex, a project accommodating over 10,000 low-income tenants in that city, was razed to the ground. It had been the target of condemnation from both the political left and right of the time as well as social workers, architects and town planners. Ugly buildings are regularly flattened, but what made this demolition job historically significant was the wide and curious alliance formed to oppose it. A consensus across the political spectrum had emerged to target the centralized bureaucratic planning frenzy of the post-war era, and the range of cognate aesthetic and political beliefs that sustained it.

The deeper meanings of this event surfaced in the arguments advanced in support of demolition. Regardless of which side of politics the critics were on – and this was a time to be on one side or the other – opponents expressed a loss of faith in the capacity of this style of *modern* architecture to advance the well-being of citizens who had no control over, or say in, the decisions of the planners and bureaucrats. Jencks argued that their technocratic mind-set was typical not only of a distinctively modernist vision developed in the early years of this century, but also some of its original roots dating from the Enlightenment. These ideas claimed that society could be reconstructed on a rational basis with tools provided by the natural and social sciences. In similar fashion the architect, as the designer of buildings and cities, could use his or her peculiar expertise to identify general human needs and satisfy them by judicious grand designs. These ideas received their most articulate expression in the architectural modernism of the Bauhaus project, of the constructions of Le Corbusier and Mies van der Rohe and their International Style. Many architectural modernists sought to develop and apply an aesthetic that celebrated reason, technology and scientific innovation as the sole source of genuine progress. As van der Rohe put it: "I see in industrialization the central problem of building in our time. If we succeed in carrying out this industrialization, the social, economic, technical, and also artistic problems will be readily solved" (1970: 71).[4] As such ideas prospered, Max Weber's gloomy prognosis of the "iron cage" of advanced bureaucratic societies became in modernity an architectural reality. Jencks concluded that this world-view was fast losing legitimacy, and that the demise of the Pruitt-Igoe complex is but one instance of that intellectual transformation:

> Alas, such simplistic ideas, taken over from the philosophical doctrines of Rationalism, Behaviourism and Pragmatism proved as irrational as the philosophies themselves. Modern Architecture of the Enlightenment was an heir to its congenital naïveties, naïveties too great and awe-inspiring to warrant refutation in a book on mere building ... but to be fair, it should be pointed out that modern architecture is the offshoot of modern painting, the modern movements in all the arts. Like rational schooling, rational health and rational design of women's bloomers, it has the faults of an age trying to reinvent itself totally on rational grounds (1977: 10).

The new architectural sensibility was partly post*modernism*, like the new forms of art and literature. But it also mounted a different attack from that directed at the modernism of high art and literature by Fiedler, Sontag and Hassan: it was a form of post*modern*ism. Architectural modernism had a different message from that of modern art and literature: it extolled industrialization and scientific progress. It followed that to react against this movement was to reject modernity itself, and its achievements. Thus Jencks' program differed significantly from that of the postmodernist cultural theorists. Aesthetic postmodernism, by contrast, was rather more concerned with rejecting the forms and techniques of modernism. To be sure, much modernist work, such as the literature of Franz Kafka, W.B. Yeats and D.H. Lawrence, and the painting of the Surrealists, was trenchantly critical of the legacy of modernity, with its alienating bureaucratization, industrialization and rationalization. But it was the elite status of such work, and its notion that art could educate by its capacity to represent reality, that the aesthetic postmodernists particularly reacted against.

Moreover, for Jencks, postmodernism was not simply a revival of a more traditionalist, anti-rationalist temper. Postmodernism had a "double coding" which involved "the continuation of Modernism and its transcendence" (1986: 14). The continuation of modernism meant that many of modernism's organizing assumptions were to be retained, such as techniques based on scientific knowledge, but much of its utopian agenda was rejected including the scientism, the sense of remorseless progress, the blind faith in expert, technical and instrumental reason. Architecture was an example of this sea-change in attitudes. The revolt against the obsession with centralized rational planning, Jencks concluded, had fostered a postmodern architecture that was informed by a different set of institutional concerns, and was marked by alternative practices. It accepted that the individual needs of human beings ought to be the driving force behind building design. And because of the vast differences between individuals and groups, the central planning model is unacceptably undemocratic.

According to Jencks, the history of architectural development hardly amounted to progress to ever higher forms of life culminating in a triumphant fusion of technological innovation and scientific method. Against this oppressive model he set the smaller, less ambitious objectives of former styles that might be more suited to the process of democratization of the built environment. To democratize does not mean the revival of a premodern nostalgia, but rather an openness to the potential value in any number of earlier traditions, which might both usefully and aesthetically be combined with modern styles to generate more user-friendly buildings. So, postmodern architecture leant more in the direction of eclecticism rather than nihilism. It was not a philosophy of anything goes; with a new-found modesty, its aim is to embrace a pluralism of styles consonant with the vernaculars and traditions of a plurality of communities. There is an analogy here with law. Similarly critical perspectives on the formal, official practices of the law as too distant from those it affects finds expression in elements of contemporary legal change, as will be explored in chapter 5.

The distinctiveness of this version of postmodernism lies in the theoretical amalgamation of a philosophical and aesthetic attack on a rationalistic modernism on the one hand, and a sociological overview of the changing practices of the institution of architecture on the other. Moreover, a progressive politics is clearly evident in Jencks' approach. It reflects a vision grounded in smaller images of community, and an emphasis on the opening up of institutions to novel forms of accountability. A very different formulation of the problems of modernity emerged in France at the same time as the above theoretical developments were unfolding. This theoretical rupture was to a similar degree a rejection of a dominant paradigm, but from very different vantage points.

Postmodernism à la Française: Derrida, Foucault and Lyotard

From the late 1960s onward, some leading French philosophers, including Jacques Derrida, Michel Foucault, and Jean-François Lyotard sought to subject the central and defining characteristics of Enlightenment discourse to radical critique.[5] The focus of analysis for these theorists was rather different in emphasis from that of their Anglophonic counterparts. The trajectory of the work from Mills to Jencks was defined by an attempt to mark off the present from the modern past by identifying some key sociological and historical changes, either in the appearance of new institutions and technologies, or in the form of a proliferation of new ideas, knowledges and attitudes, or both. The work of these French theorists, however, takes up at a more philosophical level the invitation held out by

Mills: to develop a new understanding and critical awareness of the relationship between reason and freedom. Such a project necessarily involved interrogating the key epistemological tenets of the Enlightenment philosophers whose work celebrated the techniques and promise of the natural sciences, while disparaging forms of knowledge based on religion, custom and tradition (Smart, 1992: 6-18). If the premises of natural science were found wanting, methodological prescriptions for the human sciences founded upon them would be equally suspect, as would derivative political ideologies and ethical codes. Paradoxically, therefore, in attending to the much narrower and technical question of conceptions of truth, these theorists were simultaneously paving the way for a total re-assessment of all those modern ideologies that anchored themselves in, and drew their legitimacy from, these grand epistemological theories. If the dark side of reason were exposed, the concept of "Enlightenment" would look increasingly empty.

Given the very different approaches of these theorists, it is impossible to examine them jointly. It may be more useful to identify some of the targets their analyses share, and then to investigate their separate responses. Such an approach will suggest some general conclusions about what unites them and what is distinctively postmodern about their theories. This is a matter of particular importance for the reason that two theorists typically described as postmodernists, Jacques Derrida and Michel Foucault, have not seen themselves either as postmodernists, or as advancing a postmodern position or sensibility. Rather, because the cluster of ideas represented by "structuralism" provided a point of resistance and reference for their work, the label "poststructuralism" is a label equally apt to describe their writings. Accordingly, it will be necessary briefly to analyze this philosophical forerunner first. Nonetheless, the prevalent practice of subsuming their ideas within postmodernism indicates that their concerns overlap in important respects. The writings of Jean-François Lyotard, who by contrast fashioned an explicitly postmodern perspective, will then be examined. For the purposes of my argument, the importance of surveying these theories lies in the considerable influence they have had on recent critical analyses of law and justice.

Structuralism and Poststructuralism

The generally accepted source of modern structuralism is the structural linguistics of Ferdinand de Saussure (1966). The particular novelty of his analysis lay in an emphasis on the synchronic, as opposed to the diachronic, study of language. The synchronic approach concentrates on the constant features, the systemic elements of language, examining it in freeze-frame. Diachronic studies, by contrast, focus on the origins and historical transformations of language. Diachronic approaches to linguistics were marked more by a concern with processes of linguistic change than with the nature of what it was that was changing. In developing his synchronic analysis of language Saussure rejected the common idea that meaning involves a process of assigning words to objects; rather, the meaning of words could best be understood if they are seen as signs. Signs are made up of two elements: specific sounds ("signifiers") and concepts ("signifieds"). The relationship of sound to concept is completely arbitrary: the sound "cat" could conceivably relate to the concept of a dog. Conventionally, however, it refers in the English language to the concept of a feline animal. Central to Saussure's argument is that the meaning of the sign is determined not by its connection with those particular things in the world (its "referents") but by its relationship with, or difference from, other signs in the language. Language is therefore a system of "differences" (Saussure, 1966: 120). Commonly, these differences are expressed in the form of binary oppositions. Saussure's related theoretical advance was the distinction he drew between *langue* and *parole*: *langue* is the entire system of language or its structure, while *parole* is a specific utterance, dependent for its meaning on that pre-existent structure. In this scheme, not only does structure rather than individual become the key to the analysis of meaning, but also things, or "referents", in themselves lose their centrality; the conventions and practices of communities become the decisive factors in understanding how language works.

These ideas were enthusiastically transferred to the social sciences, most notably and expressly by the anthropologist Claude Levi-Strauss (1968). In the study of alien societies, he saw this technique ("structuralism") as particularly apposite, firstly, because society is a synchronic system in Saussure's terms, best understood in its present formation, as opposed to its genetic or historical origins. The second advantage of this approach was to generate explanations of events or actions within those societies as evidence of the structure that gives them meaning, rather than the motives or intentions of the actors associated with them. This methodology led Levi-Strauss to draw connections between more and more seemingly disparate elements of social practice, embracing increasingly broader fields of inquiry. Structuralism, therefore, came to be a totalizing theory of social formations, at odds with an earlier anthropology where societies could be broken down into components, such as structure and culture, in which "structure was, for instance, whom one could marry; culture was what the bride wore" (Gellner, 1985: 136).

In its emphasis on synchronic rather than diachronic analysis, structuralism had some pertinent advice for historians and sociologists, too. The individualistic cast of histories marked by the actions of Great Men, or crucial events, should give way to the synchronic study of the determining factors that make individuals "great" and events happen. Structuralism is therefore "anti-humanist" which, as Terry Eagleton points out, "means not that its devotees rob children of their sweets but that they reject the myth that meaning begins and ends with the individual's 'experience'" (1983: 113). In a related move, structuralists rejected bare chronologies, or diachronic exercises, on the ground that they tend to produce seriously flawed *teleological* histories, that is, histories which tend to explain events as the latest effect of some originating, underlying cause or causes. In contrast, structuralist historiography placed greater emphasis on the conditions of existence of certain phenomena and the structures into which they and human subjects are inserted. Similarly, it warned against the tendencies of historians to attribute causes informed by their own system of thought and interests.

The emphasis on identifying deep structures involves persistent attempts to show how apparently insignificant phenomena reveal at least as much about an age as dramatic events do. Structuralism consequently focuses on the persistence and continuity of social practices and systems of thought. On the other hand, histories devoted to individuals and events direct attention to constant change and regular discontinuities. Yet for all these points of distinction, structuralism still retains some affinities with the classical forms of modern social theorizing. First, theory is seen to be capable of capturing the workings of the whole of society. Second, the theorist, if sufficiently sensitized to his or her own cultural prejudices, could understand another society in an objective, value-free way: structuralism had attained, or at least had the potential to attain, the status of scientific method. Third, it identifies social practices, grounded in language, as no less determinate than the meanings produced by those languages. Fourth, societies are seen to operate in an ordered, law-like way: the empirical detail which appears to differentiate various social orders points to some fundamental organizational principles or underlying logic. Their reality is "out there", capable of being uncovered. It represents a strikingly ambivalent project, therefore, with one foot in the modern social theory camp, but one somewhere in an as yet unspecified outside. It was to this ambivalence that poststructuralism was addressed.

Poststructuralism in Practice: Jacques Derrida and Michel Foucault

Like structuralism, language forms the basis of the poststructuralist project. However, where structuralism was based on the idea that the individual speech act (*parole*) could be understood in terms of a generally determinate system (*langue*), poststructuralism places emphasis on *parole* and the way in which meaning is not so much present in signs but can only be identified by examining the context in which they are used. As contexts vary infinitely, meaning itself becomes immeasurably elastic. The identity of any sign is therefore subject to endless mutations. In consequence, the stability of language as posited by the structuralists following Saussure is found to be illusory. It follows that the "logocentric" impulse – the search for a "transcendental signified" which would give meaning to and would form the basis of all others in a perfect system – must be rejected (Derrida, 1978: 280). Thus Jacques Derrida, poststructuralism's leading exponent, developed from these ideas the technique of deconstruction, which purports to demonstrate how texts subvert their own logical structure by means of identifying seemingly irrelevant details which expose self-contradictions and incoherence.

This general idea is demonstrated at its clearest in Derrida's analysis of the very process of writing. As soon as words are committed to paper, he argues, the author loses control of them and they become subject to an endless play of signification; the author, in other words, is no longer fully "present" in them. Whereas for structuralists there was a neat correspondence between one signifier (acoustic symbol) and signified (concept) by virtue of the structure of language (*langue*), the poststructuralist seeks to subvert this idea by revealing how each signifier contains "traces" of other signifiers; and the same is true of concepts, or signifieds. For instance, when someone reads a sentence they do not capture its meaning by piling its words on top of one another. Rather, its meaning is "deferred" in the sense that each word contains traces of the words which follow it and so on continuously with the sentence as a whole. In this way sentences are not unlike musical melodies: notes do not so much stand alone but refer back to the notes immediately preceding, and anticipate those to come. The meaning of signs is therefore never complete, pure or fully "present". This technique of trying to identify how meanings are laced through with other meanings is applicable to all texts: philosophical and legal texts are just as susceptible to such imprecision as works of literature. For this reason, deconstruction has informed much recent critical analysis of law. This theory of language becomes an epistemological thesis because theories of knowledge, always grounded in language, are beset by the impossibility of establishing any secure bedrock of concepts on which all others may be based. Previous philosophical efforts to secure "presence", to allow authors' meanings to be fully present in their writings, also described as the "metaphysics of presence", are accordingly seen to be impossible (Derrida, 1976: 49).

A related Derridean notion is that of the "dangerous supplement" or the "logic of the supplement". It refers to the way in which the binary oppositions favoured by the structuralists operate very differently to the way they suppose. Binary oppositions usually privilege one term over another, investing one with positive values that the other is held to lack.

Derrida sees a quite different process at work. He concludes that the devalued term performs an additive function to the other, indicating that the former lacks something. This is potentially dangerous because it can have the effect of disrupting the hierarchy that the binary code presumes (1976: 141-164).

The gist of this argument may be illustrated by an example taken from debates about gender. In a patriarchal world there is a persistent and prevailing desire to establish a secure theoretical foundation for male supremacy. Accordingly, the binary opposition man/woman is loaded with positive and negative valuations. Derrida suggests that this conceptual framework may be appropriately termed "phallogocentrism". The poststructuralist scepticism towards such absolutist thinking manifests itself in the identification of an opposite within the concept itself. So, the technique of deconstruction, would reveal that the category "man", for example, is not so much propped up by the outside world but is suffused with its opposite "woman", no-man, or in other words man's very negation. On this analysis, far from being autonomous and separate, man's being is inextricably dependent on woman's. That is, his identity is based on the renunciation and discrediting of what may be his own potentialities (Eagleton, 1983: 142). The rigidity of this binary formula operates in practice as a form of cultural policing. The ideologies of all major belief systems, regularly based on similar oppositions – black/white, civilized/barbarian, nature/culture – function in the same way for the deconstructionist, and form a collective target.

Clearly, this type of analysis is squarely at odds with the main methodological tenets of structuralism in its rejection of the idea that binary oppositions can explain the basic elements of a society's structure; but its bite goes deeper than methodology. To the extent that major political belief systems are founded upon such oppositions, they too are robbed of legitimacy by a thoroughgoing poststructuralism. It therefore has a political edge, but one which is quite at odds with ideologies explaining history in terms of dialectical struggle between one class and another, or one more advanced race triumphing over a lesser one (Ryan, 1982: ch 1). Equally, Western science's pretensions of objectivity are spurious; it is better seen as a form of "white mythology" (Derrida, 1982: 213).

But while poststructuralism is clearly "past" or after structuralism, it is quite another thing to argue that it is postmodernism. As has been noted above, a feature of the Anglophonic theorizing that proposed the term postmodernism was its emphasis on temporality: postmodernism is linked to an historically specific set of institutions and attitudes. Derrida's work, by contrast, is generally ahistorical or transhistorical after the fashion of most philosophical discourse. And the techniques of deconstruction are equally historically neutral. Of course, this emphasis on the contingent and fluid nature of language, social forms and signifiers demands a keen awareness of historical and cultural specificities; but this is a methodological premise rather than an argument about history. It represents a further dimension of the break between poststructuralism and a structuralist approach that operated with concepts of universal structures, codes and myths. As will be explored in chapter 6, the implications for understanding law are similarly circumscribed. All claims of true meaning, the right answer, and objective interpretation in legal discourse form ready targets for Derridean deconstruction.

Despite a general indifference to the question of postmodernism in the poststructuralist project, its general assault on scientism, philosophical foundationalism and rationality, puts it at odds with key elements of the modern outlook. But poststructuralist writing is a long way from advancing the sorts of analyses and critiques of the sociological and historical consequences of modernity's obsession with reason in the manner that Mills and the succeeding self-styled postmodernists have done. It is not particularly helpful, therefore, to see postmodernism and poststructuralism as co-extensive in the way many commentators have done.[6] There is merely an overlap in their central concerns. A similar conclusion may be drawn in relation to the work of another leading theorist, Michel Foucault, also identified closely with poststructuralism.

Foucault's writings involve a thoroughgoing and critical appraisal of the legacy of Enlightenment reason no less than Derrida's do. Taking his lead from Georges Bataille and Friedrich Nietzsche who sought to emphasize and valorize the irrational and the Dionysiac, and to expose the necessarily imperfect and flawed nature of attempts to capture reality by reason alone, one of Foucault's central objectives is to explore the precise manifestations of the dark side of reason. In particular, he wishes to demonstrate the spuriousness of the Enlightenment claim that only through reason is it possible to realize liberation. Indeed, quite the reverse, and recurrent, message comes from Foucault's perspective: it seeks to demonstrate that reason and freedom have neither a necessary nor even a contingent relation to one another. Behind each claim to knowledge lies an ineradicable will to power. On this analysis, reason is not to be understood as a driving force in the understanding of historical development; on the contrary, especially in the modern age, it is best seen as a tool in the service of impulses to dominate. For all the divergent themes and topics addressed in the entire corpus of his work it is possible to see an underlying continuity: to examine how the development of different forms of knowledge are implicated in the exercise of differing types of power. It may be easier to see how his studies as a whole fits into postmodernism if the major themes are outlined. These are fivefold: the critique of specific institutions; the critical overview of the human sciences; his power-knowledge thesis; his conception of the subject; and his political perspective. Each has influenced recent understandings of law.

The thread that connects each of these themes is their shared object of critique: modernity. It is evident in the argument of his first major work, *Madness and Civilization* (1967). Significantly subtitled *A History of Insanity in the Age of Reason*, it attempts to demonstrate how it is only in modern times, defined quite specifically as the period that dawns in the latter part of the 18th century, that the notion of mental illness appears. Though the study appears at first glance to be an historical analysis of psychiatry, it contains much deeper philosophical resonances. Madness, a condition which formerly was not seen as necessarily the antithesis of reason – for instance, it was often viewed as a possible source of prophetic or apocryphal truth – becomes in the modern age recategorized as mental illness. In consequence, sufferers are confined in closed institutions and subjected to relentless scientific observation and objectification. Scientific categorization through a psychiatric discourse which confines the mad and classifies them as lacking reason has the wider social function of policing the boundary between reason and its opposite. In this way madness becomes the very antithesis of reason. As Habermas concludes,

> Making madness clinical, which first renders mental illness a medical phenomenon, is analyzed by Foucault as an example of those processes of exclusion, proscription, and outlawing in whose traces Bataille had read the history of Western rationality (1987a: 239).

This theme of the centrality of the human sciences in the marginalization of other forms of knowledge and subjectivity becomes a central theme in Foucault's work.

A similar line of analysis is developed in his later studies of modern medicine in *The Birth of the Clinic* (1973a) and the modern prison in *Discipline and Punish* (1977a). In these works Foucault develops the argument about how an historically-specific reason, originally set to work within the asylum's walls, would act as template for an array of modern institutions: prisons, schools, and factories, for example, all bear the stamp of reason working hand in glove with impulses to dominate. These impulses culminate in a bio-politics which progressively subjects not merely the bodies but also the souls of deviants to myriad disciplinary strategies that have as their goal the normalization of specific populations. For this reason, Foucault claims that

> 'Discipline' may be identified neither with an institution nor with an apparatus; it is a type of power, a modality for its exercise, comprising a whole set of instruments, techniques, procedures, levels of application, targets; it is a 'physics' or an anatomy of power, a technology (1977a: 215).

These practices are shared by specialized institutions such as prisons, and other institutions that adopt them as an essential instrument for a particular end, for example schools, and even state apparatuses. In this last respect, modern societies are governed differently from premodern societies: they are "governmentalized" (Foucault, 1991).

To be sure, Foucault recognizes that there have always been institutions that subjected individuals to training regimes centred on bodily control, such as monasteries and armies; but it is only in the eighteenth century that institutions such as prisons, schools and asylums adopt analogous forms of disciplinary strategies. They do this by means of techniques afforded by the human sciences – observation, examination, classification, and record-keeping. Closer examination of the prison, the clinic and the asylum reveals broader features of modern societies: they adopt many of the characteristics of the closed institutions generally. Carceral discipline of this kind comes to pervade the whole of society:

> The movement from one project to the other ... rests on a historical transformation: the gradual extension of the mechanisms throughout the seventeenth and eighteenth centuries, ... the formation of what might be called in general the disciplinary society (Foucault, 1977a: 209).

Yet how can this style of analysis and critique be characterized as postmodern given that there is not a single reference to the term in these works? This question is answered by seeing how the modern age is treated in Foucault's narrative. To begin with, he paints a much bleaker picture of modernity than conventional, "modern" overviews do. Prisons look unattractive from all angles, but in these accounts their horror lies in the way that they deprive individuals of freedom. In Foucault's view, however, they do something much more insidious: what happens inside is anything but discontinuous with processes at work in the outside world: they form part of the same disciplinary fabric of an entire society. Jeremy Bentham's model prison, the Panopticon, which was constructed in such a way as to allow a warder to watch over many isolated prison inmates without at the same time being seen, becomes the quintessential expression of a society geared to ever more finely calibrated strategies of control. A key feature of this new modality of power is the way in which inmates become part of the apparatus of domination. Unable to tell if they are being watched, they end up being implicated in their own discipline. By this mechanism, institution and subjectivity intermesh. Modernity, as manifested in its many and varied institutions, has perfected highly distinctive forms of domination by the ruthless and ever-widening deployment of reason. In contrast, for the moderns, reason and liberation go hand in hand; they write histories that characterize modernity as liberation from feudal and customary forms of domination. In Foucault's view, this linkage between reason and freedom is no less central to critical perspectives on modernity such as Marxism than it is in liberal accounts. Capitalism is still seen as a form of liberation from feudalism. In Foucault's work, by contrast, these concepts are de-coupled; reason becomes a tool of enslavement in the modern age.

A second postmodern theme in Foucault's writing lies in his analysis of the emergence of the human sciences, in order to unmask what they conceal. This project began with *The Order of Things* (1973b) and was extended in *The Archaeology of Knowledge* (1977b). In the former, Foucault's concern is to identify "epistemes": these are the specific world-views that operate in different epochs to organize and arrange the data of different disciplines, and in consequence allow certain claims to rank as knowledge. This exercise points to a structuralism to which he was earlier attracted. He describes the emergence of knowledges not in terms of the interventions of specific individual subjects, but by means of the way in which discourses operate. For example, rather than being the subject or agent of changes in discourses and, more generally, historical change, "man" becomes the effect or object of discursive and non-discursive practices. Foucault's history therefore involves an evacuation of the human subject as creative force. Despite this apparently structuralist move, his analysis is *post*structuralist in the sense that these discourses are not immutable structures of societies but change over time. The focus on the production of knowledges has the further consequence of relativizing them; enlightenment does not so much emerge; it is produced, and it triumphs not by virtue of any inherent, scientific superiority but as the result of a successful outmanoeuvring and marginalizing of other forms of knowledge.

Foucault's critique of the human sciences is supplemented by his elaboration from Nietzsche's work of a genealogical method in historiography (1977b). Foucault sought to develop this method because it avoided the problems that beset popular approaches to writing history influenced by the modern human sciences. Genealogy eschews explanations of historical events in terms of linear processes or grand, totalizing explanatory systems by means of which key individuals or events are seen to explain subsequent developments. By contrast, genealogical analysis focuses on the singularity of events without seeking to insert them into some bigger narrative. It directs attention to seemingly marginal social phenomena and subjugated knowledges overlooked as unimportant in the general march of history. Examples of this, for Foucault, are sexuality, the body, reason, and punishment. Also, this method rejects histories that see the present as the necessary culmination of processes set in train long ago. It has an anti-teleological message emphasizing discontinuities, and it places importance on identifying the accidents and deviations that have given rise to present conditions.

Foucault's third innovation lies in his analysis of power. This focus is closely linked to his studies of institutions. Power is best understood as the antithesis of what he identifies as the two dominant models of power, the "juridical" and the "economistic". Both the juridical and economistic characterize power in a negative way; it proscribes, it forbids, it says "thou shalt not". Equally, power is seen to be located in one primary, central institution. The juridical model, typically expressed in liberal accounts of the modern state, has power located in law, and ultimately the sovereign. The economistic model, archetypically Marxism, finds power concentrated in the owners of the means of production. For Foucault, however, these approaches misconceive the way in which disciplinary power operates. Power is not a property which one group possesses and another does not. In contrast, it is productive: it moulds subjects to do, to feel, to want. Moreover, it is radically polycentric, occurring in prisons, hospitals, schools and families. Juridical and economistic perspectives simply miss this many-faceted nature of power. They are also unhelpful insofar as they see it as a property of persons or institutions; by contrast, power is best understood as relational *within* institutions.

Each of the above notions reappears in Foucault's fourth theoretical position, his conception of the subject. As a poststructuralist, he sees the subject as marginal to any understanding of historical forces or social structures; but for all that, his analyses are acutely focused on the nature of the human subject in light of the operation of institutions and discourses. For instance, reason is deployed as a mechanism to repress subjects and mould them to fit the requirements of power; and there is no escape for subjects from these forces. It follows that the question whether subjects are free, or more liberated than others, can hardly be posed within this framework; to be a subject is to be subjected to the exercise of power and the operation of institutional rationalities. Also, subjects are inherently plastic, moulded by forces over which they have little control. Certainly, Foucault adds that wherever there is power there is resistance; but this notion is a very long way from any sociological conception of agency (Dews, 1984).

The fifth theme in Foucault's work, politics, shares affinities with more explicitly postmodern theories. It is informed more by his thesis on power than by his analyses of institutions and the human sciences. In the juridical and economistic models of social action, as we have seen above, roughly translated as liberal and Marxist social theory respectively, resistance to power is focused on the centres from which it emanates: the state or the economic substratum are the sites where significant social power is located. Consequently they become central targets of political struggle. No such strategy is suggested by Foucault's analysis. Resistance takes place within the myriad institutions where disciplinary strategies are implemented. This leads to his advocacy of a form of micro-politics or localized struggle directed at specific institutions. Moreover, to the extent that power is the constant in social relations, there can be no "outside" of power in the sense of emancipation or liberation. Insofar as power-knowledge involves the subjugation of alternative knowledges and identities, moulding bodies and souls, an "identity" politics is implicitly affirmed. It follows that the promises articulated in so many modern ideological claims about progress toward freedom are replete with dangerous illusions, as are the political programs built upon them: "[T]here is no locus of the great Refusal, no soul of revolt, source of all rebellions, or pure law of the revolutionary. Instead there is a plurality of resistances, each of them a special case" (Foucault, 1990: 95-96). Modern conventional politics are accordingly displaced in this framework. As we shall see in chapter 6, this perspective calls into question mainstream understandings of law and law reform to no less a degree.

Despite their respective assaults on different elements of the Enlightenment project, Derrida and Foucault do not provide any temporalization or periodization that might locate the contemporary world by reference to modernity; whether it is to be described as late modernity, postmodernity or some other historical period is a question quite outside their studies. Nonetheless, their work is central to any discussion of postmodernism. Their particular concerns are archetypically postmodern in their repudiation of some central features of modern intellectual traditions. In summary, their shared postmodern themes include: an epistemological uncertainty about the capacity of reason to make good its promises; a deep suspicion both of the grand totalizations of structuralism on the one hand and the major intellectual currents of Western culture on the other; a disillusion with the emancipatory potential of the predominant political, historical and sociological narratives; and a conception of the individual subject and personal identity as fragmented, fluid and decentred in the social field. Additionally, in Foucault's case, his "postness" is reflected in his critical analysis of some institutional features of modernity. Their widespread influence has ensured that these are recurring themes of postmodern writings. But their work, and that of their followers, is symptomatic of postmodernity rather than descriptive of it. It is more in the nature of postmodern theory than a theory of the postmodern. The further step in the refinement of postmodern theory involved the exploration of the linkages between theories of knowledge, broader cultural changes, and the particular transformations in the contemporary structures of advanced societies, and it was taken in different ways by a group of theorists who are more readily associated with postmodernism. Moreover, these theorists have done most to make it a popular term in current theoretical debates.

From Postmodernist Sensibilities to Postmodern Societies

The shifts in sensibility (aesthetic, philosophical, historiographical, and methodological) noted above raised important sociological questions both about their causal origins and their effects. If there is a shift at the level of philosophical discourse, one question posed for sociology is, "What consequential effects appear in other areas of social life?". Equally, the impact of social transformations on the emergence of these ideas in the first place calls for explanation. The issue of the possible environmental conditions that have nourished various postmodern sensibilities, and the impact they might have on that environment, soon came to form the focus of analysis both within French philosophical circles as well as in parallel sociological theory in the Anglophonic world. In the process postmodernism spread from philosophy and aesthetics to become an identifiable form of sociological theorizing.

The work of a number of influential writers marks this process. First, Jean-François Lyotard interwove some elements of the philosophical and methodological concerns of the analyses of Derrida and Foucault with an assessment of the particularities of contemporary societies (1984; 1992). His partially sociological analyses were followed by the work of Scott Lash and John Urry's that paired postmodernism with the appearance of "the end of organized capitalism" (1987), and in Fredric Jameson's examination of aesthetics by reference to "consumer society" and "late capitalism" (1991). David Harvey extended this line of inquiry even further and linked change to "flexible postFordism" (1989). For each of these theorists, the peculiar features of present institutional change in conjunction with radical transformations of consciousness allow for the application of the completely novel *historical and sociological* category of the postmodern. It followed that it was now possible to talk about a "postmodern condition" (Lyotard, 1984; 1985), "postmodernity" (Harvey, 1989; Bauman, 1992; 1997) or even "postmodernization" (Crook, Pakulski and Waters, 1992; Inglehart, 1997). Each of these concepts are directly relevant to legal change.

The "Postmodern Condition"

Jean-François Lyotard's work represents the first systematic attempt to identify the defining elements of the new society by the express deployment of the concept of postmodernism. The current changes in the way in which knowledge is now generated and assessed, and the various contemporary technological revolutions that interact with those changes, allow us, Lyotard concludes, to speak of a new epoch. In his introduction to *The Postmodern Condition* he provides an outline of his theory:

> The object of this study is the condition of knowledge in the most highly developed societies. I have decided to use the word post-modern to describe that condition. The word is in current use on the American continent among sociologists and critics; it designates the state of our culture following the transformations which, since the end of the nineteenth century, have altered the game rules for science, literature, and the arts. The present study will place these transformations in the context of the crisis of narratives (1984: xxiii).

Lyotard emphasizes that his study is primarily concerned to examine changed attitudes to knowledge. Nonetheless, he explains those changes in relation to an unfolding "postindustrial society", where workers in technical, managerial and service employment come to be the dominant occupational groups both in numerical and sociological significance. He adds: "Simplifying in the extreme, I define postmodern as incredulity toward metanarratives" (1984: xxiv). To understand the drift of Lyotard's argument the terms "narrative" and "metanarrative" need to be defined. "Narrative" is an antonym for science. Narratives are the discourses by means of which typically pre-modern societies express truth-claims. By contrast, modern societies eschew narratives, and replace them with scientific discourse. The mark of the qualitative difference of scientific discourse lies in the way that it legitimates itself by its incorporation into some greater narrative "such as the dialectics of Spirit, the hermeneutics of meaning, the emancipation of the rational or working subject, or the creation of wealth" (1984: xxiii). As this rough range of examples demonstrates, grand narratives appear in both descriptive and prescriptive guises. It follows for Lyotard that large political visions and programs are just as suspect as macro-theoretical models of social development.

All forms of scientific discourse, whether the social or the natural sciences, are grounded in grand narratives or metadiscourses. Narratives, by contrast, such as religious beliefs, myths or legends, use different strategies to legitimate themselves by calling on sources such as revelation, nature, or divinity to validate their knowledge claims. For those of a modern, scientific frame of mind narratives are mere "fables, myths, legends, fit only for women and children". Lyotard wishes to rehabilitate these stories, the victims of "the entire history of cultural imperialism from the dawn of Western civilization" (1984: 27).

Lyotard's specific proposal in light of this crisis of metanarratives is to make use of the concept of language games derived from the later philosophy of Ludwig Wittgenstein, who foreshadowed some of the central arguments later made by poststructuralists.[7] Wittgenstein rejected the prevailing denotative theories of language that maintained that the meaning of words lay in what they stood for. Instead, he proposed a connotative conception of language that claimed that the meaning of words can only be discovered by examining the context in which they are used. Like games, one can only play if one knows the rules. Once the rules governing the use of a particular word are mastered, then and only then can its meaning be grasped (Wittgenstein, 1958). This approach to meaning inevitably induces a form of philosophical relativism since the truth value of statements is seen to depend on whether the concepts contained in them have been "correctly" used within what Wittgenstein calls a "form of life". Insofar as scientific statements are linguistic, being part of a (technical) language game, they can claim no greater validity or truth-value than narrative discourses. Lyotard concludes that "[i]t is therefore impossible to judge the existence or validity of narrative knowledge on the basis of scientific knowledge and vice versa: the relevant criteria are different" (1984: 26). Recognition of the heteromorphous nature of these language games, and the purely contingent truths they provide, opens up possibilities for resisting and subverting the oppressive and technocratic ideology that puts its faith in an omnipotent reason.

There are clear points of overlap in Lyotard's work with Foucault's analysis of the "microphysics of power" and Derrida's emphasis on the localized, contextual subjectivism of interpretive practices. Far from representing a break with their concerns, Lyotard's theory retraces and reiterates some key moves in their theories. He is comparably anti-Enlightenment in his critique of Western reason. He follows them in bemoaning the scientistic pretensions of grand social theory, preferring a set of refined methodological tools, more sensitively calibrated to reveal the microscopic detail of social practices and institutions:

> Thus the society of the future falls less within the province of anthropology (such as structuralism or systems theory) than a pragmatics of language particles. There are many different language games – a heterogeneity of elements. They only give rise to institutions in patches – local determinism (1984: xxiv).

These albeit sketchy programmatic proposals are developed further by Lyotard in his later, more philosophical works, *Just Gaming* (with Jean-Loup Thébaud, 1985), and *The Differend* (1988). In the former, he argues that justice has nothing to do with universal principles, but is always local, provisional, and context-bound. Justice is not only a move within a plurality of pre-ordained language games, but it also tests the boundaries and limits of what the game allows. In the later work, his focus is again on the unacceptability of universal notions of justice and judgement, but he turns away from language games, because they imply players, or subjects, in favour of what he calls "regimes of phrases". Relying on the Kantian notion of the incommensurability of spheres of judgement, Lyotard asserts that regimes of phrases, like language games, are also incommensurable;

and any attempts to set up hierarchies of regimes inevitably involves oppression of the weak. He celebrates the differences between these regimes, and sees in them the seeds of political emancipation. In sum, his work exhibits the "three negations" typical of postmodernism (Hebdige, 1988: 187-203), and clearly present in Derrida's and Foucault's analyses: namely, a defiant stance against science, a rejection of totalizing understandings of the social world, and a loss of faith in utopian thinking.

Despite his antipathy toward totalizing analysis, Lyotard fails to avoid formulating an albeit brief sociological analysis of the causes of the decline of metanarratives, seeing their fate as sealed in general by the emergence of the "postindustrial society", and in particular by the vast proliferation of technology. On the one hand the postindustrial society has changed the class system: a new class of experts with privileged "[a]ccess to data" has transformed the "nature of the social bond" in the postmodern condition. The old networks of allegiance and identity "represented by nation-states, parties, professions, institutions, and historical traditions are losing their attraction" (1984: 14). On the other hand, technology is much more than a mass of objects; it incorporates and gives expression to a distinctive logic or philosophy – the efficiency principle. "Technology is therefore a game not pertaining to the true, the just or the beautiful, etc., but to efficiency; a technical 'move' is 'good' when it does better and/or expends less energy than another" (1984: 46). The growing and pervasive contemporary obsession with performance improvement, or what Lyotard calls "performativity", has a corrosive effect on traditional notions of truth in the scientific language game. At the present time, any scientific endeavour that can demonstrate efficient results attracts increasing legitimacy, and thereby social power.

For all the connections between his arguments and those of Derrida and Foucault, Lyotard's work heads in a very different direction. Most significantly, he expressly defines and deploys the concept of postmodernism, which involves consideration of what it is about the modern world that present arrangements are supposed to succeed or transcend. Yet insofar as this exercise identifies the decline of the metanarrative it provides a sociological explanation of change at odds with the approaches in Foucault's and Derrida's work (though in an unsatisfactory way, as will be argued in chapter 6). Also, unlike them, a type of grand theory lurks not far below the surface of his argument. Fundamental to his thesis is an assessment about the general state of knowledge in advanced *contemporary* societies. It is in the nature, therefore, both of a sociology of knowledge, or a history of ideas and also an overview of the society in which this change in knowledge occurs. This particular feature of his work represents a very modern style of social theorizing, grounded on an assumption that macro-sociological concepts can reveal social reality and change society. His postmodernism shades into a theory of postmodernity in its attempt to give a global picture of these new cultural changes and explain how and why they have appeared. The title of Lyotard's most influential work is highly significant: the "postmodern condition" embraces institutional and structural as well as cultural factors. His focus on the dark side of reason and his concern to locate its recent historical and sociological manifestations reflects a clear attempt to identify an historical break between the present and a recent past. This project is taken up more systematically by theorists keen to analyze the broader landscape of contemporary, "disorganized" capitalist societies.

Postmodernity and Capitalist Disorganization

Theories of capitalist disorganization go beyond Lyotard's limited focus on postindustrial society and the influence of technology. They direct primary attention to the economic and political structures of contemporary society. As a secondary, subsidiary focus of study, they seek to locate postmodernism as a cultural phenomenon within broader social change. In this section I will outline the general contours of the main elements of this body of work. A restoration of focus on the spheres of the economy and the state clearly differentiates them from the theoretical priorities in the theories examined above. The importance of this body of work lies in its offering a novel conceptual framework for periodizing contemporary legal change. It is this framework that will inform the examination of the detail of legal change in chapter 5.

In *The End of Organized Capitalism* (1987) Scott Lash and John Urry argued that contemporary capitalist societies had been fundamentally transformed in the previous decade. Relying in part on Claus Offe's (1985) theory of the emergence of "disorganized capitalism", they focused separately on changes in the nature and structure of economic activity, the transformation in the form of the state, and shifts within civil society. Taking a long view of social development, they advanced a three-stage periodization of capitalist societies. Liberal capitalism, characterized by a free market economy and a weak state, represents the first stage, to be followed in the late 19th century by "organized capitalism". Capitalist "organization" in the economic domain had a number of elements: the concentration and centralization of banking and finance capital; the proliferation of cartels and the organization of markets on a national scale; and the increasing rationalization of production by the creation of ever larger industrial units which incorporated very high levels of specialization of short-cycle tasks for workers (commonly known as "Fordism" after the Ford motor company's wholesale adoption of the model) (Lash and Urry, 1987: chs 1-3; 1994: ch 5).

"Organized capitalism" is supported by an equally transformed state apparatus. The state increasingly regulates the economy in the national interest, and to do this successfully the state adopts a range of interventionist strategies. Markets are subjected to regulation to protect weaker parties, and the welfare state was expanded, usurping the market in many spheres such as the provision of transport, utilities, health and education. The emergence of corporatist styles of political organization is integral to this process. Corporatism is a system of hierarchized interest representation organized primarily around capital and labour. It is a feasible political strategy only when there is a delicate balance of power between labour and capital, and where the state is actively engaged in regulating, organizing and participating in economic activity (Cawson, 1986). Under organized capitalism collective organizations representing workers and employers grow and become nationally operational. Welfare states in part express the institutionalization of a political armistice between these two sets of antagonistic interests by the incorporation of their representatives into national governance. States also expand externally as the leading capitalist nations extend their power by establishing empires and overseas markets. In civil society, the changes are no less profound. The emergence of modern capitalist societies had the effect of pushing social groups into two basic classes defined by reference to their position in the economic process, either as owners of the means of production, or owners merely of labour power. Mass production along Fordist lines accentuates this divide and fuels the growth of representative organizations of the respective classes. As we shall see in the next chapter, legal reforms follow suit.

An array of changes, which have their origins in the period from the late 1960s to early 1980s, reverse these processes. Lash and Urry catalogue a wide range of evidence in support of this argument. In the economic sphere, there is a shift away from mass production with its inbuilt rigidities of organization, product and type of work. In its place appear more flexible industrial arrangements. Workforces are multi-skilled, there are great increases in the number of outworkers, part-timers and fractional workers, and management is reduced. In general, capitalist enterprises are disaggregated, plants are progressively reduced in size, with corresponding reductions in the number of core workers, and cartels are dismantled. The changes lead to a decline in industrial cities, combined with industrial deconcentration. Finally, product lines are increasingly differentiated: a shift is evident from mass- to niche-markets, which are geared toward more specialized forms of consumption. Technological innovations have contributed significantly to many of these changes. Advances in the area of sophisticated systems of communication, allied to higher levels of mechanization and more efficient forms of transportation have made distanced and fragmented forms of production increasingly viable and efficient. The computerization of production is one of the most dramatic in impact, with computer-aided design and planning improving not only ways of transferring and storing information, but also the very process of manufacturing (Mathews, 1989: 43). In sum, a "second industrial divide" has appeared, as fundamental in nature as the first industrial revolution (Piore and Sabel, 1984).

Economic transformation is no less pronounced in the international dimension. Not only consumption but also production is geographically dispersed so that the component parts of one commodity may be made across a number of continents. Markets are increasingly globalized, especially as capitalism extends to the Third World and former communist societies (Lash and Urry, 1994: ch 1). The ephemerality of so many forms of capital and commodity, and the velocity with which they travel corrode the comparative stability of an earlier modernity to deliver a "transformed political economy [which] is both 'post-Fordist', in that it succeeded the era of mass production and mass consumption, and postmodern" (1994: 2). These developments are not uniform; like the changes identified above, they have occurred at different tempos and to differing degrees in various countries, and within particular industries in those countries. Nor do they represent a wholesale transformation of economies. What is discernible is more of a general shift of emphasis where Fordist models of production are in some cases supplemented and in others replaced.

The state infrastructure is transformed no less than the economy. States have encouraged international developments. They reorganize their economies by dismantling many of those structures by which they were modelled along national lines. Tariffs are reduced, legal restrictions on movement of finance and capital are dissolved, and limits on foreign ownership revised or removed (Lash and Urry, 1987: chs 4-5). Domestic changes to the state are equally profound. The growing internationalization of commercial activity, later captured by the term globalization, also exerts influence on states by weakening the capacity of nation states to regulate markets given the highly territorialized limits on their jurisdictions. To advance the growing internationalization of economies "resources had in part to be squeezed out of the public sector through 'austerity' and into export industry" (1987: 235). States gradually jettison the Keynesian strategy of guaranteeing industrial harmony, high employment and steadily increasing wages. The progressive abandonment of corporatism displaces trade unions from public policy formation as governments hand over responsibility for industrial disputes to the parties, and market forces. The new regime may also be explained in part by a changed balance of power between capital and labour that makes labour compliance in many instances unnecessary for the maintenance of profit, and also by structural changes in the labour market (Lash and Urry, 1987: ch 8). Like Cawson, they conclude that because corporatism is feasible only where the three "coherent corporate bodies of capital, labour and the state" are present, disorganized capitalist internationalization has been a decisive factor in its demise (1987: 280).[8] As we shall see in chapter 4, these changes point to a need to re-evaluate theories that seek to draw conclusions about the nature of law from the many varieties of corporatism.

In the changing environment, states increasingly adopt a series of non-corporatist strategies such as the market, mass unemployment and international competition (Cawson, 1982: 80-81). In turn, the enlarged post-war welfare interventionist state is progressively reconfigured. Tight regulation of markets with its consequential redistributive regulation gives way to the steered marketization of distribution. The reduction in welfare state interventionism represents one dimension of disorganization generally at odds with the trajectory of the development of modern states, and while more rapid and advanced in some countries than others, it is sufficiently widespread to suggest a general reversal of earlier monocentric tendencies. The typically modern faith in progress and the belief in rational state-centred planning received expression in Keynesian economic policies. These policies were geared to contain business cycles by means of stimulating demand; but they started to falter as the economic environment proved too complex to manage and too volatile to regulate.

A series of exogenous economic shocks to the advanced capitalist societies in the mid-1970s prevented them from delivering the levels of material well-being which had helped to guarantee continuing legitimacy during the long boom of the post-war period. The economic recession and the oil crisis of 1973, in conjunction with increasing rates of inflation, induced a period of acute stagnation. From this time onward, the strong and relatively stable rates of post-war economic growth started to wane. As the fiscal basis for state income began to shrink, the capacity of the state to deliver adequate levels of welfare provision was reduced. The welfare state's fortunes are therefore no less tied to international developments than is corporatist governance. The domestic decline of corporatism also removes one more of the pillars of support of the welfare state (Lash and Urry, 1987: 231).

Economic reorganization of such a fundamental nature has a direct effect on the form of class structure. As mass production and mass consumption decline, the core elements of working class organization begin to crumble. The industrial deconcentration that unfolds as industrial plants reduce in size, and as production takes place in widely distributed units, leads to a spatial dispersal of the traditional working class population. Occupational communities begin to shrink and the social base of a unified working class culture fragments (Lash and Urry, 1987: 227). The recasting of work relations across the economy as a whole, in the form of outsourcing, subcontracting, self-employment, and multi-skilling, and expansion of a tertiary sector, produce an occupational complexity which undercuts the sense of shared fate conducive to traditional working class solidarity. Also, the new economy has produced long-term levels of high unemployment that keeps a huge pool of the most disadvantaged *outside* the working class.

As industrial mass production declines as a proportion of total national productivity, so do the institutionalized forms of solidarity that it fostered. The net reduction in the numbers of the working class coincides with increasing numbers in the service and managerial classes so that it ceases to be the most numerous class in advanced societies. As the traditional working class reduces both relatively and in overall numbers, so is there a decline in its industrial strength and political influence. These factors conspire to force a decentralization of industrial relations and a decline in class allegiance to political parties. Equally the growth of the tertiary sector has had the effect that

> [i]n 'postindustrial' societies the subdivision of 'workers as a whole' into 'producers' and 'producers of production' therefore undermines not merely the structural unity of social labour and its governing rationality. It also challenges the rationality standards which guide (and possibly limit) the socially mediated exchange with nature (Offe, 1985: 139-140).

One consequence of the fractured "structural unity of social labour" is that the economic interests of the various strata of workers in different sectors are often radically opposed. The rationality driving service sector labour can militate against the value-systems that play a central role in the self-identity and the political sympathies of those who are involved in the "socially mediated exchange with nature" of primary and secondary production. The increased social complexity that attends this shift in the organization of work throws major obstacles in the path of the political process of forging broad alliances. They cumulatively tend to displace work from the centre of personal identity. In the political context these changes are reflected in the decreasing influence of social categories on the work relation. Thus Lash and Urry conclude that

> There has been an extensive expansion both in the number of voluntary associations and socio-political groupings and in the significance and impact of the means of mass (rather than class) communication. Both developments mean that civil society is structured on a progressively 'horizontal' rather than 'vertical' basis (1987: 311).

A related development that is particularly relevant for understanding legal change is the weakening of labour and social rights institutionalized by the welfare state. The internationalization and globalization of the world economy systematically shift the odds in the struggle between capital and labour. While labour and citizens are still closely tied to the nation state, capital becomes increasingly footloose. This changed balance of forces corrodes many of the advances for labour and the working class in the welfare state. In consequence, new patterns of inequality have appeared to produce "a bottom and excluded third of the 'two-thirds society'" (Lash and Urry, 1994: 145).

How do the changes catalogued above bear on the question of the postmodern? For Lash and Urry the answer is that postmodernism, as a set of aesthetic and critical perspectives, is the cultural accompaniment to the underlying structural processes of disorganized capitalism. There is an "elective affinity" between disorganized capitalism and postmodernism, and they are linked in a loose causal way: the capitalist infrastructure is partly fuelled by postmodern culture, but that environment also creates the conditions that make postmodern*ist* culture acceptable (1987: 285-296).

The project of charting the main features of an entirely new social formation and locating postmodernism within it receives a further refinement in David Harvey's *The Condition of Postmodernity* (1989). As the term "postmodernity" suggests, Harvey's analysis is concerned to embrace both cultural and structural phenomena, and see them as parts of an integrated totality. The particular objective of his work is to explain the exact nature of the causes of economic, political and cultural change over the last couple of decades. By comparing how the regime of accumulation interacts with the mode of social and political regulation – "the behaviours of all kinds of individuals ... into some kind of configuration that will keep the regime of accumulation functioning" – his emphasis is on the close linkages between the various social spheres (Harvey, 1989: 122). He sees the factors that precipitated a qualitative shift from one regime of accumulation to another beginning in 1972 and ending with the economic crisis of 1973 (1989: iv).[9] His explanatory framework entails going "back to basics", in particular Marx's understanding of the dynamics of capitalism in general (1989: 179). In a more emphatic conclusion about the determinative influence of economic events than that of Lash and Urry, he suggests that the crisis dealt the decisive blow to the political and economic consensus that underpinned the institutional framework of the postwar advanced capitalist democracies.

That particular consensus received expression in Keynesian market interventionism and Fordist production methods. Like Lash and Urry, Harvey too identifies the critical elements of the new regime as being a greater role for the state. Increasingly, the state played a central role in the processes of production, consumption and exchange, by means of a combination of the ownership of significant sectors of the economy, a high level of regulation of economic activity and significant levels of wealth redistribution in the form of the welfare state. The state form reflected a unique intermeshing of the political and economic spheres. Also, the organization of production was marked by a very high division of labour: factories increased in size and scope, while their workers were deployed to perform ever more specialized tasks. Harvey emphasizes the particularly modern features of industrial techniques pioneered by Henry Ford:

> What was special about Ford was ... his explicit recognition that mass production meant mass consumption, a new system of the reproduction of labour power, a new politics of labour control and management, a new aesthetics and psychology, in short, a new kind of rationalized, modernist, and populist democracy (1989: 125-126).

Harvey's Marxism, however, with its emphasis on "the mechanisms and logic of transitions" (1989: 179) impedes the possibility of examining how far causal influences operate in the other direction, or indeed whether some of these changes are susceptible to causal analysis at all. His account remains heavily economistic, devoting comparatively little attention to the political sphere. Accordingly, wider social, political and aesthetic changes are explained almost exclusively in terms of economic determination. Unlike Lash and Urry, Harvey emphasizes not so much the disorganization but the *coherence* of the new system (1989: 174). As a "regime of accumulation" it secures continued rates of profits by means of the rapid deployment of new organizational forms of production such as: small plant size; geographically dispersed units of production; decentralized and weakened industrial relations systems; small batch production; reduced turnover time; and an emphasis on niche rather than mass-marketing and production.

Thus the condition of "postmodernity", he concludes, can be seen as resulting from responses to the organizational rigidities that flow from the high level of vertical integration of production units in Fordist economies. These rigidities rendered them acutely vulnerable to changes in the economic environment. Flexibility was seen as the only available solution to these problems if profits were to be maintained. The introduction of multi-use equipment in small plants and the revival of multi-skilled workforces gives these units the capacity to adapt quickly to changes in demand from larger producers and consumers. Relying on similar evidence to that of other theorists of post or neo-Fordism, Harvey traces a trend toward vertical disintegration in the form of subcontracting, outsourcing and decentralization from this time. In consequence, workforces are more fragmented, and individual workers are tied to employers for shorter periods of time either directly, or as self-employed contractors (Pollert, 1988: 281). The net effect of these changes is that it becomes possible for enterprises to respond ever more rapidly to changes in the economic environment, but they do so particularly by reducing the costs of production, and therefore the security of labour. The new economic environment therefore represents a significant weakening of the power of labour in favour of capital; flexible accumulation represents the latest "shift to alternative systems of labour control (with all its political implications)" (Harvey, 1989: 192).

An important aspect of Harvey's analysis is his development and extension of Lash and Urry's analytical focus on the spatial dimensions of disorganization. He examines the reconfiguration of the spatial coordinates, but just as importantly, the temporal co-ordinates within which production, consumption and exchange take place. He elaborates in detail the way in which flexible accumulation has led to "an intense phase of space-time compression that has had a disorienting and disruptive impact upon political-economic practices, the balance of class power, as well as upon cultural and social life" (1989: 285). Capitalism has always exercised a corrosive effect on traditions, institutions and ways of perceiving them; but what is unique about the present conjuncture is that space and time are related in a different way.

There are a number of aspects to this process. First, a speeding-up of connection between these separate domains has occurred. The development of a "just-in-time" delivery system which requires much smaller stock inventories, smaller batch production and reskilling of labour has become an increasingly prevalent part of manufacturing (Mathews, 1989: 79-81). Second, the half-life of consumer products reduces: over the period dating from 1973 to the end of the 1980s, for instance, the seven- to five-year span of consumer durables shrank to less than four in textiles and one and a half in video and computer software (Harvey, 1989: 156). Third, the proliferating production and purchase of services, both in absolute terms, and as a proportion of total consumption, has a temporal dimension: they are more rapidly consumed, so that consumer demand is satisfied for only the briefest of time spans, and, unlike consumer durables, are in principle infinite. Consumption patterns reflect these changes as the consumption of goods gives way to consumption of services (1989: 285).

Fourth, the time-horizons of private and public decision-making have shrunk. An increasing temporariness affects products, values and personal relationships where short-term arrangements replace more permanent ties and institutions (Harvey, 1989: 288). The recent re-establishment of contract at the centre of social order prefigures a dramatically enhanced sociological significance of contractual principles in law, as we shall see in Chapter 5. Fifth, space is annihilated by time. The increasing sophistication of communications and transportation technologies has dramatically reduced the costs and barriers to international flows of information and influence (Harvey, 1989: ch 17). This internationalization or "globalization" of relations gives rise to a profound reorganization of space: an historically unique "time-space distanciation" appears where events many thousands of miles apart can influence each other immediately, unrestricted by national boundaries (Giddens, 1990: 64). The networks of social relations that are typical of globalization are better captured by a greater sensitivity to space than to time. Where a former sociology was framed more by temporal co-ordinates, so that social phenomena are primarily explained and understood in terms of their historical origins, spatial influences are now of more significance.

Finally, the structural changes receive expression in increasingly vertiginous postmodern cultural and ideological visions. Again, the shift is explicable in economic terms, specifically by reference to "the crisis of overaccumulation that began in the late 1960s and which came to a head in 1973". The result is that

> [t]he experience of time and space has changed, the confidence in the association between scientific and moral judgments has collapsed, aesthetics has triumphed over ethics as a prime focus of social and intellectual concern, images dominate narratives, ephemerality and fragmentation take precedence over eternal truths and unified politics ... (1989: 327-328).

This conclusion follows Frederic Jameson's characterization of postmodernism's interconnectedness with economic restructuring: it is "the cultural logic of late capitalism" (1984; 1991), where pastiche and a sense of depthlessness characterizes aesthetic production, replacing a former (modern) consciousness of enduring historical narratives with their deep roots in politics and ethics. Like Jameson, Harvey decries the emergence of the newer formation.

Taken together, the changes demonstrate a decisive historical watershed: the twilight of *modern* Fordist, Keynesian welfare states. This state form, far from breaking with the organizing principles of modern social organization, marked a refinement and extension of some of its central features. Both Harvey's and Lash and Urry's largely historical periodizations provide useful conceptual ammunition for the development of a sociology of postmodernity, and the understanding of the context of recent legal change.

The Sociology of Postmodernity

A sociological understanding of postmodernity receives its most wide-ranging and sophisticated elaboration in the work of Zygmunt Bauman. In what has become a vast corpus of theoretical inquiry, Bauman has not only presented critical and incisive perspectives on many of the themes of the theorists listed above, but has extended them into the realms of sociological theory, globalization and ethics. Like Harvey, Bauman sees postmodernity as the term best suited to capture the distinctiveness of the present social constellation and, in a theoretically decisive move, he seeks to correct an imbalance of postmodernist concern with predominantly cultural questions:

> Most current concepts of postmodernity refer solely to intellectual phenomena... Rarely, if at all, they step beyond the boundary of the spiritual, into the changing social figuration which the artistic, cultural and cognitive developments, bracketed as postmodern, may reflect (1992: 26).

Postmodern society and the "randomly assembled experience of postmodern life" exert an influence on its culture; they lend it "animus and momentum" (1992: 41). But Bauman's central focus is on postmodernity as a radically restructured society. It follows that "a sociology of postmodernity" must address this novel social environment. "The changing social figuration" imposes the following requirements: 1) postmodern cultural forms ought to be viewed as "surface symptoms of a much deeper transformation of the social world"; 2) "these deeper transformations [should] ... be sought in the spheres of systemic reproduction, social integration and the structure of the life-world ..."; 3) analyses of contemporary society need to adopt "a theoretical model of postmodern society as a system in its own right, rather than a distorted form, or an aberration from another system"; and, finally, 4)

> The model of postmodernity, unlike the models of modernity, cannot be grounded in the realities of the nation state, by now clearly not a framework large enough to accommodate the decisive factors in the conduct of interaction and the dynamics of social life. This circumstance makes the task particularly complex; the reality to be modelled is both in its present shape and in its plausible prospects, much more fluid, heterogenous and 'under-patterned' than anything the sociologists tried to grasp intellectually in the past (1992: 64-65).

At a deeper level change of this nature frustrates traditional sociological strategies for understanding "society". Bauman follows Alain Touraine in concluding that, paradoxically, sociology should no longer be the study of bounded societies. Of particular importance for the study of contemporary law, it needs to abandon "the idea that social life takes place within essential limits which in practice coincide with those of the nation-state *and its juridical institutions* or educational programs" (Touraine, 1989: 8; emphasis added). The recommended shift away from an exclusivity of focus on society conceived in terms of the self-contained nation state has since led to the emergence of two further distinctively postmodern notions into sociological analysis: the problem of spatialization in social theory and the emphasis on global flows rather than national institutions (Bauman, 1997; Featherstone and Lash, 1995: 2).

According to Bauman, all forms of sociological analysis that seek to deny the novelty of the present situation display a double and misleading traditionality. First, in denying the "existential autonomy of postmodernity" they treat contemporary changes merely as temporary aberrations, crises or deviations from a basically continuous modernity; second, they imply that the old tools of sociological analysis are all that is necessary to make sense of contemporary advanced societies. He concludes that "[f]or the discursive knowledge of postmodernity with a place in history and social space one needs however to turn to other responses [than those of traditional sociology]" (1992: 41-42). Included in these traditional responses are the structurally-oriented crisis theories of capitalism, for instance, the work of Habermas (1976), Gorz (1985) and Offe (1985), as well as the more culturally-informed versions, typified by Richard Sennett (1978) and Christopher Lasch (1977).[10] As these theorists generally suggest, though it is possible to trace the beginnings of a new social configuration in advanced capitalist societies from around the mid-1970s in each of the realms of state, economy and civil society, both the old sociological concepts apply, and a modified rather than transformed modernity is in place. For Bauman, by contrast, a perspective properly attuned to the cumulative magnitude of these changes requires an acknowledgement of a decisive break with modernity as evidenced by "the *systemness* of postmodern society" (1992: 52-3; italics in original).

Bauman demonstrates the extent of change by reference to a number of social spheres. In relation to economic activity, Bauman argues that it is precisely the transformed manner in which economies function in postmodern societies that renders unsatisfactory all production-focused crisis models for the purpose of understanding contemporary social change. The organization of production and the labour relation have been so dramatically reconfigured that labour ceases to be the central determinant in social integration and control. At the present time, it is consumption that assumes increasingly greater sociological significance. Seduction through signs, images and the promise of plenty is becoming the dominant strategy of social control: consumer conduct plays an increasingly central role in the "the cognitive and moral focus of life, the integrative bond of society, and the focus of systemic management" (1992: 49). It supplants the function formerly performed by *work* in the earlier phases of capitalism. Having secured control over the level of production, the system now deploys the pleasure principle to ensure a more effectively operating realm of consumption. Moreover, a principle grounded in pleasure hardly functions as oppression; rather, "[s]eduction is the paramount tool of integration (of the reproduction of domination) in a consumer society" (1992: 97-98). System management is increasingly geared toward ensuring the maximization of commodities and opportunities to consume. Freedom of consumer choice becomes entrenched as the correlative basic organizational principle of society, which in turn leads to the cultural valorization of "difference":

> Once consumer choice has been entrenched as the point in which systemic reproduction, social integration and individual life-world are co-ordinated and harmonized – cultural variety, heterogeneity of styles and differentiation of belief systems have become conditions of its success (1992: 52).

This line of analysis puts Bauman very much at odds with Harvey's productivist approach, despite clear points of overlap between their accounts. His analysis is also separated by a critical distance from the work of Foucault. While accepting the force of Foucault's perspective on the general significance of technologies of control in the constitution of modern societies, Bauman presents a powerful argument for rejecting his model of control as quite inadequate to understand postmodern society in its entirety.[11] For Bauman, lifestyle choices centred on bodily consumption and personal development perform a more decisive role in the forming of subjectivity than do the panoptical regimes of factories, schools and barracks. And unlike their predecessors, they are not felt as externally imposed, and therefore resisted, structures of control and discipline, but as consciously chosen expressions of the postmodern agent's freedom. Accordingly, the prominence of coercion as a social force wanes. Bauman is not arguing that analyses such as Foucault's should be rejected, but that contemporary societies are distinguished by the unique interplay of strategies of seduction and repression. He therefore restores both the concept of freedom to the centre of social theory, and also offers a more complex account of subjectivity and agency.

Another key indicator of postmodernity for Bauman is the decline of the "legislative reason" characteristic of the modern age. Legislative reason, most visible in the emergence of the nation state, entailed the centralization of power and authority and the parallel destruction of local traditions, regional patterns of authority and the fragmented networks of power of feudal societies. Its key operative principles were sovereignty and designed order. It entailed the banishment of "ambivalence" from dominant forms of thinking:

> In the intellectual realm, purging ambivalence means above all de-legitimizing all grounds of knowledge philosophically uncontrolled or

> uncontrollable. More than anything else, it means decrying 'common sense' be it 'mere beliefs', 'prejudices', 'superstition', or sheer manifestations of 'ignorance' (1992: 120-121).

The connections Bauman makes between the ideological notion of legislative reason and its institutional manifestation in the "obsession with the question of legislative power" allows the welfare state and its associated mass production and consumption to be seen as broadly continuous with those earlier "foundational politics" (1997: 36).

Postmodernity is distinguished by a revival of forms of thinking which reflect this earlier ambivalence. Legislative reason comes to be supplanted by an "interpretive" reason for which "relativity is not just a transitory state, but an apodictically given existential condition of knowledge ... Pluralism is an irremovable feature of such a world" (1992: 21-22). The contemporary influence of the relativistic and pragmatist approaches to knowledge claims detailed earlier in this chapter are for Bauman sociological evidence of a changed world. He concludes that the "tables have been turned" against the rationalists and empiricists, and that they are increasingly asked to "clear themselves of the charges of dogmatism, ethnocentricism, intellectual imperialism or whatever else their work may seem to imply when gazed upon from the relativist positions" (1992: 104). The presumed supremacy and superiority of Western Enlightenment values is being eroded, along with modernity's promise to establish objective measures of truth, judgment and taste. This conclusion is affirmed by the way in which modernity's universal tendency to launch assaults on "unlicensed difference" has given way to a postmodern ethics which centres on the affirmation of differences – social, ethnic, religious, sexual – and the celebration of the "other" becomes culturally dominant. The appearance of new social and political movements reflects this development.

Unlike some of the theories outlined above, Bauman's argument is less an affirmation of relativism than an acknowledgement of its contemporary ascendancy; so he advances more a sociology of knowledge than an epistemological position. At the same time, however, there are many echoes of sympathy with postmodern approaches to knowledge. In an extended discussion of "postmodern ethics" he voices guarded support for the new pluralism and heterogeneity of the postmodern world, and commends the waning of the typically modern, scientistic certitude at the present time (1993).

In a further departure from some of the normative underpinnings of the postmodernists, Bauman's weak relativism informs a forthright critique of the novel forms of poverty and powerlessness ushered in by the more market-driven social order. As one of postmodernity's "discontents"

(1997), he laments the attenuation of the welfare state project and the politics of inequality and hence of redistribution that it fostered (1997: ch 3). The new world that celebrates freedom to a greater extent than ever before has created a conspicuous lack of freedom for those excluded from the seductive pleasures provided by the market. It is for these people that repression is reserved, so that postmodernity must be understood as a period of their distinctive symbiosis and complementarity. The new regime represents a shift "from the welfare state to the prison", where "the task of coping with the collectively produced risks have been *privatized*" (1997: 37; italics in original). If redistributional concerns surface at present, they tend to be expressed in freedom-oriented discourses of human rights, and refracted through the lenses of oppressed minorities, rather than in traditional, labour-based languages and institutions. It is but a small step from this study of the current reconfiguration of the social and political order to the focus on the complex elements in the "postmodernization" of contemporary societies.

According to Stephen Crook, Jan Pakulski and Malcolm Waters (1992) the key to understanding contemporary societies is by reference to a former "modernization". Modernization is the historically unique emergence of distinct changes in the three key realms of state, economy and civil society. In the case of the state, the progressive centralization of power, and the ensuing monopolization of violence made the democratic nation state the ultimate source of legal and political authority. Economic production was industrialized and commodified by reference to principles of private property and the market in relation to capital, labour and product. Finally, in the domain of civil society, social actors become progressively emancipated from the bonds of tradition, community, religion and custom. The changes in each of these three spheres can be measured in the rise of individualism, and its adjunct, the "expansion of options" (Offe, 1987a: 5). Postmodernization, by contrast, marks the "continuation of the processes of modernization, where those processes operate with increasing scope and intensity to erode what appears in retrospect as the regional stability of modernity" (Crook et al., 1992: 120).

Taking their cue from both Talcott Parsons' (1977) and Jürgen Habermas' (1981) analyses of advanced societies, Crook, Pakulski and Waters argue that modernization is essentially a process whereby the problems of increasing social differentiation are resolved or stabilized by means of centralized, but ultimately unstable, co-ordination. By contrast, "[t]he shift from modernization to postmodernization is related to the convergence of modernizing processes on an 'impossible' combination of hyperdifferentiation with monocentric organization" (1992: 220). The term "hyperdifferentiation" refers to the acceleration of structural differentiation in contemporary societies. They claim that this is a pervasive feature of each of the significant social domains. In the economy, for example, they expand on the capitalist disorganization thesis, concluding that the process is clearly evidenced in the contemporary structure of work. Whereas in the post-Second World War era patterns of work were increasingly organized along the lines of Fordist mass production, and so social classes were differentiated according to their *function*, differentiation is now being manifested at the level of *structure* also. Thus mass production is increasingly overtaken by niche-marketing, outworking, subcontracting, and flexible specialization. There are clear resonances here with Harvey's analysis, but they provide a more sociological analysis derived from the theoretical perspective of functionalism: "the patterns of economic production may be said to be hyperdifferentiating, providing a multiplicity of directions in the absence of a unifying structural principle" (1992: 33).

The process of functional differentiation in modern societies implies a limited range of institutions: economy, politics, law, for instance. In contrast, recent developments provide evidence of an exponential increase in social complexity which in turn induces these institutions to split into more specialized units. One direct consequence is that social organization becomes "impossible" because in the context of the increasing complexity of social life control is more hazardous, more uncertain: "[u]nder postmodernization, hyperdifferentiation ensures that the consequences of a given piece of bureaucratic or economic manipulation cannot be foreseen. States become ungovernable, economies unmanageable, and lifeworlds anarchistic" (1992: 35). As structures undergo transformation in order to confront this changed social environment a process of *de-differentiation* emerges. There is a fusion of social institutions and elements, previously differentiated, into quite novel combinations: institutions formerly characterized by ideologies and practices at odds with strictly economic criteria, begin to operate in ways analogous to the market. As the analysis in chapter 5 will suggest, law is no exception: a process of disautonomization, or de-differentiation, begins to affect it in parallel fashion to other social spheres.

Crook, Pakulski and Waters' claim that postmodernization is measured by institutional change leads them to consider the transformation of the modern state. The rise and expansion of the nation state marked the high point of one sphere of social modernization. Moreover, the establishment of the welfare state represents the culmination of this process. It follows that welfare states can only be understood as the result of an interplay of some of the variables which constitute the core elements of modernization, including the democratic, politically centralized nation state (see also Flora and Heidenheimer, 1981: ch 1). In recent times, however, a unique process of reversal of this historical trend is at work, as this form of state apparatus contracts. The historical uniqueness of this contraction can be seen in an "unravelling" along two axes. "Vertically" power is transferred upwards to supranational institutions, and downwards to the market. "Horizontally" former state functions are shed, exemplified by decentralization and the dismantling of corporatism, and the delegation of traditionally state-provided welfare responsibilities to private organizations or individuals (Crook et al., 1992: 97).

State shrinking in an "upward" direction is evidenced in the recent exponential growth of international economic activity, and the comparably increasing influence of international institutions on states and societies. The dawning of modernity is marked by the emergence of nation states as the only legitimate actors in the international sphere. In turn, the underlying principle of modern international order is that states retain sovereign power within their own territories, and are autonomous from one another. The range of recent changes to the structure of the international order and the fabric of international institutions has altered this framework and has meant that nation states are not only less significant agents within their own boundaries, but have a reduced dominance on the international stage.

In addition to the growing influence of the institutions of global or regional governance such as the United Nations and European Union over domestic matters once the exclusive preserve of the nation state, Crook, Pakulski and Waters point to the proliferation of international agencies which operate between the major trading blocs to regulate financial markets, exchange rates and monetary policy (1992: 101). As sources of supranational norms embodied in conventions and treaties they may now have an impact on domestic economies as dramatic as internal political decisions, and domestic norms. Their argument is confirmed by more recent developments, such as the expanding role of regulatory bodies such as the World Trade Organization (WTO) with jurisdiction to settle international trade disputes.

The extent of change is demonstrated by the proliferation of Non-Government Organizations (NGOs). They reflect a change in the dimensions of civil society, changing patterns of political influence, and the transformed fabric of governance. They may be effective at policing international obligations in the absence of developed mechanisms of international enforcement. In this sense it may not be appropriate to describe them as "non-governmental" at all: they are deeply imbricated in the system of international governance (Hirst and Thompson, 1996: 191). In this way, they have come to supplement, and in some instances counterbalance, the influence of another, more established, group of non-governmental players on the global stagethe transnational corporations (Santos, 1995: 268). A changed, and revised, international civil society is emerging with an enhanced influence on domestic national affairs and institutions. This new civil society co-exists and interacts with an emerging international political society.

The power of international organizations is not exercised directly as they have little scope for independent action. Furthermore, while goods, capital and finance are relatively footloose, populations are still largely tied to states, so that states retain much exclusive territorial power. But given the increased interdependency of nations, the costs of international isolation are now so high, politically and economically, that this has become an increasingly unviable option for states to take. This changed political landscape fuels the growth in normative force of agreements reached in international political forums. The "new sovereignty" therefore lies in the fact that "[n]ation states are now simply one class of powers and political agencies in a complex system of power from world to local levels, but they have a centrality because of their relationship to territory and population" (Hirst and Thompson, 1996: 190).

This brief overview of changes in national sovereignty is not meant to suggest that the internal political structures of societies bounded by the nation state have been eclipsed by the emergence of global institutions. Rather, international political institutions have developed which are beginning to wield the sorts of powers and influences historically associated *exclusively* with sovereign states. A unique overlapping and interpenetration of political power results. Law is no less transformed, as the discussion below will claim. But states still play a pivotal role in the absence of a sovereign global legislature or executive. Not only have international institutions gained their powers primarily with the consent and active involvement of states, but the efficacy and legitimacy of those institutions remains contingent both on states' support, and the extent to which states operate as conduits between them and national populations of citizens. Moreover, the emerging globalization can be seen as *post*modern to the extent that it differs from the international imperialist expansion practised by nation states. Modern imperialism consolidated the power and autonomy of those states for which it was achievable. By contrast, globalization weakens the power of states, and the contemporary interconnection and interdependency of all global areas happens in a less purposeful way.

The increasing significance of the global dimension necessitates an examination of the ways in which these influences are refracted by national forces: global inputs are re-written and displaced in many different ways within particular national environments so that the local and the distant combine in novel ways. Globalization induces a *hybridization* of political and social forms at odds with the monocentrism of modernity (Pieterse, 1995). In this context, a former sociological focus on national traditions needs at the very least to be tempered by a notion of cultural migration and interpenetration. The novel forms of social power and influence displace *society* as the central category of social theory. Where earlier sociology characterized social change as the internal development of particular societies, a more relevant consideration now is how social change is best seen in terms of "the outcome of struggles between members of a configuration of inter-dependent and competing nation-states" (Featherstone and Lash, 1995: 2). While modern nation states remained sovereign, it was entirely appropriate for social theory to assume that society, and *law*, were equally circumscribed. With the emergence of globalizing processes, however, a different set of conceptual tools is required. Legal paradigms that fail to incorporate these profound changes cannot capture accurately the nature of contemporary law.

Along the vertical axis, the unravelling of the state is evident "downwards" by the devolution of power to the market. The nationalization characteristic of welfare states was an integral element in the process of social and economic modernization on a national scale. It also furthered the project of social solidarity by reversing inequities produced by market mechanisms in areas of individual need such as utilities, transport, health and education (Crook et al., 1992: ch 3). In direct contrast, a dramatic reversal of direction of this pattern of modernization is in train at the present time. Now privatization, deregulation and marketization are the preferred mechanisms by which governance is secured. Since the late 1970s the privatization of state-owned manufacturing and trading corporations has occurred in all welfare states. Even countries such as the United States, where the state has had historically negligible ownership of industrial enterprises, have nonetheless held vast public assets (Reich, 1964), which are now being increasingly transferred to private ownership and control. Moreover, market activity is increasingly deregulated, in the sense that it is subjected to less intrusive and less redistributive forms of regulation than applied by welfare states.

A parallel development to those identified above is the selectively decreasing level of welfare provision and the progressive transfer to the private sector of the traditional welfare functions of the state. This general trend can also be seen at work in the progressive withdrawal of the state's monopoly of provision in various welfare fields, and the correlative assumption of control by the various segments of civil society, predominantly the market, though also to significant degrees, voluntary agencies, charities, and religious organizations. Also, individuals are increasingly cut adrift from universal entitlements to benefits in place of user-pays principles. More dramatic changes still are evident in housing and education where the balance of state/private support has shifted markedly in favour of private provision. The dismantling of the state monopolies of service is commonly achieved by creating market incentives to allow private providers to compete with public institutions.

Marketization increasingly replaces state provision. The influence of contractual principles does not stop there: the *contracting* state in relation to its internal functions adopts contractual models in order to achieve efficiencies and a greater level of accountability in its internal operations (Harden, 1992). Moreover, the state increasingly relies on a strategy of governance *through* contract by contracting with private providers to supply public services (Boston, 1995; Yeatman, 1995). These changes herald the emergence of a social structure (and, as discussed in chapter 5, legal regimes and doctrines) quite at odds with those definitive of the welfare state.

Though some have seen in this transformation evidence of a general crisis of the welfare state (Mishra, 1984), it is more accurate to emphasize that even if there is a dismantling of the welfare state in progress at the present time, it is still more in the nature of a goal aimed at, and only patchily achieved, than a destination reached. As Pierson notes, after a review of the literature "not so much sheer survival nor even the level of expenditure but the *type of welfare state regime*. It is this last feature that may be changing most rapidly and profoundly" (Pierson, 1991:183). New patterns of inequality emerge in this new environment as the universal benefits guaranteed by welfare states are progressively stripped away (Crook, Pakulski and Waters, 1992: 102-103; ch 4). The qualitative shift provides highly pertinent implications for change in the structure of legal rights that define citizenship.

Horizontally, the state transfers power by decentralization. Corporatism is dissolved, unions are pushed from government, and industrial relations are transferred increasingly to the local level. The size of the state is also reduced as many functions are transferred to autonomous agencies or to the local level. Both developments complement strategies of marketization. Overall, these changes to the state are:

> synonymous with a change in the general socio-economic idiom: from the 'visible hand' of politics to the 'invisible hand' of the market; from administrative-political redistribution to market-regulated provision; from authoritative commands to less obtrusive control; from centralized regulation to polycentric and consumer-oriented competition; from entitlements to provisions (Crook, Pakulski and Waters, 1992: 99).

Of course, an "unravelling", or "contracting", state (Freeman, 2000a) does not imply a shift *backward* to premodern patterns of social organization; rather, transformations reaching *beyond* the nation statein the sense of being at odds with the general trajectory of social modernizationare increasingly in evidence.

Changes at the level of the state and the economy are replicated in politics and civil society. Traditional class politics in the policies of the former representative parties are displaced by "new social movements". Like the theorists of capitalist disorganization and postmodernity, Crook, Pakulski and Waters point to the phenomenon of allegiances drifting away from the mainstream parties whose policies were geared to a class constituency defined almost exclusively in relation to the labour process, in favour of a politics which gives greater emphasis to other, non labour-related issues (1992: ch 5). The broad transfer of political allegiances results from the increasing impossibility of mass political parties to be the mouthpiece for the interests of one class. Insofar as the values espoused are largely indifferent to questions of class, they are more cultural than economic. Alain Touraine provides the following snapshot of the new environment:

> From the seventies to today, the displacement of protest from the economic to the cultural field has been linked to an opposite tendency, the privatization of social problems, an anxious search for identity and a new interest in the body, demands which can lead to the definition of new social norms or, in an opposite way, to an individualism which excludes collective action (1985: 784).

Ronald Inglehart brings to the concept of postmodernization a rich empirical analysis of how "postmaterialist" values have become dominant in the fabric of civil society in the sense of being both unrelated to transfers of material wealth, and also directed to policies which undercut the productivism of modern political movements (Inglehart, 1977; 1997). He identifies modernization as defined by the core societal project of maximization of economic growth, the key individual value as achievement motivation, and the typical authority system as rational-legal authority (1997: ch 3). Postmodernization, by contrast, consists of a core societal project of maximizing subjective well-being, the primacy of postmaterialist values and a "de-emphasis of *both* legal and religious authority" (1997: 76). This argument also locates the post-war welfare state as an advanced example of the modernization process. Inglehart tracks this widespread shift in values across 43 societies of varying degrees of economic and political modernization; it is reflected in the pruning of the corporatist and highly redistributive arrangements of the welfare state noted above. Anti-economic growth policies are prevalent, such as environmentalism, protection of human rights, indigenous rights and resistance to certain forms of technological progress. They are also more oriented to development and enhancement of experiences in the personal, the familial, the private sphere which attempt to reverse the differentiated nature of modern existence (Inglehart, 1997: chs 5 and 9).

A related manifestation of the different politics of new social movements is their advocacy of sets of policies no less at odds with those which accompany the rise of the traditional nation state: a "politics of recognition" come to the fore (Taylor and Gutman, 1992). Recognition in this context refers to a set of claims to respect based on the particular identity of individual citizens. Identity covers ethnic, racial, religious, sexuality and gender issues that define individuals. This overall movement can be described as a general shift in the grammar of political claims, from "a politics of redistribution to a politics of recognition" (Fraser, 1997). It entails

> an apparent shift in the political imaginary ... in which the central problem of justice is recognition. With this shift, the most salient social movements are no longer economically defined 'classes' who are struggling to defend their 'interests', end 'exploitation', and win 'redistribution'. Instead, they are culturally defined 'groups' or 'communities of value' who are struggling to defend their 'identities', end 'cultural domination', and win 'recognition'. The result is a decoupling of cultural politics from social politics, and the relative eclipse of the latter by the former (Fraser, 1997: 2).

In light of these changes, notions of community start to take on very different meanings: where communities were conceived in the post-war welfare state as bounded by nation-based co-ordinates, even if expressed in terms of class, such as nationally organized trade unions, bourgeoisies and political movements, these forms of identity have started to break down. In a development paralleling changes in politics, transnational organizations attract an increasing measure of support. This demographic shift away from the political, economic and social arrangements characteristic of the post-war welfare state consensus in favour of a widespread cosmopolitanism is also a decisive factor in explaining recent legal change.

Conclusion

To analyze law by reference to concepts of postmodernization and postmodernity avoids the charges of many of the critiques directed at the sociological, political, ethical and aesthetic deficiencies of postmodernism. But a different line of critique suggests that the historical or sociological concept of postmodernity fares no better for the reason that it is either unworkable or misconceived because the world has not changed to a sufficient degree over recent decades to justify the application of a revised periodization. An explicit and striking example of this argument is Alex Callinicos's *Against Postmodernism* (1989) which concludes that basically it is business as usual for capitalism, and that "postmodern" attempts to theorize "New Times", or an historical break in social and economic life, "grossly exaggerate the extent of the changes involved" (1989: 135). From this perspective, while postmodernism as a set of cultural practices might be evident (and lamentably so), postmodernity as a distinct phase of historical development has not yet appeared. Callinicos acknowledges that similar structural changes as those identified by Harvey have occurred, but argues that they have not fundamentally changed the basic capitalist infrastructure of three decades ago. Social theoretical accounts of the development of law which identify the law of the welfare state as the latest, rather than a surpassed, phase, or "paradigm", of legal evolution lend implicit support to Callinicos's thesis about a basically continuous late modernity (Unger, 1976; Ewald, 1986; Habermas, 1996: ch 9).

Against these arguments, however, lies the wide array of postmodern social theory briefly summarized above. The sheer amount and variety of evidence gathered in this body of work suggests that this type of sociological and historical critique seriously underestimates the extent of the changes that have occurred. The process of postmodernization represents a decisive historical watershed that marks a shift away from many of the institutional arrangements typical of Fordist, interventionist welfare states. David Harvey, coincidentally writing in the same year as Callinicos, after a detailed review of all the literature concludes that the "evidence for increased flexibility (subcontracting, self-employment, etc.) throughout the capitalist world is simply too overwhelming ..." (1989: 191). Anthony Giddens advances a similar position in his examination of postmodernity. One of his concerns in addressing the debate about postmodernity is to shift focus away from epistemological and methodological questions to an examination of their distinctive structural features at the present time. Though he rejects a concept of postmodernity in what he describes as its "poststructuralist" manifestations in favour of "an institutional analysis of modernity with cultural and epistemological overtones" (1990:1), he nonetheless posits a conception of "radicalized modernity" that substantially overlaps with the postmodernization detailed above. The notion of radicalized modernity emphasizes that many institutional developments have displaced key elements of classical modernity, and like the concepts of postmodernity and postmodernization, it refers to "transformations moving 'beyond' the institutions of modernity" (1990: 150). The table on the opposite page seeks to represent the extent of the contrast.

While none of these many changes alone would justify the description of a completely new system, they can be seen to contribute cumulatively to a very different, measurably cohesive and historically distinctive social environment, with its own "existential autonomy" (Bauman, 1992: 42). Moreover, the *interconnected combination of these factors* best explains the present condition, rather than a focus on one factor

Table 2.1 Late Modernity and Postmodernity Compared

Organized capitalism/ welfare state late modernity/ late modernization	*Disorganized capitalism/ flexible postmodernity/ postmodernization*
STATE	
National organization of markets; redistributive regulation	De- and co-regulation; markets globalized
Growth in size of state	Contraction of state
Consolidation of welfare state	Attenuation of welfare state
Limited restrictions on national sovereignty; imperialism	Diminution of national sovereignty; growth of global institutions
Increasing nationalization	Increasing privatization
Rise of corporatism	Breakdown of corporatist governance
ECONOMY	
Growth of cartels, Fordist production; increase in plant and workforce size	PostFordist production; outsourcing; multiskilling; reduction in plant size
Industrialized extractive and manufacturing sector predominates	Postindustrial service sector predominates
Mass production	Small batch/ niche marketing
National concentration and centralization of finance and capital	Internationalization of finance and capital
Industrial concentration in fewer firms and regions	Geographical dispersion of production
Nationally-based production and consumption	Globally-oriented production and consumption
CIVIL SOCIETY	
Class structure based primarily on capital/labour split	Class structure based on multiple identities
Political parties reflect economic class cleavages	New social movements; decline in class-based politics
Increasing influence of trade unions	Decline of trade unions
Growth of industrial cities	Decline of industrial cities
Rise of manufacturing working class	Relative/absolute decline in manufacturing working class
Work paradigm central to identity	Consumption paradigm central
Organized functional differentiation	Disorganized hyper-differentiation/ de-differentiation
Speeding up of time and consolidation of nationally organized space	Acceleration of time and fragmentation of national space
Nationally organized politics of distribution	Locally and globally organized politics of recognition

Sources: Lash and Urry (1987); Harvey (1989); Crook et al., (1992); Bauman (1992).

alone, such as the rise of neo-liberalism, the crisis of the welfare state, globalization, or even the "postnational constellation" (Habermas, 2001). The table includes a variety of labels to identify late modernity and postmodernity because they largely overlap and represent a broad consensus among the theorists referred to above. It is important to emphasize, however, that to characterize these processes as postmodernization is not to suggest the *replacement* of one set of (modern) structures by another. Rather, the concept indicates that at the present time we are witnessing practices and institutions that operate along different lines. In this way, contemporary social changes often supplement in a cumulative fashion an already secure but now reconfigured set of modern institutions.

Having drawn the conceptual boundaries it is now possible to examine how the notions of modernity and postmodernity may be useful for understanding law and legal institutions, and exactly where the legal order of the welfare state fits into this schema. To embark on this exercise first requires an analysis of the general characteristics of modern law. This will be followed by tracing how the specific social, political and economic changes ushered in by welfare states impacted on law and legal institutions. It will then be possible to address the question of the extent to which the changes described and analyzed by the theories of postmodernity and postmodernization above are reflected in a process of legal postmodernization.

Notes

1 This distinction has also been used in various formulations by many other leading commentators. See, for example, Jameson (1984; 1991); Lash (1990); Harvey (1989).

2 I am using the phrase in a somewhat different way to that of Jameson (1984). He defined "cognitive mapping" as an aesthetic perspective oriented to the incorporation of a spatial understanding of contemporary change. Nonetheless, to the extent that this also requires critical examination of the divergent theories of change, it entails the location of theories of the postmodern at the same time.

3 Toynbee (1963). See also Best and Kellner (1991: 6).

4 Cited in Jencks (1977: 15). This statement originally appeared in an article by van der Rohe in the magazine *G*, Berlin, 1924.

5 I am all too aware how abbreviated this discussion is. Also relevant to any examination of the French development of poststructuralism and postmodernism are the works of Roland Barthes, Gilles Deleuze, Felix Guattari, Jacques Lacan and Jean Baudrillard. I have not discussed them here both for reasons of space, and the fact that the relationship and relevance of their work for law is less obvious. For an excellent and critical overview of this broad intellectual movement, see Dews (1984; 1987); Best and Kellner (1991). For an argument identifying elements of Lacan's work of possible relevance to law, see Barron (1993).

6 For a thoughtful examination of the distinctions, and linkages, see Huyssen (1984).

7 See on this point Redding (1986).

8 Obviously there are large differences across national boundaries. On the reasons for the comparative absence of corporatism in the United States, see Salisbury (1979), and generally, Lash and Urry (1987: ch 8).

9 This point is strikingly evocative of Charles Jencks' (1977) identification of the timing of the seismic shift in architectural practice, and Lash and Urry's timing of the emergence of "the end of organized capitalism" (1987).

10 Bauman is prepared to concede that Offe does not quite fit this bill: he is much closer than any of these theorists to being a theorist of postmodernity insofar as his later work is keenly attuned to certain epochal shifts consistent with Bauman's own account. See generally, Bauman (1992: ch 2).

11 The difficulties with Foucault's work will be examined in more detail in chapter 6, at pp 207-221.

3 Modern Law and the Welfare State

> There was no canned soup in the middle ages (Friedman, 1986: 18).

> Then imagine, after a while, all this changing. The snake enters the garden; the middle classes start to rise; thoughts fall apart from feelings, so that nobody thinks through their fingertips any more; and history starts out on its long trek towards Mr George Bush (Eagleton, 1990: 366).

> The cricketers of today play the cricket of a specialized stratum, that of functionaries in the Welfare State (James, 1963: 211).

Introduction

The concept of postmodernity as elaborated in the previous chapter, with its historical and sociological resonances, offers a periodization that will allow a distinction to be drawn between the legal structure of the "modern" welfare state on the one hand, and a putatively postmodern present on the other. But before the extent of the differences between these two historical stages can be identified it is necessary to define with some precision what is embraced by the term "welfare state", and how it is to be distinguished from earlier, liberal societies. The term has acquired a wide variety of meanings in the literature. At its narrowest it simply means a range of state policies directed to the provision of some basic welfare services such as income maintenance, health care, housing and education. More generally, it can refer to a particular form of state apparatus that has welfare policies as its central or defining feature. Alternatively, it may designate a particular kind of polity where that state is seen to be linked to other institutions of government.

In its broadest sense it describes a specific type of society with a distinctive mode of governance, where political authority, economic power and social structure are interconnected (Pierson, 1991: 7). It is this last definition that will be used throughout this chapter in order to capture the widest range of factors that have influenced law, and to identify a number of variables that reveal a clear dividing-line between the typical institutional features of modern societies (both in their liberal and welfare state phases), and their counterparts in this later historical period. The focus of this chapter will be first, on the continuities between liberal societies and welfare states, and the changes that distinguish them, and second, on parallel developments in the legal domain. The general conclusion is that the manifold changes introduced by the welfare state amount to a shift from the "liberal paradigm" of law to a "social welfare paradigm" (Habermas, 1996: ch 9). In spite of the extent of this transition, they are both paradigms of modern law.

Much of the postmodern*ist* theoretical literature appears indifferent to this question, and applies a very gummy analytical bite in relation to understanding the distinctively modern features of the welfare state and the transformation of its central institutions. Foucault's work, for instance, in its focus on the shift from "classical" to "modern" societies, assumes a continuity between liberal and welfare states: either the "disciplines", or a creeping "governmentality", are the defining features of an essentially unitary modernity. For Lyotard, the emergence of post-industrial society with its associated world-views is the key historical moment setting the postmodern era apart from a modern past; but as we have seen above, this is but one of many developments which mark the appearance of welfare states. Of itself, it is quite insufficient to provide a comprehensive understanding of a postmodern condition far more complex than Lyotard's account describes.

Postmodernist positions make strong objections to the style of theorizing proposed here. The general approach of identifying stages of historical development, of which the marking of successive "paradigms" of law might be said to be an obvious example, results in a level of generality akin to the much discredited "totalization", or "metanarrative" (Foucault, 1980; Lyotard, 1984). In chapter 6 further criticisms of various forms of this objection will be canvassed. At this point I would merely argue that developmental models of large-scale social and legal change can help to delineate the distinctive characteristics of the object in view, and then allow legitimate generalizations to be made. The plausibility of those generalizations will depend on how they are framed, the extent to which they admit of revision, whether they overreach the available evidence, and whether the evidence they rely on adequately justifies any evaluative assessments made. But theory-building in general should not be dismissed *a priori* any more than small scale images of narrowly circumscribed localities should be considered to be intrinsically more informative than large-scale maps (Santos, 1987).

A compelling example of this argument comes from a feminist perspective. To understand the general nature of male domination in a satisfactory way, argue Nancy Fraser and Linda Nicholson, it is quite insufficient, though nonetheless important, to analyze local, particular and historically specific conditions. To present a more complete picture of historical processes, such detailed, empirical approaches need to be supplemented by "large narratives about changes in social organization and ideology, empirical and social-theoretical analyses of macrostructures and institutions" (1988: 91). Moreover, analysis pitched at a high level of generality can yield important ideas for institutional reform. In the case of law, the elaboration of macro-conceptual legal paradigms is an important step in "illuminat[ing] the horizon of a given society" and thus exposing key elements of the legal landscape in order to advance legal rights by revealing opportunities and possibilities for change (Habermas, 1996: 437).

To describe shifts from one legal paradigm to another is not to imply that each period of legal development entails the simple displacement of an earlier legal paradigm by a later one. My argument is less ambitious; it suggests that the restructuring of one phase of legal development marks an "additive, or cumulative, rather than substitutive" process of transformation (Willke, 1986: 286). A stress on the "additive" nature of change represents an attempt to avoid a common weakness in historical, or evolutionary, models of law which tend to over-emphasize the extent of change because of a zero-sum presumption that the appearance of a new legal form involves the destruction of another (Blankenburg, 1984: 273, 283). By contrast, the following chapters will emphasize the extent to which typical features of earlier paradigms live on within new frameworks. If evolutionary models exaggerate the causal factors at work in social change they deserve to be rejected. Equally, general theories of evolutionary development are inappropriate if they imply an inexorable advance towards higher forms of life, or marshall evidence too selectively to fit a particular political vision, or even where the direction of change is exaggerated and counter-tendencies are ignored. Absent these failings, broad developmental or evolutionary narratives of legal change are instructive and inescapable (Nonet and Selznick, 1978: 19).

Any examination of the links between social and legal change raises the thorny question of the causal priority of one over the other; but the preferable position is to see them as inextricably intertwined so that in advanced societies, social change cannot occur without parallel changes in the legal sphere. Legal change and social change are functionally interdependent so that "law is, as an indispensable element of the social structure, always cause and effect simultaneously" (Luhmann, 1985: 227). The discussion below will examine how modernizing social processes are reflected in change both at the level of the general structure of the legal system, and in the content of legal norms. And legal change is a necessary factor in, and thus contributes to, broader social transformation.

Modern Society, Modern Law

Modern societies can be identified by the appearance of a cluster of historically unique features, each of which is reflected in fundamental transformation of law. The most striking indicator of the emergence of these societies lies in the change in their political and administrative structures. Feudal patterns of political organization were completely transformed as the nation state came to be the centre of political power. In the place of the fractured and overlapping sites of authority of feudal societies, where monarchs, aristocracy and the Church competed for allegiance, modern societies are marked by an historically unique centralization of political authority. In consequence, the notion of sovereignty is a dominant theme in modern political theory (Bodin, 1955 [1576]; Hobbes, 1968 [1651]). The economic infrastructure of feudalism was transformed to no less a degree. In the place of traditional, local and household-based patterns of production and consumption, markets came to be the dominant mechanism of economic organization in modern societies. The market, with its commodification of production and consumption, proved to be corrosive of the customary forms of feudal economic relations. It both required and fostered the growth of individualism. The capitalist economy was consolidated further by the industrialization of production, and with the development of markets in finance and capital.

Modern societies are also historically distinctive by virtue of the differentiation of their various subsystems. Differentiation refers to the process by which societies are organized into separate spheres. In contrast to feudal societies that were hierarchically differentiated, with the various strata of society allocated different social tasks (knights for military service, serfs for manual labour, for instance) modern societies are functionally differentiated, with subsystems such as law, politics, economy, science, religion and art, characterized by their own distinctive and autonomous functions. Each of these differentiated social spheres requires distinctive types of rationality in order to perform their separate functions at an optimal level. This process of rationalization comes to regulate all modern social subsystems. It involves the development of forms of instrumental rationality concerned exclusively with the solution of specific problems by resolving the best means of achieving particular ends rather than by assessing the desirability of those ends by a broader reference to custom, tradition or ethical value, as was typical in feudal societies. Also, in modern societies rights of participation in social subsystems are not confined to particular social strata, but are progressively extended to citizens as a whole.

Related developments appear in the spheres of knowledge and culture. They also become differentiated from one another, gradually splitting into a number of separate fields that operate according to their own inner, distinctive modes of rationality. The philosophical project of modernity can be described as a general program of developing objective science, universal morality and law, and autonomous art, according to their separate, inner logics. One aspect of this process is the progressive secularization of values and norms: they are systematically and progressively decoupled from any unitary religious or traditional world-view. The general objective of the Enlightenment philosophers was to utilize this accumulation of specialized knowledge and culture for the rational organization of society (Habermas, 1981). Of course, this general process did not unfold with any consistency or uniformity across time and place: in every society modernization has progressed at different rates and to different extents, and its constituent elements are blended in unique ways in various countries. Yet in spite of its varying and uneven paths of development, modernization has invariably advanced at the expense of traditional forms of social organization, and by means of replacing the structures of feudal societies with historically unique institutions.

The general advance of social modernization was reflected in profound changes in law. Feudal societies were marked by multiple and overlapping legal orders. A complex patchwork of legal jurisdictions, originating in a range of sources, governed every stratum of feudal society. Customary law regulated relationships at the community or local level; a separate system of royal law subjected freemen to monarchal authority; municipal law regulated relationships within towns; and *lex mercatoria*, or law merchant, applied to certain classes of trading relationships. Finally, each of these orders operated under canon law (Bloch, 1961; Berman, 1983). Not only were each of these sets of substantive legal norms different, inconsistent and incompatible, but they were also governed by their own forms of procedural law administered by separate systems of courts without any unifying administrative apparatus, shared interpretive techniques or common professional expertise. And these distinct legal orders mirrored the disaggregated and diffuse centres of political power in feudal societies – local, aristrocratic, monarchal and papal.

Legal modernization was registered by transformations of each of these elements of feudal law. Most distinctively, modern law breaks with feudal law in respect of a general transformation of the sources of legal norms. The centralizing ambitions of emergent nation states were expressed in a general strategy of marginalization, destruction or assimilation of the conflicting, contradictory and pluralistic sources and aggregations of norms typical of feudal society. The confused, "ambivalent" character of the legal landscape demanded decisive action on the part of states to suppress competing sources of legal authority:

> In the political realm, purging ambivalence means segregating or deporting strangers, sanctioning some local powers and delegalizing the unsanctioned ones, filling the 'gaps in the law'... [I]ts correlate [lay] in what may be called the *foundational politics* of the rising modern state; there was a striking symmetry of declared ambitions and practised strategies, as well as a similar obsession with the question of sovereignty of legislative power expressed as the principle of universality of legal or philosophical principles (Bauman, 1992: 120-121).

Over time in modern societies, the making and repeal of laws came to be monopolized by national sovereigns. Central to the enforcement of uniform laws applicable throughout the national territory is the monopolization of violence by states. Without effective mechanisms of enforcement, a drastic curtailment of the role of legal rule-making institutions below the level of the nation state followed. The multiple, overlapping legal orders typical of feudal societies operating within a shared geographical space were gradually replaced by national law applying uniformly within the spatial confines of the state's borders.

The emergent internal sovereignty of nation states in the early modern period influenced external developments. As authority was centralized within the territorial confines of the sovereign nation state, the relationship between domestic legal orders and supranational norms changed. An important historical watershed is the Treaty of Westphalia (1648) in which leading sovereign European powers expressed mutual recognition of each other's legislative supremacy within national borders. In consequence, laws enacted extraterritorially could not bind citizens or states unless and until incorporated into domestic law by an act of the sovereign, and the only legal rights and obligations enforceable by citizens within nation states were those that the sovereign had agreed to recognize. Eventually the influence of canon law dwindled in all countries. With both external and internal sources of law drained of their independent normative force, modern law is marked by a shift from a polycentric to a monocentric legality as sovereign nation states assumed exclusive lawmaking power, and a unified judiciary as part of the state apparatus gradually acquired sole authority over legal interpretation. This process of systematization and rationalization of law achieved by modern nation states emulated the Papal Revolution of the 11th century, by means of which the Church of Rome secured autonomy from secular powers, while the papacy achieved internal legal sovereignty over all aspects of the Church's affairs (Berman, 1983).

Modern law is not only distinctive by virtue of the source of its legal norms, but by the manner in which they come into existence. It is typically in the form of positive law, and an object of human creation through the agency of a unitary sovereign state. This "positivization" of law (Luhmann, 1985: 147-158) was certainly present in feudal law; but in modernity it becomes the most prevalent type of law, and is the mechanism by which sovereign states asserted their authority against competing normative orders. Because of the legal supremacy of the sovereign, a related innovation in the structure of modern law was the centrality of sovereignty in legal interpretation. In order to find the law, the key to legal validity lay in whether particular norms had been sanctioned by the sovereign: only these norms could attain legal status. In this respect modern law shared similar objectives to modern philosophy and science. The self-professed aim of modern philosophy was the establishment of unassailable foundations upon which the rational ordering of society might be possible:

> Modern rulers and modern philosophers were first and foremost *legislators*; they found chaos, and set out to tame it and replace it with order. The orders they wished to introduce were by definition artificial, and as such had to rest on designs appealing to the laws that claimed the sole endorsement of reason and by the same token de-legitimised all opposition to themselves (Bauman, 1992: 119).

Insofar as positive law was an "artificial" creation, law was substantively autonomous from other types of norms. To discover law required a different test from the reference to, or deduction from, moral, customary or religious norms.

The artificial nature of modern law and the demands of unitary sovereignty required a distinctive style of legal hermeneutics for the purpose of interpreting the law. Consistent with the rationalization of different social spheres, modern law developed its own, peculiar methodology, an "artificial reason" (Coke, 1642), which was autonomous from other forms of practical reasoning. Modern law can also be distinguished by means of the institutions with authority to identify and develop legal norms. A unified system of courts came to replace the divergent and chaotic feudal institutions for declaring the law; they operated according to their own internal principles and acquired independence from other social spheres. This institutional autonomy is affirmed by a professional autonomy: a distinct professional group of practitioners emerges to monopolize legal knowledge and expertise. It follows that the autonomy characteristic of modern law has substantive, methodological, institutional, and occupational dimensions (Unger, 1976:

52-57). In consequence, it becomes possible to describe modern law as a distinct, functionally differentiated social subsystem.

The structural transformation of modern law is marked by a range of novel transformations of substantive law. The break with feudalism entailed a progressive removal of traditional restrictions placed upon citizens from participating in economic life. In order for markets to function, individuals regardless of status or social position are granted general, universal rights to own property, to enter into contracts, and to sell their labour power. An adjunct of these rights is a general right of freedom of movement beyond the immediate community throughout the national space (Marshall, 1963). Modern law is therefore "transactional": legal relationships, rights and responsibilities are determined largely by consent rather than by the imposition of local traditions or customs as in feudalism (Galanter, 1966). Contract rather than status becomes the legally dominant mechanism for the creation, transfer and enforcement of legal rights (Maine, 1917).

It would be a mistake to see the emergence of modern liberal societies as defined simply by the appearance of markets with increasing, universal rights to participate in them, and the modern legal subject as essentially the abstract bearer of economic rights. The formal equality represented by these economic rights was progressively supplemented by general rights to participate in the political sphere with the extension of universal suffrage, freedom of speech and rights of assembly and association. Moreover, the creation of these equal political rights necessitates the imposition of significant restrictions on the operation of market activity to prevent their frustration by economic power. Hence, the historical advance toward formal equality has both economic and political dimensions so as to furnish the idea of the generality of law and the abstract legal subject with both a public and private law character. As Paul Starr concludes

> The rise of the liberal state specifically entailed a sharpening of the public-private distinction: on the one hand, the privatizing of religious and moral belief and practice and of economic activity formerly regulated by the state; on the other, a commitment to public law and public political discussion. Classical liberalism is often represented as a purely privatizing ideology, but liberals were committed to suppressing markets in votes, offices, and tax collection, not to mention human beings (1988: 10).

One further feature of the positivized nature of modern law is that it is separate from society; by contrast, traditional or customary law, which represented a significant element in the fabric of feudal law, was secreted in the interstices of society. It followed that law could never be seen to change society; rather, law changed imperceptibly as society changed. In modern societies, law is characteristically an instrument of change so that

> [p]ositive law – which is formally cut off from its roots in 'custom and habit' – ... creates in modern societies a capability, still hardly imaginable only a century ago, for the state executive to bring authority to bear comprehensively and reliably on highly specific groups, matters, etc. with a multiplicity of prohibitions and commands (Offe, 1987a: 4).

The institution of markets formed part of the "multiplicity of prohibitions and demands" introduced by modern states: without strong states with a monopoly of violence and an effective system of courts, free markets cannot function effectively. From the very beginning of the emergence of market economies, they were underpinned by a firm regulatory framework (Polanyi, 1944). Moreover, the freedoms presupposed by market behaviour require the enactment of laws, and the establishment of institutions of enforcement, to regulate disruptive and dysfunctional practices.

Another distinctive characteristic of modern law is the institutional development of the legal concept of citizenship. Citizenship is the right to participate fully in the life of a body politic. It represents what T.H. Marshall famously described as a "status bestowed on those who are full members of a community. All who possess the status are equal with respect to the rights and duties with which the status is endowed" (1963: 92). It only begins to make an appearance as a universal right with the innovations introduced by modern law. For instance, the removal of traditional restrictions on rights to own property and to enter into contractual relations, are the "civil rights" component of citizenship. Examining the English experience, Marshall found that these civil rights received mature expression in the 18th century. Comparable developments are evident in other modernizing societies. Moreover, the modern legal framework of citizenship is essentially tied to the nation state: "When freedom became universal [with the demise of villeinage], citizenship grew from a local to a national institution" (Marshall, 1963: 84). The problems of legitimacy posed by the emergent nation state gave rise to the demand and ultimate recognition of general, universal rights of political participation. Marshall's conclusion is that the constitutional reforms of the 19th century that led ultimately to universal suffrage, rights of freedom of speech and to stand for public office, supplemented the earlier civil rights of citizenship with a secondary layer of "political rights".

Marshall's evolutionary typology of modern law parallels that of Jürgen Habermas who identifies a similar process of expansion of legal rights for citizens in modern societies; but he prefers to describe these rights by reference to "waves of juridification" (1986: 208; 1996: 77). He analyzes the evolution of modern law by examining changes in state form, and sees three stages of development in contrast to Marshall's two. He draws a distinction in the emergence of modern states. The modern state's first manifestation is in the form of the bourgeois state that oversees the emergence of the market economy (Marshall's "civil rights"). The next two stages of development are the constitutional state, or *Rechtsstaat*, to be followed by the democratic state that accelerated the appearance of the abstract legal subject (in sum, Marshall's "political rights"). Despite their different perspectives, the authors offer strikingly complementary analyses for understanding the development of modern law.

These elements of modern law are neatly captured by the concept of the rule of law. The rule of law expresses both an ideal and a description. Prescriptively, it demands that all individuals should be equal before the law, and that the administration of law be free from outside influence. These requirements entail the generality of law as marked by the appearance of the abstract legal subject; that the state be subject to law in its dealings with subjects; and the autonomy, or differentiation, of law from other social domains such as politics or morals. The rule of law also insists on a separation of powers within the state for the reason that the autonomy of law cannot be achieved unless the judicial branch is institutionally separate from the executive and legislature. Descriptively, modern societies that institute these principles are held to function under the rule of law.

A dramatic reconfiguration of the spatio-temporal co-ordinates of law is also evident with the emergence of modern law. As noted above, law's reach ultimately becomes co-extensive with the territorial boundaries of nation states. This development accompanies a profound re-orientation of the temporal vision within which modern law unfolds. Feudal law and customary law operate with an overwhelmingly backward-focused temporality: the past exerts enormous normative pressure on the present, and is the central legitimating mechanism for the legal order. Modern law, by contrast, increasingly dispenses with legitimation based on tradition: in place of the "medieval idea that old law is better than the new one ... positivization is incompatible with a qualitative differentiation between old and new law" (Luhmann, 1985: 161). Moreover, modern law increasingly adopts a future orientation. Legislation is overwhelmingly an exercise of normatively guiding future behaviour, and of calculating the nature of prospective events and environments. Because legislation becomes the dominant form of production of laws, a general future-mindedness typifies modern law.

Institutions can only survive if they are supported by a culture that values and nourishes them. In the case of law, a "legal culture" mediates the relationship between social change and legal change. One element of legal culture is the professional attitude to law (Friedman, 1986). A distinctive professional ideology accompanies the changed structure of modern law. A central component of this attitude is the dominant critical vocabulary that each age applies to existing positive law. Thus for premodern law the prevailing critical attitude is natural law, either in a rationalist or theological form. In the case of modern law, legal positivism, which emphasized the essentiality of sovereign command or formally posited laws as master tests for legal validity, became a dominant jurisprudential vision for the legal profession (Cotterrell, 1989: chs 3-4).

To be sure, the empirical and historical reality of the development of modern law belies this general picture of the evolution of modern law. In spite of its ambitions to guarantee freedom and equality under the law, modern law has never been able to contain completely the competing normative orders and resistant practices within modern societies. Legal pluralism has operated to greater or lesser degrees in all modern societies (eg Arthurs, 1985), and the formal legal equality promised by modern law has regularly proved to be much more of an aspiration than a concrete reality, as all those disadvantaged on the basis of gender, race and class would attest. And unofficial violence of some degree has always accompanied the state's claimed monopoly of violence. So it is misleading to suggest an unambiguous triumph of formal, centralized, rational modern law over all the plural forms of norms that surface from below the level of the sovereign state. In this sense, in the domain of law, no less than other social spheres, "we have never been modern" (Latour, 1994). Despite these caveats, the appearance of modern law represented a radical transformation of the legal order of feudal societies, as sovereign nation states acquired historically unprecedented law-making power at the expense of other sources of law. Of course, the emergence of this new legal order was built on, and necessitated, the destruction of local customs and traditional law, with consequential losses for the communities that lived by them. But it offered at the same time some very material gains for citizens in terms of rights to political and economic freedom and equality.

In one significant respect the advances in citizenship and equality uniquely achieved by modern law had limited success in advancing justice. The two early waves of citizenship rights made little impact on addressing the social injustices that flowed from the economic and social inequality within modern liberal capitalist societies. Though the first wave of civil rights described by Marshall conferred real power upon citizens, this power was restricted by an entrenched class system and sparse economic opportunities. Subsequently, "[p]olitical rights gave potential power whose exercise demanded experience, organization and a change of ideas as to the proper functions of government" (1963: 105). The "potential power" of this second wave of citizenship rights ultimately fuelled the introduction of the very different institutional infrastructure, and legality, of the welfare state.

The Welfare State: What and When?

Welfare states were established in order to redress the social and economic inequality pervasive in liberal capitalist societies. To achieve this aim, they were built on a number of organizational principles at odds with central liberal tenets. First, in the economic sphere the welfare state introduced a more systematic and intrusive regulation of markets. The regular dysfunctions of the weakly regulated markets of liberal societies, most obviously evident in recurrent boom-bust cycles with consequential and widespread unemployment and poverty, were seen to be morally unacceptable. There are many dimensions of the novel array of regulatory techniques deployed by the welfare state. Certain economic activities were completely removed from the market, as in the case of the provision of certain public goods and utilities, where state monopolies in the form of nationalization were imposed. Changes in the nature and scope of the state in relation to the economy through nationalization policies were complemented by restructuring of the private sector of the economy. Tighter regulation was introduced to prohibit and dismantle monopolies, and to restrict the production of dangerous and defective goods. These reforms show the welfare state to be a *regulatory* state.

Second, market-based processes of accumulation and distribution tend to impoverish some citizens and aggrandize others in a manner which seems to be only tenuously related to individual merit, and largely at odds with popular conceptions of economic justice. In order to reverse vast inequalities in the distribution of wealth and power the *interventionist* welfare state widely steered the market, routinely deploying strategies to equalize bargaining power in economic relationships, to impose duties on more powerful parties, and to fix prices, particularly in the case of necessities such as housing, income and health.

Third, the general welfare of citizens came to be seen as one of the central concerns of the state. Society as a whole assumes a general responsibility for providing for the welfare and well-being of the population by removing these functions from the private sector. Following Goran Therborn (1987), welfare states can be identified by reference to levels of welfare provision. The most comprehensive welfare states are defined by Therborn as "strong interventionist welfare states" which have extensive social welfare entitlements and a strong commitment to full employment. At the other end of the spectrum are the least welfare-committed states; they are market-oriented welfare states with limited social welfare entitlements and a comparatively low commitment to full employment. In each manifestation, welfare states are *redistributive* states.

Clearly, the divergence in forms of welfare state ought to induce caution about making overly broad generalizations about the nature of such states. Nonetheless, some notable points of overlap between the various regimes can be identified. First, the historical trajectory of post-war welfare states is the same: despite clear differences in policy across parties and countries, welfare states reached their zenith in advanced industrialized societies in the post-war period. Regardless of whether right- or left-leaning governments were in power, there was a steady increase in the range and extent of benefits until roughly the middle of the 1970s (Pierson, 1991: ch 5). Second, for all the national differences, the benefits were extended across the categories of welfare provision. The welfare state dramatically increased forms of provision of health, education, housing, unemployment and disability benefits for those who failed to acquire the basic human needs from the market or other (private) mechanisms of distribution. Each of these principles (market regulation, interventionism and welfare provision) manifests an overall conception of society that stands in stark opposition to the individualism of liberal societies: in the welfare state, a strong sense of inevitable social *interdependency* pervaded both public policy and popular consciousness (Lowi, 1987: 30-32).

This account of the distinctiveness of the philosophical underpinnings of welfare states should not be taken to imply that the development of the welfare state appeared as a sudden, revolutionary transformation. As Flora and Alber note, the emergence of the welfare state can be traced to origins much earlier than many standard accounts assume (1981: 37). The seeds of the modern welfare state were sown last century. Even Bismarck's welfare innovations in 19th century Germany, commonly seen as a starting point in the history of the welfare state, were modelled on earlier Prussian welfare and insurance legislation. Equally, depictions of Victorian Britain as the classic liberal *laissez-faire* polity seriously underestimates the legislative framework of factory regulation, housing provision, extension of local public services, free public education and health care, and introduction of workers' compensation which was introduced during that period (Evans, 1978). In the three decades preceding the First World War comprehensive systems of social insurance were introduced in most of the advanced industrialized nations. To be sure, these were meagre and ungenerous systems when set alongside 20th century welfare states. But they were *welfare provision*, and often under law.

To recognize the long history of the welfare state has the important consequence of correcting the periodization of many of the welfare state theorists who exaggerate the changes that the appearance of that state is supposed to have introduced (Pierson, 1991: 102-116). The welfare state is best seen both as a quantitative extension of those initiatives that are consistent with the enhancement of democracy and citizenship within the modern state, as well as a remodelling of some of their key features. If these continuities are examined by reference to the structure and institutional forms of the welfare state, it can be seen that the welfare state falls squarely within the traditional parameters of the societal modernization described by sociologists and historians.

The Welfare State and Modernization

For theorists of modernization, the welfare state is generally seen as a distinctive feature of modern societies. It retains the key features which differentiate a modern from a traditional society, despite exhibiting features that clearly distinguish it historically from the liberal state. According to Flora and Heidenheimer's formulation, the welfare state is "a general phenomenon of modernization". In particular, the welfare state is defined by reference to the following variables. It is the result of

> the increasing differentiation and the growing size of societies on the one hand and of processes of social and political mobilization on the other ... [T]he historical constellation in which the European welfare state emerged ... [is one] of growing mass democracies and expanding capitalist economies within a system of sovereign nation states (1981: 8, 23).

On the basis of a detailed analysis of various legislative schemes covering typical welfare benefits (sickness and accident benefits, unemployment, and pensions) across the 12 most economically advanced European nations, Flora and Heidenheimer reach the broad conclusion that the more developed each of the elements of modernization are in a particular country, the more advanced the growth and spread of the welfare state will be. If we look at the changes in each of the domains identified earlier in this chapter as essential to modern societies it is possible to see the extent to which welfare states display all the hallmarks of the process of modernization notwithstanding their newly acquired regulatory, interventionist and redistributive functions.

For instance, the state apparatus characteristic of societies described as welfare states is markedly different from the states of liberal capitalism. The state increasingly steers society by means of more regulation and intervention in the economy, especially in the form of nationalization to "provide a nucleus for the economic expansion of the nation and offer the advantages of large-scale operation, without the disadvantages of private monopoly" (Friedmann, 1971: 54). As it did so, the nation state unquestionably consolidated its power, and often in ways that supplanted the influence of local communities, and patterns of "indigenous" ordering throughout civil society. The monocentric organizational structures of modern societies noted, driven and underpinned by a remorseless and universalizing "legislative reason" (Bauman, 1992: ch 1), reach their apogee in this state form, with their increasing reliance on technical rationality and the capacities of scientific knowledge.

A further aspect of this feature of welfare states lies in its accentuation of the centripetal tendencies of the modern nation state as the formerly more territorially dispersed power of markets, regions and local governments is centralized. As the nation state is an essential component of modern societies, the changes referred to above represented a dramatic enhancement of its power and influence. In particular, the executive arm of the state grew exponentially, as large bureaucracies emerged to manage newly acquired industries, regulate the economy, and to administer the wide array of welfare functions. In assuming greater control of the economy the state also increased the share of the total national resources it consumed and the extent of provisions and benefits it distributed so that "[a]nywhere from half of the gross national product flows to and through the central government" (Friedman, 1986: 18).

One of the pillars of modern societies is industrialized production. Late modernity witnesses the dramatic expansion of industrialization across the economy as a whole, and a net aggregation of enterprises into ever larger conglomerates and cartels, as Fordism comes to be the dominant form of production in the economies of industrialized societies in the post-war period. Indeed, consistent with the general process of social modernization, it represents the high point of the *industrialization* of production. And as economies become progressively spread over national spaces, capital and labour develop their own, nationally oriented political structures: unions cease to be purely local and craft-based, and capital takes an increasingly national perspective with national institutional co-ordination (Lash and Urry, 1987: chs 2-3). This process coincides with, and to a degree reflects, a parallel increase in the state-managed organization of production in the private sector along *national* lines. As we have seen in the previous chapter, Fordist production techniques further this development: the distinctively local patterns of solidarity in small industries were weakened. The novel massification of workforces contributed to a different worker ideology. The more collective experience of life-chances grows, the more workforce solidarity is fuelled (Offe, 1987b). It can be seen therefore that in the welfare state the class structure of liberal capitalist societies was not fundamentally altered but in many respects sharpened. This development is evident as the *economic* class cleavage in welfare states in part accentuated the class divisions of modern liberal capitalist societies and gave rise to clearly demarcated forms of *political* representation as corporatist forms of governance were established.

A further consequence of the larger scale of Fordist economic organization is the appearance of a distinct managerial class whose interests are different from those of capital and labour. Equally, "extensions of state activity into arenas of social reproduction tend towards the development of credentialized professional fragments of this new middle class" (Crook et al., 1992: 21). This novel social structure sets the welfare state both apart from and yet continuous with modern society. The functional differentiation of modern societies persists; but it is now more systematically the object of state guidance as "organized functional differentiation" appears.

In conjunction with high levels of employment, and state-driven policies of redistribution of national wealth, ever greater proportions of citizens were able to become active consumers of material goods in the market. In this way, the welfare state represented a significant *extension of the market*. Now "affluent workers" were able to attain levels of material well-being formerly the preserve of only the wealthier strata of society (Goldthorpe et al., 1968). Accordingly, market relations, though more regulated, and restricted in some areas, greatly expand in number in others, so that in this respect also the welfare state represents an advanced example of the economic structure of modern societies (Esping-Andersen, 1990). Welfare states only appear in expanding capitalist, market economies, at a late stage of the modernization process (Flora and Heidenheimer, 1981: 23).

Modernity, as we have seen, was marked by an historically unique re-organization of time and space: polities, economies, classes, and societies generally, were all, with greater or lesser degrees of success, structured along lines consistent with the spatial and geographical boundaries of nation states. The welfare state was marked by an even more comprehensive organization and domination of national space. The advance of "Fordism" in the private sector was reflected at the level of the state by the development of institutions that were more closely attuned to national, rather than regional, or local conditions. So, nationalized industries provided goods and services of uniform standard and price, while welfare provision was similarly set by reference to national benchmarks. As the state assumed responsibility for health, education, transport and welfare, increasingly centralized planning resulted in redistribution within and between regional sectors. This process involves the "disembedding" of social relations from their local contexts, which is a characteristic element of modern societies in general (Giddens, 1990: 21).

This necessarily brief overview of the structurally transformed welfare state provides a background for examining how late modernization was evidenced in the sphere of law.

Late Legal Modernization: The Legal Order of the Welfare State

Law and the Changed Structure of the Welfare State

The legal structure of the welfare state displays close parallels with wider social change. In general the law of the welfare state has three basic characteristics. First, it continues to exhibit the key features of classical modern legal systems: insofar as the welfare state retained the general character of modern capitalist societies, many central features of modern, liberal law remained untouched by the waves of reforms that it introduced. Law remains generally autonomous, or differentiated, from other social subsystems, and it takes the predominant form of positive law. Also, like the law of liberal states, the law of the welfare state displays a striking monocentricity: the sovereign nation state retains exclusive rights to make and enforce law. Second, the welfare state ushered in many changes to law that furthered and enhanced the underlying aims of liberal law. Third, the law of the welfare state radically transformed some domains of modern, liberal law, as society progressively shed its liberal character.

To recognize this diversity of elements suggests that the changes implemented by nations in their welfare state phases, viewed as a whole, manifest *both an enhancement and a revision* of their (modern) liberal legal underpinnings. It would be a misleading exaggeration to suggest that the law of the welfare state simply *reforms or replaces* liberal law. The edifice of modern law was not so much demolished as refurbished and extended. To be sure, it looked and was different; but it was reformed, not dismantled and therefore is best described as "late legal modernization". If the "additive" legal change in the welfare state is examined in detail (Willke, 1986), and the extent of both its continuity and *dis*continuity with the law of modern societies is borne in mind, the dimensions of legal postmodernization to be examined in later chapters may become clearer.

The transformation of the liberal state into a welfare state pushes law in directions that give expression to the distinctive functions and aspirations of the newly emergent society. This is not to imply that there is a simple causal relationship between forms of state and forms of law. Rather, a distinct normative affinity links the values that underpin the welfare state and the legal reforms that appear within it. The welfare state should be seen as a state as much constituted by changes in the law, as effecting legal change. As we have seen, one of the central features of the new social formation is its assumption of far greater regulatory responsibilities over all aspects of life. But given that all states regulate by means of law, and at all times, it is necessary to identify the distinctive nature of the regulatory framework of the welfare state. Regulatory styles can be divided into four different ideal-types. The first type of regulation is self-regulation, in which the relevant sector establishes and enforces its own regulatory rules, which may or may not be buttressed by law. Second, there is "general regulation" of which liberal contract and property law are paradigm cases. This type of regulation takes the form of general rules that govern private interaction and are enforced by the courts at the suit of individual litigants. T.H. Marshall's (1963) category of "civil rights" to participate freely in market relationships captures the bundle of rights established by this regulatory model. Third, regulation may take the form of interventionist legislative reform of these general rules to achieve procedural or substantive justice. Fourth, regulation may be effected by state agency. In this mode, the legal framework is no less interventionist: the agency sets command and control standards and regulations, and assumes some responsibility for enforcing the legislation (Bradgate et al., 1994: 158).[1]

The rise in the welfare state is marked by the progressive, but selective, abandonment of the regulatory framework characteristic of liberal societies. In general, it entails the overhaul of the first and second types of regulatory strategy in favour of the third and fourth examples: self-regulation and general regulation were gradually supplanted by regulation in the form of legislative rules and regulation by the creation or enlargement of separate governmental agencies with substantial powers conferred on officials in the form of broad discretions to investigate, to make regulations, issue and revoke licences and to prosecute. So, in the United States' New Deal legislation, for instance, the enlarged administrative powers granted to regulatory agencies heralded an era of "administrative autonomy" (Sunstein, 1990: 29-30). The process is replicated to greater and lesser degrees, though in different institutional forms, in other welfare states (Majone, 1990: 2; Friedman, 1986: 14).[2]

This use of law on the part of the welfare state to direct social life – its "legal instrumentalism" (Teubner, 1986) – clearly represents a break with the prevailing style of general legal regulation characteristic of classical liberal societies. But in another respect, legal instrumentalism is not at odds with the general ideology, and function, of modern law. On the ideological level, it represents an advanced stage of a legal world-view that mastery over the external world can be achieved by rationally informed state interventions by means of positive law. On the functional level, as we have seen above, modern law, freed from the restrictions of custom, is marked by a capacity to bring public authority powerfully to bear on all social spheres (Offe, 1987a: 4). The law of the welfare state takes this project to a higher level by means of a closer coupling of legislative activity and social change. Moreover, if modern law is particularly notable for its positivization (Luhmann, 1985: ch 4), the burgeoning mass of legislation characteristic of welfare states puts it squarely within the modern mould.

A further dimension of this new regulatory role is that in order to be most effective it needs ever more detailed levels of legislative specificity: if certain practices in markets and other regions of society are to be successfully managed, they must be identified with precision by the legal regimes devised for them. This requirement led to an increasing mass and density of legal rules. A process of the "juridification of social spheres" follows, whereby increasing categories of economic and social activities come under the shadow of the law (Teubner, 1987). The general pattern of regulatory transformation is manifested in legal change in five distinct areas: private law, the state apparatus, welfare rights, the spatial and temporal co-ordinates of law; and access to formal justice.

Reform of Private Law

The regulatory and interventionist innovations of the welfare state can be seen most clearly in the transformation of private law. The private law of liberal societies is the body of general rules that govern dealings between private individuals. The general regulatory framework in liberal societies governing economic relations appeared in the form of legal rules that expressed the values of individual autonomy and the formal equality of subjects. A central element in the regulatory regime of welfare states is the introduction of legislative reforms of these rules. Among the various indicators of this development, two of the most important were the increasing restrictions imposed on individual freedom in the allocation of legal rights and responsibilities, and the declining sociological role played by contract in the social distribution of goods and services.

As part of a general policy to redistribute wealth and power in pursuit of a more egalitarian society, the welfare state enacted a series of wide-ranging legislative schemes that targeted the central principle of free choice and consent in classical contract law. This principle was subjected to historically unique restrictions for the reason that the generous freedoms offered to all participants in a free market tend to operate in practice as a key mechanism of exploitation, wielded by wealthier and more powerful owners of property against the weak and the poor. The steep power gradient often separating contracting parties had the effect of routinely rendering the notion of "free" choice and consent illusory. Accordingly, legislative reform removed many matters entirely from the parties' determination that were formerly the subject of notionally "free" private agreement. In particular, widespread reforms of the general liberal rules that governed private interaction appeared in the form of legislation designed to equalize the bargaining power of parties to commercial transactions. For instance, the form and content of certain types of contract – in the areas of employment, credit provision and residential leases, for example – were largely fixed by legislative fiat. Moreover, the scope to introduce onerous terms for consumers was substantially restricted, and expansive disclosure requirements, and product standards, were imposed on producers giving rise to a set of protections under the heading of "consumer law" (Mooney, 1995: 1132). At the same time, legislative reforms enhanced certain distinctively liberal, rather than welfare, principles. For example, the modern concept of equality of civil rights was furthered by means of the enactment of extensive anti-discrimination laws directed at removing prejudicial judgements by the owners of businesses and property from imposing arbitrary barriers to economic participation.

An even more intrusive interference with market mechanisms was discernible in the introduction by welfare states of laws to compel transfers of rights from property owners to the disadvantaged to advance policies of redistribution of wealth. Prices of certain key commodities were fixed, such as residential rents, transport costs and interest rates on loans. These general developments were evident no less in the doctrinal change elaborated by courts, representing a general replacement of a market individualist paradigm with a consumer-welfarist one (Adams and Brownsword, 1987: 156-165; Mooney, 1995). Another factor in the transformation of private law was the "corporate state" marked by ever larger corporations, unions and governments where relations are regulated more by administrative law than contractual rules (Atiyah, 1979: 601). As these organizations and the state increased in size, contracts between individuals reduced in both quantitative and qualitative significance in the economy and society as a whole; terms of employment, for instance, were determined by negotiations between large unions and corporations often on an industry-wide, and national, basis rather than in individual contracts. In the case of classical contract law – the area of law that is the privileged site of the expression of liberal values – commentators have identified in these general shifts, the pervasive "fall" or "death" of freedom of contract with the onset of the welfare state (Atiyah, 1979; Gilmore, 1974).

In addition to reform of the general rules governing private dealings, a second type of regulatory strategy was implemented: state agencies were set up, and were empowered to regulate consumer relations by means of licensing, certification, standard-setting and prosecutorial functions (Sunstein, 1990: 18-31, Bradgate et al., 1994: 158). This process combines with the reforms above to represent a break with the fundamental, modern principle of generality in law. Put another way, the formal, abstract law of liberal societies comes to be *materialized* in the welfare state. Under the new regime, the formerly abstract legal subject of modern law has his or her material context and identity taken into account in the framework of legal rules, so that whether a legal subject was a consumer, a producer, a tenant, a landlord, a worker, an employer, infirm, powerful, a small businessperson, or a commercial monopoly became legally relevant in ascribing rights and responsibilities (Weber, 1978: 894). Equally, in addition to enhanced private remedies, the environment, workplace safety, protection of consumers from both defective products and the predatory practices of monopolies, and employment relations were subjected to agency control, rather than by an exclusive regime of private property and contract law.

One further cause of the declining social and economic function of classical, modern contract law lay in the roles played by the expanded welfare state which became the dominant mechanism for allocating resources in the new economy through strategies of nationalization and enhanced welfare provision. Where the state wholly funds and controls the health, education and welfare sectors, relationships between individuals and institutions are governed by statute and administrative regulation, not contract. Even where public authorities were formally bound by a contract, as in the case of public housing tenancies, in reality the relationship was of a public law kind. For Atiyah, freedom of contract, as a principle of private law, did not disappear in this context. Rather, it was displaced from its central place in the social distribution and allocation of property and entitlements (1979: 726-727). In its place, the legal focus shifted from binding agreements and promises to duties of officials, expectations of the relevant public, and the fairness of decision-making processes, that is, a general shift from private to public law unfolds.

Another factor in the changing legal order was the appearance of the "corporate state" marked by ever-larger corporations, unions and governments where relations are regulated more by administrative law than contractual rules (Atiyah, 1979: 601). As these organizations and the state increase in size, contracts between individuals reduce in both quantitative and qualitative significance in the economy and society as a whole. Terms of employment, for instance, are determined by negotiations between large unions and corporations often on an industry-wide, and national, basis rather than in individual contracts. These legal changes were not confined to the United Kingdom, which was Atiyah's focus of study. They represented a consistent feature of advanced capitalist societies at the time (Gilmore, 1974; Preuss, 1986: 163; Ewald, 1987: 40; Wilhelmsson, 1994: 63).

The welfare state also subjected property law to historically unprecedented pressures. According to Charles Reich, "new property" had appeared in the wake of post-war regulatory and welfare reforms (1964). In the liberal state property was typically in the form of tangible or intangible things created or transferred by individuals in the market, and protected from infringement by the state. By contrast, the welfare state functioned to create positive rights in individuals to resources that were obtainable from, and enforceable against, the state. This novel "public interest state" operated as an enormous fountain of rights and benefits, showering its citizens with "largess":

> The wealth of more and more Americans depends upon a relationship to government. Increasingly, Americans live on government largess – allocated by government on its own terms, and held by recipients subject to conditions which express 'the public interest' (1964: 733).

In common with other commentators on welfare state reforms, Reich identified the tripartite domains of regulation, welfare and enterprise as the growth areas of definite sites of welfare state activity. Examples of "new property" that derived from the state's regulatory functions were franchises for specialized forms of economic activity such as mass communications, licences to ply particular trades, and subsidies to vulnerable industries. These rights had become just as valuable in economic terms as shares of tangible wealth. The state's welfare functions led to a complex web of income support and unemployment benefits; and its entrepreneurial activities made it the source of lucrative business opportunities for the private sector. Where an individual could claim such rights against the state they were directly analogous to traditional property rights because they performed broadly similar social functions: individuals who were entitled to them acquired the same means of basic survival, and the sort of autonomy and well-being, as conferred by traditional ownership of wealth.

One major distinguishing characteristic of the "new property" rights was that they came with a reduced measure of protection for those intended to benefit from them. Unlike "old" property which was protected by a range of measures against state intrusion, even in cases of compulsory acquisition by the state, in the case of "new" property rights the state was subject to comparatively limited legal restrictions in determining whether to withdraw or modify them. In consequence, the individual citizen stood in a position of some vulnerability to a Leviathan-like state apparatus that by means of administrative decision now had the power to directly undermine or withdraw the sources of an individual's livelihood.

Reich's solution was to propose that the constitutional protections safeguarding private property should be extended to new property; without such a change, a new form of dependency and insecurity would attend the otherwise beneficial effects of welfare state reforms. Under Reich's suggested changes, the state would be prevented from withdrawing licences, welfare benefits or contractual rights from private individuals to further the public interest without being subject to stringent procedural safeguards, or even obligations to pay just compensation. Only by these means would the autonomy of the citizen guaranteed by traditional property law be adequately protected under the welfare state. Reich's complaints about the present legal framework were so persuasive that they quickly received legal expression in the United States as the Supreme Court tightened constitutional due process requirements on welfare and other state agencies such as prisons when carrying out their statutory functions (Glendon, 1981: 185-192; Pierce, 1996: 1973). Moreover, the analogy of welfare rights to property rights was generally, if loosely, applicable in all welfare states given the growing universality of entitlements to state largess (Macpherson, 1973). In providing additional legal rights to public benefits, the welfare state in its redistributive role advanced another principle: it gave a richer meaning to the legal concept of citizenship. No longer was citizenship reducible to a set of public rights to vote, reside, and private rights to participate in economic activity; it also embraced "social" rights to minimum wages for the workforce; rights to pensions or benefits for the sick or unemployed; and universal rights to healthcare and education (Marshall, 1963).

New property also appeared as a direct result of the state's tight regulation of certain "contractual" relationships. The employment contract, for example, in light of constitutional, legislative and doctrinal changes wrought by the welfare state to afford employees a measure of security of employment, rights to join unions, and statutory entitlements to pensions and severance pay, introduced a form of "occupational bonding" that moved this nominally contractual relationship ever closer to the category of traditional property (Glendon, 1981: ch 4). Comparable accretions of rights in favour of tenants (in terms of notice rights, security of tenure, and rights of habitability) consequent on a tighter regulation of residential leases had the effect of giving tenants quasi-property rights (Gray, 1979: 38; Atiyah, 1979: 727-729). And as the state and private organizations such as insurance companies and banks invested savings and pension funds in large enterprises in the private sector of the economy, so that shares in companies were increasingly owned at least indirectly by large numbers of citizens, a process of socialization of production occurred. Of course, this overall picture differed significantly in detail and degree across the various post-war welfare states, as Therborn's (1987) classification of the types of various welfare states above implies. But the general trend was clear, especially in Western Europe, where the welfare state was more entrenched and developed.

The distinctive features of the legal infrastructure of the welfare state cannot be understood by exclusive reference to its novel economic regulation. It also introduced significant reforms of other features of the liberal legal order. Prior to the establishment of the welfare state a free market stood in stark contrast to a set of rigid legal rules governing intimate relationships. What is often overlooked in accounts of the liberal state, is its imposition of very restrictive, strikingly *illiberal* legal controls on intimate relationships. Just as far-reaching as the changes in the economy over the period of the development of the welfare state were transformations in the legal regimes that regulated sexual and family relationships. The welfare state's "new property" was paralleled by the emergence of the "new family". The new family was governed by legal principles diametrically at odds with those that produce new property rights described by Reich. The greater security afforded citizens by the welfare state in the form of enhanced protections of workers in their employment and extensive provision of social welfare benefits, was matched by a corresponding diminution of the security of family members where "couple relationships are distinguished by the role of choice in their dissolutions, transitions and substitutions" (Glendon, 1981: 30). As the right to opt out of marriage became more widely available with the easier availability of divorce in the family law of welfare states, the once solid nuclear family that stood as a haven in a heartless, free-market world, began to fracture. In consequence, on a global view of welfare state policies, there are both gains and losses in overall personal security.

It is possible to see in these general legal changes the welfare state's novel realignment of the "public/private" distinction. For earlier liberal societies, expansive notions of individual freedom were deemed appropriate for market relations, but not for the spheres of sexual and family relationships. This bivalent standard of freedom was reflected in a loosely regulated regime for contractual relationships in the economy on the one hand, and a dense network of much more restrictive laws governing the intimate sphere. For example, liberal states afforded enhanced legal privileges to marital status by comparison with other relationships, the right to divorce was highly restricted, while abortion and homosexual behaviour were proscribed with criminal penalties. By contrast, in post-war debates about marriage, divorce, abortion and homosexuality on the one hand, and market relations on the other, this dual standard of freedom was turned on its head. Increasingly the policy debate shifted from a concern about what citizens were doing in their bedrooms, to what the so-called "night-watchman" state was doing there. The distinctively modern individualistic rhetoric of the liberal marketplace came to be directly applied to the intimate sphere (Atiyah, 1979: 726-727). Also, as freedom of choice came to guide family law, it can be seen as a fulfilment of the individualistic values of the Enlightenment (Glendon, 1981: 44), and thus quintessentially modern. Legal reforms gave citizens far greater freedom to divorce, re-marry and (to a substantially lesser degree) to form homosexual relationships. The process of freeing crime from sin (Hart, 1963), represented another wave of legal modernization: the differentiation of legal from religious authority, and the progressive secularization of law.

With this development, welfare states effected two distinct reversals of the underlying values of liberal societies: first, the economic individualism of the marketplace gave way to a form of collectivist ideology that subjected economic relations to tight control. Second, the field of sexual conduct and marriage relations was subjected to a looser style of legal regulation, articulated in the former modern liberal language of an anti-statist individualism and free choice. This is not to suggest that gains in freedom in the private sphere are *paid for* by losses in the public sphere of economic relations; or that the appearance of one makes it easier for the implementation of the other. Rather, this was a politically driven policy mix, "an attempt to articulate a culture, a 'civilization', a moral economy for an emergent state capitalism" (Hall, 1980: 35), where a highly regulated market stands alongside an increasingly de-regulated private sphere. As we shall see later, postmodernity registers a striking legal reconfiguration of these policies.

The Entrepreneurial and Corporatist State

The welfare state developed an historically unique structure of government. In order to pursue a strategy of systematic modernization, it took on entrepreneurial functions by means of assuming ownership of vital sectors of the economy. These roles can also be seen as further aspects of the state's regulatory functions insofar as the impetus that gave rise to them was the correction of earlier market failure. By nationalizing key industries and utilities, the welfare state created novel legal entities to control and manage their activities. Where these entities operate, the processes of production, consumption and exchange are to a significant degree exempted from the legal rules that govern market relations. Nationalized industries exhibit some of the features of private business organizations; but they are also responsible to governments that have political as well as economic objectives to fulfil. In this way their legal form evades the traditional categories of public and private law. The public law that governs the realm of politics and state activity becomes fused with private law that regulates the economy to the extent that the distinction between the two categories of law is "blurred" (Friedmann, 1971: 39, 57). For instance, where the state provides utilities such as gas, electricity and water to citizens, it does so not by means of contract – though at the point of delivery it concludes an agreement which has some of the superficial appearance of being contractual – but more in the exercise of public statutory powers and obligations (Prosser, 1986).

A further legal change that follows policies of nationalization is the emergence of novel forms of accountability to the public. Where nationalization removes an economic activity from the market, the former mechanisms of private law, such as contract, tort and property law are displaced. Under the new regime, a more public law-governed system comes to prevail (Aubert, 1986: 35-36). The nationalization of industry can equally be seen as part of a process of legal modernization: to the extent that it articulates broader Fordist visions of economic and social development, it is intimately bound up with the emergence of "organized capitalism". Government policy in the form of public law, rather than the network of private contractual agreements, is the dominant engine driving social interaction. In conceiving legal rights and obligations in these circumstances, "the whole conceptual apparatus of the lawyer changes as he moves from private to administrative law" (Atiyah, 1979: 719). Moreover, the relevant administrative law, unlike contract law, is cast in a national mould, with the duties and powers of relevant officials attuned to the demands of a modernizing, Fordist and corporatist welfare state.

The nationalization and regulatory strategies of welfare states dovetailed into corporatist policies. As we have seen in the previous chapter, when industries came to be increasingly organized along Fordist, national lines, representatives of capital and labour became similarly realigned. One consequence of this development was that the legal pattern of governance of liberal societies was reformed. Peak national employer associations and trade unions tended to hammer out compromises on legal rights under the auspices of the state, so that incomes and prices came to be set less by the market, but more by a tripartite alliance of representatives. The resulting accords commonly took on legal form in the shape of collective bargains or awards enforceable in the courts. These bargains expressed the general post-war truce between capital and labour, that is, between private property rights and political rights, in a "Keynesian accommodation" (Bowles and Gintis, 1987: 55-63).

Second, corporatist arrangements also had the effect of unbalancing the liberal state's legal separation of powers. The legislature came increasingly to endorse law rather than make it in an environment where bargains were struck by the executive, and the peak organizations of capital and labour, the new centre of gravity of political power (Cawson, 1986).

Welfare Provision and Welfare Rights

The welfare state's economic interventionism was based as much on a principle of redistribution of wealth as industrial modernization. This principle was reflected in a host of social security and welfare reforms. A torrent of legislation was enacted to confer rights on qualifying citizens to a range of monetary and in-kind entitlements in order to alleviate or remove poverty and disadvantage. Unemployment benefits, pensions, and state-funded compensation schemes for various misfortunes came to replace the partial and haphazard support given by charities and communities; and health and education systems came to be increasingly, sometimes exclusively, state-funded and controlled.

This extension of universal legal rights to health, education and welfare radically transforms the relationship between citizen and state: the state becomes subject to novel legal obligations, and the citizen is the bearer of a whole new set of rights in the form, not of rights to participate in economic and political activity as was the case with the advances of the modern package of citizenship rights, but to a universal right to a minimum level of security. The new package of rights replaces the privileges and unrestrained discretion inherent in the fitful and haphazard practices of charities, family and community in the alleviation of poverty. Equally, because these rights were geared to the elimination of harms that affect all or large numbers of citizens, not merely individuals, they "were collective rather than individual in character ... The government was thus managing risks rather than vindicating individual rights" (Sunstein, 1990: 29).

In reconfiguring the legal position of citizens, especially the disadvantaged, in this way, the state achieved two simultaneous results. First, by providing pensions and unemployment benefits, welfare states were re-adjusting the public/private distinction characteristic of liberal societies where the private institutions of civil society such as family and community played a more central role. Second, according to T.H. Marshall (1963), the bundle of universal entitlements that the welfare states accorded their citizens amounted to deepening of the concept of citizenship. These "social" rights formed part of citizenship because they had become no less universal than the political and civil, or economic, rights won by citizens in earlier stages of development of the modern state. But this social citizenship was successful in a way that civil and political citizenship was not: it reversed many of the class inequalities of capitalist societies. The diminution of inequality in the welfare state was achieved

> by incorporating social rights in the status of citizenship and thus creating a universal right to real income which is not proportionate to the market value

> of the claimant. Class-abatement ... is no longer merely an attempt to abate the obvious nuisance of destitution in the lowest ranks of society. It has assumed the guise of action modifying the whole pattern of social inequality (Marshall, 1963: 106).

When taken together, the regulatory reforms ushered in by welfare states in conjunction with the enhanced social rights enforceable against governments, constitute a novel "social welfare paradigm" (Habermas, 1996: ch 9). And insofar as these newly won rights could be characterized as aspects of citizenship, they fitted neatly into the modern political project of strengthening the rights of the individual against the state.[3]

Reconfiguration of the Spatial and Temporal Co-ordinates of Modern Law

The historically unique monocentricity of modern law derives from the fact that nation states are sovereign states, and exercise exclusive law-making power within their boundaries. By this characterization, the welfare state is an essentially modern state to the extent that its legal order is monocentric to an even more striking degree than that of liberal states. The vast increase in legislative and administrative activity required by the expanded regulatory and welfare functions of post-war nation states represented a dramatic rise and centralization of their power. They were larger, consumed a greater share of national resources, and both made and administered more law than ever before. This development was strikingly evident in all branches of law: legislation increased exponentially, state bureaucracies proliferated and the legal system processed more litigation, employed more staff, and fuelled an expanding legal profession. A growing proportion of social life became subject to legal control as the welfare state took over subsystems that were previously left untouched or at best barely regulated by the law of the liberal state. So, poverty, ill-health, market dominance and inequality, unemployment, environmental degradation and homelessness, once seen as accidents of fate, the result of misfortune, the blind interplay of market forces or individual fault, and left to be remedied by individual effort, or local collective action, now came to be seen as a direct legal responsibility of the state (Friedman, 1986: 20). As modern states, including welfare states, must act by law as required by the rule of law, the implementation of these responsibilities was governed by a complex web of public duties and citizens' rights.

As a result of these developments the unfolding welfare state contributes to the juridification of social spheres noted above in the context of its increased regulatory role (Teubner, 1987: 3; Partington, 1987: 419). In its extension of the law in this way, the centralized, welfare state effects a striking spatial reorganization of legal jurisdiction: nationally uniform rules gradually supersede – though, of course, never totally replace – local norms, institutions and arrangements. Other reforms similarly adjusted the spatial co-ordinates of welfare states from a local to a national frame. Where sectors of the economy are exclusively owned and controlled by the state, the legal relationship the citizen has with them will be governed by the nationally defined statutory powers and duties vested in those who manage them, rather than by the form of any private (local) binding agreement.

The consolidation of the legal sovereignty of the nation state in the form of the welfare state coincided with the emergence of international institutions such as the United Nations and the European Community that pulled in the opposite direction. As institutional mechanisms directed to imposing legal limits on national sovereignty they represent the beginnings of a break with one of the defining features of legal modernity. Yet for all their promise these law-making bodies had little initial effect on the form and content of domestic law, largely because the underlying interventionist philosophy of welfare states is at odds with the volatility and unpredictability of international influence. Accordingly, as long as welfare states jealously guarded their sovereignty, these emergent international institutions were able to exercise very limited influence over domestic affairs at the very time when those states extended their regulatory reach within the confines of national borders.

The spatial re-organization of law that followed the introduction of welfare state reforms was accompanied by the re-casting of the temporal co-ordinates of law. The separation of powers, as one of the cornerstones of the modern law and the liberal state, implied very different temporal visions for functionaries in its constituent branches. The legislature operates by looking to regulate the future, the judiciary applies law by relying on past rules and doctrines, and the executive implements those rules by reference to present circumstances. In the welfare state this delicate temporal balance between the state's branches is strained. Given the new state's imperative to achieve a fairer redistribution of resources, impose ever tighter regulatory controls over the economy, and integrate increasingly complex social subsystems to further wealth generation, and in a rapidly changing environment, legal rules developed in an earlier age are rendered increasingly obsolete, and with growing alacrity. With each change in the environment, law must be changed, so that legislative output increases exponentially (Galanter, 1992). But even swift legislative reform is not enough to meet regulatory needs in this context. In order for legal rules to regulate and steer social change more effectively, each branch of the law, legislature, executive and judiciary, is called on to look to the future impact of legal decisions and the context of the application of law. It follows that defining features in the law of the welfare state are

> problems of time and of speed ... Sufficient speed can be achieved only by legislation and legislation will change the law again and again without leaving time for court traditions and for dogmatic [doctrinal] refinements to settle down. Within the legal system the priority passes onto the legislature. This means, to some extent, a new primacy of cognitive over normative considerations (Luhmann 1986: 119).

The "new primacy of cognitive over normative considerations", that is, the importance of fitting rules to the changing empirical context in which they are to operate (always typical of legislative activity) imposes analogous demands on the judicial and executive branches of the state. It is reflected in the case of judicial reasoning, for instance, by a keener attention to the purposes lying behind the law to see if they can be effectively carried out by instant decisions in an increasingly volatile social environment. This "sovereignty of purpose" is reflected in "the waning of 'artificial reason'", in the form of the traditional, deontological style of legal interpretation more concerned to look to the formal meanings of terms (Nonet and Selznick, 1978: 78, 83). This development also appears in the growing need for legislators and law reform agencies to make use of other knowledges (economics, sociology, politics) in order to understand the interaction between, and interdependence of, law and other social domains.

A second way in which the temporal dimensions of law are changed is evident in the transformation of certain types of legal relationships. An important dimension of the security guaranteed by welfare states was its restriction of the rights of more powerful parties to bring contractual relationships to an end. Contracts "at will", especially in the areas of employment and housing, were the source of greater insecurity and therefore impoverishment in the liberal state. In the welfare state, regulatory and interventionist reforms were particularly pronounced in labour law, where employers in both the private sector, and especially in the much-enlarged public sector, were subjected to increasingly stringent legal requirements before dismissing employees. Given the other benefits in terms of leave and pension entitlements, jobs came to provide the long-term stability. Glendon notes that this position stands in stark opposition to new opt-out, legally "at will" family (1981: ch 4). "Altered patterns of legal bonding" result: in the world of work, jobs and employees came to be bound in more secure, and therefore enduring, ways than in earlier times when the contract of employment much less resembled a property right, because it could be terminated at will, and did not bring with it extensive pension and other benefits associated with broader welfare state reforms. In combination, the reforms held out powerful incentives and pressures for workers to remain with particular employers.

Employment security also reflects the rigidities of corporatist and Fordist economic organization: it represented a bargain struck by strong unions with employers strategically weakened by low historic rates of unemployment and the organizational power of workers in mass production enterprises with a very high division of labour. Comparable changes were evident in other contracts, such as residential leases, so that security of tenure, like stability of employment, particularly when linked to fair rent rules, tied the tenant to the lease as much as the lease to the tenant (Glendon, 1981: 176-185). As a result, "the secure tie to rented housing, like new property in jobs or welfare benefits, is one that may lock in both sides" (Glendon, 1981: 184). From a broad sociological perspective, the short-term contracts typical of legal relations in liberal society gradually gave way to the more stable, status-related arrangements of the welfare state.

The changed time/space orientations of the law of the welfare state refine rather than completely transform the structure of modern law. National space is more systematically subject to legal regulation; a more entrenched future-orientation appears within legal institutions; law is more contingent in nature as rapid social change requires accelerating legal change; and secure status-type legal relationships in economic relations come to replace the pure contractual dealings of the liberal state. These legal changes form part of the historical and sociological uniqueness of the welfare state.

Access to Justice

The legal order of the welfare state demonstrates both continuities and discontinuities with the trajectory of modern law by providing for greater levels of access to the legal system on behalf of its citizens. As we have seen, modern law is archetypically formal, positive law, with its own distinctive profession and unified system of courts. It was also characterized by its recognition of the abstract legal subject, a bearer of universal rights of access to the formal courts. But treating citizens of unequal power and resources equally is ultimately to treat citizens on an unequal basis. In consequence, alongside the formal equality of access to formal justice lay dramatic substantive inequalities of access in liberal societies. Consistent with the redistributive politics that formed part of the ideological bedrock of welfare states, public funds were increasingly directed into schemes to make formal justice more accessible to the poor and disadvantaged. In this way, legal aid programs entailed a specific type of regulation of, and intervention in, the market for legal services. "Unmet legal need" was a common catchcry from the beginnings of the welfare state, evoking the notion of state responsibility to redress injustice.

This "first wave" of access to justice (Cappelletti and Garth, 1978) coincided with the rise of the welfare state. Notwithstanding great differences across states, steadily increasing proportions of public funds in advanced industrialized societies were channelled into legal institutions, with corresponding increases in the numbers of legal personnel, courts and lawsuits, in order to make them more accessible for all citizens. This particular type of market intervention is entirely consistent with the organizing principles of modern law in three respects. First, it extended the reach of formal, national law, replacing private, informal mechanisms of dispute resolution. Second, the modern principle of equality before the law was directly fostered through legal aid programs (Sackville, 1975: 9). They purported to render the identity and position of parties irrelevant to the dispute and so achieve "'equality of arms' – the assurance that the ultimate result depends only on the relative legal merits of the opposing positions" (Cappelletti and Garth, 1978, vol 1: 10). To the extent that state-funded legal aid "fitted snugly into the developing post-war welfare state" (Smith, 1996: 571) it provided particularly compelling evidence of the emergence of social citizenship (Marshall, 1963: 101-105).

Third, legal aid represents an increase in the legal monocentricity and centripetality typical of modern societies. As legal aid provision expanded (eligibility for legal aid for some matters extended to 60–80% of the populations of England, Wales and the Netherlands by the 1970s, for example, (Parker, 1999: 33)) access to justice could be said to have become a predominantly national concern. On a broader level, general increases in wealth, and a public commitment to redistribution, combined with legal aid policies to put recourse to legal redress within the reach of a much larger proportion of the population than before (Galanter, 1992).

Somewhat later than legal aid initiatives, a "second wave" of access to justice is evident in the emergence of the "public interest law" movement which sought to represent large classes of litigants to achieve lasting reforms of a public, rather than largely private, benefit. Through the use of class actions, and reform of procedural rules, the movement linked with social movements to advance the rights of the disadvantaged, especially in the United States (Parker, 1999: 35-36). Public interest law also targeted the administrative powers of state agencies and bureaucracies and so led to the expansion of administrative remedies against the state. The net effect of these changes is that the formal law of the nation state occupies an increasingly central place in the social order and normative architecture of welfare states. A further reflection of this development is that legal professions grow in size, courts proliferate, and court lists lengthen

(Galanter, 1992). As Cappelletti (1993) concludes, legal aid provision is a key feature marking the modernization of societies.

A paradox of the legal landscape of welfare states is that alongside the rapid growth of the apparatus of formal law and the widening of access to it, a "third wave" of more informal mechanisms of dispute resolution starts to emerge. A broad array of informal tribunals with informal procedures and limited rights to legal representation in areas such as social security, employment and housing began to appear, as well as centres directed to provision of "community justice". This heterogeneous third wave of access to justice encompasses incongruous aims. It increases access to legal redress. But it also threatens to disrupt the centripetality and monocentricism of the legal systems characteristic not only of welfare states, but modern societies generally. Informalism opens disputes to norms that have their origin not in the state but in the murkier waters of civil society. Coming from below rather than above they represent, in their institutional guise, the appearance of the ambivalent legal pluralism that modernity sought to erase. It follows that this particular feature of legal change in the welfare state cuts against the grain of modern formal, autonomous, law. However, while the welfare state was in its ascendancy, the appearance of state-sponsored informal justice (alternative dispute resolution, or ADR) lay only at the margins of the formal legal system. It was very much weaker in effect than the first and second access to justice waves: apart from the state-funded tribunals, generally "ADR options were slow in gaining popularity and were not publicly funded" (Parker, 1999: 38). We shall see in chapter 5 that as ADR dramatically increases in legal and sociological significance, it forms a central feature of a broad process of legal postmodernization.

Conclusion

The range of reforms of both the legal systems and legal doctrines characteristically introduced by welfare states were sufficiently profound to justify their being described as representing an historically new paradigm of law (Habermas, 1996: 402). At the same time, welfare states were identifiably modern in character; they both revised and enhanced liberal law in equal measure. Also, the overall pattern of change reflects a widely held belief in "total justice" (Friedman, 1985). Governments and populations at large generally came to expect that the various social misfortunes could be contained by legal remedies, and that the courts had the capacity to deliver them. The general confidence of the time that economies could be successfully managed by centralized planning, funding and guidance had its counterpart in attitudes to law. Law could be the tool by means of which state policies could achieve such goals, but they would only be capable of doing so if the appropriate levels of empirical information about society were available to inform legislative and judicial judgment. In this context, the critical vocabulary of both legal realism and earlier sociological jurisprudence assumed a far greater influence in normative discourse about law than the legal positivism that accompanied the rise of the liberal state (Cotterrell, 1989: chs 6-7). These schools of thought emphasized that law needed to take account of a much wider range of empirical social facts in order to deliver justice more effectively (Nonet and Selznick, 1978: 73). At the same time, the re-deployment of liberal values to the private sphere that valorized choice and pleasure – "the social-democratic variant of 'economic individualism'" (Hall, 1980: 34) – had the effect of paving the way for a range of later postmodern discourses directed at analyzing the social forces and policies of both liberal societies and welfare states seen to suppress identity and difference.

The broad political and popular consensus underpinning these legal changes was partially reflected in the appearance of many and varied theoretical understandings of the legal reforms of the welfare state. Also numbered among these theories were critiques from the political left and right who saw the new developments as reflecting a more sinister turn. An assessment of some of the more influential of these writings, particularly from the perspective of whether they provide insights into more recent reforms, will be the focus of the next chapter.

Notes

1 Bradgate et al. (1994) suggest three types of regulation. They exclude my third example, the legislative variation of general rules. I have added it to attempt to clarify the distinction between liberal forms of modern law on the one hand, and welfare state styles of regulation on the other.

2 Majone (1990: 1) makes the important point that regulation in the United States is generally seen as intimately tied to the structure and practice of regulatory agencies. In Europe, by contrast, regulation is seen more as "the whole realm of legislation, governance and social control. This broad use of the term makes the study of regulation coextensive with law, economics, political science and sociology ...". Throughout the book, I use the term in the latter sense.

3 For more detail of Habermas' perspective on this, see below at pp 112-116.

4 Old Theories, New Paradigm

> The characteristics of these [postliberal] societies undermine the rule of law and they strengthen tendencies in belief and organization that ultimately discourage reliance on public and positive rules as bases of social order (Unger, 1976: 192).

> Regulatory law – the most ambitious, modern, goal-oriented, sociologically informed type of law representing a political mechanism of social guidance – is said to be in deep crisis, or at least in a state of institutional failure (Teubner, 1986: 305).

Introduction

The rise of the welfare state provoked many theorists to examine the extent of the changes introduced into modern legal institutions. These analyses yielded rich and diverse empirical evidence about the nature and extent of legal change, and its relationship to broader social change. They also provided a range of critical perspectives on these developments, as theorists sought to offer evaluative assessments of the advantages and disadvantages of the reforms that defined the new legal order. But the more recent wave of manifold and convulsive social transformations catalogued in chapter 2 tends to show the theories of the law of the welfare state in a very different light. Because they purport to draw conclusions from the array of very different empirical features of the welfare state they raise questions as to how valuable their insights are for the purposes of understanding the nature of law, with its "opaque and inconsistent structure" (Habermas, 1996: 390), at the present time.

This chapter will examine some of these theories. I will argue that the more their focus is directed to the empirical detail of welfare states, the less capable they are of offering clear understandings of the legal structures of present societies where that particular state form, and its law, is substantially transformed. In this endeavour it will be necessary to examine separately the work of some of the leading theorists for the reason that they each emphasize different aspects of the novelty of the changes ushered in by the new state's regulatory, interventionist and redistributive policies. It is also important to consider critically the sociological presuppositions that lie at the heart of many of these analyses. They constitute one element in a sociology that features as "an adjunct of modernity", and expresses a distinctive intellectual project. This type of social theory

> translated the 'rationalization spurt', the disciplinary practices, the uniforming ambitions of modernity from a normative project into the analytical framework for making sense of reality, and thus made the 'structure' those pre-individual forces which bring order into the otherwise chaotic and potentially damaging drives of the free agents – the pivot of its discourse. It drew its cognitive horizons with the leg of the compass placed firmly in the very spot from which the levelling, uniforming, proselytizing tendencies of modern times emanated – and thus identified 'society', the largest analytical totality meant to incorporate and accommodate all analysis – with the nation state (Bauman, 1992: 54).

The centrality of the notion of "structure" in social theory is now subject to unprecedented doubt. To problematize structure in this way makes obvious sense given the less exclusive contemporary influence of the nation state; but it is also justified by the lack of stability of those very institutions by reference to which modern societies are typically identified. In a more fluid and chaotic world, a rigid concept of structure must give way to a recognition of the present "systemic indifference to cultural plurality and, indeed, ... the waywardness of constitutive agencies. It seems unlikely, therefore, that ... the business of sociology can go on 'as usual'" (Bauman, 1992: 54).

This chapter will generally examine the social context and the specific legal change that the theorists analyze rather than gauge their arguments by reference to more recent legal change. This latter subject will be addressed in detail in the next chapter. The sample of theorists to be examined here is necessarily limited. I have chosen those whom I believe to have been the most influential, and the most perceptive and representative in analyzing the structural changes in law in the welfare state. The discussion will be divided into two sections. The first will deal with some of those theorists whose work appeared at the high watermark of the welfare state. The second will survey the work of theorists who have attempted to analyze law in the context of emergent changes to the structure of the welfare state. Neither, I will argue, offer sufficiently comprehensive understandings of society to explain the entire range of influences on *contemporary* law and legal institutions.

Theorizing the Law of the Welfare State

Theories of the law of the welfare state have, in general, aimed to show how the changes ushered in by the welfare state had transformed law no less than other spheres such as the economy or the state. While a measure of consensus links the wide array of theoretical perspectives developed to explain and critically evaluate these legal changes, there are significant differences of emphasis. These differences relate to the sociological perspectives employed, the political and critical assessments as to the desirability of the novel developments, the identification of the most significant components of the new legal orders, and the social impact of the various legal reforms.

The Rule of Law and the Mixed Economy

Among the earliest and most influential analyses of the historically unique legal changes ushered in by the welfare state are Wolfgang Friedmann's *Law in a Changing Society* (1959), and *The State and Rule of Law in a Mixed Economy* (1971). In these works, Friedmann combined an examination of the relationship between advanced post-war states' greater involvement in social and economic activity and the legal system. He also made no secret of his admiration for the achievements of the welfare state and the mixed economy, though he urged legal reform in many areas. The starting point of his account is the "social ideal of contemporary democracy" (1971: 20-23). It is in this ideal that the four core elements of the welfare state are to be found. First, the welfare state performs the function of a provider, by guaranteeing minimum income levels and the satisfaction of basic needs; second, the state assumes the role of entrepreneur, by means of involvement in, and ownership of, substantial public enterprise; third, the state becomes a regulator, through the increased intervention in the formerly private areas of freedom of contract and property rights, the management of private organizations, the control of competition and the systematic containment of socially harmful activities. The state's fourth role is that of umpire. This role differs from the others in that it is not specific to the welfare state: it is part of the general legal fabric of liberal societies captured by the notion of the rule of law. The rule of law requires that the law must apply equally to the state as to private individuals; the state is *subject to law*. For this purpose to be achieved, the judicial arm of the state must be autonomous from politics and administration. And, as we have seen in chapter 3, autonomy can be achieved if law operates with a distinctive, "artificial" reason, which is different from the rationality that drives other social subsystems.

To play the umpire is considerably more difficult in light of the welfare state's other functions because of potential conflicts of aims that the various roles require. For example, can competition policy be fairly pursued if the state has a direct economic interest, as producer and distributor of resources, in the outcome of such a dispute? Such dilemmas pose particular problems for public law: how can it effectively ensure equality of treatment between state officials and private persons if its rules are not sufficiently sensitive to the power imbalances between the citizen and the administration? And where regulators are given wide discretion to achieve their statutory purposes more effectively, the power gradient separating the private actor and the public officials steepens dramatically, especially as this discretion is inherently less capable of judicial control than rule-based behaviour is. For some, these social and economic changes presented conundrums that even a reformed law could never resolve; and for this reason they had a deleterious, if not fatal, effect on the rule of law as a principle that upholds a commitment to clear, abstract rules which purport to treat all legal subjects equally (Unger, 1976; Kamenka et al., 1978; Hayek, 1982; Walker, 1988). Friedmann showed no such pessimism. He argued that by formulating a revitalized set of public law principles, the state could be effectively shackled to ensure an appropriate balance between liberty and prosperity, and so preserve the delicate equilibrium required by the separation of powers.

Although there is no social theoretical framework developed in this account, many of the empirical factors identified in the previous chapter as being characteristic of the welfare state are central to Friedmann's analysis. In general, they indicate a process of social and economic modernization. So, the growth in monopoly power of corporations and unions is seen to be the key element driving a "steadily increasing" role for the state, "even in Britain[!]" (1971: 37). Widespread nationalization produces previously unknown forms of public law, which he identifies as symptomatic of the nation-building and modernization initiatives of the last century (1971: 54). A further manifestation of this process is an increased centralization of state control in economic and social planning in ways similar to what Lash and Urry describe as "organized capitalism" (1987).

Friedmann's analyses of the welfare state and the law that both defines and regulates that state are highly convincing, and largely uncontestable. Yet they now seem outdated given the range of changes that have occurred in the state and society over the last twenty years or so. With the advent of widespread privatization, and the corporatization of so many state enterprises, with their attendant return to a marketplace governed more by principles of private than public law, it is more difficult today to point to the distinctiveness or the relative significance, legal or otherwise, of the "entrepreneurial" state. The datedness is particularly evident in light of the fact that many *pre*-welfare state functions have since been progressively privatized, such as transport, utilities and prisons, with consequential adjustments to the legal regimes that govern their delivery.

Furthermore, the dramatic changes in the regulatory mix of contemporary societies are at odds with what Friedmann outlines as his "regulator" state. The welfare state's command and control strategies have been progressively jettisoned in favour of reforms that privilege market discipline. Equally, the general thrust of the redistributive role of the state has changed. As the state partially retreats from these areas, the relevant regulatory instruments are comparably re-calibrated. It follows that Friedmann's account of how the heavily centralized welfare state operates to give law a distinct sociological complexion, has a largely historical, rather than contemporary, ring to it. It also exhibits the characteristic optimism of that time when it appeared impossible to envisage the fragility of this historical compromise. Hence Friedmann concludes that "[t]o me it is inconceivable that, in the foreseeable future, the role of the state could be reduced" (1971: 98), and "[i]n the years ahead, the active intervention of government in the economic affairs of nations is certain to increase greatly" (1971: 52). This point is underscored by his postscript to the book where he sounds a note of despondency, in the British context, about the plans of the then Conservative Government to clip the wings of some nationalized industries with the aim of conferring greater incentives and benefits on the private sector. This strategy was no less than a "half-baked compromise between a *laissez-faire* philosophy and public responsibility for vital sectors of the national economy" (1971: 101).

The Rule of Law and "Postliberal Society"

A more sociological understanding of the law of the welfare state in light of the state's changed responsibilities emerges from Roberto Unger's *Law in Modern Society: Toward a Criticism of Social Theory* (1976). Squarely within the Weberian tradition (Parsons, 1977-78: 147-148; Duxbury, 1986: 659-665), Unger's analysis identifies similar changes to Friedmann's, but he seeks to go back further in time, and locates them in a more developed theoretical scheme. Unger understands the transformation of the law in the welfare state in terms of how it relates to, and deviates from, the entire historical trajectory of legality in Western societies. In a very general historical periodization, he sees Western societies as demonstrating a transition from the tribal to the aristocratic, then liberal and finally to the "postliberal" stage. Each of these societies is distinguished by, among other factors, its legal order; indeed, for Unger, a society's legal order is the key to its inner essence. Thus for tribal societies, an unwritten, implicit customary or interactional law is central. In aristocratic societies a "bureaucratic law", marked by public and positive rules holds sway. Liberal societies are distinctive by virtue of their supplementation of the public and positive rules of aristocratic society by the rule of law, defined by its autonomy from other social spheres on the one hand, and the generality of its legal rules on the other.

Although Unger's theory operates at a high level of abstraction, and the empirical evidence he relies on is highly elusive, he nonetheless provides a general picture of the essential elements of the final phase of social and legal development – postliberal societies, which roughly equate with the broad definition of welfare state used in the previous chapter. For Unger, postliberal societies have two key components: first, a welfare state "involved in the tasks of overt redistribution, regulation, and planning", and second, "corporatist tendencies" which require the state's abandonment of its role of "being a neutral guardian of the social order" and a correlative "effacement both in organization and in consciousness of the boundary between state and society, and therefore between the public and the private realm" (1976: 193, 200-201). As with earlier societies, the general sociological features of postliberal societies leave their mark on the legal order. Overall, they effect a decline of the rule of law. Because the welfare state is the site of political struggle around "the problems of unjustified hierarchy", it develops policies of tight regulation of the economy and substantial redistribution of wealth (1976: 193). These policies are manifested legally in three forms: first, laws that exhibit open-ended standards and general clauses in legal rules; second, a more policy-oriented legal reasoning; and third, a shift away from "concerns with formal justice to an interest in procedural and substantive justice" (1976: 194).

The first and third types of laws offend the rule of law's central principle of generality. The wide discretion conferred by open-ended standards and general rules entails an ad hoc, particularistic application. This means that the law is progressively *less general* in nature: there is more focus on the empirical characteristics of parties and groups in dispute rather than the treatment of them as formally equal, abstract subjects in the manner typical of the legal orders of liberal societies. Also, the welfare state's increasing managerial responsibilities call for vague standards, rather than hard and fast general rules, given the complexity of the social and economic environment. The shift from formal to procedural and substantive justice corrodes the principle of generality in a similar way. Formal justice requires "the uniform application of general rules", whereas procedural and substantive justice demand that "rules be interpreted in terms of ideals that define the conception of justice" (1976: 194-195). And in the welfare state the distributive effects and welfare consequences of legal rules loom large in general ideas about justice. Policy-oriented legal reasoning, the second feature of the law of the welfare state, offends the rule of law's principle of autonomy from other social spheres. As policy intrudes, legal reasoning appears less "artificial"; it begins to look more and more like political or moral argumentation (1976: 199).

Corporatism is considered by Unger to have even more significant consequences for law. He defines the term somewhat vaguely, and idiosyncratically, as the interpenetration of state and society, and the ensuing generation of institutions "that rival the state in their power and take on many attributes formerly associated with public bodies" (1976: 201).[1] Unger seems to see corporatism as a particular form of regulation of the structures and operations of large organizations. This development corrodes the public and positive character of legal rules because large, nominally private, organizations are regulated by means of "state-authored rules and ... privately sponsored regulations or practices" which "are less and less capable of being separated" (1976: 202). Further, corporatism is implicated in "the growth of a body of rules that break down the traditional distinction between public and private law" (Unger, 1976: 201). A form of "social law" results.

For all the sociological and historical grounding of his thesis, Unger's analysis of postliberal societies does not look any more relevant than Friedmann's for the purposes of understanding the social and legal landscape of contemporary societies. Can his analysis of the sociological phenomenon of corporatism, for instance, be relevant to an understanding of legal systems in societies where corporatism, even in his restricted sense, is so visibly on the wane? As former welfare states retreat from restrictive regulation, yielding ever-greater control to the market, the growing fusion of public and private law that Unger details is being steadily reversed. This point is underscored by Unger's reliance on Philip Selznick's (1969) empirical study of industrial relations law that identified the increasing intrusion of public interest considerations, and a corresponding public law dimension, to employment relations. As we have seen in chapter 2, and will examine in more detail in the next, in a post-Fordist industrial setting, this type of legal regime is subject to significant modification in the light of a changed social environment.

Unger's account of the welfare state appears equally unsuited to offering a theoretical understanding of the current conditions. The welfare state's policies of "overt redistribution, regulation and planning" have been substantially modified since Unger's book appeared. Redistribution appears as a less pressing goal for most states in contemporary advanced capitalist societies, while strategies of regulation and planning have been entirely recast. To be sure, the revitalized interest in procedural justice to which Unger refers is still present, but, as will be seen later, it is expressed in ways which differ from the policies adopted, and the philosophies cherished, at the height of the welfare state. And the welfare state's concern with substantive and distributive justice is a much less prominent feature of contemporary *post*-postliberal societies. Moreover, the causes Unger identifies as the major factors fuelling the changes – "the problems of unjustified hierarchy" and "the vicissitudes of the class struggle" (1976: 193, 197) – have been displaced at the present time to a significant degree by a politics of recognition, where different political players have influence, and by a revised faith in market mechanisms. This changed political and sociological environment has subjected legal forms to a range of divergent influences. In particular, the deregulatory developments of the last couple of decades have had the effect of displacing much of the regulatory law that Unger sees as undermining the rule of law's principles of generality and autonomy. As we shall see in the following chapter, the general dismantling of corporatism (in both Unger's and the more widely accepted meaning of the term) and the paring back of the welfare state have produced a legal landscape far removed from the one Unger understood. In turn, the pressures facing the rule of law are radically different in nature and effect.

A more significant factor in registering the limited utility of Unger's approach for understanding contemporary society is the closed nature of his central concept, "society", which is fundamental to his analysis of forms of law. Tribal society, feudal society, liberal society, postliberal society – all alike are held to capture neatly the boundedness of the context from which legal norms originate, and their sphere of operation. In the nature of ideal types, they serve to make sense of the normative orders of earlier societies; but even here they seem to be far too unitary in approach to offer clear understandings of the complexity of legal orders. This weakness becomes dramatically pronounced at the present time when the normative reach of global institutions is historically unprecedented. Unger's operative social theory cannot offer adequate assistance to understand the contemporary array of influences on law and legal institutions for the reason that so many of these originate *outside particular societies*.

Unger's concept of society, both in *Law and Modern Society* and in his later *Social Theory: Its Situation and Its Task* (1987) which revises some of his sociological ideas, implicitly assumes that it is a "sealed totality" (Bauman, 1992a: 57). This renders it particularly unhelpful in the context of a dramatically more fluid political, economic and legal environment, where the welfare state unravels, and globalization intrudes, with all their attendant diversity of influences on legal systems and doctrine. Central to his approach is an equation of modern liberal and postliberal societies with the nation state. The generality of Unger's concepts might seem to protect him from these criticisms, but if anything it renders his argument even more vulnerable: the concept of "society" simply rules out of account in theoretical terms the issue of *degrees* of external structural determination. His later acknowledgement of how nations can borrow from the legal and political traditions of others, and produce historical "surprises" (1987) might suggest a way forward, but his examples predate and cannot accommodate the complexity of contemporary developments. As Bauman describes this general methodological approach,

> the nation state prototype for the concept of society endowed the latter with a visible *developmental tendency*; a self-sustained and self-propelled tendency, with all its relevant explanatory factors to be found *inside* the society in question – so that all *outside* factors could be theoretically reduced to the role of environment... (1992: 57).

However adequate this methodological assimilation of society and nation state is for modernity generally, and "postliberal" society in particular, where national legal sovereignty was pre-eminent, it is unsatisfactory for societies with legal systems subject to strong supranational influences. So, Lawrence Friedman identifies a central contemporary challenge for legal sociology: "For all its achievements ... the social sciences are best at studying what occurs within a certain legal system (usually the United States) ... In spite of the globalized *practice* of law, the study of transnational legal processes is barely beginning" (Friedman, 1996: 65). Despite its evolutionary, comparative and historical focus, Unger's work offers no conceptual tools for this task.

Of course, it would be unfair to blame Unger for this oversight. His work was written at a time when many of the central elements of the corporate welfare state were still either in their ascendancy or were at least intact, and the sorts of disintegrative processes outlined in chapter 2 had hardly begun. But it is not inappropriate to challenge Unger's approach on the same ground that he finds the "classical" social theorists wanting. He argues that classical social theory was crafted for a world very different from the one he occupied: on the one hand, modern Western societies had become "postliberal", and on the other, non-Western societies had adopted industrialization but retained traditional values and institutions. As he powerfully argues, an examination of legal change in modern societies could shed critical light on the inadequacies of traditional social theory. This same argument is just as relevant to his revised social theory: it is no less immune from obsolescence by the processes of historical change. Law in *post*modern society opens a window onto some very novel, yet different, problems for social theory. Society has changed to such a degree that its new structures and institutions pose very different questions for, and apply very different pressures on, that central feature of Western legal systems, the rule of law.

Neil MacCormick makes similar criticisms in relation to "standard positions in legal theory" – which must include Unger in this respect – in the contemporary legal environment that he characterizes as being "beyond the sovereign state" (1993: 1). These standard positions mirror sociological traditionality insofar as they typically display a monocentric view of law. To remedy this defect, a focus on the sociology of globalization is necessary for the purposes of more effective contemporary socio-legal scholarship. Such an approach might begin to explore the contours of an emerging social and political polycentricity, and how that phenomenon affects and is affected by law. In conducting this exercise, the implicit, static *spatial* co-ordinates of Unger's approach need to be re-examined. And an analysis of this nature might be complemented by considering the different *temporal* co-ordinates of postmodern societies where the nature of the social bond is rather different to what Unger sees as the key to understanding the welfare state. At present the temporariness of relationships is supplanting permanent institutions, and one social mechanism that commonly facilitates this change is contract (Lyotard, 1984: 66). At a deeper level, the notion of solidarity which Unger sees as receiving expression in postliberal societies in the form of a shift to substantive justice must be reconsidered in the light of another level on which modernization and postmodernization are separable: that of a shift from materialist to postmaterialist values (Inglehart, 1997).

Finally, Unger's attempt to draw distinctions between the different types of contemporary "modern" societies and their laws, by means of a trichotomy – the traditionalistic, such as Japan, the revolutionary socialist, such as Communist China, and the postliberal, such as Western capitalist democracies, as a supplementary way of looking at the variety of legal orders – also begins to look increasingly shaky. The recent dramatic changes to former communist societies and the Eastern traditionalist societies as they move in a capitalist direction, the development of global communications networks, and the increasing economic interdependency between nations, tend to level distinctions between cultural and national traditions, as well as political ideologies. Unger's difficulty is reflected in his speculations for legal change: that in a "circular" progression, the welfare and corporatist tendencies of postliberal societies will lead them, and their legal institutions, back toward custom, and the "logic of tribalism". Or in his other model, that of the "spiral", the undoing of the rule of law might lead to "individual freedom [being] brought into harmony with the reassertion of communitarian concerns" (1976: 238-239). Neither option appears remotely close to the polycentric legal structure of contemporary societies, where some features of political and economic liberalism have become re-established. This process in turn may provoke varied forms of resistance and interplay with local and regional traditions in a way that provides another inflection to the term "postmodernity",

> not as a 'countermodernity' or a nostalgic recalling of a 'premodernity', but perhaps as a way of describing experiences of, relationships to, and

struggles with the diverse and complex manifestations of a modernity that is still very much with us (Smart, 1993: ch 6).

The resultant effects of this new patchwork quilt of social forces is far more complex, and historically advanced, than Unger's rigid typologies are capable of accommodating.

Postliberal "Responsive" Law

A comparable attempt to locate law in an historical, evolutionary sequence is Philippe Nonet and Philip Selznick's *Law and Society in Transition: Toward Responsive Law* (1978). They attempt to understand changes both in popular consciousness, society and law by means of a condensed evolutionary typology which has three phases: repressive law, autonomous law and responsive law. Roughly speaking, these forms of law correspond to types of society: the late feudal/early liberal, the liberal and the welfare state respectively. Repressive law is marked by a very weak, or illusory separation of powers at the level of the state, a pervasive authoritarianism, a high level of indifference to popular opinion and no real accountability. Nonet and Selznick see it as characteristically present in the formative period of nation states, though it has contemporary manifestations in totalitarian states (Nonet and Selznick, 1978: 29-42). They acknowledge that this type of law closely parallels the "bureaucratic law" identified by Unger (1976) as typical of feudal societies (1978: 54).

Autonomous law, by contrast, is based on a clear division between the political and legal spheres. Like Unger's legal order of liberal societies, typical of this type of law is its independence from direct political interference and the immediate demands of the state. It is also characterized by a rule-based formalism administered by an identifiable group of professionals: law is a distinct system with its own internal rationality and personnel. Nonet and Selznick link this development with wider social change. It is seen as evidence of functional differentiation: "The social process of differentiation, which brings into play new groups and vested interests, completes the job of forming the institutional system we call autonomous law" (1978: 57). It follows that autonomous law is intimately bound up with the emergence of social modernization. Under autonomous law the power and authority of the state is significantly restrained, while "the obligations of citizens are limited" (1978: 70); it follows that at the very least it reflects the values of a liberal state and liberal society.

Responsive law, as the historically most recent type of law, is more sensitive to, and thus less autonomous from, social needs and contexts. In tones reminiscent of Friedmann's "social ideal of contemporary democracy", and Unger's "gradual approximation of state and society"

(1976: 193) the appearance of responsive law can be measured by how "[l]egal institutions give up the insular safety of autonomous law and become more dynamic instruments of social ordering and social change" (1978: 74). Yet the essential features of responsive law are not directly produced by the operations of a changed state, or transformations in the nature of society, as is the case of repressive law or autonomous law. Rather, it is an *internally-generated* response to external problems: responsive law "*perceives social pressures as sources of knowledge and opportunities for self-correction*", and "[t]he dynamics of legal development" come to give priority to the very general ends of legal principles over particular rules, policies and procedures (1978: 77-78; italics in original).

Responsive law, therefore, in its social dimension, has an affinity with the law of the welfare state analyzed by other theorists, though Nonet and Selznick refrain from making a close alignment between this type of law and the form of state and society. One of the reasons for their stance is that responsive law, like autonomous and repressive law, is more of an ideal type than it is a description of an existing legal system. It is also the model of law that they propose as the most desirable legal framework for advanced societies. However, they do identify some general patterns of legal change as evidence that responsive law has an historically unique prominence in post-war American law. First, there is a greater level of participation in the legal system. This is evidenced by what they describe as social advocacy that was permitted by more relaxed rules in relation to standing. Second, a preference for regulation over adjudication starts to appear (1978: 108). Third, informal dispute resolution mechanisms that give greater emphasis to the social context of disputes and the re-establishment of relationships have become integrated into the legal system. It follows that for all the stubbornly persistent presence of repressive and autonomous elements in the contemporary legal system, responsive law has staked a sure foothold. Their perspective differs from that of Friedmann's particularly in its implicit criticisms of the legal structure of contemporary modern societies. Far from comforted by the idea that the modernized structures of the welfare state, in delivering increased levels of well-being to all citizens, will equally enhance their legal status, they see formal law as commonly obstructive of genuine justice, and so requires supplementation with some "postbureaucratic" openness.

This general argument is linked to, and builds on, the thesis of Selznick's earlier work, *Law, Society and Industrial Justice* (1969) which is a study of the emerging principles underpinning the industrial law of the post-Second World War period. These principles were quite at odds with traditional private law concepts of freedom of contract and property insofar as they had the effect of infusing public law "due process" obligations in the context of the "private government" of large industrial enterprises (Selznick, 1969: ch 7). The industrial and political environment they identify as inducing and sustaining these changes – hierarchized management, large-scale industrial organization, heavily unionized workforces, a mixed economy, higher levels of government intervention and welfare provision – captures the characteristics of the "Fordist" patterns of industrial organization, underpinned by a regulatory welfare state, as outlined earlier. These changes were replicated in the context of other large organizations such as universities where a new law of governance was beginning to appear. It conferred increased participatory rights on citizens most directly affected by the activities of organizations that had a public or "governmental" character, or wherever the "social function of governing" is present (1969: 259).

These analyses are beset by similar problems as those of Unger and Friedmann though their reluctance to draw close linkages between responsive law and changes in the nature of the state and society absolves them from some of the charges of datedness detailed above. In a number of respects the analytical thrust of their argument seems to have been overtaken by events. Thus, responsive law is no less unitary, or monocentric, in dimension than the other theories examined above: the influences on, and problems of, legal systems are determined by the particular, singular societies and states within which they are situated. Their recommendations also appear as very much internal to particular systems: a "postbureaucratic" model is urged, but this has little of the recommendations for adoption to solve wider social problems as is found, for instance, in Friedmann's account. And even as viewed as a set of internal prescriptions, it still appears more suited to an earlier phase of legal development. There is a complete absence, for instance, of any consideration of an international dimension where a responsiveness to principles, policies and values created and developed beyond the boundaries of specific societies might be desirable. Human rights discourse, shared international norms, harmonization of rules – all these are presently pressing concerns which feature nowhere in their proposals for law reform.

As regards the emerging "industrial justice" that Selznick identified, the decline of this pattern of production in favour of post-Fordism and postindustrialism has had the effect of modifying or reversing many of the institutional changes represented in his model of industrial justice. Selznick's labour paradigm starts to look seriously out of place with the emergence at the present time of patterns of production where a much more extensive freedom of property and contract regime seems to be taking hold. This point is especially relevant with the decline in the power of unions, and the loss of their privileged place in the formulation of policy and law.[2] A similar process has affected other organizations engaged in the "social function of governing" where market mechanisms have intruded to supplement or even replace those of welfare state-inspired due process reforms. The exact nature of this new legal framework will be explored in the next chapter; however, it is enough to emphasize here that the sorts of structural changes which Nonet and Selznick are pointing to appear to be receding into a past age.

Not all of what Nonet and Selznick argue seems ill-suited to describe the present landscape. Some of their evidence of the "responsiveness" of the legal systems of the welfare state, such as the increasing openness of the legal system and the growth of informal dispute resolution mechanisms has become substantially more entrenched in postmodernized legal systems, as will be seen later.[3] But these changes also are now driven by different values, and therefore take different directions. Increasingly the language of the market and the consumer has begun to replace the critical vocabulary of state regulation and control. The consumer has become the agent of accountability to the extent that the institutional design which Nonet and Selznick write of has been influenced along very different lines. This is not to suggest that there is a complete break with the past; rather, it is merely to say, as Ayres and Braithwaite suggest in their later overview of regulatory law, that there is a quite novel reconfiguration of the law and institutions of the welfare state at the present time (Ayres and Braithwaite, 1992). Accordingly, a new paradigm, if not actually established, is in the making.

A transformation in the structure of legal rules is also central in Francois Ewald's analysis of the law of the welfare state, where "social law" makes its appearance for the first time (Ewald, 1986; 1987). The primary emphasis in Ewald's scheme is on only two functions of the welfare state: regulation and wealth redistribution. But he shares with the theorists above a sense of the unique pressures that the welfare state imposes on legal systems, and is fundamentally in agreement about the direction they take. In his evolutionary scheme, Ewald sees the welfare state as displacing the law of the liberal state. With the rise of liberal societies, the prevailing legal order is remarkable for its "reciprocal" character. In welfare states, by contrast, the underlying philosophical principle of "solidarity" takes hold. It reflects a heightened concern for the social impact of formal, abstract rules. Solidarity manifests itself in law by means of the "norm". The norm is much more than a rule; it is a principle which "socializes judgement and identities ... [and] defines the conditions of what takes the place of the social contract in the solidarity societies: *consensus*" (1987: 108; italics in original).

More specifically, the "norm" comes to influence legal doctrine by taking ever more detailed account of sociological facts in the target area to be regulated. So, unlike modern law, which posited an abstract subject removed from his or her context, social law puts the context back in, treating the subject

> in terms of its concrete characteristics. The legal subject gives way to the wage earner, the consumer, the professional; the notion of contract breaks down into a multiplicity of types of contract, each capable, like the labor contract, of being governed by a special regulation (1987: 109).

Equally, the norm requires that justice not be formal, but substantive, with heavy reliance on discretion (1986: 68-70). Despite the different theoretical vocabulary, there are clear resonances in Ewald's analysis with each of the theories above that identify a drift away from legal formalism in the welfare state. And for the same reasons, the concepts central to his analysis are equally unsuited to explore the changed social and legal environment of the present.

Juridification and the Colonization of the Lifeworld

One theorist of the law of the welfare state who is rather more critical than the theorists discussed above of the reforms ushered in by welfare states is Jürgen Habermas. Simplifying greatly, Habermas sees modern capitalist societies generally as characterized by a fundamental cleavage between "system" and "lifeworld" (Habermas, 1987b: ch 6). The "system" is composed of the two great social subsystems, the state apparatus and the economy, which are distinguished by the currencies they deal in, power and money respectively. These subsystems typically function by using strategic or instrumental rationality. By contrast, the "lifeworld" is composed of the various subsystems such as family, culture, associations, and the various public spheres that operate primarily by means of consensus-oriented communicative interaction. Though both lifeworld and system are mutually interdependent, modern societies, for Habermas, are constantly threatened by the domination of lifeworld by system: economic inequality and state domination tend to corrode, or "colonize" the public spheres of the lifeworld. The welfare state represents the latest, highly developed phase of this general historical process.

Habermas sees in typical welfare state legal reforms the latest stage of the development of modern law. It amounts to a "*freedom-guaranteeing juridification* ... [which] bridles the economic system in a fashion similar to the way in which the two preceding thrusts of juridification bridled the administrative system" (1987b: 361; italics in original).[4] But Habermas identifies a dark side to this freedom. For instance, legal rights to income support and pensions deliver a capacity on the part of officials to intervene in an undesirable way in the lives of claimants. In particular,

> The more the welfare state goes beyond pacifying the class conflict lodged in the sphere of production and spreads a net of client relationships over private spheres of life, the stronger are the anticipated pathological side effects of a juridification that entails both a bureaucratization and a monetarization of core areas of the lifeworld. The *dilemmatic structure of this type of juridification* consists in the fact that, while the welfare-state guarantees are intended to serve the goal of social integration, they nevertheless promote the disintegration of life-relations when these are separated, through legalized social intervention, from the consensual mechanisms that coordinate action and are transferred over to media such as power and money (1987b: 364; italics in original).

A "therapeutocracy" comes to deliver welfare benefits to those who are legally defined as being in need; and in performing this role the law simultaneously creates dependencies on the state and corrodes the autonomy and self-reliance of recipients that are essential for an effectively functioning lifeworld. As an example, Habermas offers the case of a person who establishes a legal entitlement to geriatric care. Once defined in legal terms, this right

> has burdensome consequences for the self-image of the person concerned, and for his relations with spouse, friends, neighbours and others; it also has consequences for the readiness of solidaric communities to provide subsidiary assistance (1987b: 362).

A similar effect occurs in relation to other areas of law transformed by the welfare state. Relying on detailed empirical research on family law and school law, Habermas sees in the tendency of welfare states to regulate more closely domains considered private in liberal societies, a process of juridifying relations previously governed by informal norms. So, in the family, the former "traditional, economically grounded, patriarchal power relation in the family" (1987b: 368) is replaced by legal rights of children, of wives against husbands, while in the school, pupils', teachers', and school administrations' activities are increasingly subjected to legal regulation. The net effect of this panoply of legal remedies is to marginalize the *communicative* action that underpins the socialization of children: "The formalization of relationships in family and school means, for those concerned, an objectivization and *removal from the lifeworld* of (now) formally regulated social interaction in family and school" (1987b: 369; italics in original). But despite these pathological side-effects of welfare state law, Habermas acknowledges that a great proportion of the welfare state's interventionism operates in the opposite direction. Legislation that guarantees freedom to form unions, shortens working hours, or provides security of employment, embodies power-balancing principles, and therefore adds to the freedom afforded in earlier, liberal societies. It follows that the advance of the welfare state is a contradictory affair, with both gains and losses registered on freedom's scorecard.[5]

Unlike the theorists of the law of the welfare state above, Habermas has returned recently to the subject of the general nature of contemporary law, and so has had the opportunity to address possible empirical changes to the earlier paradigm. But despite this move, he does not address in any detail the more significant of recent changes to the welfare state. In his *Between Facts and Norms* (1996), Habermas introduces the notion of a "proceduralist" legal paradigm to resolve what he sees as the problems with both the liberal and the social welfare paradigms of law. But this paradigm does not seek to identify the *empirical* characteristics of a legal order that has moved beyond its liberal and social welfare counterparts. Rather, it is pitched at the *normative* rather than the sociological level; that is to say, his proposals centre on the articulation of "a convincing understanding of law that is connected with a constitutional project tailored for complex societies" (1996: 391). The proceduralist theory is therefore part of a reform agenda. It has much to commend it as an aspirational goal, and in chapter 7 it will be possible to see how it might form part of a general program of legal reform. But as a sociology of the present it is no less overtaken by recent change than the other theories examined above.

In elaborating the proceduralist paradigm, and setting the context in which it might operate, Habermas substantially retains a perspective of contemporary societies that sees them as conforming to "the social-welfare model". Thus contemporary law operates in a social environment of "an organized capitalism dependent on the government's provision of public infrastructure and planning" (1996: 402). The distinctive feature of that contemporary law is "the materialization of formal law" (1996: 392-409). He gives as examples the familiar doctrinal reforms in the "classical areas of property law and contract law". In the case of property these developments are evidenced in the expansion of the category of property to encompass various monetary entitlements, and the limits imposed on property holders, for instance, in the context of management prerogatives in employment law (1996: 403). In contract law, consumer protection and the adjustments to inequalities of status and market power demonstrate the appearance of a "compensatory law". The changes reflect an overall "ideology of a more managerial, redistributive, and welfare state" (1996: 404-405).[6] Further examples of the workings of the welfare state on legal doctrine lie in procedural change, as demonstrated in the opening up of the legal system by means of strategies concerned with "the actionability of rights" in the form of class actions and informal tribunals to resolve disputes (1996: 411).[7] Habermas' argument here is essentially the common one of theorists of the legal structure of welfare states: that is, that it can be gauged to the extent that it increasingly takes account of the substantive characteristics of participants in market relations – landlords, employers, corporations, producers, for example – in the process of formulation of legal rules, and it starts to make the legal sphere more "responsive" to disadvantaged groups.

Equally indicative of the extent to which Habermas' theory is still grounded within the empirical framework of liberal and welfare understandings of law is his criticism of both paradigms as limited by their "*productivist image* of capitalist society", which means that they "lose sight of the internal relation between private and *political* autonomy" (1996: 406; italics in original). This criticism derives from his understanding of these paradigms as equally concerned, though in different ways, with establishing individual autonomy by securing the material preconditions for equality. The ethical thinness of this project is evident when measured against a proceduralist paradigm that insists that

> legitimate law reproduces itself only in the forms of a constitutionally regulated circulation of power, which should be nourished by the communications of an unsubverted public sphere rooted in the core private spheres of an undisturbed lifeworld via the networks of civil society (1996: 408).

To understand the bureaucratic structure of the welfare state as being insufficiently sensitive to democratic pressure is by now a widely held belief, as was seen in chapter 2. However, the historically unique legal features of the welfare state are an inappropriate yardstick for measuring postmodern, as opposed to late modern, legal systems. In this way Habermas' argument falls prey to exactly the same problems as those of Friedmann, Unger, and Nonet and Selznick. Continuing to see the contemporary state as essentially a *welfare state* which operates in an environment of "organized capitalism", his social theoretical concepts are tied to a time which historically predates the disorganizing tendencies of the last couple of decades or so. Moreover, his empirical reference points in the sphere of legal doctrine are still interventionist contract, property, family and labour law, emphasizing as he did in his earlier work on the law of welfare states the threats they pose to a fully functional lifeworld by encouraging "passive followership" (1996: 414-416). Even if one accepts his thesis about the law of welfare states as at least in part corroding the communicative structure of the lifeworld, it is still necessary to examine the postmodern context, where the market, or neo-liberal principles, hold greater sway, and the state increasingly pares back many of its earlier ambitions. There is a strong case to be made that there is now a decolonization of some aspects of the lifeworld, or that there are processes of colonization at work that are radically reconfigured.

This argument remains pertinent in relation to other factors that cause the welfare state to unravel such as transnational forces and changes in civil society. In the case of the latter, the empirical findings of Ronald Inglehart's extensive cross-cultural researches are surely relevant. Inglehart identifies a widespread emergence of "postmaterialist" values in the culture and institutions of contemporary societies (Inglehart: 1997). Could this development be reflected in law? Habermas criticizes the liberal and social welfare paradigms as equally "productivist" and implies that in combination they exhaust the character of contemporary law, and therefore is theoretically closed to this possibility. As we shall see in the next chapter, a significantly changed legal landscape poses very different questions even for the critical "proceduralist paradigm".

Of course, it would be a mistake to imply that Habermas' criticisms of the functioning of welfare bureaucracies are irrelevant for contemporary societies. Substantial welfare law survives, with its associated institutions and practices. And it is clear that Habermas is acutely aware of the problem of the most recent social policy changes, emphasizing that his critique does not imply an argument in favour of a neo-liberal model of reform (1996: 414). Yet there is little in his model designed to comprehend the wide range of complex developments outlined in chapter 2 above. This is especially problematic given the "scant attention" he pays "to controlling private market powers" in this work (Parker, 1999: 226). His most recent work on the "postnational constellation" (2001: 58) cannot be accused of this weakness given its extensive analysis of how the entrenchment of market mechanisms at the global level have had a dramatically enhanced influence on all aspects of domestic social relations. But how this might connect with, and might inform, the proceduralist paradigm in the domestic legal context has yet to be worked out.

The most influential theories of law in the welfare state do not provide the necessary conceptual tools to offer an understanding of the law of contemporary societies. We can now turn to some theories of law and social change that have attempted to theorize the transition from the regulatory, interventionist and redistributive welfare state.

Postmodernization and Theories of the Decline of the Welfare State

A body of neo-evolutionary theory postdates the work analyzed in the previous section. In similar fashion, it has descriptive and prescriptive dimensions. It differs in its historical approach by attempting to understand some of the factors that signal a retreat from the high-water mark of the welfare state. My focus in this section is on the adequacy of these historical exercises, especially as some of them frequently deploy the term postmodern, if in an ill-defined way, to describe those changes.

Reflexive Law, Juridification and Autopoiesis

Gunther Teubner's work offers a number of different theoretical perspectives to update and revise the "neo-evolutionary" analyses of the law of the retreating interventionist welfare state. Each of Teubner's critical perspectives on recent legal change, in various ways, focus on a post-welfare state paradigm. Teubner's studies of law initially led him to identify the emergence of a new form of law, "reflexive law", which heralded the twilight of the welfare state's regulatory law (Teubner, 1983). Later, he deployed the not unrelated concept of "juridification", and thereafter "autopoiesis", to understand problems facing the regulatory law of welfare states. Most recently, he has advanced a type of legal pluralist analysis to understand "global" legal trends.

For Teubner, "reflexive law" was the historical successor to the welfare state's substantive legal rationality devised to achieve substantive justice by reform of legal rules. The key to the *Zeitgeist* regarding the state's extensive social responsibilities lay in "increasing disenchantment with the goals, structures, and performance of the regulatory state" (1983: 239). Unlike Nonet and Selznick's no less evolutionary responsive law, which unfolded primarily in consequence of internal change, even if some of the stimuli were external, Teubner's central concern is the "relationship between legal and social processes in the evolutionary process", or the "covariation of legal and social structures" (1983: 257, 259). The origins of the disenchantment for Teubner were to be found in the welfare state's regulatory failures that were caused by "the complexity of socio-economic processes, the contradictory imperatives of economic crisis management, and the cognitive limits of our mechanisms of politico-legal control". In combination, these factors dramatically reduce the capacities of the substantive legal rationality of the welfare state (1983: 268).

Teubner's theory of reflexive law relied heavily on the sociological theories of Jürgen Habermas and Niklas Luhmann. The work of Habermas provided Teubner with the concept of recurrent crisis in welfare states. The welfare state can be seen, Habermas argued, as an attempt to deal with economic crises (Habermas, 1976). When the welfare state becomes less successful in resolving these crises, the crisis shifts to the political realm, corroding the legitimacy of state interventionism. The solution for Habermas is for the state to develop a different rationality from that which guided welfare state interventionism. Only if procedures to guarantee rational, non-coercive deliberation are introduced into all social subsystems, can meaningful legitimation of decisions be possible.[8] To supplement this line of analysis, Luhmann's neo-functionalism supplied Teubner with the notion that all social subsystems (law included) must operate with internal "reflexion structures". These structures ensure that subsystems can successfully integrate with each other in "functionally differentiated societies" by resolving conflicts between a subsystem's general function and its performance (Teubner, 1983: 272-273). Otherwise, over-performance would jeopardize relations with, and the operation of, other subsystems. In societies where functional differentiation is extreme (as in welfare states), their integrative role is paramount because "[c]entralized social integration is effectively ruled out today and cannot be achieved by legal, economic, moral, or scientific mechanisms" (1983: 272).

Teubner deployed both lines of argument to criticize the materialization of formal law in the welfare state, and to advance the cause of reflexive law. Reflexive law had a descriptive dimension also: it had become an empirically demonstrable feature of the law of late welfare states. He noted that the liberal state developed a formal legal rationality to organize its economic and social environment, and the welfare state "rematerialized" law by introducing an increased measure of substantive rationality into the legal system. By contrast, the drift of support away from the welfare-regulatory state can be measured by the appearance of both a more legitimate and also functionally effective reflexive law which places greater emphasis on procedural, and less on instrumental, goal-oriented, rules. Thus, reflexive law

> will neither authoritatively determine the social functions of other subsystems nor regulate their input and output performances, but will foster mechanisms that systematically *further the development of reflexion structures within other social subsystems* (1983: 275; italics in original).

The law fosters these "reflexion structures within other social subsystems" by imposing restrictions on its own potential over-performance. To do this, substantive legal rationality, which all too "authoritatively determine[s] the social functions of other subsystems ...", was being gradually replaced with forms of procedural law: "reflexive law tends to rely on procedural norms that regulate processes, organization and the distribution of rights and competencies" (1983: 255). Examples of reflexive law given by Teubner were: 1) labour relations, where the legal rules did not so much direct specific results (as substantive legal rationality would) but provided the ground rules for collective bargaining; and 2) consumer law, where procedures guarantee the representation of consumer interests in various public policy contexts (1983: 276-278).

For all these original insights and theoretical innovations, Teubner's assessment of the crisis of regulatory law, from the vantage-point of the present, appears insufficiently related to, or explained by reference to, the dramatic social transformations collected under the label of "postmodernization" that have been already addressed in chapter 2. This is despite the fact that Teubner repeatedly refers to "postmodern" society and claims to be "[b]orrowing ... 'external' variables from concepts of postmodern societies in critical theory and neo-functionalism" (1983: 276). Given the outline of postmodern theory in chapter 2, it is far from clear what strand of postmodern theory is being invoked here. For instance, the critical sociological theory of Jürgen Habermas, as we have seen, does not offer any in-depth analysis of *postmodern* society. Teubner sees the key structural feature of societies where this changed climate of opinion about the welfare state has appeared as one of "a 'legitimation' crisis in *organized* capitalism" (1983: 264; italics added). Yet this line of analysis clearly fails to provide a firm basis for understanding the very different empirical factors of postmodernity's "disorganized capitalism" (Offe, 1985; Lash and Urry, 1987). This pattern of change puts pressure on those two areas of law Teubner sees as examples of embryonic reflexive law. Thus, disorganized capitalism with post-Fordist styles of production tends to push labour law in the direction of traditional contract law on the one hand, while the globalization of markets induces harmonization of consumer law across national boundaries on the other.[9] Moreover, the centrality of this notion of legitimation crisis demonstrates an "unfortunate timing" in postmodernity insofar as "the evident weakening of systematic legitimation could be a symptom of the *falling significance of legitimation* in integrating the system, rather than a manifestation of crisis" (Bauman, 1992: 46).

As for Luhmann's work, Teubner deploys his concept of "functional differentiation" to explore the distinctiveness of law as a separate, social subsystem, with its own internal rationality. But functional differentiation is a general sociological feature of modern societies; it is not capable of capturing the forms of differentiation of postmodern societies, and what effects they may have on law. The specific changes which appear in postmodern societies – the reconfigured power of the nation state, globalized economic and political institutions, postindustrialism, and a starkly reconstituted class system and civil society – do not feature in the social theoretical basis for reflexive law. They are at least as significant as "cognitive limits", "crises of economic management" or the "complexity of socio-economic processes". Teubner's use of the adjective "postmodern" to describe them rightly periodizes the changes; but it does not explain them. It functions in the argument to mark a temporal, or historical, phase of social change, while at the same time it delineates a qualitative transformation of the legal system: "reflexive law ... may emerge as the dominant form of post-modern law" (1983: 246). That the term imprecisely straddles both the rise and decline phases of the welfare state is suggested by Teubner's description of Nonet and Selznick's responsive law, more identifiably associated with the welfare state, as dealing with "trends in post-modern law" (1983: 245).

The theory of reflexive law was later supplemented by Teubner's development of two related concepts, "juridification" and "autopoiesis" (Teubner, 1987; 1988; 1993). Both are equally relevant to the regulatory crisis of the welfare state. Societies are increasingly turning away from state regulation in favour of mechanisms that are more *internal* to the subsystems formerly targeted by the state for overhaul:

> Recently, the most striking change in direction in politics, social science and law has been the tendency to replace the concept of regulation by that of evolution. It is not only with the 'de-regulation' movement that concepts of active guidance of society are being renounced as constructivist, interventionist and are being replaced by evolutionist concepts. The legalization/delegalization debate calls into question the regulatory effectiveness of politically instrumentalized law and tends to favour autonomous processes of social evolution. And one of the most fascinating theoretical innovations in systems theory – self-reference and autopoiesis – is considerably involved in this change of direction (1988: 217; references omitted).

"Juridification" refers to the process whereby social spheres become subject to excessive legal regulation at the expense of the internal, that is, local, indigenous or customary norms and procedures by which they previously operated (Teubner, 1987: 3). In general, the term juridification has a quantitative aspect: the amount of law vastly increases, and the number of disputes processed in the courts grows exponentially. A related development is the inappropriate removal of conflict from the political to the legal realm. But for Teubner, juridification defined in this way is too amorphous and abstract to be usefully analyzed. The real problem is posed by that more specific form of "juridification which occurs in the welfare state ... [where] law is used as a control medium for state intervention and compensation" (1987: 12). Importantly, his is not a nostalgia for the liberal past; he acknowledges the freedoms the welfare state has advanced, but indicates that "reforming attention should be directed to compensating for negative side-effects ..." (1987: 13).

"Autopoiesis", by contrast, is the analytical concept which, for Teubner, best describes the detailed process of self-regeneration by which social systems adapt. "An autopoietic system produces and reproduces its own elements by the interaction of its elements" (1988: 3). It follows that "an autopoietic legal system is seen as operationally closed". To avoid the charge that this notion is merely traditional legal formalism by another name, the legal system is also characterized as marked by "openness toward social facts, political demands, social science theories, and human needs" (1988: 2). In this way the law is paradoxically both open and closed at the same time, but in respect of different functions. Legal norms are developed and applied internally, closed off from outside *non-legal* influence, while legal systems readily absorb the empirical facts that register external processes and social change. Consequently, the legal system exhibits, in common with other social systems, the couplet of "operative closure and cognitive openness" at the same time (Teubner, 1993: 84). Equally, the concept has a critical, normative dimension: it points to the value of autonomous social subsystems.

In the context of late welfare state critiques of over-regulation, the theory of autopoiesis has obvious appeal: by focusing on the importance of internal processes of regeneration it implicitly resists proposals for rigid external control by the state. Traditional socialist command and control economic policies most obviously fall foul of its normative assumptions; but so too, Teubner suggests, do those of the traditional political right because autopoiesis places importance on regulation (1993: 65, 68). This is not to say that autopoiesis can be readily aligned to a particular political position. Teubner points to elements of autopoiesis that offer implicit support to the disparate ideals cherished by neo-conservatives (subsidiarity), by neo-liberals (market self-regulation), by neo-socialists (democratization of subspheres), and by neo-ecologists (autonomous networks) (1993: 64). Each of these divergent political ideologies share an ideal that autopoiesis speaks to: the need to prevent the state from monopolizing regulation, and in the process suffocating local, contextualized patterns of interaction, operation and control. Of course, to valorize the local in this way echoes many postmodern*ist* themes.[10]

The concepts of reflexive law, juridification and autopoiesis are quite distinct, but they each form part of a general sophisticated theoretical framework. For instance, juridification and autopoiesis intersect insofar as juridification has the tendency of undoing autopoietic operations: over-regulation can produce "disintegrating effects on the area of social life ..." (1987: 21). Also the concepts have historical resonances no less than reflexive law. As the welfare state develops, it juridifies increasing numbers of social spheres by subjecting them to layers of legal regulation, and in so doing stifles the autopoietic capacities of those spheres: "law intervenes in self-regulating situations in a way which endangers the conditions of self-reproduction" (1987: 24). In turn, autopoiesis is intimately related to reflexive law because reflexive law can only be effective if it is developed in a way that is aware of, and sensitive to, the delicate self-referential mechanisms of relevant subsystems (Teubner, 1993: ch 5).

But for all their innovation, these concepts seem neither jointly nor severally capable of capturing the historically unique configuration of elements that characterize the contemporary legal terrain. Some indication of the weaknesses of autopoietic understandings of contemporary societies can be gleaned from the fixed nature of societies that underpins the theory. So, Teubner's starting-point that "society is an autopoietic system of recursively self-reproducing communication" (1988: 3) looks seriously deficient in the context of the unravelling of the nation state, and the society that it encompasses and defines, where *external* pressures increasingly determine *internal* change. More tenaciously than many of the theories noted above, the conceptual framework of autopoiesis affirms the system-ness of societies; but a theory so steadfastly wedded to the metaphors of "evolution" and "self-reference" is clearly unsuited to the radical nature of the present changes in law's environment. To an historically unprecedented degree, the contingent and shifting nature of social institutions defines the contemporary social landscape.

In the legal sphere, the interpenetration of different normative codes ushered in by transnational developments on the one hand, and the reconfiguration of the welfare state on the other, requires a greater emphasis on how powerful external forces mould the content of legal norms, as well as the broader architecture of legal systems. How these processes are felt, and managed internally, is an important question; but it is surely *now* less significant than the historical question: Are social subsystems at present *less systematic* in their modes of operation? In the context of moves toward deregulation, it might appear that internal mechanisms prove more decisive in effecting change, and more likely candidates for examination, as the theory of autopoiesis urges. But the evidence discussed earlier, which points to an array of external social forces applying *disorganizing* pressures on all social subsystems, suggests otherwise. Moreover, an indifference to the concept of *spatial restructuring* of legal systems renders the concepts of juridification and autopoiesis unable to deal with many of the most recent changes which reflect an increasing interpenetration of *legal systems* and pluralization of forms of law as much as covariation between legal and other subsystems. In fairness, it should be noted that Teubner never claimed to be engaging in such a macro-level analysis, and his theories were elaborated before the dramatic recent transformations; but this point should not obscure the limited usefulness of his "modern" social theoretical concepts at the present time. These criticisms are only to a small degree remedied in Teubner's recent work on transnational legal developments, which will be discussed below.

Despite these criticisms, Teubner's work marks a valuable break, on both a theoretical and an empirical level, with the analysis of theorists of the law of the welfare state. Reflexive law, as we shall see in the next chapter, does capture one significant strand of contemporary legal change, and identifies some important social factors that trigger it.[11] Also, the general tenor of Teubner's analysis of the interventionist strategies of welfare states, in focusing on the question of regulatory efficacy, is consonant with the themes of socio-political stability and the effective performance of public policy that are characteristic of contemporary critiques of the welfare state (Offe, 1985: 228-229). By contrast, in earlier times the reforms introduced in welfare states were more commonly criticized at a *normative* level: that is to say, the welfare state was objectionable because it violated fundamental constitutional principles (Hayek, 1982). This shift in the vocabulary of critique reflects the postmodern emergence of "performativity" as a dominant contemporary political criterion (Lyotard: 1984).

The Appearance of "Relational Programs"

The extent to which problems arise in relation to the application of understandings of the law of welfare states to present conditions where state and society have undergone dramatic change can be seen in the attempt by Helmut Willke to identify paradigms of law by relation to forms of state on the one hand, and structural principles of social organization on the other. His categories evoke some of the key factors identified as marking off different historical phases as premodern, modern and late modern noted in chapter 3. For Willke, the welfare state works a change in the structure and nature of the legal norms that operate to create the conditions and the rules by which its policies are carried into effect. Simple societies are characterized by a preponderance of simple norms that take the form of straight commands: "Do X", or "Don't do Y". The liberal state supplements this type of norm with a "conditional program". The conditional program is the structure of a fairly simple norm that takes the form of, or can easily be reformulated as, an "if-then" sentence. So, "if you do X, punishment Y will follow" is an example of such a rule. The formulation is equally relevant to civil law rules: "If a will is not witnessed, it is void" is no less a conditional program. And as any parent (or child) will attest, being able to move from outright prohibitions to bribery represents a very real evolutionary gain.

At a later stage of historical development, the liberal state's typical conditional program is supplemented by the welfare state's "purposive program" tailored to implement its policies more effectively. In the case of purposive programs "the rigid connection between the factual preconditions of a norm and its consequences are loosened" (Willke, 1986: 287). They are of the form "Y may do Z in the following circumstances". Clearly, this latter rule is considered to be most suitable for the responsibilities imposed on regulators of economies, and welfare bureaucracies. The complexities of the field to be regulated make it impossible for legislators to predict the precise practices that may fall foul of the objectives behind regulatory schemes. Accordingly, discretion to deal with them as they arise, in line with some general principles, becomes the most effective legal strategy. The purposive program proliferates as target environments become more volatile and unpredictable because

> it permits a degree of flexibility in state actions and reactions, it introduces a limited learning capacity into the law (eg choice of means and intensity of means), and it certainly expands the time perspective of law from the present structure to future processes (1986: 287).

Examples of purposive programs are typically evident in planning, environmental and welfare law where agencies are given wide discretion to achieve certain policy objectives.[12] With the decline of the welfare/ regulatory state, the purposive program is itself surpassed by a more sophisticated instrument, the relational program (1986: 290-294). The relational program seeks to incorporate into the state-centred purposive program "societal commonsense" in order to make up for deficiencies inherent in purposive programs in regulating complex environments. It tends to "improve the guidance capacity of exceedingly complex societies" and is "prototypical for 'reflexive law'" (1986: 296). In historical terms, it is a response to the regulatory crisis or failure of the purposive programs characteristic of advanced welfare states. Willke gives an example of an embryonic form of a relational program: the "Concerted Action" policy introduced by the Social Democrats in West Germany in 1967. He sees it as different from traditional corporatist strategies by virtue of its "main conceptual target ... to combine comprehensive ('global') guidance of economic macro-relations with a decentralized decision-making in the area of micro-relations" (1986: 296). In this way it represents a "neocorporatist discourse system", and despite its distinctiveness it ultimately exhibits the features of a general "reflexive law".

Even though Willke identifies crisis elements in a similar fashion to Teubner, the sociological reference points for his theory are still squarely within the late modernity/welfare state paradigm. For instance, relational programs emerge to deal with the problems of societies marked by "organized differentiation" and the guidance capacities of "welfare states". This evolutionary model attempts to identify the particular obstacles faced by late welfare states. Though attentive to the crisis of the welfare state it fails to identify either deeper changes to the forms of social differentiation, in particular tendencies toward "disorganization", or to the general and pervasive "retreat" of the state (Strange, 1996). These failures prevent it from comprehending postmodern law. These weaknesses are clear from Willke's tabular representation of his argument extracted below. I have added the final row to his table so as to pose the question of how his model needs to be updated. This subject will be addressed in detail in the next two chapters. I have also inserted in parentheses the labels "modern" and so on, both to spell out what appear to be implicit historical phases in his argument, and to link his typology more closely to my argument. Willke emphasizes that these categories should be seen as "additive" rather than as mutually exclusive. Accordingly, societies with welfare states "include all four types of differentiation, legal forms" (1986: 286).

Table 4.1 Co-evolution of Social Structure, Role of State and Legal Form

Structural principle of society	*Role of the state*	*Legal form*	*Type of legal rationality*
Segmentary differentiation	---	Archaic, Religious	Magic, Reciprocal
Stratificatory differentiation	Repressive state [feudal]	Customary, Natural law	Material, Substantive
Functional differentiation	Liberal state [modern]	Secular, Positive law	Formal, Procedural
Organized differentiation	Welfare state [late modern]	Reflexive law	Systemic, Discursive
Disorganized/ Hyper-differentiation	Contracting state [postmodern]	---	---

Source: Adapted from Willke (1986: 286).

It follows that these ideal types merely seek to show the *dominant* forms in each historical and sociological phase. However, while this framework offers a succinct snapshot of social and legal change, it is not sufficiently attuned to the recent sociological analyses of postmodernization to offer an analysis of contemporary legal change, despite his description of welfare states as "postmodern societies". Willke actually goes further than this and talks about a "postmodern welfare state" characterized by "organized differentiation", and that "[a]n outstanding example of this is the trend towards neo-corporatist intermediation in the economic sphere" (1986: 286), which evokes the Fordist industrial paradigm. This particular usage of the term "postmodern" obscures the extent to which present law and its social environment differs from that of the welfare state.

If the differentiating process operates, in Willke's terms, as a "structural principle of society", and therefore dovetails with a particular legal form and type of legal rationality, then the question to be explored is how the most recent shifts in social differentiation are reflected in the dominant legal form and legal rationality, and possibly in other dimensions of contemporary law as well. By contrast, as the disorganization theorists affirm, postmodernity registers a pronounced breakdown of these macro-level policies; they give way to a very differently configured range of more polycentric, market-driven initiatives. These policies operate with quite distinct organizational principles and are of no less profound effect on the restructuring of the welfare state. Yet it is this traditional notion of the welfare state that lies at the centre of Willke's analysis.

Willke introduces an additional element into the analysis, complexity, in order to explain the sociological factors that produce this type of law but it, too, suffers from a periodization problem. It appears as a feature of the problems faced by welfare states, and poses intractable problems for regulatory strategies.[13] But problems of complexity take on an increased significance for law where economies and the division of labour are worldwide rather than nation-bound, where regulated fields are subject to increasingly rapid technological change, and where institutions are more fluid and unstable. Willke's analysis reveals too little of the transformation of the welfare state to capture the extent of that change.

"Global Law without a State"

Gunther Teubner's more recent researches have taken him beyond the confines of the nation state to examine the impact of globalization on law. He sees globalization, which has "certainly now become a reality" (Teubner, 1997: 5), as evidenced by, among other things, a "global law without a state" (1997: 3). The most visible form of global law is a revitalized *lex mercatoria* (law merchant), which first made a premodern appearance to govern the trading practices of medieval merchants. As an example of transnational law governing economic relations, it represents law being made, applied and enforced without any significant state action. Teubner identifies the internal operations of multinational enterprises as typical sites for the application of *lex mercatoria.* It is also evident in labour law where "enterprises and labour unions as private actors are dominant law-makers" (1997: 4). The emergence of this type of law poses problems for traditional ways of seeing law; it is no longer mapped by reference to the co-ordinates of the nation state, but by means of the global institutional settings in which it occurs. Equally, it is not marked by structures but by processes and transactions.

If global law without a state is now a meaningful feature of legal development, then we need a revised notion of legal pluralism to understand its operation. For Teubner, non-state law at the global level is radically de-centred: it originates in diffuse contexts. Traditional theories of law that emphasize institutions and legal autonomy are too tied to nation states and international relations to be able to register its efficacy. The character of the new *lex mercatoria* is its essentially indeterminate quality: it consists not so much of clear rules but broad principles, it is "soft" rather than "hard" law, "more flexible and adaptive to changing circumstances" (1997: 21). For this type of subject matter, postmodernist and related examples of the "linguistic turn" in sociology "promise a deeper understanding both of *lex mercatoria* and global legal pluralism" than do either classical sociology's "core concepts" of "rule, sanction and social control", or the traditional positivist focus on legal institutions (1997: 6-12). Insofar as global economic law has a weak centre, "*global law will grow mainly from the social peripheries, not from the political centres of nation-states and international institutions*" (1997: 7; italics in original).

Generally, Teubner and his collaborators focus on the largely informal dimensions of the spread of global law (Teubner, ed., 1997). In the communications of executives and managers within and between multinational enterprises, in the emergence of non-state actors in the implementation of human rights, and in the rule-making of accountants and lawyers in mega-insolvencies, it is informal, peripheral law, largely isolated from political processes, that is seen to be the decisive indicator of global law. On both the methodological and the empirical level this line of analysis uncovers some important features of contemporary law not addressed by earlier neo-evolutionist theories.

Yet what Teubner describes as poststructuralist and postmodernist concepts would appear to be insufficient by themselves to untangle the complexities of contemporary global law. As we shall see in the next chapter, distinctly determinate "hard" legal rules and sanctions issuing from international institutions form an increasingly dominant part of the present global and domestic legal landscape. This development is possible in large measure because of the proliferating institutional mechanisms and bodies designed to give effect to them, even if they operate on an overwhelmingly national basis. They demonstrate considerably greater effectiveness and enforceability than Teubner seems prepared to acknowledge. And attention to these *structural* features of global law might offer deeper insights into the operation of non-state laws, and the pluralistic interplay between the formal and informal in this historically unprecedented transnational environment, than the exclusively hermeneutic strategies of a linguistically informed, post-*structuralist* sociology is able to. Moreover, the process whereby the nation state is overshadowed by processes of globalization needs to be understood as coinciding with, and in significant ways linked to, changes to the state from within, so as to achieve a more complete picture of recent legal change.

Law in the "Paradigmatic Transition"

A more self-consciously postmodern temporalization than is evident in Teubner's and Willke's work appears in the writings of Karl-Heinz Ladeur's work on postmodern legal and constitutional theory (Ladeur, 1995; 1997), and Boaventura de Souza Santos' assessment of law in the "paradigmatic transition" (Santos, 1995). For Ladeur, the empirical factors that register a new environment for law are: striking increases in social complexity; the waning of the power of large enterprises with their repositories of knowledge and influence; and the "Pyrrhic victory" of the breakdown of communism, which produced a more searching examination of the workings of late liberal societies. In sum, these factors produce the need for a "postmodern legal theory" that might point the way out of present difficulties. Among the constituent elements of this theory are some usual suspects: a systems-theoretical framework of analysis; a proposal for a much more open-ended approach to deal with social complexity; and procedural changes that might allow deliberation about change. But Ladeur goes further. He wishes to introduce a "proceduralization" different from Habermas' preferred model that posits an inherent rationality or consensus-oriented character to speech-acts. By contrast, he prefers the systematic production of models that might generate further options for change and "presumes a process-like organized, experimental mode of procedure":

> Proceduralization in the version argued here does not bet on the open process of discussion as criterion of truth, nor on the rationality of procedural law as guarantee of a most comprehensive taking into account of the arguments for the decision ... The new variants of complexity distinguish themselves by the fact that practical decisions can no longer be based on available, yet fragmentary knowledge, but have to explicitly turn to the *formation of models* and to the generation of knowledge by the process of decisions themselves (1995: 237).[14]

While Ladeur clearly evokes some postmodern transformations, such as post-Fordism ("[m]ass production in the big enterprise loses its paradigmatic force" (1997: 623), and the decline in political significance of this economic form, there is still no extended analysis of the precise effects these changes have on law. Like Habermas and Willke, his major focus of analytical study is at the normative level. And though his suggestions provide innovative and thoughtful proposals for dealing with the capacity of law to regulate effectively the rapidly shifting sands of contemporary social problems, there is still little evidence of what the relevant legal changes should be, or exactly what the problems are.

The theorist who has gone furthest in identifying the interplay between the sociological developments outlined in chapter 2 and contemporary law is Boaventura de Souza Santos. Santos sees in recent social change a "paradigmatic transition" to a wholly different law, science and politics. As the title of his book on the subject suggests, *Toward a New Common Sense* (1995), the major thrust of his wide-ranging and ambitious analysis is the elaboration of a set of criteria, both political and methodological, with which to assess contemporary law, and so develop a "postmodern critical theory [which] is ... an emancipatory common sense" (1995: x). His concept of postmodernity focuses much more on changes in ideas than it does on changes in social structure. As his preferred reading of the contemporary social environment concludes:

> modernity is collapsing as an epistemological and cultural project and such a collapse opens up a range of possible futures for society, a noncapitalist, eco-socialist, future being one of them (oppositional postmodernism) (Santos, 1995: 92).

The "new common sense" has a number of dimensions. Politically, it rejects the notion that modern science and institutions retain emancipatory potential. Santos elaborates this common sense by reference to three concepts, the "frontier", the "baroque" and the "South". In keeping with his primary focus on changes in consciousness, each of these concepts refers to a contemporary attitude, or an "emergent subjectivity". The "frontier" dimension of this subjectivity is characterized by a preference for the institutional and social ferment of life on a frontier, that is,

> very selective and instrumental use of the traditions brought to the frontier by pioneers and emigrants; invention of new forms of sociability; weak hierarchies; plurality of powers and juridical orders; fluidity of social relations; promiscuity of strangers and intimates; mixes of heritages and inventions (1995: 491).

The "baroque" is a "cultural metaphor", "essentially a Latin and Mediterranean phenomenon" intended to valorize eccentricity and "a temporary suspension of order and canons" (1995: 499-500), while the South, connoting the Third World, "signifies the form of human suffering brought about by capitalist modernity" (1995: 507). There are familiar traces here of some elements of the postmodernist sensibilities analyzed in chapter 2.

In its methodological dimension Santos' vision embraces a concept of "interlegality", which seeks to reveal the way in which state law and other normative orders interact (1987: 279; 1995: ch 7). This methodology is closely related to the political vision, because it underpins his concern with the way law is used and impacts on oppressed peoples, as well as informing detailed empirical studies of contemporary law. It also has a postmodern flavour; it rejects the "liberal" (and therefore modern) legal vision that ignores the inter-relationship between state and non-state law. Santos provides three studies which deploy the concept of "interlegality": first, the intra-class informal law of Pasargada, a squatter settlement in Rio de Janeiro in 1970; second, the inter-class formal legal contests between squatters and property owners in Recife in the late 1970s; and third, an overview of how the process of globalization subjects formal state law to historically unique pressures. The third study is the most relevant for the purposes of this chapter, because it specifically addresses the wider historical and sociological question about the extent to which contemporary law and legal systems are transformed by broader social changes.

Santos concludes that "the national legal field is increasingly interpenetrated by transnational legal forms which unfold in complex relations with both the state legal order and the local legal order" (1995: 250). In a remarkably rich and insightful overview, among the indicators of this process he identifies are: the emergence of a new transnational *lex mercatoria*, a global human rights regime, transnational influence on national regulatory rules and laws of regional integration. These factors are centrally important elements in postmodernity's legal landscape and represent a decisive advance on the theories examined above in analyzing legal postmodernization. They will be examined in detail in chapter 5, though with somewhat different emphases, and will be supplemented by the identification of other factors and additional data. As Santos readily admits, it is not his purpose to offer "a full description of each period" of legal modernity (1995: 72), but in addition to his extensive analysis of globalization, he also provides a brief sketch of some of the social changes detailed in chapter 2, and some of the attendant legal shifts (1995: 71-90). His major focus is a critical rather than descriptive one, and is directed more at transformations in consciousness rather than social change. Moreover, in its critical dimension, Santos' argument in general finds little of value in the framework of modern law; and his utopianism is geared to the construction of a new common sense about law in contrast to activating in the present any possible positive contributions that it might make.[15] Accordingly, while his work offers valuable pointers in the direction of registering the nature of the comprehensive empirical legal changes evident in contemporary law and legal institutions, it is – with the exception of his in-depth study of globalization and law – suggestive only in relation to the profound changes in other areas of the domestic law of contracting welfare states, and how they might be interconnected. Nonetheless, his methodological notion of interlegality, in conjunction with his historical and anthropological approach, offers the most instructive guidance for marking the contours of contemporary law.

Conclusion

The theorists considered above in general do not provide, either singly or collectively, a complete set of conceptual tools to understand the nature of contemporary law. The reasons for this absence can be traced to three factors. First, some of the theories focused exclusively on welfare states, and so predate the latest social and legal changes. Second, those theories that have attempted to theorize a transition examine only some elements of change; either one factor of legal change such as juridification, or a particularly novel form of law, be it a "relational program" (Willke: 1986) or a reinvigorated *lex mercatoria* (Teubner, 1997), has been identified to the exclusion of many others. Third, postmodern approaches to legal change have addressed transformations in structures of consciousness and ideologies rather more than institutional developments. How this gap might be filled is the subject to which we now turn.

Notes

1 In the conventional meaning of this term, corporatism never existed in the United States (Salisbury, 1979). Unger appears to treat corporatism purely as a form of regulatory intervention, as opposed to a specific form of governance (cf Cawson, 1982; 1986). For a general discussion of corporatism in the context of the welfare state, see chapter 2, pp 42-44, and chapter 3, pp 88-89.

2 For a detailed discussion of this point in relation to recent legal reforms in the United States, see Bainbridge (2002).

3 Robert Kagan makes the important point in his preface to a new edition of *Responsive Law* that responsive law in the European context finds its expression rather more in the political system and legislative reform, in contrast to the American preference for legal change through the courts (2001: xxii-xxiv). I am indebted to my colleague Martin Krygier for drawing my attention to this reference.

4 See chapter 3.

5 As noted in chapter 3, in many ways the welfare state represented in its reconfiguration of the public-private divide a *de*-regulation of certain aspects of the liberal state, and so, if anything, *de*-colonization of some dimensions of the lifeworld. Habermas gives scant attention to this aspect of welfare state reforms. This omission is common to each of the theorists considered in this chapter. On this point, see Blankenburg (1984: 278).

6 Citing Steiner (1987: 92).

7 This argument evokes Nonet and Selznick's analyses of "responsive law". See above, pp 108-111.

8 Clearly there is the germ here of what was later to become the "proceduralist paradigm". As to which, see pp 114-116 above.

9 These changes will be examined in more detail in chapter 5.

10 See generally chapter 2.

11 See p 191.

12 The concept of "purposive program" comes from the work of Niklas Luhmann (1985), and has also been deployed by Habermas to refer to the paradigmatic character of welfare law (1996: 390).

13 See also Gagné (1992), whose focus on the crisis of the rational law of modern societies in postmodernity is insufficiently directed to post-welfare state transformations.

14 The translation is by Sabine Pittrof.

15 The general trajectory of his critique overlaps with some of the themes of legal postmodernism discussed in chapter 6.

5 Legal Postmodernization

> Is it possible that the post-war era of the Welfare State will prove to have been but a brief interlude in the history of Western capitalism? (Cawson, 1982: 1).

> Contract is dead – but who knows what unlikely resurrection the Eastertide may bring? (Gilmore, 1974: 103).[1]

> The nation state has become too small for the big problems in life, and too big for the small problems (Bell, 1980: 225).

Introduction

This chapter offers an overview of some of the empirical evidence indicating the general direction of the most recent phase of legal development. The evidence suggests that law has changed in ways that closely parallel trends in other social spheres, and to a sufficient degree as to transcend the paradigm of law in welfare states. In keeping with the argument in chapter 2, the transformation is best captured by the concept of "legal postmodernization". Given the range of evidence to consider, and the number of jurisdictions from which it is derived, I can only offer a thumbnail sketch of recent developments. Furthermore, I am painfully aware of the common law bias of much of this data. It may well be that in certain jurisdictions, and in some domains of legal doctrine within particular jurisdictions, much counterfactual material can be produced. But the conclusions advanced here are not fatally undermined by the existence of such material. As the many and diverse theories of legal change in welfare states discussed in the previous chapter demonstrated, reliance on selective and impressionistic empirical evidence can nonetheless produce valuable insights into the thematic elements of the law at particular stages of its historical development. In the analysis that follows a comparable measure of unavoidable selectivity will be evident. Despite this, I will argue that the evidence clearly reveals the overall direction of legal change.

The general concept of postmodernization has placed emphasis on the *inter-related* nature of change in the spheres of state, economy and civil society, and the impact of influences above and below the level of the state. The state is transformed no less by domestic developments than by supranational forces. Unlike welfare states, contemporary states participate in a cycle of international competition, in attempts to attract investment and multinational corporations. In the economic sphere, the currently prevalent policy preference for markets drives both trade liberalization at the global level as well as domestic deregulation and privatization.[2] Local marketization therefore cannot be seen in isolation from changes in the supranational field. The interconnectedness of the elements brought together in the concept of postmodernization offers a more updated explanation of the general direction of contemporary legal change than the theories examined in the previous chapter.

Legal postmodernization displays many of the characteristics of institutional change at the level of polity, economy and society. The unravelling, or *contracting*, of the welfare and nation state is particularly evident in five separate, but connected, transformations of its legal order: 1) privatization, that is, the transfer of legal ownership or control of a wide range of assets and functions from the public to the private sector; 2) the deregulation and marketization of the economy; 3) the reduction of the welfare role of the state, with consequential modifications in the structure of welfare rights; 4) a significantly enlarged third wave, and a novel fourth wave, of access to justice that jointly redirect welfare state access to justice policies; and 5) the growing influence of supranational legal norms on domestic legal systems. These recent developments do not exhaust the extent of contemporary legal change; they are merely identified here as offering some of the most convincing evidence of its overall direction.[3] In each of these domains can be seen the displacement of some of the defining features of legal modernization in both its earlier and later forms.

Privatization

Privatization and deregulation are commonly discussed together because they tend to be linked elements in political programs that privilege market mechanisms over state methods of distribution and exchange (Swann, 1988). They jointly advance the "hollowing out" of the state (Rhodes, 1994), and the reduction in the scope and intensity of centralized legal control. But they represent very different reform strategies. In this context, deregulation does not imply the removal of regulation, because all states regulate; instead, it suggests a *relaxation* or *reconfiguration* of the rules that govern the operation of actors and institutions in the marketplace. Privatization, on the other hand, refers to the transfer of state-owned assets and functions to the private sector, which may or may not render them subject to market principles. Because this distinction has important consequences for law, deregulation will be examined separately.

It is important to emphasize the extent of national differences in terms of the mix of privatization and deregulation. In the United Kingdom privatization has been the major element in the reconfiguration of the welfare state, with deregulation secondary. The German example has shown that deregulation has been prominent, with limited privatization; while in Italy has been comparatively slow to move in either sphere (Prosser and Moran, 1994: ch 1). In the United States, where the state has traditionally held a limited range of public assets, deregulation has been the dominant policy (Freeman, 2000a: 846). Furthermore, privatization and deregulation have advanced unevenly *within* states. For instance, even in the United States deregulation has been less readily pursued in areas such as health, safety or product liability where the free market offers few credible alternatives to traditional forms of state regulation (Breyer, 1990: 17). Accordingly, any firm conclusions about a wholesale rush to privatization and deregulation ought to be avoided. But to note these complexities should not obscure the general drift of recent policy change.

Privatization dramatically transforms the structure of legal obligations and entitlements characteristic of the welfare state. As we have seen in chapters 3 and 4, where the state became deeply immersed in the production of commodities, had extensive ownership of utilities, and significantly expanded its welfare functions, its legal powers necessarily increased, and in ways that simultaneously enhanced, and restricted, the rights of the individual citizen. The preservation of the rule of law in this changed context required "the maintenance and protection by the law, of a balance between public and private power" by means of the "fuller development of administrative justice" (Friedmann, 1971: 98). An alternative solution proposed that legal protection could be constitutionalized by the adoption of a broader concept of property to encompass the welfare state's provision of income and entitlements (Reich, 1964).

Yet for all the unease about the growing legal powers of welfare states, a broad political consensus supported an enlarged public sector grounded in the belief that public ownership, as one dimension of the state's expanded functions, meant public control in the public (national) interest (Prosser, 1986). The public interest reflected the post-war settlement: public goods and services were provided to all as legal entitlements on an equal basis regardless of cost of delivery by means of extensive cross-subsidization (Graham, 2000: 12; Taggart, 1991). Uniformity of provision was an integral element of this legal universality and equality; with the state as the sole provider, services tended to be delivered in a standardized manner throughout the national space.

The recent waves of privatization are no less grounded in broad popular support straddling traditional political divides; but the present consensus valorizes private, rather than public, sector provision. In consequence, privatization in its various forms has reversed many of the welfare state reforms. The most obvious manifestation of privatization is the direct sale of public assets to the private sector. But the term also embraces: the practice of contracting out public functions; the private provision of formerly public services; the exposure of state monopolies to competition from the private sector; the application of private sector management practices into the state bureaucracies; and the introduction of "user pays" policies in the sphere of public provision (Jackson and Price, 1994: ch 1). For all these differences, and the great variations in implementation from state to state, there is one consistent factor: the legal changes under newly privatized regimes clearly differentiate them from their predecessors. They are sufficiently similar in trajectory to provide the basis for some direct comparisons with the general legal structure of welfare state public ownership. In general, they represent on a global scale a dramatic reduction of government involvement in national economies, and a corresponding abandonment of the legal forms to implement such policies.

Where privatization is effected by the direct sale of public assets, states have adopted a number of novel regulatory options to replace the universal rights to provision of services or goods under exclusively public regimes. One common method, consistent with neo-liberal economic theory, is the establishment of competitive markets by means of allowing third party access to service delivery. For example, in the case of utilities, formerly monopolized facilities, such as transmission lines, pipes and cables, have been made available to new entrants (Malbon, 1998: 24-31). These markets, in which a state-owned enterprise may still be a player, afford consumers a legal right to choose providers, and "exit" from the relationship if levels of cost or service are unacceptable, in ways alien to the operations of public monopolies (Hirschman, 1970). The pricing strategies, the quality of service and the range of products available, are set by reference to market forces in the form of contractual agreements between two formally private parties, provider and consumer, in contrast to the executive oversight or statutory framework which typically sets price caps and service standards for state monopolies. The overall effect of these regimes is to transform legal relations in the direction of contract, or private law, rather than public law: legal rights to services flow from private arrangements, rather than public duties.

This is not to argue that the new regulatory regimes are strictly contractual in the traditional doctrinal sense. Agreements tend to be highly structured and regulated to limit complete contractual freedom. Legislation commonly imposes controls on pricing and service provision in the form of ministerial or regulator oversight, or in the statutory licensing agreement, or both (Malbon, 1998: 9-33). In turn, these obligations are reflected in the terms of the relevant agreement between consumer and provider. A considerable measure of consumer protection is therefore built into these contracts. But they are still contracts (Shames, 1998: 119-123). So, prices may vary considerably between different private providers, as may the range and quality of services offered. Contracts of this nature have now become a dominant form of legal regulation in privatized industries and services, replacing the public law models of the welfare state. Moreover, the function of contract in this context is to regulate by means of market pressures exercised ultimately by *citizens recast in law as consumers*. In the place of public services provided to citizens as free or subsidized legal entitlements, services increasingly are redefined as private commodities to be purchased in the marketplace by economic actors. One direct consequence of this change is that the social *role* of contract – much reduced as a result of welfare state provision (Atiyah, 1979: 726)[4] – greatly expands. This development sits comfortably with the deregulatory changes identified below where contract is the model for much legal reform.

The re-characterization of the legal subject from citizen to consumer, to citizen *as* consumer, also represents a shift in emphasis in the substantive content of citizenship rights. The redistributive aims of the welfare state received legal expression in universal and collective *social* rights to the satisfaction of needs. The welfare state's strategy to achieve this result was marked by a gradual advance towards the socialization of production, consumption and exchange. Contemporary states prefer to marketize these domains. Accordingly, the newer arrangements give priority to particularistic and individualistic rights to purchase goods and services for the satisfaction of preferences in the package of rights expressive of citizenship.

This reversal of policy direction is further reflected in the differences in the nature of governance within nationalized or public systems and their privatized counterparts. In a comparative study, Graham and Prosser found that the legal structure of the nationalized industries in the United Kingdom and France (in quite different ways) enshrined a notion of the public interest that had identifiable, though basic, mechanisms for accountability and representation (1991: 14). Citizens played a formal policy and advisory role by representation on consumer councils; and to the extent that these industries were in public ownership there was a measure of democratic influence over their operations through the political system. Such arrangements were buttressed by corporatist forms of interest representation that provided for institutionalized input into the state's prices and incomes policies (Cawson, 1986). By contrast, under privatization where competition is the preferred legal mechanism to protect the interests of the citizen/consumer, attention is diverted away from institutional mechanisms that might allow consumers a formal policy-making role (Graham and Prosser, 1991: 12). Where consumers can legally exit, the appeal of voice rights is inevitably weakened.

A further legal characteristic of privatization, which bears directly on the declining social rights of citizens, is a weakening of the social responsibilities of public enterprises once they pass into private hands. Privatized entities are expected to operate on the same footing as other operators in the private sector, which means that their activities are governed by reference to exclusively commercial considerations (Jackson and Price, 1994: 7-14). To advance this policy, the former social obligations of state-owned corporations, devised to advance a general, national interest, such as regional development, provision of low-cost housing and employment creation, are typically no longer imposed as legal duties. In other instances, states have recognized a significant public dimension to the operations of newly privatized bodies and have imposed community service obligations. But in practice, the duties required have often proven so vague as to be illusory, or easily avoided because impossible to enforce, as in cases where they only apply when a minister so decrees. Also, courts have found that they are so close to policy matters as to be not justiciable; and regulators, with or without statutory direction, have generally determined that they are "secondary" and rank behind primary "economic" duties (Aronson, 1997: 66-69; Graham, 2000: ch 2).

The attenuation of social responsibilities has also been evident in the field of utilities in relation to dealings with the most disadvantaged of consumers. Increasing rates of disconnection for failure to pay, and reduced rights of universal access are common features of privatization, because commercial considerations generally require such policies (Prosser, 1994: 15; Graham, 2000: 101). Another typical feature of the market-driven privatized sector is that citizens/customers in different regions of the national territory may have very different levels of costs and services (Meek, 1998: 113). This development mirrors on the legal level the disorganization characteristic of contemporary capitalist societies, where uniform nationally regulated processes progressively give way to more local conditions and patterns of control. A comparable diminution of social obligations has occurred with the corporatization of state-owned enterprises.[5] For instance, in New Zealand, the subsequent shift from corporatization to privatization has been found to strip away "most of the accountability mechanisms we observed in operation during the corporatization phase" (Taggart, 1991: 107).

Generalizing very broadly, the legal changes represent a significant diminution of the redistributive functions played by such institutions at the height of the welfare state. The shift from universal state provision on an equal basis to market distribution can lead to certain classes of citizens benefiting to the disadvantage of others. If the consumer is defined in abstract terms, with no legal distinction drawn between different types of consumers, he or she is "dematerialized" in the marketplace; in this environment, powerful consumers may be able to negotiate more generous terms. So, in some cases, large industrial consumers have been able to secure preferential pricing arrangements at the expense of residential consumers (Prosser, 1994: 14; Meek, 1998: 113; Shames, 1998: 125-126).

The processes of sale of public enterprises tend to offer no greater benefits to consumers at large, but are more likely to favour large, established corporations or institutional shareholders more than individual citizens. Even where a broad public right to purchase shares on privatization takes place, the poorest in society are unable to participate. In this regard, privatization can be seen as a re-ordering of legal claims in society, whereby the legal entitlements of all are transformed into the private property rights of a much smaller number of institutions and citizens; where strong public sector unions with entrenched rights and conditions are progressively replaced by private sector workforces with lesser individual, contractual rights; and where safety nets are stretched too widely to catch the weakest and the most disadvantaged (Starr, 1988: 38-41). Perhaps the disproportionate and uneven benefits of privatization, distributed in ways that appear to reverse the accretion of social rights typical of the welfare state, ironically provide the clearest proof of the public choice theorists' conception of the democratic process: that the legislation that brought it to fruition was driven by rent-seeking *par excellence* (Starr, 1988: 34).

In some instances, privatization does not involve the transfer of state assets to a number of private sector players. It may also be effected by the sale of a state monopoly as a private monopoly, as in the case of gas and electricity when they were first privatized in the United Kingdom. This method of privatization is far removed from the neo-liberals' preferred market mechanism and demonstrates that privatization does not necessarily mean replacing state provision by the market. Rather, this particular model of privatization is more suited to the very different policy of reducing government overload and costs: selling a state monopoly is generally more profitable than breaking one up (Jackson and Price, 1994: 11). In this context, without a market mechanism to regulate prices and levels of service, states have had to set up specialist regulatory regimes to ensure that prices remain fair and services even to replace control through ownership. Indeed, it requires the setting up of regulatory machinery that neo-liberals have consistently seen as vulnerable to "rent-seeking" behaviour from powerful private organizations. This novel complex system of regulation of "private" monopolies clearly contradicts simple conclusions about a remorseless deregulatory shift in the contemporary legal landscape. But despite regulator oversight, similar problems have beset this model to the marketized variant in relation to weaker social responsibilities, and patchy mechanisms for consumer representation (Graham, 2000: chs 2 and 5). According to one assessment of the United Kingdom experience, regulators have had some "isolated successes" but "are constrained by statute which stacks the odds against low-income groups in particular and the domestic user in general" (Meek, 1998: 117).

Where privatization is introduced in the form of contracting out, or "outsourcing", a service or performance of a function formerly carried out by the state, the state becomes a purchaser of a service provided by a private sector contractor. In turn, the traditional, public agencies that delivered those services are transformed into "transactional bureaucracies" (Boston, 1995: 78). Former, exclusively public, functions such as welfare services, prisons and waste management are increasingly provided by the private sector. The legal framework that governs this process also greatly differs from the standard statutory "command and control" duties and powers imposed on welfare state bureaucracies. Typically, the legal mechanism that ensures satisfactory performance of the service is a contract struck between purchaser and provider in a manner analogous to the relations between actors in the marketplace (Campbell and Vincent-Jones, 1996; Harden, 1992). Under these arrangements citizens may be deprived of traditional administrative law remedies against the private provider without any compensating contractual rights. As citizens are not parties to the contract between the state purchaser and the private operator to provide public services, they cannot sue on it. It follows that if the state, for its own legitimate reasons decides not to seek enforcement of contractual obligations, for instance where levels of service are inadequate, the citizen is effectively left without remedy. These questions are of particular concern where the private organization's functions impact directly on the liberties of citizens, as in the case of private prisons. In general this mode of privatization is only weakly informed by public law values such as accountability, openness, fairness and participation (Aronson, 1997: 65; Taggart, 1997: 3).

The process of contracting for services can also exist *within* the state (contracting in), for example where internal markets are instituted to regulate dealings between different bureaucracies. Though this is not strictly an example of privatization, it is nonetheless evidence of the extent of the penetration of private sector principles into the public sector. The contractual device in both cases has been deployed as a mechanism for reducing the discretion of public authorities. The requirement to contract has commonly brought a clearer definition of public goals, and sharper mechanisms for accountability (Harden, 1992: ch 4). However, in contrast to official rhetoric, this is not to imply that consumer sovereignty is enhanced, or that the individual citizen's rights are enlarged, because in this case also, the citizen, not being party to the contract, is unable to derive enforceable rights under it (Harden, 1992: 44-45). Moreover, contracts of this nature may not be the source of justiciable rights even for the parties to them.

One further initiative in the context of privatization, which may either be a substitute for, or complement, market-driven regulation, is the introduction of novel quality control mechanisms. In the United Kingdom this objective was initiated by means of the Citizen's Charter program, now renamed as Service First, and later extended to the operations of utilities (Graham, 2000: 87). The charter system and its successor are intended to require public service providers, whether privatized or not, to set measurable service delivery standards. If met, these standards merit an award that can be advertised by the provider. This initiative is clearly an advance on the limited range of accountability mechanisms for welfare state bureaucracies. But as with the introduction of marketization, this regime provides no place for the consumer boards that offered some, albeit limited, degree of collective, democratic input under the old nationalized regimes (Barron and Scott, 1992: 526). Under the Charter, the citizen who once received services based on a notion of need, is now reconceived as a consumer of services based on payment of taxes. Accordingly, the relevant notion of citizenship is a narrow one, with a very constricted notion of freedom. To be free is not so much to receive a basic minimum to which all are entitled; rather, it is freedom to choose (Barron and Scott, 1992: 543). Consistently with other aspects of privatization, the concept of citizenship that is evoked here is, in T.H. Marshall's terms (1963), a civil, rather than social, citizenship, and it is consequently indifferent to questions of substantive inequality.[6]

Privatization in general has the tendency to transform the public/private distinction in law. To label an entity or activity "public" implies that it affects many people, or it is done on their behalf, or both. It also imports a number of prescriptions, such as that it should be open to general scrutiny, and that those who act on behalf of the public should be accountable for their actions. Welfare state reforms introduced a public element into what were previously considered "private" domains: the process of nationalization and regulatory reform, for instance, expressed a general belief that economic activity was a legitimate concern of the state as guardian of the public interest. The new order radically refashions the legal framework within which the welfare state's public interest was achieved. Now, to be private is to raise a presumption that an activity should be beyond scrutiny by the state, and be free of responsibilities to the public, so that when a public asset is approved for transfer to the private sector, a similar set of normative presumptions are usually implicit.

The legal rules relevant to the operation of privatized bodies reflect this problem. As Paul Starr concludes, "[a]s a general movement of institutional design, privatization undermines the foundation of claims for public purpose and public services" (1988: 38). For instance, many aspects of dealings between state purchaser and private provider escape parliamentary scrutiny, or freedom of information legislation, as do the internal operations and policies of privatized institutions. But to what extent should contracts between a private utility provider and a customer be treated in law like other (private) contracts? Is a commercial agreement which imposes obligations of confidentiality between a government and a company that operates a prison appropriately treated as private matters, and so legally avoid public scrutiny and accountability, given the legitimate public interest in its operation? The language of privatization is quite misleading because it conceals the extent to which public and private sectors jointly share in the function of governance under the new regimes (Freeman, 2000a). Indeed, the problem for administrative law has now become the exact reverse of that identified by Friedmann (1971) for welfare states with large public sectors. The vast and proliferating privatization programs worldwide are confronted by the problem of how to infuse this enlarged private sector with the public law values of accountability, due process and fairness to the same degree that those values have operated, if fitfully, to impose limits on the powers of public bureaucracies (Taggart, 1991: 108; Aronson, 1997: 69-70).

As the private sector delivers progressively more of those former state functions, from production to welfare, there is a "passing of the old regime" to the extent that it is inappropriate any longer to be referring to a "public interest" state (Aronson, 1997: 40). It does not follow that no vestige of the public interest remains in the legal structure of privatization; even in the context of marketized privatization, it is common to find obligatory public service duties imposed on private bodies in terms of universality of access, price caps and customer service levels. But in general the notion of the public interest is now a more fragmented matter and is to be achieved by means of the aggregation of a range of private interests, in ways directly analogous to the market of liberal societies. In the context of outsourcing, for instance, Harden concludes that this fragmentation comes from

> the fact that the parties to the contract have separate interests. ... The public interest – ie the overall functioning of the public service in question – is not the responsibility of a single unitary organization, but instead emerges from the process of agreement between separate organizations, none of which has responsibility for the public interest as a whole (Harden, 1992: 33).

The progressive dismantling of the "public interest" state tends to outstrip many theoretical analyses of shifts in core concepts of legal doctrine in the welfare state. Thus, Nonet and Selznick's description of the emergence of a pervasive "public interest" element in law (1978: ch 4) seems unsuited to describe current developments.

If these changes have problematized the boundary between public and private law, they have equally created the conditions for a revitalized role for contract law. As contract becomes the preferred mechanism for regulating the relations between individuals and the state and larger organizations, then contract law itself becomes more significant both in terms of its sphere of operation and also in the re-emergence of notions of free choice as the decisive factor in ascribing legal rights and responsibilities in society. This is a central sociological characteristic of postmodernity: individual consumer choice, driven by specifically individual and differentiated needs and desires, rather than universal state provision of standard, uniform goods and services, becomes the axial principle of public policy and social organization (Bauman, 1992). As noted above, there is some doubt as to whether all such contracts confer rights that can be fitted neatly into traditional contract doctrines, especially as far as the "consumers" of the public services are concerned (Harden, 1992: 61; Taggart, 1991: 99). Nonetheless, the conceptual vocabulary of contract is becoming appropriate to describe an ever-widening category of legal relations and marks an historic point of departure from the legal structure of the welfare state.

The recent widespread deployment of contractual mechanism to solve regulatory problems suggests not so much the fall, but the *rise*, of freedom of contract. Formerly, the conceptual outlook of the lawyer is transformed from private to administrative law (Atiyah, 1979: 719). The relevant administrative law was cast in a national mould, with the duties and powers of relevant officials attuned to the demands of a modernizing, Fordist welfare state. At present, contract reclaims much lost ground, so that "[t]he scope of contract law has ... expanded, with novel and interesting contractarian solutions proposed for regulatory problems ... in fields once thought the exclusive province of mandatory rules" (Buckley, 1999: 23). In turn, the state is now neither "corporate" (Unger, 1976: 200), nor "entrepreneurial" (Friedmann, 1971: ch 3) in the sense of owning vast industrial complexes. And to describe contemporary society as "postliberal" (Unger, 1976: 192) seriously misdescribes its pervasively contractual character consequent on recent changes.

By contrast, a "contracting state" in the fullest sense has appeared: it is shrinking in overall size, capacity and reach, manages its internal operations by recourse to contractual instruments, and increasingly governs by *contractual* means (Harden: 1992; McPherson, 1999; Freeman, 2000b).

Relations between citizens move closer to the short-term, conditional nature of contract, rather than the fixed, long-term entitlements characteristic of property. Without much exaggeration, as in the case of deregulation to be discussed below, it is possible to conclude that a "new contract" has emerged to replace the "new property" as Reich described the pattern of legal entitlements typical of the welfare state (1964).

Despite the changes, it would be wrong to conclude that all the consequences of privatization have been negative, or that the changes ushered in by privatization *necessarily* corrode the legal entitlements of citizens, or particular classes of them. For some, privatization is valued merely as a different means to the achievement of welfare state egalitarian ends, and in some circumstances may be a more effective mechanism (Howse et al., 1990: 511). The welfare state with its uniform and standardized services was beset with rigidity, insufficient accountability and negligible transparency in many of its activities. These design faults can be attributed to the paternalism characteristic of many welfare state policies, and its concomitant, the pervasive faith in the technocratic expertise characteristic of state instrumentalities (Habermas, 1976). Also, it makes little sense for governments to be providing services such as refuse collection "if the cost of government provision exceeds the inefficiencies of market imperfections" (Freeman, 2000a: 826), with the result that taxpayers in general have to foot the bill. By contrast, both the process of privatizing institutions, and the subsequent experience of their operations have offered much evidence of an expansion of legal rights and remedies for citizens/consumers. For example, a direct result of the process of selling public assets was the provision of unprecedented levels of information about their internal operations, and this continues to be the case (Prosser, 1994: 6; 1999). Equally, a recent overview of the performance of utilities after privatization in the United Kingdom has concluded that generally prices in real terms had dropped (Meek, 1998: 111-113), while some of the consumer representation models set up are more effective than their counterparts under the nationalized regimes (Graham, 2000: 96).

There is also evidence that some contracting out policies have not necessarily been at odds with increased levels of service to the legitimate interests of citizens. They may even contribute to a more "responsive law" as advocated by Nonet and Selznick, as in cases where citizens such as public housing tenants are incorporated into the process of awarding government contracts to private operators (Vincent-Jones, 1998: 370-372). And where the diminution of the social rights of citizens could be reversed by grafting contractual or administrative law remedies onto present structures, or by the statutory imposition of more stringent community service obligations, privatization could express some inherent "progressive potential" not possible by simply reverting to the former regimes

(Donnison, 1984: 41; Ehrenreich, 1996: 1235). So there is no reason in principle why forms of privatization could not be designed so as to be progressive in terms of cost recovery (and therefore income distribution), the provision of genuine universal access and local empowerment, and by offering more responsive mechanisms for accountability (Starr, 1988: 39).

The problem with many of the privatization strategies to date is that their chief proponents and supporters, scattered across the broad political spectrum, have shown a generally reduced measure of concern about these regressive consequences when compared with the redistributive political consensus of the welfare state. Until the legal rights of all citizens, rich and poor alike, under the new regimes become an improvement on welfare state redistribution, the suspicion remains that if there has been an enlargement of rights and benefits, they are being unequally and unfairly (re)distributed. The more general recourse to contractual mechanisms is no less evident in the legal regimes governing deregulation.

Deregulation

As was noted in chapter 3, the regulatory innovations typical of the welfare state in the economic sphere are twofold. First, private, formal law is "materialized": the social characteristics of economic actors come to figure increasingly in legal rules both to equalize bargaining power, protect consumers and to redistribute resources. Second, regulation is conducted with an increased level of intensity by state agencies; they are pro-active, set "command and control" standards in the form of rules and regulations to govern prices and operators, and take responsibility for enforcing the legislation.[7] Overall, such reforms express "governmental efforts to control the individual price, output or product quality decisions of private firms, in an avowed effort to [advance] ... the public interest" (Breyer, 1990: 7). Both these reform strategies have been significantly transformed in recent years.

Deregulation I: The New Private Law[8]

Deregulation, in the sense of a relaxation of former regulatory controls, has appeared in the form of a reversal of the materialization typical of the welfare state reforms of private law. The welfare state's legal doctrines that were crafted to achieve first, procedural justice (by equalizing bargaining power), and second, substantive justice (by the imposition of restrictive controls on prices and the quality of commodities, and the capacity to "exit" from certain contractual relations) are steadily being pared back. In consequence, there is a significant *dematerialization of law*. This change is occurring in a number of domains of law.

In labour law, for instance, the transformation is already far advanced. The deregulation of labour markets is central to the legal transformation of the Fordist welfare state. As we have seen in chapter 2, one key element of the process of postmodernization is the shift from Fordist to post-Fordist patterns of production, where plant size is reduced, mass production is less pronounced, union membership decreases and workforces become, or are forced to become, more "flexible". Further, the widespread rejection of collectivist solutions to social problems in favour of individualism assists in corroding the legal entitlements of employees in the workplace (Rood, 1994: 85). The political power of unions decreases in direct proportion to the size of their membership, so that if, as is now the case in most tertiary sector-dominated "postindustrial" economies, the rate of union membership drops well below half of the workforce (and outside the public sector less than one quarter) they have greatly reduced influence over public policy. Such demographic shifts mean that the collectivist model is circumvented as the dominant model of rights and obligations in the workplace, both in terms of its effective practical influence, and its legitimacy, however much legislation may seek to protect workers by privileging the status of unions.

In general, even though the structure of labour law differs markedly from state to state,[9] a striking consistency is evident in the overall pattern of change. The new model is manifested by principles that give greater primacy to *individual* rights in the workplace, and "the rediscovery of the individual in labour law" (Simitis, 1994: 183). These rights include the right of individual employees not to be members of unions, and the right to negotiate directly with an employer as to rates of pay and conditions of work without union representation. As union monopolies over worker representation are reduced, and these changes become standard features of the legal relationship between employer and employee, rights and obligations become more individualistic than collectively determined. In the absence of collective bargaining over rights and obligations in the workplace, the labour contract takes on more of the characteristics of the traditional contract. The freer, contractual rights tend to be accompanied by a reduced package of statutory rights in relation to such matters as redundancy payments, minimum wage constraints and protections against unfair dismissal.

In the United Kingdom, these changes are evident in the shape of employers' rights to induce employees not to join unions (Wedderburn, 1994: 16). Similarly, in New Zealand, reforms have emphasized the centrality of the contract of employment between the individual employee and employer. This contractualization of relations has been encouraged by restricting unions to the role of employees' agents, and then only if chosen by the employee. A direct consequence has been that "the service and retail sectors are now effectively deregulated, apart from the Minimum Wages Act" (Wilson, 1997: 141). Australia, which traditionally has had a more centralized wage-fixing system, has witnessed a revision of this legal framework, so that terms and conditions of employment are increasingly set at the local industrial level, with greater freedom to negotiate away formerly fixed award conditions, in exchange for higher rates of pay or other benefits (Creighton, 1997: 120-125). In Germany, where the labour market has been historically heavily regulated, comparable though less far-reaching reforms have been introduced to restrict the right to strike, and to allow employers greater power to determine employment contracts (Leaman, 1994: 17-20). Not only does the contractualization of relations in the workplace tend to reduce the former array of statutory legal protections for employees, but it may also usher in diminished access to the courts where a dispute arises. In the United States, for example, compulsory private arbitration of industrial disputes, with minimal appeal rights to the courts, is now a common, and legally permissible, feature of employment contracts (Stone, 1996: 1017; Nolan, 1997: 147).

Individualist rights are further enhanced by means of concerted assaults on the mechanisms for collectivist advancement of workers' rights. The legal priority conferred on unions to represent workers in negotiations with employers, to pursue better conditions, and to enforce rights has been curtailed, as in the abolition of the closed shop in the United Kingdom, and restrictions on the rights of unions to enter workplaces in Australia (Creighton, 1997: 107, 124). Ever more stringent conditions have been placed on unions to take strike action, by the imposition of procedural hurdles such as postal ballots, as well as the re-establishment of civil liability for loss caused to employers resulting from industrial action (Wedderburn, 1994: 23). A general strategy of "union exclusion" is directed at dismantling the collective power of workers; at the same time it affords a commensurate increase in employer prerogatives and discretion (Wedderburn, 1994: 24). In this way, the policy of equalizing bargaining power typical of welfare state reforms is being slowly eroded, and with it the procedural justice at the heart of labour law. The new, more contractual, regime in principle can, and in practice often does, bring additional benefits to some workers; but it does so *individually* rather than *collectively*. And as the power of workers to organize for a collective defence of rights is eroded, the broadly redistributive features of post-war entitlements in the sphere of employment fade in favour of marketized and individualized contractual rights. Such a legal framework both fosters and institutionalizes greater levels of inequality than under the former, more restrictive regulatory regimes (Wilson, 1997: 146).

Closely related to the changes in employment law is the transformation of corporatist structures of governance. As they decline, unions lose their privileged place in the hierarchy of interest-group pluralism; in turn, they have less influence over states wishing to legislate to scale back worker entitlements. In a general overview of developments in labour law in "post-industrial societies" Wedderburn concludes that the increasing focus on the "individual" rights of employees particularly in countries such as Britain, New Zealand, the United States and Australia, represents

> an opportunity to disestablish collectivism, roll back the frontiers of workers' collective organization, fragment employment protection laws and dismantle machineries of corporatist consensus in the name of 'competitiveness', even to the point of restricting the scope of consensual, tripartite machinery, such as ACAS in Britain (Wedderburn, 1994: 37).

In this changed landscape, the "occupational bonding" characteristic of the enhanced legal security given to employees in welfare states (Glendon, 1981: 143-170) becomes one of the more obvious casualties of a shift to the incorporation of more visibly non-corporatist, individualist market-oriented principles into labour law. Moreover, the temporal and spatial co-ordinates of legal relations are strikingly re-fashioned. Where once labour unions, usually within a corporatist political framework, would offer nationwide representation to workers, in the newly disorganized, postFordist environment, workplace agreements, and therefore wages and conditions, reflect local, and increasingly individual, circumstances (Ben-Israel, 1997: 55). The new legal order looks very different from the collectively deliberative "reflexive law" of the early 1980s (Teubner, 1983). And we seem further than ever from the heavily due process-driven "industrial justice" widely supported at the height of the welfare state (Selznick, 1969).

Another field where the process of dematerialization is already advanced is that of housing law. The rights of tenants, much expanded in the welfare state, particularly in the immediate post-Second World War period, have been widely reduced in a manner generally consistent with the above developments. First, state provision of public housing has been significantly curtailed. In contrast to the post-war boom in public housing provision for the poor at heavily state-subsidized rents, states now have reduced or even reversed these policies. The most dramatic example is the United Kingdom where a comparatively large public housing stock has been heavily sold off in recent years so that tenants' rights in the nature of public law against the state based on need have become private rights of ownership in the property market (Forrest and Murie, 1988). At the same time, this shift in the direction of the market has been complemented by greater reliance on market rents by public housing authorities in many countries (Kemeny, 1995: 114-125).

In the private sector, the former redistributive features of laws that gave tenants security of tenure and rights to affordable rents have been diluted. Increasingly, security of tenure is measured not by legal rules limiting landlord's rights to terminate based on a tenant's long-term need, but simply by contractual agreement between landlord and tenant (Cranston, 1985: 116; Bradbrook, 1998). Equally, rents are determined by market pressures, as mechanisms for rent control are gradually dismantled (Cranston, 1985: 116-117). The picture is not uniform, however, as many of the welfare state's fair trading reforms such as disclosure obligations, and duties to provide adequate and safe premises remain. Thus the process of dematerialization is less advanced in this domain than in labour law, where advances in both substantive and procedural justice have been reversed. Nonetheless, the changes move in the same general direction. Norbert Reich (1992) finds a similar alteration of a regulatory framework is evident in European consumer law, whereby the "pre-interventionist" 1950s and 1960s and the "interventionist" 1970s were overtaken in the 1980s by "post-interventionist" reforms.

There is increasing evidence that these fundamental changes in the regulatory framework of particular social subsystems, largely introduced by legislation, are being reflected in general doctrinal developments in law. So, in Australia a process of contractualization in the law governing commercial leases is unfolding with the result that statutory protections of tenants are supplanted by contract remedies (Effron, 1988: 83). In the United States, as Mooney concludes, in a broad survey of changes in contract law principles over the last couple of decades in nine states, there is "a resurgence of individualist, laissez-faire ideology" (1995: 1133).[10] He identifies in recent revisions to rules governing contract formation, interpretation, implied terms and warranty disclaimers, a trend of doctrinal departure from welfarist concerns for weaker parties. Courts are gradually showing a greater reliance on classical concepts of contractual freedom, abstract equality between the parties, and decontextualized interpretations of language and intent. The consequence of this "conceptualism" is a shift to a less materialized form of regulation, where "sellers, employers, insurers and banks have become again the principal beneficiaries"; and it represents a "judicial tilt away from underdogs ..." (1995: 1148, 1170). In a more recent survey, (in the aptly-titled *The Fall and Rise of Freedom of Contract*), F.H. Buckley examines the era when judicial and legislative interference with freedom of contract was the norm, in every sense of the term, a little more than two decades ago, and concludes that that time now seems like a distant past (1999: 2).

It is important not to over-emphasize the extent of change. There has been no systematic return to pre-welfare state liberal principles in law. Considerable evidence of materialization in law persists, with important and extensive legal protection for workers, consumers and tenants still in place. My argument is rather that a significant reversal of the more extensive forms of materialization is in evidence at the present time. In general, these developments represent a break with one component of the welfare state's "new property" (Reich, 1964; Macpherson, 1973: 133-140) in the direction of what might be described as "new contract". Welfare state modifications of a wide range of contractual relationships created new legal entitlements that came increasingly to resemble traditional property rights in favour of particular groups such as workers or tenants (Atiyah, 1979; Gray, 1979).[11] The creation of new property rights to achieve a measure of substantive justice equally represented a general expansion of property principles into contract law within the general sphere of private law (Glendon, 1981: ch 5). Now, by contrast, as the legal rules that defined these rights are progressively repealed, contractual rights expand *at the expense of "new property" rights*. Rights are determined increasingly by reference to private contractual agreement rather than public regulation so that contract once more, as in the 19th century, "swallows up" much of the subject matter it was seen to "disgorge" with welfare state developments (Friedman, 1965: 17-26; Atiyah, 1995: 27-36). Consequently, the "judicial tilt" of rights moves in the direction of the advantaged; there are less forced (property) transfers, and ever more strictly contractual ones.

The broadening sweep of deregulation and contractualization is not confined to the economic sphere; it also comes to assume growing importance in the sphere of intimate relationships. One paradox of the welfare state legal reforms in the sphere of intimate relationships where, in stark contrast to economic relations, a modified form of "deregulation" occurred, with the removal of legal restrictions on rights to divorce and abortion, and the decriminalization of homosexual activity. But the welfare state was marked by a tainted liberalism as long as homosexuals could be discriminated against in the public sphere, and heterosexual marriage remained legally privileged in the private sphere. Genuine legal equality for sexual "marginorities" (Ertman, 1996) would remain a distant reality as long as the two spheres remained regulated by such discriminatory rules.

A measure of the advance of contemporary identity politics is reflected in the legal advances achieved in both directions. First, homosexuals have gradually been granted more equal legal rights under anti-discrimination legislation enacted in many countries (Waaldijk, 2000: 75-79). Second, the legal rights of partners in same-sex and de facto heterosexual relationships have been brought much closer into alignment with those of partners in marriage. The changes are evident in relation to property distribution on separation, inheritance and custody rights (Waaldijk, 2000: 79-85). The extension of contractual remedies has been another mechanism for the achievement of legal equality. For instance, there is increasing recognition of private contractual arrangements between partners in homosexual relationships, and in de facto relationships (Ertman, 1996; Becker, 1996). The changes have been extended to married partners in many jurisdictions, so that "the welfarist paternalism of family law characteristic of the mid-1970s is increasingly giving way to private norm formation" (Dewar, 2000: 73). The gradual equalization of legal protection of an increasing diversity of relationships reflects the way in which "marriage has become increasingly a matter of private ordering, of setting one's own ground rules – in short, of contract rather than status" (Dewar, 2000: 65).

In another respect the contrast with the welfare state is striking. The freedom enshrined in the 1970s legal reforms governing marriage – "the attenuation of the ties that bind" – was accompanied by a strengthening of security in the economic sphere (Glendon 1981: chs 1, 4). But there now appears to be a loosening of rights in all spheres, and for all types of relationships. Changes in family law therefore do not stand at odds with those that underpin the increased marketization of the economy; rather, they mirror those changes. The new world of social reproduction parallels the new world of economic production, a world of more unstable employment and more diverse families, where

> the policy of deliberate 'precarization' conducted by the operators of labour markets finds itself to be aided and abetted (with its effects reinforced) by life policies, whether adopted deliberately or embraced by default. Both converge on the same result: the fading and wilting, falling apart and decomposing of human bonds, of communities and of partnerships (Bauman, 2000: 163).

Other features of social postmodernization are reflected in these developments in the "moral economy" (Hall, 1980: 35). Thus, the general rejection of welfare state paternalism inherent in the contractualization of relationships expresses the same rationality of refusal to allow some to speak on behalf of others that is a distinctive feature of claims to recognition in intimate relations. In each sphere, freedom of choice is at a premium. So, Anna Yeatman concludes that

> the so-called 'new social movements' – feminism, the gay and lesbian movements, the various anti-racist, multicultural and indigenous people's movements, have all contributed to the resurgence of contractualist principles (1995: 126).

Given this diversity of sources of support for change, it would be a mistake to characterize it as simply "neo-liberal" or conservative. Rather, there is a wider acknowledgement of some progressive potential in contractual mechanisms to further decentralization, localism or indigenous rights. And this shift in sentiment is in general context-dependent and pragmatic more than ideological and *a priori* (Peller, 1996: 1003).

Deregulation II: The Attenuation of Agency Command and Control

In the case of regulation by state agencies or ministries, recent reforms have restructured their duties, powers and resources, consistent with the widespread loss of faith, and an ensuing crisis of legitimacy, in the capacity of centralized planning to successfully co-ordinate the triple objectives of growth, welfare and freedom. The changes in the United States have been the most dramatic, and have led the way for other jurisdictions. From the period of the Carter administration onward, there has been substantial deregulation of most industries, starting with the airline, transportation and telecommunications sectors. In the case of airlines, by the mid-1980s routes and fares were deregulated, and the legal restrictions on the entry of new carriers were greatly relaxed (Breyer, 1990: 16). The transportation industry was substantially deregulated by the introduction of looser legal requirements governing the licensing of operators, prices and routes. At the same time, the setting of oil and natural gas prices was removed from statutory control, and the financial services sector was progressively deregulated so that by the enactment of legislation in 1988 commercial banks were free to participate in investment banking (Howse et al., 1990: 503). During this period, the heavily monopolized telecommunications industry was broken up, and new entrants encouraged. Canada deregulated the airlines and financial services sector in similar ways and to a comparable degree. For instance, legislation was introduced that allowed any carrier meeting safety, insurance and Canadian ownership requirements to be granted a licence (Howse et al., 1990: 503).

In Western Europe the detail differs, and the extent of change was less dramatic, not least because legal control in many sectors was effected through the mechanism of state ownership, but a similar theme is discernible. Moran and Prosser conclude that by the 1970s a widespread, if uneven, search for "soft" regulation was evident because "[t]he systems being regulated were so complex, and changing so rapidly, that control was limited, ineffective and prone to breakdown" (1994: 10). The Australian experience is comparable. By the mid-1980s, telecommunications, airlines and international cargo shipping industries had been largely deregulated (Ayres and Braithwaite, 1992: ch 1).

The transformation in regulatory practice in this way does not in any way amount to the complete removal of legal rules governing the operation of these industries, as the term "deregulation" implies. Rather, I am using it in the sense that it describes a progressive shift away from centralized bureaucratic command and control of legal rules capping prices and rates, in favour of increasing supplementation or even replacement of direct regulation by market mechanisms. The market is further nurtured by reductions in regulators' rights to control entry into the industry. So it would be a mistake to see changes of this order as deregulation pure and simple. In the United States, for instance, deregulation has brought more extensive application of antitrust law, and equally rigorous enforcement of product safety legislation in the deregulated sector. As one analyst has put it: "[t]he successful deregulation of airline rates does not lead to a sense that we should leave to the free market the question of whether DC-10 engines are attached in a proper way" (Steiner, 1983: 1304).[12] Deregulation in one domain can therefore require more extensive forms of regulation in another (Rose-Ackerman, 1990: 520). Where regulation has been perceived to have been largely successful, as in the case of anti-discrimination legislation, it has been retained, and even extended.

The European experience more clearly evidences this trend, where formal mechanisms have had to be set up to replace the earlier structures of informal regulation. The financial services sector is a particularly noteworthy case where deregulation was accompanied by legislative schemes imposing a complex regulatory structure on financial markets (Moran and Prosser, 1994). These new regimes are not merely transitional arrangements: marketized systems of production, distribution and exchange routinely require continued policing in order to promote competition (Prosser, 1999: 197).[13] In Australia in the late 1980s, for example, the Trade Practices Commission, as it then was,[14] required more resources to police antitrust laws in the deregulated telecommunications, airlines and international cargo shipping industries after deregulatory reforms were introduced. The Commission, as a regulatory agency, was even responsible for encouraging many professions to *deregulate* in the areas of advertising, fees and entry barriers (Ayres and Braithwaite, 1992: 15). Thus the general, and overall, drift of deregulation often simultaneously produces market-affirming forms of reregulation.

A different way of restructuring command and control mechanisms is to replace them with more flexible, incentive-driven, consensual instruments. Regulatory strategies are increasingly implemented with a heavy dependency on the input of private agents. The essence of this style of soft regulation is that it affords greater autonomy to the private sector. The pattern is evident across many jurisdictions, though manifested in differing forms. Environmental regulation is a typical example of the novel regulatory practice. The change in the Netherlands, for instance, has been described as a "paradigm shift" away from "end of the pipe" regulation directed simply at preventing pollutants entering the environment, toward in-plant practices to prevent the production of such materials in the first place (Hanf, 1994: ch 9). In order to intervene earlier in the production process, agencies have to work with more sophisticated instruments that enlist the efforts of industry in a concerted manner. Manufacturers are given greater scope to define their own ways of achieving the state's environmental policies, and are offered more market-sensitive incentives to that end, in place of the direct proscriptions of the former regulatory regimes. One model of such instruments is the "contractarian" paradigm in the United States and Europe, where agreements are struck between regulators and polluters on either an industry-wide or case-by-case basis that certain legal requirements are not to be enforced in exchange for the fulfilment of duties not imposed by existing law (Dana, 2000: 35).

In Australia, the trend is already entrenched. In some states consumer law embodies a form of co-regulation where codes of practice are formulated, under government auspices, by peak bodies comprising industry groups, consumer organizations and members of the public to control practices within an industry. The governing instrument then is enforceable ultimately by the Minister or commercial tribunals. In the mining and aviation industries, companies write the rules that are ratified by the regulatory agency. Initial responsibility for enforcement lies with private compliance units, with back-up public enforcement in cases of weak or ineffective local compliance (Grabosky and Braithwaite, 1986: 228). One former member of the Commission described the newer arrangements as reflecting a general transformation of the agency "from legalistic enforcer to facilitator of deregulation and self-regulator (and law enforcer when these approaches fail)" (Ayres and Braithwaite, 1992: 15).

Deregulatory tendencies can also be seen in the waning enthusiasm for pro-regulatory "New Deal Constitutionalism" in the United States, exemplified by the appearance of increasing Congressional and presidential control over regulatory agencies, so as to rein in the broad "administrative autonomy" characteristic of the post-New Deal federal bureaucracies. Shifts toward principles of construing regulatory statutes restrictively apparent in Supreme Court decisions in the 1980s consolidated this trend (Sunstein, 1990: 29-31). Over the same period, many federal agencies suffered substantial reductions in funding and staff and so were unable effectively to perform their statutory obligations (Rose-Ackerman, 1990: 524). Though much regulatory machinery was retained, and in some cases even enhanced, the net effect of these developments was to signal the end of the "rights revolution" that characterized the 1960s and 1970s regulatory reforms (Sunstein, 1990: ch 1).

Deregulation in the few typical forms outlined above connotes reliance on market mechanisms rather than direct state control; but the reality is more complex. In many cases the rules devised, implemented and policed rely first, on *non-state institutions* as much as private actors in the marketplace, and second, on differently constituted agencies and instruments, tailored to the specific context of the target industry. Ayres and Braithwaite have concluded, in an assessment of the changes in regulatory policy in a number of common law countries in the 1980s and early 1990s, that forms of "responsive regulation" are emerging in advanced capitalist societies (1992: ch 1) where regulatory legal regimes are not top-down but respond "to how effectively industry is making private regulation work" (1992: 4). To achieve this result, states increasingly rely on consumer and producer representatives to frame workable compromise regimes for organizing the market. A form of "conciliated regulation ... less goal-directed than command and control regulation" ensues (Grabosky and Braithwaite, 1986: 229).

Because the "deregulatory" changes have in general not merely removed regulation, but reconfigured it, and in some cases have produced even more regulation, it has been argued that reference to a sea-change in policy-making is inappropriate (Laux and Molot, 1988). But the evidence against this view is far too weighty. The sheer scale of legislative, institutional and doctrinal change suggests that the regulatory landscape is sufficiently transformed to suggest a "non-incremental" shift has occurred (Howse et al., 1990: 506-522). The extent of the shift is also quite consistent with the postmodernization thesis. Insofar as "[p]rocesses of postmodernization 'shrink' the corporatist state, causing a shift from centralized to decentralized apparatuses and from authoritative to manipulative forms of control" (Crook et al., 1992: 221), deregulation affords a typical example. The pattern of recent change casts doubt on Habermas' typology of modernity's four general "waves of juridification" which culminate in the welfare state's "constitutionalization of the economy" (1986: 208-212). The less directive, "new regulatory state", that "steers rather than rows" (Osborne and Gaebler, 1992), is evident not only in the sphere of civil law; in the criminal sphere, too, a gradual, and selective, process of withdrawal is evident in crime control strategies. Not only are restorative justice strategies growing in number in various jurisdictions, but also increasing reliance on community, local and individualistic "prudentialist" policies are drawing responsibility away from state control to greater reliance on institutions of civil society and individual citizens (Braithwaite, 2002; O'Malley, 1992).[15] A comparable, general reordering of legal entitlements is evident in the sphere of welfare.

Contracting Welfare Rights

Welfare states have always differed in the extent, reach and universality of welfare provision. They can be located on a spectrum ranging from universalism to particularism, where universalism refers to the provision of benefits in money or in kind to all citizens regardless of wealth and position, and particularism entails the rationing of benefits by reference to closely defined categories of need. By this measure, the welfare states of countries such as the United States and Japan have featured at the particularistic end of the spectrum, while the northern European social democracies have been at the other. Despite these historically large differences, in recent years there has been a pervasive shift away from former welfare principles across the domain of welfare rights in all countries. Contemporary welfare states are marked by a growing rejection of the principle of universalism to selective provision, and by a departure from optimal to minimal levels of service, and from tax-funded to user-pays schemes (Pierson, 1991: chs 5-6). Welfare rights are greatly attenuated as the welfare state safety net is residualized. These general developments are manifested in the appearance of a very different legal regime governing welfare rights.

The move in the direction of more particularistic regimes is strikingly evident in the increased conditionalization of welfare provision. Benefits are not only increasingly harder to obtain, but also more difficult to retain. An ever-widening range of welfare benefits are hedged with conditions, time-limits, and mutual obligations, so as to erode progressively the principle of universal entitlement that underpinned the welfare state. In Australia, for instance, the provision of unemployment benefit has been substantially revised in the last couple of decades in this direction. Beginning with the imposition of tighter conditions for eligibility such as participation in vocational training, the changes have culminated in the requirement that claimants enter into agreements with caseworkers to prepare more actively for work, and to accept a wide range of jobs. The former centrepiece of income support based on meeting uniform qualifying conditions has been replaced by more diffuse, flexible and subjective criteria where a caseworker with delegated power is in an individual contractual relationship with the "client". The role played by these "case management contracts" is to structure with precision the terms on which benefits are to be paid, and the obligations of the claimant (Carney and Ramia, 1999). The case management of welfare introduces a novel set of principles into the structure of welfare law: unemployed citizens are not so much entitled to benefits as of right, but only on condition that they fulfil the obligations on their side of the welfare bargain, which may now require working for the dole. The development from "entitlement to contract", or the contractualization of welfare, parallels the reforms in the law and governance of the economic sphere.[16]

In the United States, comparable, if more extreme, revisions of welfare provision have been introduced. They include restrictions on access to many programs; reduced eligibility to food stamps; comprehensive work requirements; narrower standards of physical disability for pensions; and tight time limits on financial assistance (Quigley, 1998; Diller, 2000). These regimes share the policy objective of shifting more responsibility onto citizens to provide their own welfare, as "workfare" comes to replace "welfare". And an overview of recent trends in Europe suggests that a process of convergence of welfare state regimes is at work, also with a new "workfare state" replacing the variety of welfare state reforms of the post-war period (Kosonen, 1995: 99-103).

A related development is the progressive dismantling of strategies formerly adopted by welfare states to entrench welfare rights by minimizing state discretion to reduce or withdraw benefits. The notion of welfare entitlements as enforceable claims against the state is giving way to a more fluid sense of entitlement. In Australia, the "robust public law culture of the 1970s" has been replaced by wider discretion to reduce and withdraw entitlements; also, agreements concluded between clients and caseworkers are "less accessible to tribunal review" (Carney and Ramia, 1999: 135). A clearer example of the changes at work is the United States where, as was outlined in chapter 3, the 1970s saw the extension of constitutional safeguards for the rights of welfare recipients by analogy with property rights (Reich, 1964). In recent years, the Supreme Court has led a "due process counter-revolution" which has largely undone the reforms inspired by Reich's critique (Pierce, 1996: 1973). This trend is confirmed by legislative reform of the legal infrastructure of welfare provision. The new regime emphasizes discretion on caseworkers, conferring greater powers on them in their dealing with clients, at the expense of due process protections. Diller examines the detail of the new system, whereby the former "legal-bureaucratic model" with its centralized and hierarchical structure is replaced by discretion-driven welfare administration (2000: 1141-1166). Welfare workers are given greater discretion as benefits are no longer dispensed on the basis of simple criteria, but on condition that the claimant engage in a range of employment-related activities. A pervasive "delegalization" results, consistent with developments in other spheres (2000: 1187). The earlier emphasis on the security of the entitlements of claimants as expressed in the language of property rights has been eclipsed by contractual principles, market-oriented rhetoric and a correspondingly weakened sensitivity to individual need. In sum, the new regime is "the antithesis of the social, political, and legal philosophy espoused by Reich and adopted by the [Supreme] Court as the foundation of the due process revolution" (Pierce, 1996: 1993).

As was noted in chapter 2, post-Fordism is not merely an economic development; it also captures change in the structure and functions of the state and wider society. The modern assumptions of the "organized" welfare state, consistent as they are with the "organized capitalism" which nourished it, have been measurably reversed. The state is now called upon to reflect the differentiated, fragmented, flexible and market-driven nature of the transformed economy. The "mass" system of notionally uniform, universal welfare rights extending across the entire national space is being replaced by localized and differentiated forms of provision which vary both with the particular contractual arrangements concluded between state purchaser and private provider on one level, and the contractual rights and obligations tailored to individual claimants on another. The more localized and particularized regimes represent a shift away from the mass welfare state bureaucracies and their distinctive pattern of alienation, where "[t]hese organizations add a spatial and temporal element to the social and psychological distance of the client from the welfare bureaucracy" (Habermas, 1986: 210), though not by any means for the better. The temporal dimension of welfare provision is no less transformed. In the place of lifelong entitlements, implicit in the "cradle-to-the-grave" metaphor of welfare state citizenship, stands a framework of discretionary, restrictive and finite provision. This progressively contingent and obligation-based structure of welfare rights introduces a novel precariousness into what were only recently solid social rights. It is an exaggeration to describe the new legal environment, even in the United States, as resembling the medieval and early modern Poor Laws (Quigley, 1998); but in the pervasive policy themes of local provision, increasing responsibilities of the poor, and a more punitive regime, there are eerie parallels with the welfare state's ungenerous ancestor.

With traditional welfare services increasingly provided by the private sector, the legal relationships that govern responsibilities veer away from public law and toward contract. When welfare law moves from "'status' to 'contract'" (Carney and Ramia, 1999: 135), similar problems identified with the use of contractual solutions in the wider context of privatization and deregulation arise. Claimants face new obstacles to realizing rights: the vocabulary of agreement conceals a more discretionary regime which poses grave difficulties for those with weak bargaining skills because claimants' benefits are dependent on dialogue and negotiation with local provider agencies and caseworkers (Cox, 1998). Also, where services are contracted out to private providers, the legal relationship that welfare recipients have with state is transformed. If the private agency performing the welfare function breaches its contract with the state, the aggrieved recipient has no automatic remedy against it, but must depend on the discretionary action of the relevant state agency. As another example of "entrepreneurial government", there is a general reduction in public accountability in a "delegalized" environment where delivering benefits and services to which individuals are entitled takes second place to achieving "efficiency" outcomes such as caseload reduction and employment (Diller, 2000: 1183). It may be that in some cases the new regimes reverse a debilitating dependency by encouraging a more active citizenry to participate productively in labour markets; but much of the empirical evidence suggests that the primary consequence of getting claimants off the register leads to a substantial growth in the number of the working poor (Matsuda, 1997).

A cumulative effect of these changes is a transformation in the nature of citizenship. One measure of the extent of structural change is the disappearance of the language of citizenship from policy discussions about the direction of the welfare state (Ignatieff, 1989: 72). In an era of declining welfare expenditures, less generous provision for the disadvantaged, and curtailment of universal rights to minimum levels of welfare, yet another element in the social dimension of citizenship rights is being whittled away. The deepening of the concept of citizenship in the welfare state is dramatically reversed in postmodernity when new legal arrangements replace the scope and solidity of social rights with a widening span of duties and obligations. A new model of citizenship matches citizens' rights with responsibilities that derive "from the contractual metaphors of activity, reciprocity and mutuality" (Carney and Ramia, 1999: 139). Welfare has ceased to be an entitlement or benefit owed to the citizen unconditionally on the establishment of legally predetermined need, but rather forms one part of a mutual bargain creating rights and duties.

The recent legal changes have a greatly different impact on poverty from welfare state reforms. The welfare state's universalized social rights achieved a significant reversal of class inequality (Marshall, 1963). By contrast, Kosonen concludes, in summarizing trends in Europe, that the former capacities of welfare states to ameliorate class disadvantage has faded where "unemployment rates and poverty rates have increased, public social security has weakened, and a shift toward private arrangements has occurred" (1995: 99). Moreover, the general diminution and conditionalization of welfare rights reflect an attitude to the poor which combines to characterize recipients as undeserving or marked by moral failure (Carney and Ramia, 1999: 138; Diller, 2000: 1111; Quigley, 1998): "as a result, welfare provisions have been transformed into the stigma of the impotent and the improvident" (Bauman, 1997: 37).

Beyond the provision of welfare benefits, other realms of welfare entitlement such as education, health care and pensions have been similarly transformed: public policy increasingly favours rights to purchase in the private market over collective provision. A civil, consumer citizenship steadily corrodes a former social citizenship. This is not to argue that the post-war welfare state has disappeared. Rather, a radically reconfigured state regime has appeared, nowhere more discernible than in its changed pattern of welfare entitlements. The changes combine to outstrip Habermas' account of legal change, which sees the latest wave of juridification as conferring a package of social rights accompanied by an administrative "therapeutocracy" (1986). A fragmented and market-driven network of institutions is replacing significant parts of the former state system, and they operate within a very different legal framework. Contemporary legal systems are no less transformed, and in analogous ways, in their provision of access to justice.

The Domestic Fragmentation of Legal Systems

As noted in chapter 3, a distinguishing feature of modern law was its historically unique project of centralization and monopolization of justice. Although this project was only ever partially successful, local jurisdictions were in general increasingly absorbed and subjected to closer supervision and control by the nation state's expansionist legal apparatus. The term "system" came to be an appropriate epithet for the legal order, as it became a unified structure, was governed by a distinctive type of reasoning, and came to be formally accessible to all citizens, however much in practice the ideal was unequally enjoyed. This historical pattern accelerated with the rise of the welfare state that substantially fuelled the increase in access to justice in the form of "three waves" of reforms in the form of legal aid, public interest law, and informal justice respectively (Cappelletti and Garth, 1978).

This package of reforms has changed in three separate dimensions in the restructured, contracting welfare state. The reforms are sufficient in extent to support the conclusion that in this domain also, a significant historical shift has occurred. The most noteworthy development is a dramatic growth in, and reconfiguration of, the "third wave" of informal justice. Also, a "fourth wave" of access to justice emerges in the form of competition policy. Finally, state resources directed toward the comparatively generous provision of legal aid are subjected to significant cutbacks and revision. The changes, though occurring in different ways, and to different degrees in various jurisdictions,[17] replicate the broader policy preferences of contemporary advanced capitalist societies. They will be considered separately.

The "Explosive" Rise of Informal Justice

The recent expansion of informal justice is evident in a number of domains. They include the development of court-annexed alternative dispute resolution and diversionary strategies; the proliferation of specialized informal tribunals; the incorporation of third parties such as victims into the legal process; the rise of community-based initiatives such as justice centres; and the emergence of private adjudication and mediation services that compete directly with the formal justice system. The predominant policy underpinning the access to justice movement in the welfare state was the opening up of the formal legal system to a wider cross-section of citizens. Legal aid and public interest law clearly express this objective. But informal justice is based on a different philosophy; its fundamental guiding principle is the *diversion* of disputants away from the formal, legal process. As we have seen, it was the third, and weakest, wave of the reform movement. In the early years it failed to attract public funding and commanded little popular support because it was seen to be inadequate to protect citizens' rights, on the ground that it was a mechanism for privatizing justice so that domination was perpetuated rather than opened up to the scrutiny of public legal justice (Parker, 1999: 38). In consequence it appeared as a second-class type of justice (Cappelletti, 1993: 288). With the exception of the expansion of tribunals, what initiatives there were tended to be privately driven, and were generally confined to disputes about less important matters.

Current developments reveal a very different picture. Informal justice now stands at the very centre of access to justice reform, so that it is coming to overshadow, rather than simply supplement, other mechanisms of access to traditional formal law. Initiatives in the United States have been the most dramatic, where, starting in the 1980s, an "alternative dispute resolution explosion" has occurred. It represents "a wave of antagonism against litigation" and the formal processes of the courts (Nader, 1988: 269-270).[18] Now, as the "Prince Charming to a court system in distress", it has become the preferred justice strategy for both public and private initiatives (Wald, 1997: 1445). Many parallel developments have taken off in other jurisdictions (Astor and Chinkin, 1992; Cappelletti, 1993; Genn, 1999b).

The informal justice movement is composed of a similar blend of mutually inconsistent ideological strands as characterized the general search for alternatives to the legal structures of welfare state. It is far from an exclusively grassroots campaign for change. The growing numbers of advocates for reform of the legal system who demand the removal of the traditional trappings of legal formality, with its concern for right answers and legal truth – Bentham's "rectitude of decision" (Zuckerman, 1999: 4) – are as likely to be among the ranks of the legal profession, as outside. And though the reform movement seeks a shared goal, its members have different interests to pursue. Thus for governments, and the senior judiciary,[19] the problem is primarily one of system overload. Informal justice becomes a way to deal with the problem of increasing demand for formal legal services by means of diversion to a cheaper form of justice delivery. From below, the push for informal justice is consistent with the broader trend described as "democracy against the welfare state" (Offe, 1987b), where the formal justice system is attacked variously for being beset with inefficiencies and delays; being so costly as to be within the reach of only the more affluent of citizens; and offering an inferior type of justice because it is bureaucratically insensitive to, and corrosive of community, local, private or broadly "indigenous" solutions. The dramatic institutionalization of these demands reflects the nature and extent of contemporary change.

There are a number of characteristic traits that these various informal innovations share. One of these is the appearance of a process of hybridization of the legal system.

Hybridization The familiar metaphor of the "justice pyramid" with formal justice at the tip, and levels of increasingly informal justice below, captures the atypical nature of the disputes formally adjudicated in the courts (Parker, 1999: ch 4). The related metaphor of "the shadow of the law" expresses the way that formal law operates to structure and influence, if not necessarily determine, disputes resolved outside the courtroom (Mnookin and Kornhauser, 1979). Formal dispute processing has therefore always been an exceptional event. The access to justice movement claimed impressive victories in breaking down financial and other barriers to the courts, and so both metaphorically lengthened the shadow of the law, and expanded the pyramid's tip. The terms "juridification" and "litigation explosion" capture the development (Teubner, 1987; Galanter, 1986). Recent changes point to a different process at work. A distinctive change since the first appearance of "third wave" alternative dispute resolution is the institutionalization of its role *within* the formal legal system. There are now a multitude of ways in which legal disputes are *officially* processed by means of recourse to alternative dispute resolution. Formal courts increasingly have alternative dispute resolution annexed to their day-to-day operations and are imposing ever-widening obligations on parties to attempt to resolve their differences by alternative means before a formal hearing. Family courts have routinely operated in this way. But they are now a standard feature of the general judicial process, so much so that it is "no longer a question of mediation in the shadow of the law, but of the law and the courts in the shadow of negotiation" (Dezalay, 1994: 175).

Some of the examples of entire jurisdictions "moving in the 'third wave' direction" are collected by Cappelletti (1993: 288-294). In 1987 in France, for instance, a nationwide system of conciliators was established. Appointed by the President of the Court of Appeal, their function is to meet parties in the attempt to secure a pre-trial conciliation agreement, after examining the evidence intended to be presented to the court. The legal systems of Germany and Italy have introduced similar institutions. In the United States, reforms to procedural rules require federal district courts to consider using a formal alternative dispute resolution program for pre-trial referral in certain cases. The result is that over 80 per cent of the courts have programs in place authorizing judges to use alternative dispute resolution in the form of court-annexed mediation programs, mandated arbitration, early neutral evaluation or arbitration under an existing statute (Wald, 1997: 1445-1447). In Australia, pre-trial conferences and judicial mediation are now common, and compulsory court-annexed civil arbitration has been introduced in some states, with disincentives against appeal to the referring court such as costs rules (Astor and Chinkin, 1992: ch 8). A similar trend is indicated in the recent wave of reforms of the civil courts in the United Kingdom which give judges various powers to suspend proceedings to allow mediation of disputes, and allocate cases to various "tracks" depending on amount of claim and complexity of subject-matter (Genn, 1999a: 59; 1999b: 2-3). The result is that in many jurisdictions the phenomenon of the "multi-door courthouse" has appeared where a wide variety of legal and non-legal mechanisms co-exist to resolve disputes (Solum, 1993: 2146).

The effects of this general transformation have led to the appearance of a distinct judicial managerialism. First evident in the United States, where it has advanced the furthest, it has been replicated in other jurisdictions (Zuckerman, 1999: 51). As the Supreme Court has shifted from disdain for alternative dispute resolution methods in the courts, to enthusiastic endorsement, alternative dispute resolution has been progressively incorporated into the formal courts. In turn, the traditional adjudicatory function of courts is being overtaken by the requirement to reduce court lists as a predominant judicial responsibility. This leads to the appearance of "managerial judges"; far from attempting to be "Hercules" in pursuit of the right answer (Dworkin, 1977; 1986), judicial work has increasingly involved the management of caseloads, which necessarily entails bringing influence to bear on parties to settle rather than proceed to trial (Reznik, 1982). Insofar as this confluence of systems takes place with the increasing official involvement and even encouragement of the legal system, there is a hybridization of legal and non-legal norms.[20]

In the "marriage" of the traditional legal system with alternative dispute resolution, as in all marriages, both parties are transformed (Reznik, 1982). As disputes are diverted from the formal judicial process to meditation or conciliation, a legal discourse based on objective rights and obligations is typically mingled with, or even replaced by, moral, economic and other discourses, where subjective interests, needs and relationships assume priority (Merry: 1990). The process corrodes the autonomy, or in Teubner's terms (1988; 1993), the "autopoietic closure" imposed by legal processes on disputes; what would otherwise be a closed universe of strictly legal communication becomes an intersection of a plurality of values and norms. A related development is that the autonomy of negotiation from the legal process is structurally compromised, as the dyadic format of private negotiation is replaced with triadic mediation giving rise to a form of "litigotiation" (Galanter, 1985: 1). This pattern contains contradictory elements: the state is both enlisted, as where a settlement is buttressed by means of a formal court order, but it is also kept at a distance from the actual process of resolution.

A less dramatic example of this trend, but no less significant, is the increasing use of tribunals that operate with looser and more informal legal procedures. Though a typical feature of welfare state access to justice reforms, they have proliferated as the welfare state recedes (Genn, 1993: 393). Their character, as with the multi-door courthouse, is also essentially hybridized: legal representation is commonly restricted or absent, and other legal forms such as the rules of evidence are limited. Moreover, they regularly provide for disputes to be mediated or conciliated in preference to adjudication. The linkage between the formal and informal is evident even in cases of community or neighbourhood justice centres. They formally operate outside the formal court system, and their work is routinely conducted in relatively close functional proximity to the formal justice system by receiving a large proportion of their clients as referrals from the police, lawyers and the courts (Astor and Chinkin, 1992: 30).

The new landscape of disputes therefore looks more diversified than ever. The historical development of modern law is registered in its formal institutional separation from other normative orders.[21] Of course, such a separation has never been fully realized, and even within the court system; wide divergences of practice have always been present (Arthurs, 1985; McBarnet, 1981). But modern law is distinctive for its sharp differentiation of the formal courts, the legal profession, and its lawyers' law, with its specialized formal rationality, from the "indigenous law" of groups, communities and associations. In the emerging policy of coupling formal and informal law, a continuum connects the various norms of dispute resolution as opposed to an institutional barrier that keeps them apart.

It may therefore be inappropriate to describe this development merely as the rise of "informal" justice. Instead, the legal system as a whole becomes *de-differentiated*: the norms by which disputes are resolved are now much more difficult to classify with precision as legal and non-legal discourses become institutionally intermeshed. Thus "[l]aw is less autonomous, less self-contained, more absorbent, more open to methods and data from other disciplines" (Galanter, 1992: 24). To be sure, litigants unhappy with informal resolutions may still go to court; but they are institutionally discouraged from doing so. Accordingly, modern law's metaphors of autonomy, unity and closure give way to plurality and openness. Sociologically and historically, postmodern law comes to operate with a "porous legality" (Santos, 1987: 289).[22] In this respect legal change reflects the transformations of other institutions in postmodernity. Max Weber characterized the rise of modern institutions as being marked by a progressive rationalization of internal practice. At present, by contrast, traditional institutional policing mechanisms, and in law – this means the autonomy or closure of its discourse – are being applied in a looser, more flexible fashion.

Privatization Alternative dispute resolution is also an example of the growing privatization of justice. If the welfare state was typified by the pursuit of "total justice" (Friedman, 1985), to be dispensed predominantly by the public, state-funded legal system, the primary objective of the present access to justice policies is increasing reliance on the private realm for delivery. The private nature of the alternative dispute resolution is manifested in a number of ways. First, there has been a dramatic proliferation of private dispute resolution organizations in recent years, which offer their services directly to private disputants. In the United States, a partnership of private corporations and foundations that set up the National Institute for Dispute Resolution in 1982, has played a major role as catalyst for other private initiatives (Fn'Piere and Work, 1992-93: 960). Comparable developments have occurred in Canada (Arthurs and Kreklewich, 1996: 25-28), the United Kingdom (Genn, 1999a), and Australia (Astor and Chinkin, 1992). As these organizations grow in legitimacy, and take a greater share of the dispute resolution market, the private sector becomes institutionally, and legitimately, entrenched.

Second, the personnel who perform the function, even if as is usual they are legally qualified, are not constrained by public legal norms in resolving disputes, and so may be bringing a different set of other, private values to bear. In the case of community-based justice schemes, for instance, their private nature is also reflected in the fact that volunteers are prominent in the delivery of services (Fn'Piere and Work, 1992-93: 960; Astor and Chinkin, 1992: 24). These features of privatization are no less a mark of alternative dispute resolution when it is court-annexed, and disputes are effectively diverted from judicial determination.

Third, the reasons for settlement are generally not revealed, and so remain private, even where alternative dispute resolution forms part of a court-administered regime, or is buttressed by court order. The function of alternative dispute resolution is exclusively the settlement of the *individual*, and therefore private, dispute. If decisions cannot be subject to public scrutiny, they cannot serve as public norms for the purpose of resolving other disputes (Fiss, 1984: 1085; Sander et al., 1996: 885, 893). Of course, settlements have always greatly exceeded the numbers of adjudicated disputes in the legal system; but where settlement becomes an overwhelming concern of the judicial system, the publicity of law – a central feature of modern legality and the rule of law – is displaced.

Fourth, where the formal system with an impartial judge treats parties as equal, the practice of settlement is indifferent to questions of inequalities of power and influence, and personal or private differences between the parties. Largely hidden from public judicial scrutiny, informalism can become second-class justice for the poor, the badly advised and the powerless. Fifth, issues of great public significance, such as liability for mass torts or involving the accountability of public servants, may be concealed (Fiss, 1984: 1089).

One of the most visible manifestations of the growing role of the private sector can be seen in the rise of dispute processing mechanisms in particular industries and institutions. These are sometimes given encouragement and support by governments; but they are very different from the formal legal process, or indeed state-run informal adjudicative bodies. Many industries and businesses, such as insurance and banking, have established and funded positions of ombudsman to deal with complaints (Cappelletti, 1993: 290-291), and large corporations have started to make alternative dispute resolution pledges binding them to use informal mechanisms to resolve disputes before resorting to litigation (Adler, 1995: 74). Changes in strategies for the provision of legal aid replicate the trend: applicants are increasingly directed toward alternative dispute resolution mechanisms as part of the state's attempts to reduce expenditures (Blankenburg, 1995; Dewar et al., 1999: 13; Genn, 1999b: 4). In consequence, even the first wave of access to justice is being redirected by a countervailing, and expanding, third wave.

The valorization of the private sphere as a site for the production of norms is consistent with the more general trends towards privatization. And advocates for the private sector echo the criticisms of other features of the welfare state examined above. So, formal justice is seen to be too bureaucratic, and therefore too costly, slow and rigid. It is deemed ill-suited to the individual needs of parties to disputes, who may need a speedier remedy, or one more suited to sustaining rather than fracturing an ongoing relationship. By contrast, private dispute resolution offers a wide range of different and flexible solutions. In a manner not dissimilar to the shift from Fordism to post-Fordism in the economy, the mass production of justice through the formal legal system is being matched by mechanisms for more diversified (private) products. The subtle shift in the discourse of access to justice from citizens to "customers" reflects this general trend (Genn, 1999b: 5). Inglehart's wide-ranging empirical study of recent changes in community values across a number of countries identifies the broad decline of legal-rational authority as typical of postmodernization, and is consistent with debates about access to justice (1997: ch 3). Such attitudes to the law have always been present in debates about the delivery of justice; but it is their prevalence and pervasiveness in reform strategies that marks out recent developments.

Both the public and private expansion of alternative dispute resolution, and informal justice generally, contribute to a further innovative feature of the new landscape, that of the reconstituted legal subject.

From a rights-bearing to an interests-bearing legal subject The legal subject of modern law is a rights-bearing citizen who can call upon the courts to declare and enforce legal rights. Those rights operate as "trumps" that are enforced by the state, and enforceable against the state (Dworkin, 1977). The extension of this image in the 1970s by the widening of access to formal justice under the banner of equality of rights contributed to the prevalence of "rights-talk" (Silbey and Sarat, 1989: 476). This development is to be contrasted with the present spread of mechanisms of alternative dispute resolution. Where official policies emphasize the centrality of settlement, induce parties to resolve differences in private, and to use the courts only as a "last resort" (Woolf, 1999: 9), the "interests" or "needs" of parties, and the "harmony" of their relationships (Nader, 1988), come to overshadow their formal rights. Those interests and needs extend from individual requirements to have disputes resolved quickly, effectively and justly with the minimum of cost, to the wider social interest of ensuring that community-based, private, and non-legal sources of authority play a greater role. The emphasis on a needs-sensitive informal justice tends to elevate the needs- and interests-bearing subject to be the primary figure of reform strategies, displacing the central rights-bearing subject of modern law (Silbey and Sarat, 1989: 479-496). In turn, the discourse of legality, rights, and "rights-talk", comes to play a secondary role.

In this context, formal adjudication is seen as merely another form of dispute resolution mechanism not necessarily suited to the overall benefit of the legal subject. By contrast, the central concern of rights talk, or legalism, is with the rights of the parties, and to the extent that formal adjudication is primarily concerned with defining those rights, deciding which party's rights have been infringed, and articulating *public* legal values (Fiss, 1979: 161), it is seen as the highest form of justice. Hence, legalism shows disdain for "arbitration, negotiation, bargaining as mere politics arbitrary and expedient" (Shklar, 1964: 10). This philosophy was clearly evident in the welfare state's access to justice movement given its primary emphasis on formal justice and rights. In the present climate, however,

> [r]ights talk and the conception of the juridical subject as a rights holder has been an important part of ADR's critique of adjudication ... From this perspective, rights are associated with litigiousness and blamed for a variety of social and institutional disorders (Silbey and Sarat, 1989: 476).

The trend has been identified by Garland in the emergence of economic modes of rationality in public policy in recent years (1997: 185-186). Though his particular focus is on criminal justice, his conclusions are relevant to legal systems in general. Economic modes of rationality refer to much more than a preoccupation with value for money, though this concern is certainly prominent. They are also demonstrated in the analytical language by which the field is assessed, in terms of supply and demand, and targeting of resources; in an increased focus on objectives such as effectiveness, consumer satisfaction and outcomes; and in the growing use of mechanisms such as auditing, fiscal control and devolved management. Rights talk is largely indifferent to questions of economics and accounting, relying more on rule of law or constitutional principles which attach primacy to the vindication of legal rights in the courts (Fiss, 1984; Silbey and Sarat, 1989: 471). By contrast, this type of economic perspective dovetails more neatly into the needs and interests of the legal subject. In the place of the analytical language of rights, it substitutes a broader problem-solving discourse where proportionality of procedure to dispute, compromise, cost-effectiveness and flexibility become paramount to further a range of objectives beyond the simple determination of the right legal answer (Silbey and Sarat, 1989: 487).

The shift in cultural attitudes to favour informal law both within and outside the legal system demonstrates a different way in which basis for legitimacy of law is established, and reflects wider cultural change (Inglehart, 1997). The legitimacy of modern law lies in its distinctive, formal rational character. Welfare state reforms enhanced this legitimacy by extending citizens' access to formal justice. But now, the discourse of efficiency comes to infect law no less than other social spheres. The change is captured by the contemporary emergence of what Lyotard (1984) describes as the "performativity" generally characteristic of postmodern societies. He argues that the legitimacy of social institutions is no longer to be found in their capacity to establish truth or falsity, but in resolving input/output problems. Law is a particularly apposite example of the process: as he concludes, "in postindustrial societies the normativity of laws is replaced by the performativity of procedures" (1984: 46).

A measure of the extent of change lies in the difficulty of fitting this shift into the framework of "responsive law". Its "master ideal" of "legality" emphasized the sovereignty of purpose with its analogue, purposive reasoning, and the rise of public interest law with its wider distribution of legal authority (Nonet and Selznick, 1978: ch 4). Thus, responsive law captured descriptively and prescriptively reforms typical of the welfare state. But those genuinely novel innovations now seem to be giving way to a different language of reform, both official and unofficial, where "the notion of what is threatened, has shifted from constitutional *norms* to the requirements of socio-political *stability* and the effective performance of public policy" (Offe, 1985: 229). If a social contextual or sociological perspective – "a broadening of the field of the legally relevant" (Nonet and Selznick, 1978: 73; Ewald, 1986) – was the dominant legal reform narrative of the welfare state, an economic mode of rationality or procedural performativity has become its contemporary successor.

The "justice of proximity" Modern formal justice operates by reference to specific temporal and spatial horizons: the system of justice was centralized and exclusively enforced the positive norms of the sovereign nation state. Welfare state reforms extended this process of centralization and juridification on a national scale. The broad thrust of recent developments heads in the opposite direction: the centripetal tendencies of the welfare state are being overshadowed by centrifugal forces which drive the resolution of disputes away from formal justice to local, private and communal forums. A "justice of proximity" emerges to render the resolution of the disputes closer to the context in which they arise (Wyvekens and Faget, 2001). There are three dimensions to this "proximity". First, in alternative dispute resolution there is proximity of geographical space. So community justice centres, industry-based ombudspersons, and professional experts function to resolve disputes in closer physical proximity to their origins. Not only are the detailed factual contexts relevant in such inquiries; "local" norms also assume greater importance in determining outcomes. To be sure, this type of informal justice is wholly different to the resolution of disputes in traditional, pre-modern societies where the community collectively or through an authoritative figure mediates by reference to some subjective, traditional or transcendent image of justice (Merry, 1979). But whether mediators and adjudicators are volunteers or professionals, or whether they operate within the courts or beyond, they are closer to the dispute by virtue of outlook, experience, and perspective. They operate by not abstracting the dispute from its context as formal legal adjudication requires, but by relocating it into its original environment. In consequence, the spatial confines within which law operates become more fragmented.

Second, recent changes evidence a "human proximity". The focus of alternative dispute resolution on the wider relationship of parties has been extended to a broad array of disputes to incorporate a more diverse range of considerations relevant to the need to sustain a continuing relationship or the repair of an existing one. Consistent with a more personalized "harmony ideology" (Nader, 1988), the parties to a dispute play a more active, participatory role in its resolution. To the extent that the individual needs and interests of parties are allowed to intrude more prominently into proceedings, "the juridical subject is provided with a more complicated, richer human character" (Silbey and Sarat, 1989: 491). An analogous principle of "restorative justice" has appeared, particularly in the context of criminal justice, where the emphasis is on guilty parties to compensate victims directly, and receive personal forgiveness (Umbreit, 1994; Braithwaite, 2002). Third parties to the dispute may be incorporated, as in community conferencing where family members and others may be joined, so that matters are brought closer to the intimate relational sphere than formal court processes allow (Blagg, 1997). The "new paradigm" of justice (Zehr, 1990) characterizes crime both in terms of interpersonal violation and resolution, and as an offence against the state. This development fits into the wider popular disillusionment about the effectiveness of the formal justice system and cynicism about the state's capacity to redress problems like crime (Strang and Braithwaite, 2001: 2-3).

Finally, justice is reconfigured in the temporal dimension. Where the system of adjudication dominates the justice system, a past-oriented temporality prevails. The courts focus on what has happened formerly in order to establish liability or guilt. By contrast, in each of the cases of settlement, restorative justice or diversionary strategies, a present-oriented administrative temporality prevails, requiring a swift, efficient and timely resolution of matters, at the expense of a rights-based rationality. Further, the future becomes an equally important factor in dispute resolution to the extent that questions such as how a particular resolution can fit into future relationships are crucial (Zehr, 1990). A final temporal change is evident in the increasing prominence in contemporary justice administration on the rapid transit of cases through the system. Informalism allows disputes to be resolved quickly and so achieves both the more efficient and cheaper management of caseloads, and the greater satisfaction of parties to the dispute. There is a wider context to the use of streamlined procedures: the general acceleration of social and economic relations puts pressure on legal systems to respond. So Lash and Urry note that "postmodernism hyperbolically accentuates the processes of increased turnover time, speed of circulation and the disposability of subjects and objects" (1994: 2-3). Thus, the *contemporary* pressure to incorporate more actively alternative dispute resolution processes into the formal justice system expresses "a duty to find alternatives of better accommodating the urgent demands of a time of societal transformations at an unprecedently accelerated pace" (Cappelletti, 1993: 296).

The general time-space reconfiguration involved in the incorporation of informal mechanisms within the legal system is evocative of the changes in architecture as described by Jencks (1977). The rhetoric and practice of postmodern architecture represented a revolt against the rational planning and scientistic pretensions of modern architecture with all its destructiveness of traditional and small-scale urban forms. For its proponents, the aim is a city of smaller scale structures, more responsive to local needs, less monumentalist, and more attuned to "respect the vernacular of the ... city fabric" (Jameson, 1991: 39). As we have seen in chapter 3, one effect of the expansion of modern formal law was to dominate and undermine traditional normative codes and local laws; while welfare state developments extended the process of juridification in ways that involved an even greater measure of colonization by law. Recent changes to the legal architecture, however, offer an environment more conducive to the flourishing of local, "indigenous" norms. The emergence of enhanced, officially-supported informal, delegalized justice reflects the growing legitimacy of legal pluralism; and it reflects, at least in part, a popular concern to revive informal norms marginalized by modern law's abstraction of individuals from their lived context, community and society.

Whether this overall development generally advances or impedes the delivery of justice is a matter of conjecture. There is much weight in Fiss's (1984) criticisms of a legal culture of "settlement", if it serves to divert important matters from public scrutiny and resolution by reference to legal norms. A related argument presumes that ADR is invariably "alternative" to the formal courts, and therefore sacrifices the strengths of the rule of law. In many cases, however, because the courts are practically inaccessible, informal justice is alternative to coercion in its various forms by more powerful parties, and insofar as it opens disputes to some form of public scrutiny "and thereby makes room for social norms to operate, [ADR] may be preferable" (Woodman, 1991: 30). The answer would seem to depend on the form of ADR and *its* alternatives in particular contexts. Likewise, though the growth of settlements may appear to represent an "erosion of the public realm" they may still offer weaker parties strategic, rational and just resolution of disputes (Luban, 1995: 2621). This question will be examined further in chapter 7.

The developments in the direction of informalism should not be interpreted as being purely at the expense of the formal legal process. As Galanter notes in a wide-ranging empirical study of recent legal change (1992: 1), the formal apparatus of the courts – judges, caseloads, lawyers, officials – has continued to expand in recent years despite the exponential rise of informalism. The explosion of alternative dispute resolution is therefore a novel additional element in the legal landscape, so that it is possible to talk of the phenomenon of "law abounding" with an enlargement of *both* formal and informal spheres:

> A generation later, the preference for case-by-case treatment and enthusiasm for the claim-counterclaim structure is undiminished, perhaps expanded. But the other features [the autonomy and predictability of law, formal legal rationality] are no longer evident: negotiation has been embraced as part of the legal realm; politics is no longer something alien, and the 'thereness' of law is in some doubt (Galanter, 1992: 22).

What marks this new abundance of law is its difference in overall character from its welfare state predecessor. In particular, the institutional interpenetration of the formal and informal, and a pervasive official and unofficial ideology of support for strategies of diversion signals a decisive historical break. This point is underscored by a further development in contemporary access to justice strategies: competition policy.

The Fourth Wave: Competition Policy

A fourth wave of access to justice, "competition policy", has recently complemented the widespread enthusiasm for informal justice. It expresses the policy preference for a deregulated market in legal services rather than a monopolistic legal profession as the key institutional mechanism for delivery of less costly formal justice. It differs from the first two waves of access to justice insofar as it is driven by the philosophy that cheaper formal justice is a key factor in widening access. Competition policy manifests itself in two different forms. First, greater competition is fostered *within* the legal profession, and second, the profession is subjected to competition from other professions. Competition within the profession is exemplified by the progressive introduction of market principles into the operation of professional practice. From the new perspective, lawyers are seen as providers of services like other service industries, rather than merely members of a public service-minded profession. Accordingly, they are encouraged to offer services at prices that the public is prepared to pay in a competitive market.

One of the first reforms in this mode was the relaxation of advertising rules for legal professional services. It gathered momentum in the United States in the 1970s, to be followed soon after in most of the other common law jurisdictions (Parker, 1999: 40). A later development has been the breakdown of traditional monopolies of certain functions within the profession, such as barristers' monopoly of the right to appear before higher courts. Another form of innovative market provision of legal services is by collective financing, as in group plans, where a class of potential clients is able to exert the pressure of numbers to obtain more favourable rates, or by legal expenses insurance (Pfennigstorf, 1975: 452). More recently, pro-competition legislation in various countries has introduced prohibitions on cost-fixing. Empirical studies suggest that some of these strategies have reduced costs and so have widened consumers' access to justice (Parker, 1999: 39).

A significant impetus for competition policy comes from supranational developments. The World Trade Organization (WTO) General Agreement on Trade in Services, for instance, through its core principle of non-discrimination requires national borders to be lifted to allow foreign firms to compete with local, often restrictive, practices. Though initially "a very guarded and tentative move in the direction of liberalization" it is likely to have considerable influence on the deregulation of traditional restrictions on competition given "successive rounds of commitments" to opening up markets in legal services (Arup, 2000: 145). One detailed study suggests that the North American Free Trade Agreement significantly advanced the liberalization of the Canadian legal profession (Paterson, 1996: 147),[23] while the general process of globalization introduces much greater levels of competition between lawyers and firms with very different cultural practices and expectations (Dezalay and Garth, 1996).

Second, the extensive intrusion of competition policy lies not so much within the legal system but by professional groups who are in competition *with* the legal system. An example of this reform has been the gradual introduction of non-lawyer professionals into areas formerly monopolized by lawyers, such as conveyancing. Equally, the alternative dispute resolution mechanisms referred to above directly compete with the official system by drawing clientele away from formal justice. The independent, vigorous growth of private alternative dispute resolution services is the most obvious example of this process of struggle within the legal field between different professional groups (Dezalay, 1994). The result is that the provision of legal services has become driven more by consumer preferences and less by professional expertise: as clients are offered a wider range of services and dispute resolution mechanisms, they put pressure on all branches, the formal and informal, to become more responsive (Robertson, 1998: 4). A more significant development, as noted above, is the active encouragement by the state of the incorporation of these services into the official system. In this way the alternative competes with the formal on the same terrain, and therefore with greater effectiveness. At base, competition policy is an aspect of deregulation, and so connects with the wider policies pursued by contracting welfare states. This trend is also evident in recent policies toward legal aid.

Legal Aid

According to T.H. Marshall (1963), the widespread availability of free or heavily subsidized means-tested legal aid and assistance had the effect of reversing the entrenched inequalities of liberal societies, and so was a typical example of the welfare state's "social citizenship". With its connotations of rights and entitlements to be guaranteed by the state, and available to a large section of the population, the "access to justice" movement resonated well with the welfare state's redistributive politics, where the state was the primary engine for intervention in the legal services market through strategies of direct financing and/or the employment of salaried lawyers to assist the poor. Since the 1980s, however, "the rhetoric of 'access to justice' seems to lose its power ..." (Parker, 1999: 38), only to be replaced by a very different set of discourses. In the context of legal aid, this loss of power is evident in the progressive restrictions imposed on legal aid from the late 1980s onward.

Contemporary strategies pursued to advance avenues of formal legal redress for injustice tend to emphasize other priorities, many of which are consistent with the deregulatory and privatization thrusts identified above. From the 1980s onward, legal aid has been subjected to significant restrictions. This development is particularly evident in countries with generous welfare states and historically strong commitments to publicly funded legal aid and assistance schemes (Blankenburg, 1995: 177; Regan and Fleming, 1994). And it expresses policy preferences that cut across political divides (Smith, 1996: 578). Reductions have been achieved in two dimensions: by reference to financial status of the recipient on the one hand, and to subject matter on the other. The net result is the exclusion of large sections of the population. In England, for instance, access to some legal aid was available to around 80% of the population in 1949, had declined to just above 50% by 1989 because of the application of the lowering of income levels in means tests (Rickman and Gray, 1995: 317). At the same time, clients have to pay increasing contributions and charges to receive legal aid, with greater exposure to costs orders (Goriely, 1995: 351). A similar story emerges in Canada, Sweden and the Netherlands (Regan and Fleming, 1994: 184).[24]

In relation to the eligibility of the matters capable of attracting legal aid, criminal matters tend to consume an increasing share of legal aid budgets at the expense of broader access to civil justice. Paradoxically, despite these overall changes, legal aid expenditures in England and Wales *in absolute terms* have risen significantly since the 1980s (Genn, 1999b: 3). This phenomenon is to be explained by the growing numbers *within* the reduced proportion of the populations now eligible for aid, and the more costs consumed by individual matters, particularly in criminal law. Thus growing levels of poverty and inequality, and high unemployment have been offered as explanations for the increases (Rickman and Gray, 1995: 318). They indicate a broader trend: that legal aid is now predominantly for the poor. It therefore represents an increasingly *residual* form of welfare state provision, and the replacement of the principle of entitlement to legal aid with discretionary benefit (Zander, 2000: ch 1). This point is even more pertinent for those more numerous countries where legal aid funding has declined overall (Blankenburg, 1995: 182-183).

A supplementary strategy employed by states to reduce legal aid expenditures is in the form of diversionary schemes toward alternative dispute resolution, and the more widespread use of market mechanisms. This development parallels the general access to justice policy changes noted above. Both carrots and sticks are deployed to direct applicants to alternative dispute mechanisms. Thus in the United Kingdom, for example, recent reforms have introduced private arbitration and mediation service providers into the legal aid system, while at the same time exposing more recipients to potential liability for costs in the event of failing to win cases (Smith, 1996: 575-576; Genn, 1999b).

The market mechanism has also appeared in wider deployment of franchising, whereby the state contracts with private law firms to provide legal aid services. The contracts impose upper limits on the amount of public legal aid available in specific areas (Goriely, 1995: 351). The net effect of this strategy is also to ration public funding. Another way to limit state spending is by means of increasing the use of legal expenses insurance, as has been pursued in Sweden and the Netherlands (Regan and Fleming, 1994: 184). The "ebbing tide" of support for legal aid means that states increasingly offload responsibilities for access to formal justice by the less advantaged to the private sphere (Smith, 1996: 570). Overall, these changes reflect the user-pays, "consumer" citizenship policies evident in other spheres so that legal aid appears as but "a microcosm of a wider process of change in the provision of services in society" (Regan and Fleming, 1994: 184). One overview of developments in the United States concluded that access to formal justice was increasingly seen less of a social right as a social problem, in preference to privatized models (Garth, 1992). In consequence, a general survey of international trends has concluded that "[i]n some important respects, eligibility provisions in the late 1990s bore a striking resemblance to those of the charitable schemes prior to World War II" (Regan et al., 1999: 2). These conclusions capture the extent of recent change both at the level of philosophy and policy toward legal aid provision in contracting welfare states.

In general, the transformation of the welfare state in each of the dimensions examined so far in this chapter – privatization, deregulation, the attenuation of welfare rights, and the re-direction of access to justice strategies – reflects the general, dwindling faith in the bureaucratic centralism of a welfare state organized along national lines. A more fragmented, contractualized and pluralistic legal order has started to make a clearly identifiable institutional appearance. This novel "legal polycentricity" (Petersen and Zahle, 1995) is resonant of the broader fragmentation, or disorganization, characteristic of advanced capitalist societies (Offe, 1985; Crook, Pakulski and Waters, 1992). Support for this conclusion is provided by another recent element in the reconfiguration of modern law, linked to the changes detailed above: the rapidly growing penetration of domestic law by supranational legal norms. As Jürgen Habermas has recently argued:

> The welfare state mass democracies on the Western model now face the end of a 200-year developmental process that began with the revolutionary birth of modern nation-states ... The phenomena of the territorial state, the nation, and a popular economy constituted within national borders formed a historical constellation in which the democratic process assumed a more or less convincing institutional form ... Today, developments summarized under the term 'globalization' have put this entire constellation into question (2001: 60).

Supranational Law and Increasingly Permeable Domestic Law

Sovereignty lies at the heart of modern law. As we have seen in chapter 3, it has a domestic and an international dimension. Domestically, nations were legally sovereign within their own territories, monopolizing both the power to enact laws, and the means of enforcement. Laws that emanated beyond the nation's borders did not bind citizens unless they had been incorporated into domestic law by the sovereign. Given this exclusive legal monocentricity it was understandable for both legal theory and sociological approaches to law generally to ignore legal norms originating beyond the territorial boundaries of the nation state (MacCormick, 1993; Friedman, 1996). The second dimension of sovereignty lies in the notion that the sovereign nation state was the basic unit, or subject, in international law. No law could bind a state unless in the form of custom which it participated in creating, or by treaty which it made in the exercise of sovereign powers. The emergence of welfare states did not change this underlying framework.

The picture is rapidly changing as the contraction of welfare states in a "downward" direction is matched by developments "upwards". The domestic laws of nation states, in a manner unprecedented in the modern era, operate in the shadow of international law as "globalization" unfolds. Globalization refers to a spatially and temporally shrinking world in which an increasing interconnectedness between societies results in events in one part of the world influencing peoples and societies great distances away

(Baylis and Smith, 1997: 7). The legal sphere is affected no less than others by these developments. Nation states exhibit growing restrictions on their domestic sovereignty in the face of legal norms emanating from supranational institutions. This is not to assert that the nation state is becoming obsolete, either as an entity or as a tool of analysis; as Hirst and Thompson (1996) emphasize, only states represent entire populations, and they generally continue to be the exclusive site for the application and implementation of laws. Rather, it is the extent of the centrality of the nation state in the legal domain that has been put into question by recent developments. Sovereignty is also transformed to the extent that states cease to be the sole actors on the international stage. Now, an array of new legal subjects, from individual citizens, to non-governmental organizations (NGOs), international non-governmental organizations (INGOs) and multinational corporations (MNCs) participate *both* in an international "civil society", and also have formal rights of access to a range of supranational legal institutions (Steiner and Alston, 2000: ch 11).[25]

The evidence suggests that the modern conceptual frameworks of sovereignty on the one hand, and citizenship on the other, are inadequate to understand the complex, fragmented landscape of contemporary law. Only a brief overview of some of the vast empirical evidence of change will be attempted here. Accordingly, the focus on the various dimensions of the globalization and law will be confined to: 1) the sharing and pooling of sovereignty with supranational institutions which either have direct law-making power over nation states, or have great strategic influence on the domestic legislative agenda; 2) the broadening of the interpretive norms of domestic courts to incorporate supranational legal norms into domestic law; 3) a reinvigorated informal *lex mercatoria*; and 4) the emergence of a concept of citizenship de-coupled from the institutions of the nation state. Each of these developments reflects the growth of an historically unique phenomenon of "interlegality" (Santos, 1987; 1995), or "overlapping" systems of law (MacCormick, 1993: 18).

The Sharing and Pooling of Sovereignty

Two separate factors appear at present to drive nations to share or surrender voluntarily some of their sovereignty. First, the sense of social interdependency that Lowi (1987) identified as a characteristic underpinning of the welfare state has now shifted to the global level. This interdependency is evident on two levels. First, international co-operation is increasingly perceived as essential to further *national* objectives. One of the most significant of imperatives is economic, so that globalization is most evident in the economic sphere. The state cannot any longer pursue strategies for general welfare as if it were a purely domestic problem. It is compelled to behave like a participant in a market, crafting its policies to maximize profits in the global marketplace. The welfare state becomes a "competition state", contracting with other states and organizations for domestic advantages, and competing with them to secure investment on a global stage within and around supranational institutions (Cerny, 1990: ch 8). Once the nation state competed for territory to extend its power and wealth; it now competes, not for territory, but for wealth in order to enhance its power (Braithwaite and Drahos, 2000: 475). The transformation of the state is furthered by the increased interconnectedness provided by communication technologies. According to Ruggie, a new spatiality characterized by "flows" is replacing one of "places" (1993). Whilst it may be argued that the nation state and sovereignty remain unambiguously paramount given that there are no mechanisms of compulsion on states to force domestic compliance, it remains the case that the need to enter into such legal obligations is stronger than ever before, and it imposes almost insuperable obstacles to withdrawal.

Second, states are interdependent at the level of vulnerability. Where productive and technological capacities are so potent as to be able to cause, if unregulated, irreparable damage to environments at vast distances beyond the confines of national borders, states collectively face unprecedented dangers. And as transnational flows of capital, goods, people, finance, business and information increase at an exponential rate, and the boundaries of states become more difficult to guard, international co-operation becomes an essential component of regulatory strategy. The emergence of a global community of risks (Beck, 1992) impels states to participate in transnational law-making structures to secure effective regulation beyond its borders to protect domestic policies, resources and institutions. In turn regulatory spaces (Hancher and Moran, 1989) have been significantly reconfigured: the actors, the institutions, and the operative principles of economic and political activity no longer operate in a predominantly national space to further national objectives.

These factors combine to replace the traditional contractual basis of international law, which had the bilateral treaty as its typical instrument, with multilateral treaties so that "bilateralism is no longer appropriate as the paradigm model for the regulation of activities in the international arena" (Chinkin, 1993: 2). A typical feature of multilateralism is the creation of new institutions to deliberate, implement and monitor the treaties' principles and rules. Earlier mechanisms of incorporation of treaties into domestic law are unsuited to the operation of such institutions. One such model, exemplified by the United States, Germany and Italy, confers on treaties the same binding force as domestic statutes. In this case, they will override earlier statutes, but are capable of being overridden by later legislation. In a second example, demonstrated by the United Kingdom,

Australia, and some Scandinavian countries, domestic legislation is needed to give treaties the force of domestic law (Buergenthal, 1997: 213). Each of these models proves too unwieldy where multinational treaties create supranational institutions with autonomous legislative and judicial powers. In consequence, many states have opted for constitutional change to give treaties in general priority over domestic legislation enacted both before and after the treaty. A more recent trend has been to afford special status to human rights treaties, so that they acquire "a normative rank higher than that of other treaties and ordinary domestic law". In some cases those treaties have constitutional status (Buergenthal, 1997: 217). In this context, the evolving jurisprudence of supranational institutions becomes directly incorporated into domestic law.

The most advanced example of the creation of supranational institutions with law-making powers at the regional level is the European Union with its "pooling or a fusion within the communitarian normative order of some of the states' powers of legislation, adjudication and implementation of law in relation to a wide but restricted range of subjects" (MacCormick, 1993: 16). The legal authority of the European Court of Justice has grown to the extent that it is not unlike a supreme court enforcing a federal constitution (Schachter, 1997: 11). As a result of these developments it becomes impossible to determine a single location where sovereignty lies. By any traditional jurisprudential test, neither member states nor the Union is demonstrably sovereign. And to the extent that the production of legal norms binding citizens is no longer monopolized by modern nation states, a supranational, regional order "beyond the sovereign state" has emerged (MacCormick, 1993).

Outside the European Union, even where nations have not formally ceded sovereignty to a supranational constitutional body, or have not modified their constitutions to give treaties direct effect, increasing interdependency has contributed to a greater sense of obligation to incorporate supranational norms into domestic law. As these norms grow, the international component of domestic law increases. For instance, by 1994 Australia was a signatory to approximately 920 treaties, 235 of which were signed in the previous 4 years (Saunders, 1995: 150). In New Zealand by 1992, out of almost 600 statutes in force close to one quarter were enacted to comply with the nation's international obligations (Keith, 1995: 283). Because many such treaties create supranational institutions, the range of sources of influence over domestic legislation necessarily expands. When states enact legislation to regulate particular activities such as telecommunications, airline safety or protection of copyright, they are increasingly implementing standards that have already been certified and promulgated by international institutions over which they may have little influence, and may have little option but to comply. As Braithwaite and Drahos conclude:

> The upshot of the activities of international organizations is that today ... most nations' shipping laws are written at the IMO in London, air safety laws at ICAO in Montreal, food standards at the FAO in Rome, intellectual property laws in Geneva at the WTO/WIPO, banking laws by the G-10 in Basle ... and motor vehicle standards by the ECE in Geneva (2000: 488).[26]

These international institutions have become in a short time the forums where some of the most significant contemporary domestic lawmaking takes place. Moreover, the rules they draft do not merely reflect the will of nation states, they also incorporate recommendations from MNCs, NGOs, INGOs and professional associations.

Supranational developments propel the harmonization of municipal laws. Modern sovereignty contributed directly to the phenomenon of national legal uniqueness; as states pursued their own distinct domestic policies, they were unimpeded in framing regulation by reference to exclusively local conditions and requirements. Now, however, the network of supranational norms combines to obstruct tendencies toward differentiation and induce nation states to harmonize their laws. Where technological advances, such as the internet, allow a citizen in one country to commit crimes or civil wrongs in another, both countries have an interest in making the acts illegal. In a detailed survey of the recent reforms to the international regulation of banking, money laundering and copyright, Wiener (1999) found that the United States and countries of the EU had developed strikingly similar domestic legislation governing each of these domains.

Again, the role of international organizations is central to the process, with the World Intellectual Property Organization (WIPO) and the Basle Committee on Banking Regulation and Supervisory Practices providing the institutional mechanisms for intergovernmental exchange and ultimate agreement. Moreover, even though a "race to the bottom" might be expected in a more liberalized economic environment, the magnitude of shared risks has fostered "proactive" regulatory regimes, so that for the regulation of banking, for instance, "sound and prudential supervision" has been introduced (Wiener, 1999: 10). Insofar as the process of harmonization is concerned with the reform of municipal law, it demonstrates the centrality of municipal law in the mechanisms of international governance. The "globalization" of law is therefore represented by a change in the range of sources of national law, and the interpenetration of national and supranational legal orders.

Harmonization is not confined to legislative schemes to regulate novel global risks facilitated by technological change. In the case of consumer law the United Nations Guidelines for Consumer Protection (1985), though not binding as international law, have been highly influential in the reform of municipal laws on consumer rights (Harland, 1997). Traditional categories of private law may be similarly transformed, though to a lesser degree (Braithwaite and Drahos, 2000: ch 7). In an overview of American contract law, Farnsworth concluded that the internationalization of contract law represented one of the major changes to American contract law in the previous decade, both because the United States had ratified the United Nations Convention on Contracts for the International Sale of Goods, helping it to come into effect in 1988, and because judicial law-making had been influenced by international developments (1990: 227-230). In Europe, contract law displays growing evidence of harmonization with pressures as diverse as EU Directives in relation to consumer protection, the development of EC-sponsored Principles of European Contract Law, and in the case of the UK, the wider common law world, to introduce shared principles of contract law (Brownsword, 2000: ch 7).

Harmonization may also take place at the level of the practices of regulation. In North America, for example, anti-trust laws are being progressively co-regulated by virtue of joint activities between the Canadian and US regulatory agencies (Slaughter, 2000: 114). More fundamentally, harmonization is encouraged by the convergence of laws between the broad international trade law regimes of the EU, the General Agreement on Tariffs and Trade (GATT), the World Trade Organization (WTO) and the North American Free Trade Agreement (NAFTA) which "seem to be making increasingly similar offerings to the God of Free Trade" (Weiler, 2000: 3). In their voluminous study of international business regulation, Braithwaite and Drahos have identified harmonization as one of the most decisive factors contributing to the decline of national sovereignty (2000: 511-512).

The spread of legal norms that operate in a global dimension is uneven: the globalization of economic activity has developed at a far greater speed than other spheres, so that while the governance of globalized economic sectors is highly advanced, globalized political institutions remain underdeveloped. It follows that the tendency of supranational legal norms to permeate domestic law is more pronounced in the regulation of the economic sphere than any other. Moreover, the economic values that the legal rules express are neither pluralistic nor Keynesian, as demonstrated by the evolution of the GATT/WTO, and the practices of development banks such as the World Bank and International Monetary Fund. In general, these institutions combine to advance a free-market agenda, by pushing privatization and deregulatory reforms at the municipal level. For instance, a core principle underpinning GATT and the WTO is non-discrimination on the basis of nationality, so that corporations cannot be disadvantaged in law if they seek to trade in foreign countries.

This principle directly challenges the notion of nationally configured regulation in favour of local industry, a policy that was particularly fostered and enhanced by welfare states. According to one commentator "the WTO agreements can be linked to neo-liberal reforms. The aim is not just to ease conflicts between foreign and local legalities but to promote 'efficient regulation' around the world". The effect of this principle in the areas of intellectual property and services is that the WTO favours "the private property right" (Arup, 2000: 9-13). To the extent that the agreements not merely open national borders, but protect foreign businesses, they require reform of local laws in a manner "more market sympathetic than the old fashioned, nationally based legalities of industry-specific and foreign investment regulation" (Arup, 2000: 307). Domestic policies to deregulate and privatize therefore dovetail with the influence of supranational legal norms. A measure of the influence of the emergent supranational legal order is that it has played an important role in the fundamental restructure of the domestic law, and the formerly definitive command-and-control economy, of the People's Republic of China (Man, 1997).

Human Rights

One of the most significant contemporary transformative influences on the legal doctrines of municipal legal systems is international human rights law. Human rights principles originating in the international sphere date from the Universal Declaration of Human Rights (UDHR) in 1948, and the European Convention on Human Rights (ECHR) in 1950, to be followed by many others.[27] Human rights challenge the traditional, post-Westphalian framework of international law. They are not concerned with the international distribution of power between states, such as control over resources or people (airspace, the seas, alien populations) or reciprocal rights (sovereignty, diplomatic immunity). Rather, they address primarily the *internal* relations between citizens and state, and therefore directly threaten sovereignty (Steiner, 1991: 929). Human rights law can also be differentiated from other supranational norms by reference to the balance of forces that exert pressure on states to comply. For governments, there are fewer incentives to incorporate human rights norms into domestic law, or to make domestic practices of governance conform with them, in comparison with supranational economic law: human rights reduce states' powers, and often represent embarrassing findings of domestic injustice. Therefore, rather than governments, the prime movers in this development have tended to be alliances of citizens, NGOs and combinations of heterogeneous groupings within civil society, typically by means of alliances that cross and transcend national boundaries.

In an empirical study of the embedding of human rights in formerly authoritarian regimes, Risse, Ropp, and Sikkink (1999) deploy the concept of "world time" to explain the process. "World time" refers to the era of progressive international institutionalization of human rights and their dissemination into the domestic law of nation states from the mid-1970s onward by a complex network of political pressures from other states, citizens and NGOs at both the domestic and international levels. These diverse coalitions have successfully contributed to the enactment of specific human rights legislation not merely in former authoritarian states, but across the globe in the last couple of decades or so, to give effect to the broad principles contained in the UDHR and ECHR. The effect of this movement is a "growing robustness of the human rights regime itself in combination with the increasing strength of transnational advocacy coalitions" (Risse and Ropp, 1999: 264). As noted above, many countries have formally incorporated their provisions into their constitutions or have otherwise given them priority over domestic statutes (Buergenthal, 1997). In countries that have not directly incorporated human rights into domestic law, sovereignty prevails in theory to the extent that states may ignore adverse findings; but new practicalities and social forces push powerfully in the opposite direction. In Australia, for example, under the influence of international human rights instruments, many human rights principles are scattered across various legislative schemes (Kinley, 1998). As will be seen in more detail below, human rights have also been substantially advanced globally in the domain of judicial lawmaking.

Even where international instruments have not been incorporated into domestic law, and so do not give specific rights to individuals enforceable in any domestic court, nations may confer on their citizens a right of petition to a supranational body, such as United Nations Human Rights Committee under the International Covenant for Civil and Political Rights (ICCPR). These institutions can exert significant influence on domestic lawmakers. Adverse findings fuel domestic support for reform,[28] and they may also put pressure on governments to change their laws given the growing cultural and political legitimacy of international obligations, and the greater legitimacy afforded by citizens to the shared positive norms of the international community. Though the term "globalization" is more likely to evoke economic activity and corporations rather than law and legal systems, and the "compression of distance and the dissolution of borders that drives globalization has proved far more efficient at producing global markets than global justice", the spread of human rights norms and their incorporation into increasing numbers of the world's legal orders suggests that this image is too one-sided (Slaughter, 2000: 1103). At a more fundamental level, the sociological shift in favour of the normative domestic force of international obligations is evidence of a transformation in the *Grundnorm* (Kelsen, 1967) or "rule of recognition" (Hart, 1961) that underpins domestic law: when citizens, including judges and legislators, invoke supranational norms in legal and political argument, the map of legality, of what is "law, properly so called" (Austin, 1954 [1832]), has correspondingly broadened.

Though the first international human rights instruments are now over 50 years old, the global consolidation of human rights jurisprudence is a more recent phenomenon. It both coincides with, and is related to, the decline of the welfare state. The social solidarity characteristic of the legal structure of welfare states (Ewald, 1986) receives institutional expression in social rights and the universalism of social citizenship defined within a national framework. The principle of social solidarity also operates as a normative concept to criticize governments that fail to promote social justice. But as the welfare state weakens, along with the nation state that underpins it, social solidarity within a national framework is increasingly overshadowed by a sense of solidarity that transcends national borders. The new "imagined community" (Anderson, 1983) of international society displays a different normative principle: in the form of human rights discourse an "ethic of humanity" has become a dominant cultural norm (Heelas, 1996). This "postnational" development has an elective affinity with attitudes of scepticism about the welfare state, which see it as too unwieldy, bureaucratic and insensitive to individual needs and preferences, and to the interests of communities and groups. Human rights give expression to a very different universalism from that of welfare states. They propose standards that force states to align their laws with very general concepts of human dignity. Here is a universalism asserted *against the particularistic norms* of states.

A clear example of the progressive effects of this universalism lies in the influence of international human rights norms in the recognition and advancement of the rights of indigenous people in domestic law. Though international law has historically been no more generous than modern domestic law in its treatment of indigenous peoples (Barsh, 1994), the equality principles of the UDHR, the International Convention for the Elimination of All Forms of Racial Discrimination (CERD), and the ICCPR have each given an impetus to the enhancement of the legal rights of indigenous people.[29] The establishment of the UN Working Group on Indigenous Populations has provided an opportunity for indigenous peoples to organize collectively for the advancement of their rights, in ways impossible at the level of the nation state. More recent instruments assist to address the particular injustices suffered by indigenous communities, such as the International Labor Organization's Indigenous and Tribal Peoples

Convention, No. 169, agreements signed at the Earth Summit in Rio de Janeiro in 1992 and the Draft Declaration on the Rights of Indigenous Peoples (Nielsen and Martin, 1998). In the international sphere, the effect of these developments is that "indigenous peoples are gaining recognition of their legal personality as distinct societies with special collective rights" (Barsh, 1994: 34).

Domestic legal protection is achieved by the enactment of legislation recognizing traditional customs in relation to landholding, or by the incorporation of customary norms into the sentencing practices of domestic criminal courts. Traditional norms are also revitalized by enlisting traditional communities into the administration of justice (Blagg, 1997). In some instances, as in Australia, Canada and New Zealand, substantial legal powers in the form of local governance and management have been delegated by states to indigenous peoples (Nielsen and Martin, 1998). Constitutional transformation of this order is notably at odds with the modernizing zeal of the nation-building states that wrought destruction on traditional laws. Indeed, in their assertion of the revival of their traditional law, "the claims of indigenous peoples represent the most far-reaching challenge to the modern equation of nation, state and law" (Santos, 1995: 318) for the reason that the re-appearance of indigenous law contributes to the greater polycentricity of contemporary law and to the fragmentation of legal systems. The resulting mix of normative codes, where premodern custom co-exists with municipal law and supranational norms, represents an historically unique legal framework; it is described by Santos as a form of "neo-law" (1995: 325-326).

As we have seen in chapter 3, modern law is characterized by its "positivization": the active creation by the sovereign came to be the litmus test for law and legality (Luhmann, 1986: ch 4). At present, by contrast, "states have become rule-takers rather than rule-makers", with the rules of supranational organizations increasingly pervading and dominating domestic law (Braithwaite and Drahos, 2000: 3). In consequence, the novel legal superstructure of "global regulation" represents a third type of sovereignty: the sovereignty of global regimes "of other states' markets and other actors' regulatory standards" displaces both national and popular sovereignty (Braithwaite and Drahos, 2000: ch 26). The gradual extension and infusion of supranational norms into domestic law is no less evident in the sphere of judicial law-making.

Globalized Legal Hermeneutics

In separating the functions of adjudication and legislation, modern law requires a distinctive hermeneutics for finding and interpreting law. The various modern formulations of interpretive principles, from Coke's "artificial reason" (1642) to Nonet and Selznick's "sovereignty of purpose" (1978), fit neatly with national sovereignty: on the one hand they presuppose a unitary sovereign will, and on the other hand notions of community, society or public interest, ultimately grounded in the nation state, as the exclusive sources of interpretive guidance. Those formulations were buttressed in jurisdictions that required norms contained in international treaties to be formally incorporated into municipal law by legislation before they could bind domestic courts and citizens.

Over the last couple of decades or so, there has been a marked growth in the preparedness of judges to look beyond the interpretive rules provided by domestic positive law. The normative horizons of judges in domestic courts are widening to include laws of supranational rather than exclusively national origin. Rights and principles contained in supranational instruments are increasingly relied on by judges to resolve interpretive difficulties in domestic law in cases where those instruments have not been formally incorporated by legislation. Examples of the process abound in contemporary legal systems as international legal discourse seeps into both domestic law and politics.[30] The transformation is occurring not merely in nations such as the member states of the European Union, but is affecting countries that are not part of a supranational constitutional system. For example, in New Zealand there is now wide judicial support for the principle that international obligations are a legitimate influence on the development of the common law (Richardson, 1995: 65). In Australia, the practice is already entrenched, so that hardly any branch of the law has remained unaffected (Kinley, 1998). Even in the United States, where a culture of resistance to international norms is more widespread than in many jurisdictions (Buergenthal, 1997), a recent frequency of reference to international norms suggests an incipient "judicial globalization" (Slaughter, 2000).[31]

The clearest example of this process lies in the growing influence on domestic judicial reasoning of international human rights norms contained in international treaties. In common law jurisdictions, for instance, norms emanating from supranational sources infiltrate domestic law "vertically" by offering interpretive guidance in five separate areas: first, in the resolution of ambiguities in statutes; second, in the development of the common law and equity, particularly where principles are uncertain; third, in the review of the exercise of executive discretion; fourth, in the general exercise of judicial discretion; and fifth, in the development of public policy (Cunningham, 1994: 553). The effects of this modification of judicial reasoning practices are exemplified in the United Kingdom where Murray Hunt (1997) has charted in great detail the domestic influence of international human rights law. He identified 473 cases in English courts where reference has been made by judges to the European Convention on

Human Rights and decisions of the European Court of Human Rights (ECHR) from 1953, when the Convention was ratified by the United Kingdom, to the end of 1996. He also examined the use by English courts of human rights provisions in other international human rights instruments that had until that time remained unincorporated into domestic law.[32] A measure of the exponential nature of the increase in influence is suggested by the fact that the first substantive reference did not occur until 1973, and that more than half of the total number had been decided in the last five years of the period under examination.

The impact that these norms have on judicial decision-making may operate quite independently of the legislative process. For instance, Hunt's study revealed that the enactment of the European Communities Act 1972 had no significant impact on the judicial use of the Convention's provisions (1997: ch 3). It seems therefore that the shift in interpretive norms evidenced in the judicial sphere represents a separate mechanism for the globalization of law. Of course, this process is not a simple and straightforward one. Judges remain bound by national interpretive principles, and so must proceed gradually when making use of international norms, and some judges remain resolutely opposed to any such change. The result, as Hunt points out in the English context, can be a confused and sometimes contradictory vocabulary of the old and the new, where it may be difficult to determine the precise impact of extraterritorial laws. But in general, developments of this nature demonstrate the complexity of the interpretive and normative interdependence of national and international institutions, and the overall direction they are taking.

The influence of the ECHR does not stop at the territorial boundaries of the over 40 nations that have already ratified the Convention. The Court's decisions have influenced the reasoning and the interpretive norms of both the Inter-American Court of Human Rights, and the United Nations Human Rights Committee (Merrills, 1993: ch 1), as well as the constitutional courts of other nations. Moreover, where states enact domestic human rights legislation, they open another door for the entry of international human rights norms, given the established jurisprudence on the Convention. In consequence the Court has been described as "becoming a sort of world court for human rights" (Attanasio, 1995: 16). The proliferation of supranational judicial tribunals sustains and promotes the consolidation of extraterritorial jurisprudence. The incremental establishment of an international criminal jurisdiction as represented by the ad hoc Rwanda and Yugoslav Tribunals by the United Nations, as well as the new International Criminal Court reflect the general trend.

As in other developments captured by the term globalization, common factors explain how supranational norms permeate national borders in the sphere of judicial reasoning. The generally burgeoning commerce across national borders extends to lawyers and judges. In consequence there are increasing instances of the "horizontal" sharing of legal principles and values, which in turn may come to influence domestic practice. Constitutional "cross-fertilization" provides an example of this practice (Choudhry, 1999; Slaughter, 2000: 1116). While the exchange of laws has always been a feature within families of legal systems, especially between imperialist powers and their colonies, the present patterns of interchange are different. Starting in the 1990s, Choudhry notes an increasing propensity on the part of constitutional courts in various countries to refer to judgments in other jurisdictions. This tendency is partly explained by the appearance of nascent democratic polities after the fall of former communist regimes as their legislatures adopt constitutions in the liberal mould, but the process is a much broader one. It encompasses the notion that constitutionalism is a concept that stands above national boundaries so that it becomes possible to talk of "the rise of world constitutionalism" (Ackerman, 1997).

Transnational judicial consensus as expressed in instruments that enshrine fundamental principles and desirable goals affirm this development. In 1988, the Bangalore Principles concerning the domestic application of international human rights norms were promulgated by a number of appellate judges from many common law jurisdictions. They uphold the importance of human rights principles in guiding judicial interpretation in cases concerning fundamental human rights and freedoms, especially where local laws are "uncertain or incomplete" (1988). In the Western Hemisphere, the Organization of the Supreme Courts of the Americas has been established, and in 1995 delegates from 25 countries approved a Charter affirming a commitment to the rule of law and judicial independence (Slaughter, 2000: 1120). Weak as such supranational norms may be when set alongside traditional forms of law, they nonetheless exert an historically unique influence over domestic law, and foster a general judicial autonomy from governments. Perhaps their greatest significance lies in this unique transnational expression of judicial consensus about human rights norms.

As the growing face to face contact between judges from different jurisdictions becomes institutionalized in the form of "summits", conferences, and less formal intercourse, judges no longer see themselves "only as servants of a particular government or polity, but as fellow professionals in a profession that transcends national borders" (Slaughter, 2000: 1124). A related development is a "judicial comity" that crosses national boundaries. As economic activity becomes fragmented across many jurisdictions, so do the possible legal norms governing disputes. Opportunities for forum shopping are augmented exponentially. One response to this problem is greater transnational judicial co-operation and dialogue. It is not so much expressed as deference to foreign law, but to foreign courts as courts, rather than as agents of another state, and a general predisposition to international judicial co-operation in the resolution of disputes that straddle jurisdictions (Slaughter, 2000: 1112-1116).

A direct consequence of such evolution is that it seems increasingly inappropriate to use the traditional dichotomy between monism (international and municipal law form part of the same system) and dualism (that they are separate systems) to understand the domestic relevance of international norms (Hunt, 1997: ch 1). Grounded as these notions are in the modern positivist vocabulary of national sovereignty they cannot capture the vastly more complex processes of reception of international norms by domestic courts. The recent changes also pose serious problems for "modern" understandings of judicial reasoning at both the level of prescription and description, and in particular, the debate about judicial creativity and activism fuelled by the legal reforms of the welfare state. Domestic law no longer functions exclusively by reference to home-grown rules or background principles located in the interstices of a particular jurisdiction when deciding cases where the law is unclear or inconsistent. Rather, reliance on supranational norms, either derived from a regional instrument such as the ECHR, or a global instrument such as the UDHR or ICCPR is growing rapidly. In the present context, the store of the community's principles, domestic public policy, the public interest, or legislative purposes do not exhaust the resources available to judges. They are increasingly likely to be overshadowed by recourse to norms of extraterritorial origins.

The notion of "community", so securely centred in some forms of modern legal theory (Dworkin, 1986; Cotterrell, 1995), starts to look increasingly unreliable, both normatively and descriptively, in a world of overlapping, and provisional, "communities". Surely, it can no longer be enough for Dworkin's fictional judge, Hercules, to look to the background principles of a particular community's jurisprudence to resolve interpretive difficulties in "hard cases" (1977). Both Nonet and Selznick's recommendation of the "sovereignty of purpose" (1978), and Hart's preference for judges to refer to public policy in cases where meanings are "penumbral" or unclear (1961) seem equally unsuited to capture recent developments, or insufficient to advise on best practice. In keeping with the times, Herculean activity may require a different set of reference points. This question will be explored further in the final chapter.

This general change in interpretive practices parallels the general postmodern drift towards spatial rather than temporal modes of experience where the "spaces of very different worlds seem to collapse upon each other" (Harvey, 1989: 301). Modern law was uniquely confined within the territorial boundaries of the nation-state. Within that framework the spatiality of law was rendered unproblematic: its sphere of enforceability ended at national borders. The temporal dimension of judicial interpretation was expressed in the requirement that judges look to the past for normative guidance. More controversially, welfare state reforms led to calls that judges more openly embrace purpose and policy in their reasoning, and so look forward to the different consequences of various interpretations, or try to second-guess what legislatures were purporting to do. Regardless of temporal perspective, interpretation was determined by reference to the norms of a particular polity.

In contrast, the impact of recent supranational developments is to provide a different set of reference points by transforming the temporal and spatial co-ordinates within which interpretation takes place. In this environment, neither the weight of the past, nor the requirements of the future, play as important a role in the binding force of law. Spatiality has come to be a far more relevant co-ordinate, so as to raise very different problems of how to integrate and reconcile norms that originate out of very different institutional mechanisms. The contrast with the debates around judicial activism in the welfare state is striking in another respect: where judges adopt a purposive approach to interpretation, or look to policy, legal reasoning takes on a more political or economic character (Unger, 1976: 199-200). In the case of human rights norms, however, because they are ultimately grounded in the essential dignity of human beings, legal reasoning veers towards moral reasoning, or natural law. And given the generality of the relevant norms, the new interpretive approaches are no less capable of avoiding the charge of allowing judges too much flexibility than the recourse to policy or purpose. A related development is that a more highly differentiated judicial discourse appears, where judicial reasoning comes to be influenced by a range of authoritative materials more diversified than ever, so contributing to the disintegration of national law (Wilhelmsson, 1995).

Global Informal Law

With the recent exponential increase in international commerce, a reinvigorated international *lex mercatoria* has appeared. *Lex mercatoria* is distinctive by virtue of its being a form of supranational law that does not derive from international institutions or treaties created by nations. Originating in the trade usages of medieval merchants, it has come to assume a new importance with the recent rapid expansion of international commerce. This new corpus of law is not "custom" in the sense of an embedded practice over time, as in the case of the old *lex mercatoria*; rather it derives from newly constructed cultural practices attendant on the particularities of contemporary transnational trade. Moreover, it is deliberately created and codified in model laws by authoritative agencies such as the International Chamber of Commerce.

The primary site for the new *lex mercatoria* is international commercial arbitration. International commercial arbitration is distinctive for its independence from the law of municipal legal systems. Its emergence reflects the construction of a novel transnational legal order, where a whole new class of legal practitioners, drawn mainly from large international law firms ("technocrats"), have come to dominate a field that has spread across the globe (Dezalay and Garth, 1996). There has been a dramatic proliferation of agencies that specialize in this type of work, and large increases in caseloads, so that for instance, by 1998 there were over 100,000 commercial contracts in China that specified the Chamber of Commerce in Stockholm as arbitrator (Banakar, 1998: 347). Significantly, another factor identified as generating the demand for this type of dispute processing is "the interventionism of welfare states", so that this layer of legality also represents an attempt to undo the regulatory strategies of states seeking to control commercial dealings more restrictively (Dezalay and Garth, 1996). In consequence, "the ideal of social law has been killed off, replaced by the *lex mercatoria*: the transnational law of market relations" (Dezalay, 1990: 280). Given its supranational and domestic origins, it reflects both the "upward" and "downward" contraction of the contemporary nation state.

International commercial arbitration is another type of private dispute resolution. It demonstrates many of the characteristics of ADR at the domestic level, and is supported by many of the same principles. The cost of arbitration is borne by the parties to the dispute, and the procedures and substantive rules are the subject of private agreement. Unlike proceedings in courts, resolution is private, so unwanted publicity is avoided. It also operates in closer "proximity" to the dispute: justice is delivered more quickly than formal court procedures allow, thus reducing the time between alleged breach and resolution; and it embraces principles that are both closer to the parties, and to the context of the dispute. Importantly, the norms governing disputes are not those of state-based law, and so they have a legal status that is autonomous from national legal systems. Procedurally and substantively the regime is essentially one of private norm-creation.

A related feature of this new law is that, as an autonomous legal subculture, its legitimacy derives from sources beyond formal law. Legitimacy does not reside in its rational character, or that it is the expression of popular will. Instead, legitimation is to be found in its reflexivity, that is, its capacity to advance the principle that the subsystem should generate the substantive norms to regulate itself (Banakar, 1998: 361). But this particular type of "reflexive law" is relatively impervious to questions of inequality and redistribution. The substantive justice incorporated into domestic contract law by welfare states has a very weak footing in the international commercial arena, so that protections of weaker parties provided by local law are substantially reduced within the law of international trade (Banakar, 1998: 381). The unfolding jurisprudence of this supranational legal regime is strikingly consistent with the renaissance of freedom of contract at the local level.

As we have seen in the previous chapter, Gunther Teubner sees in the new *lex mercatoria* the key to "global law without a state" (1997). This form of law is resolutely at odds with the positive law of states. In particular, it is deterritorialized, floating above and beyond states; its sources are pluralistic, located in a range of international institutions and practices; it has autonomy from states; and it lacks the unity of national law, and necessarily so, given the predominant function of regulating flexible, volatile and fragmented domains (Teubner, 1997: ch 1). This autonomy means that it is self-validating. By implication, the use of the essentially modern concept of a hierarchy of norms to understand law must now give way to the notion of the "heterarchy of legal discourses" (1997: 14). Because global law is not created by global political institutions but by the institutions of civil society, Teubner sees that global law will develop "mainly from the peripheries, not from the political centres of nation states and international institutions" (1997: 7). Teubner's overview undoubtedly captures the essential sociological features of *lex mercatoria*, but he overplays the extent of the significance of *lex mercatoria* in the present reconfigured legal landscape. The importance of this "living law" is overshadowed by the spread of *formal* legal globalization, enforced and developed by states and supranational *institutions*. Nonetheless, Teubner makes a valuable point about the pluralistic nature of the transnational legal order in his identification of an historically innovative form of non-state law creation.

Global Citizenship

Recent developments have added an international dimension to the bundle of entitlements traditionally considered to constitute citizenship. Individuals and organizations have increasing layers of legal rights that neither have their origin in the positive law of sovereign nation states, nor are exclusively exercisable before municipal courts. This phenomenon is intimately related to the corrosion of sovereignty: as states cease to be the sole source of legal rights, citizenship – "by definition national" (Marshall, 1963: 72) – is no longer monopolized by the laws of nation states. A separate development concerns rights of participation beyond the confines of national borders. In modern law, only nation states could be legal subjects, or bearers of rights, in the international sphere. At the present time, however, these rights are being institutionally decoupled from nation states.

Again, the most advanced example of the process whereby citizens have legal rights derived from supranational institutions is in the European Union where each of the waves of citizenship typical of the emergence of the modern state have been instituted, if in different sequences, and to lesser degrees, within the Union's legal structure. A civil citizenship affording individuals market freedoms such as freedom of movement, and rights to work in other member states has gradually been elaborated and extended to all citizens. By Article 8 of the Treaty of the European Union, citizens of member countries are also citizens of Europe. European citizenship has a political form in the rights of all citizens of member states to vote for representatives to the European Parliament. Citizenship is also enhanced by rights of petition to the European Court of Justice, and in the case of human rights, to the European Court of Human Rights. But because the European Community and Union is not a state, when this form of citizenship is compared with the rights commonly associated with its domestic counterpart, it "is doubtless a 'thin' citizenship ... [which] depends on pre-existing statehood and membership of the Union only via the member states" (MacCormick, 1997: 342).

Comparable, if embryonic, versions of such rights to petition international adjudicative bodies, and rights of participation of citizens in international forums, have appeared beyond the European Union. International human rights law has added to supranational citizenship, as in the case where a country accepts international obligations, and the right of individual petition, to the United Nations Human Rights Committee (UNHRC) under the ICCPR. Moreover, institutions such as the UNHRC or the ECHR may give standing to those who fall outside the formal state-based definition of citizens, and who therefore could not claim automatic entitlement to the rights and benefits afforded by nation states. Refugees, migrants, ethnic minorities, and indigenous communities have come to be afforded increasing protection in the form of human rights in circumstances where the domestic law of particular nations has sought to withhold and reduce rights. So, in the United Kingdom, Hunt's assessment of the development of human rights discourse found that complaints by prisoners and immigrants accounted for a third of all cases where human rights norms were cited (Hunt, 1997).

New legal subjects, distinct from individual citizens, appear in the form of NGOs, international non-governmental organizations (INGOs) and multinational corporations (MNCs) in the growing evolution of an international "civil society" (Otto, 1996). For instance, the legal framework of the UN's Economic and Social Council (ECOSOC) allows for the participation of NGOs in its proceedings. And a plethora of NGOs participate in "secondary international law", that is, the international law implemented by INGOs. Many such organizations provide for NGOs to participate in decision-making processes. And in the absence of global compliance mechanisms, NGOs play a significant role in the enforcement of international obligations, most notably in environmental law (Hobe, 1997: 202-207). In the domain of business regulation, a broad array of actors operates on the supranational stage in addition to the above organizations. As well as individual states and organizations of states, they can be divided into corporations, national and international business associations, individuals and various "epistemic communities", that is, collections of knowledge-based experts with shared world-views (Braithwaite and Drahos, 2000: 501). This plurality of participants contributes both to the strengthening of international institutions and to the weakening of national sovereignty. But it would be a mistake to see the diminution of national sovereignty simply as a general loss of *popular* sovereignty over markets and corporate power. Many global institutions have increased the transparency of policy-making when compared to previous national regimes, and so have enhanced, if only to a limited degree, the rights of citizens. And where mass publics can fuel alliances with NGOs and some nation states, market power can be significantly curtailed (Braithwaite and Drahos, 2000: ch 26).

A striking example of the changed notions of citizenship in law is the new status afforded indigenous peoples. As noted in chapter 3, modern law was characterized by the destruction of indigenous, premodern forms of law, a phenomenon not impeded but furthered by emergent, modernizing welfare states. But now, according to Barsh (1994), indigenous peoples have moved from being "objects" to "subjects" in international law as the unfolding jurisprudence and practice of international institutions allow them a place to participate, and so assume a distinct legal personality. Starting with the UN Working Group on Indigenous Populations established in 1982, indigenous peoples "have gained recognition of their collective legal status in the decisions and reports of the UN treaty bodies, but have gained direct access to aid programs and a greater role in UN decisionmaking" (1994: 58). To be sure, such human rights-driven developments often merely reflect domestic legal change; but in many instances they have advanced where the domestic demands of nation states attempt to curtail dramatically rights of those determined as outsiders. In the cultural and ethnic sphere, an analogous process of change is reflected in the resurgence of particularisms below the level of, and antagonistic to, the modern nation state (Schachter, 1997: 12).

These changes supplement and enhance the citizen's former exclusively national package of rights and duties. A no less significant consequence of the emergent transnational citizenship is the creation of new obligations that bind citizens extraterritorially. If citizenship is measured by the extent to which state power is legally restrained where the rights of individual members of a polity are infringed, the waning of sovereign immunity as demonstrated in the appearance of ad hoc War Crimes Tribunals, and the International Criminal Court significantly enlarges and vindicates citizenship rights. The Pinochet and Milosevic cases are perhaps the most glaring examples of how the spread of human rights law imposes extraterritorial fetters on those who have perpetrated gross violations of the entitlements that citizenship brings (Slaughter, 2000: 1123).

The supranational evolution of citizenship rights appears to parallel the historical development of citizenship within modern states: civil and political rights have assumed not only temporal priority over "social citizenship", but have gained a much more secure institutional foothold than social rights. In Europe, for instance, the social citizenship characteristic of the modern welfare state may be based on principles at odds with the unfolding polity of the integrated European Community. Thus, high levels of civil rights (in the form of rights of movement, contract) supported by human rights (such as anti-discrimination, privacy, procedural fairness) are accompanied by low levels of political rights, and even lower levels of social rights, particularly in the industrial context. In a political environment where a former national corporatism is replaced by transnational pluralism, it may be that the modern European welfare state is heading in the direction of a pre-Second World War liberal state with substantially curtailed entitlements for citizens. Moreover, international human rights jurisprudence, both in the European context and beyond, has progressed nothing like as far in the social dimension as it has in the sphere of civil rights. Accordingly, a supranational social citizenship appears to be an improbable development in the foreseeable future, though as Santos notes, notions of the common heritage of mankind as expressed in international treaties provide pointers to a possibly more redistributive future regime (1995: 365-373).

Outside the European context, the recent attenuation of social entitlements within the package of citizenship rights domestically have remained largely untouched by the general legal transformations at the supranational level; indeed, both spheres reflect and confirm that broader trend. It demonstrates the unevenness of the contribution of international norms to domestic law. Great emphasis has been placed on trade liberalization, property rights and the free movement of capital, while comparatively few advances have been made in social rights; strategies for economic redistribution and welfare rights have been feeble; and the regulation of minimum standards and conditions of work has been weakened. As Wedderburn (1994: s 14) shows, supranational instruments from European Community law to the ILO Conventions have generated relatively little jurisprudence to provide minimal protection to workers in a changed context where multinational corporations can readily shift plant to jurisdictions with less stringent legal obligations. The collectivist principles that underpin the freedom of association in the ILO Conventions are inevitably at odds with the more liberal labour markets that appear domestically (MacDermott, 1998). Moreover, the "denationalizing of urban space" which attends globalization starkly demonstrates the profound inequalities that result: it brings together global capital and immigrant workforces in the world's major cities under a new legal regime that underpins a distinct imbalance of legal rights and social power (Sassen: 1998: ch 1).

The new configuration represents a very different clash of rights from that which typifies welfare states: the social rights formerly pitted against political and civil rights (Marshall, 1963; Bowles and Gintis, 1986) have come to be overshadowed by a revitalized set of civil (economic) rights outstripping human, political and social rights in both the domestic and supranational domains. One result of this unequal contest is that the redistributive gains achieved by the establishment of universal social citizenship in the welfare state are gradually and systematically reversed. Furthermore, as privatization shrinks the domestic foundation of "public goods" upon which the welfare state was erected, institutions such as global communications and transport networks, stock exchanges and dispute-settlement institutions, have become the new "public goods" required by global capitalism and transnational investment and trade (Schachter, 1997: 10-11). They reflect the changed order of property rights in the reconfiguration of the welfare and nation state, where public goods were predominantly associated with national ownership for the furtherance of national objectives and policies within a redistributive framework. Perhaps this picture suggests a tentative conclusion about the present dynamic of the contemporary globalization of law, even in its more advanced European regional version, namely, that

> the removal of barriers to cross-border trade and mobility is less threatening to national sovereignty and less demanding of democratic legitimation than the creation and enforcement of rights and obligations of citizenship, especially the modification of property rights and institutionalization of social rights to a minimum level of subsistence (Streeck, 1996: 67).

A legal order that places a high value on substantive equality and meaningful popular participation in governance requires a more secure institutionalization of political and social rights. Many critics have therefore argued compellingly for a greater accessibility of supranational institutions, and wider forms of participation in their proceedings. This question of reform will be pursued in chapter 7.

The unfolding of a supranational dimension to rights has important consequences for conceptualizing the legal subject. Recent developments at the domestic level noted above have left the legal subject fragmented in ways that parallel the characteristic "disintegration" of contemporary societies, so that the rights of the subject are difficult to square with the modern concept of citizenship. The subject is no longer the abstract rights-bearing subject of early modernity, nor the more complex bearer of social and civil rights in the welfare state. In addition to changes at the domestic level, now the juridical subject is also a bearer of emergent rights exercisable in the supranational domain. The appearance of this more complex bundle of rights raises the question of its impact on the rule of law.

Globalization and the Rule of Law

The concerns of many of the theorists of law in the welfare state about the impact of change on the rule of law must now address a wholly different set of influences. The convulsive changes ushered in by globalization have important and novel effects on the rule of law. One of the most important of these influences is the appearance of international human rights law. If one of the requirements of the rule of law is taken to be that states must be subject to law in their dealings with citizens, it necessarily overlaps with human rights discourse. Human rights are primarily rights enforceable *against* governments to preserve human dignity and autonomy, so that where they become domestically entrenched they operate to confirm the rule of law. To the extent that they extend to all citizens, formerly marginalized minorities may be given rights absent from domestic law. The decline of the doctrine of sovereign immunity noted above also furthers the rule of law by bringing dictators and ruthless officials to account. A general assessment of the European experience with the ECHR might plausibly suggest that as nations lose sovereignty in this process, both human rights and rule of law make advances in Europe (Attanasio, 1995: 16).

The recent emergence of the domestic use by judges of international human rights norms reflects a greater measure of judicial independence, and therefore autonomy of law from politics. This is another core element of the rule of law. The formation by judges of global and regional networks and institutional arrangements fosters allegiances that cut across any sense of uncritical adherence to domestic political objectives, and so provides additional support for an independent judiciary. A global constitutionalism, and the spread of constitutions along liberal lines, appears to be advancing this process (Ackerman, 1997; Slaughter, 2000). Furthermore, the "good governance" conditionality increasingly imposed on developing nations from state and non-state aid donors and development banks (Risse et al., 1999: ch 1) encourages some of the basic requirements of the rule of law such as an independent judiciary, and transparency of governmental decision-making.

One optimistic line of thought suggests that globalization will encourage the deepening of the rule of law, and its spread across more nations as market relations come to dominate "underdeveloped" economies (Jones, 1994). As Max Weber noted, market relations require stable, predictable rules, for which autonomy of law from politics is a necessary if not sufficient condition. As Western influences such as economic liberalism increase, local practices and norms could be expected increasingly to give way to Western legal institutions. Yet the global spread of the market economic model around the globe has not produced the kind of uniform legal changes anticipated by the Weberian thesis. Advanced capitalism has penetrated, and in some cases even taken over, some Asian and East European economies, but it has not yet corroded the informal and authoritarian nature of those societies, nor appears likely to do so in the foreseeable future (Jones, 1994; Krygier and Czarnota, 1999). Those societies demonstrate that the relationship between aspects of the rule of law and the development of market economies is a highly contingent one: markets exist alongside legal systems that are neither autonomous nor generate rules of general applicability (Jones, 1994: 210-216).

Global law also erodes the rule of law in at least two respects. The first relates to the vagueness of the standards that govern the operations of many supranational institutions. Much international *lex mercatoria*, as applied in international commercial arbitration, is a type of informal law, and so suffers from the defects of ADR in the domestic sphere: its norms are of a very general nature, any rulings are secret and procedure is flexible (Scheuerman, 1999: 6-8). Given the homogeneity of participants (MNCs and their advisers) it is hard to imagine that any meaningful consideration of the public interest features in proceedings or rulings. These concerns appear to be supported by Braithwaite and Drahos' empirical study of the norms that underpin international business regulation. They describe them as more in the nature of Dworkinian "principles" that pull in a particular direction rather than legal rules that apply to specific sets of facts in an all-or-nothing fashion (2000: ch 26). This vagueness tends to work to the advantage of the most powerful. A legal structure with indeterminate norms leads to minimal and ineffective regulation, and widespread evasion. In the context of international business taxation, for example, for MNCs, unlike private citizens, the payment of taxes is in many countries almost optional (Picciotto, 1992). If an element of the rule of law is to bring all private and public power under law, then the vast powers of MNCs are in need of restraint when at the present time they surpass all but the largest nation states to make up the majority of the world's largest economic entities (Anderson and Cavanagh, 1996). Framed by the most powerful and affluent, unaccountable to the most vulnerable, it is hard to see in this legal framework much evidence of "responsive" law.

Second, recent changes also raise important and novel philosophical questions about the nature of the judicial role, and the general constitutional balance within the domestic separation of powers. Given the broad generality of the norms contained in international human rights instruments, do they confer too much (undemocratic) power on domestic judges? Should international human rights norms have special normative force, and therefore be more binding than other supranational norms? Or do judges owe a special loyalty to local laws even in the case of human rights norms? These are questions too large to be addressed in this selective snapshot of recent change, but they pose dilemmas not easily resolved by traditional theories of judicial reasoning, and so suggest the need for new conceptual frameworks. One objection is that these norms are all too malleable, affording broad scope for ideologies or politics to fill out their meaning. On the other hand, the advance of human rights norms domestically may be both a consistent and principled implementation of the democratic sovereign will, as expressed both in the original ratification of international human rights instruments and their incorporation into domestic law, as well as with the rule of law. They may also more adequately express fundamental common law principles, and give effect to international obligations to protect the rights of vulnerable minorities (Hunt, 1997; Kirby, 1995: 88-92).

Conclusion

Towards the end of *Law in Modern Society* Roberto Unger gloomily described the impact of the welfare state on the modern legal ideals of generality and autonomy. It had left "the entire conception of legality peculiarly associated with modern European history ... shaken and perhaps mortally wounded" (1976: 220). The necessarily impressionistic and selective overview of some of the more significant recent legal changes advanced in this chapter indicates that the legality identified by Unger has been substantially transformed, in response both to internal and external pressures, and in largely unforeseeable ways. The far-reaching transformations that have occurred in the last couple of decades are of comparable magnitude to those which accompanied the rise of the welfare state, and demonstrate that a new legal paradigm, and, by implication, an entirely new "conception of legality", has emerged to overshadow the legal infrastructure of the welfare state. Those changes are summarized in the fifth column of Table 5.1 below, by way of a contrast with the core elements of feudal, modern and late modern law, as outlined in chapter 3.

Table 5.1 Paradigms of law

	Premodern-Feudal	*Modernity-Liberal*	*Late Modernity-Welfare State*	*Postmodernity*
Structural principle of society	Stratificatory differentiation	Functional differentiation	Organized differentiation	Disorganized hyper-/de-differentiation
Form of state	Repressive Disaggregated	1 Liberal 2 *Rechtsstaat* 3 Democratic*	Expanding welfare state	Contracting welfare state
Sources of law	Tradition Custom Religion	National Sovereign	Interventionist National Sovereign	Supranational National Local
Legal system	Decentred Diffuse	Monocentric	Highly monocentric	Polycentric
Legal subject	Particularized	Abstract	Materialized Rights-based	Complex Dematerialized Interests-based
Citizenship	----	1 Civil 2 Political	Social	Consumer Conditional Supranational
Regulatory form	Traditional Religious Communal	Free market	Command and control regulation Nationalization	Deregulation Coregulation Privatization
Legal rationality	Customary Substantive	Formal Rational	Purposive Substantive Policy-driven	Managerialist Polyphonic Hybridized
Ideal of justice	Tradition Custom	Formality	Redistributive Substantive	Human rights
Legal temporality	Retrospective	Fragmented by separation of powers	Prospective	Spatialized Accelerated
Dominant legal philosophy	Natural law	Legal positivism	Soft positivism Legal realism	Human rights Normative legal pluralism

* These represent different phases of development (Habermas, 1986; cf Marshall, 1963).

This is not to argue that the present legal environment is a wholly different system in form and function from its modern predecessor. The less ambitious claim is that it presently exhibits symptoms indicating that many of the truly modern features of law are in the process of being transformed in a manner that mirrors the broader postmodernization of contemporary advanced societies. In law, no less than in other spheres, the shift can be identified as having its origins in the 1970s. Taken together, these sociological changes offer strong evidence to suggest that it is by now appropriate to talk about *both* postmodern law as well as postmodern commentaries *on* law (cf Post, 1992: 396).

If the development of modern law can be measured by a pervasive centripetality of normative ordering, present indicators point in the opposite direction. A postmodern centrifugality is increasingly evident at the level of norm-production and adjudication. Almost any region of municipal law could yield evidence of the general pattern of change by means of which global influences from harmonization treaties to human rights norms play their part, but no less than domestic developments that provide for the diversification of sources of norms. Influences flow in the opposite direction with the same intensity: domestic developments sway the activities of supranational institutions where a localism is "globalized" (Santos, 1995: ch 4), as in the case where a dominant (local) industry's safety standards commonly become the global legal norm (Braithwaite and Drahos, 2000: ch 26). As the multiple sources of norms both at the local and global level combine to challenge the dominance of national law, it is possible to register not so much the globalization, but a possible "glocalization" (Robertson, 1995) of law, where local, national and global norms operate in overlapping or mutually exclusive fashion.

Two brief examples of broad overviews of change within particular domains of law may suffice to indicate how much distance separates the regulatory forms of the welfare state from the complexity of the new structures of governance. In the area of private law, Dewar notes a process of "fragmentation" of Australian family law, where "norm-creation is pushed 'down' to the parties through the encouragement of private contracting, so also is it being imposed from 'above' domestic legislatures by human rights norms" (2000: 72). In public law, utilities once exclusively regulated by national laws, and often nationalized, expressed the redistributive politics of the welfare state: universal social rights were reflected in cross-subsidized provision and extensive community service obligations, and in the same stroke, citizenship rights were amplified. By contrast, now utilities are privatized, governed by market principles, fragmented within national spaces, and often in foreign ownership. Specifically in the case of the EU, an additional layer of supranational regulation is imposed on their operations (Graham, 2000). In aggregate, the combined impact of the widespread shift to ADR, deregulation and privatization, at least in some of their manifestations, have no less an influence on the "conception of legality" than welfare state reforms did, but in very uneven fashion. In equal measure, the nation and welfare state are now radically different from the "corporate state" (Unger, 1976: 200), or "entrepreneurial state" (Friedmann, 1971: 39) of only a generation ago.

As law is reconfigured the problem of justice is equally transformed. The marketized systems by which social spheres are increasingly regulated are purged of "social" obligations to significant degrees, and in general they have not yet been moderated by the emergent supranational citizenship. In this context, the conceptual vocabulary of human rights may provide not merely the critical tools for assessing the appropriate levels of protection to the poor and disadvantaged, but also ultimately the legal mechanisms for affording them. At the same time, global developments seem to offer highly uneven legal benefits: the expansion of human rights may have some successes in advancing equality and the rule of law, but trade and financial deregulation has conferred greater economic rights on the already wealthy and powerful. As with the first waves of citizenship rights at the domestic level, civil (property) rights linked to the operation of free markets seem to dwarf other rights in the new constellation. And the proliferation of novel, more diversified dispute resolution mechanisms, both beyond and below the nation-based systems, makes it more difficult than ever to capture these developments within the conceptual framework of modern law.

It would be wrong to conclude that such developments are happening in all countries, and at the same pace; but the general drift in this direction is unmistakable. The emergent legal landscape with its *unsystematic* plurality of sources of law is reminiscent of pre-modern law. To suggest that it presages "A New Middle Ages of Law" (Hicks, 1995: 13) surely overstates the matter. Nationally based law and legal institutions are hardly being marginalized; they remain the core mechanisms for promulgating and enforcing rights, so that

> even though transnationalism and deregulation have reduced the role of the state in the governance of economic processes, the state remains as the ultimate guarantor of the rights of capital [and citizens] whether national or foreign (Sassen, 1998: 199).

But how the contemporary state enacts, reforms and implements law has radically altered. The cluster of changes is too multidimensional to be explained by reference to the range of general concepts offered by the theorists of recent legal change identified in the previous chapter. Innovative and insightful as many of their concepts are, they at best offer only partial understandings of the present legal landscape. The overall trajectory of developments here suggests that another "thrust" of "juridification" is emerging to supplement the four earlier thrusts Habermas (1986) describes as capturing the evolutionary development of law in modern states. The overall picture suggests the need to explore the very different framework from that which, in light of a long historical perspective, uniquely marks out modern legal systems. This chapter has attempted to identify the extent of those changes by reference to some insights from postmodern sociological theoretical accounts of comparable developments in other social spheres. In a highly differentiated society changes in other domains both affect and are affected by legal change. As Dezalay concludes: "But the law is no different from other social institutions which only endure by transforming themselves in the wake of political changes" (1990: 290). In light of this elaboration of the paradigm of legal postmodernization, it is now possible to examine the extent to which the critical perspectives on law influenced by postmodern*ism* offer the conceptual tools necessary to examine, descriptively and prescriptively, these heterogeneous developments.

Notes

1 Cited in Mooney (1995: 1131).

2 The link is enhanced when powerful international institutions promote such changes, as where the International Monetary Fund makes privatization a factor in approval of loans (Starr, 1988: 35).

3 Arthurs and Kreklewich (1996: 44-60), for example, provide an illuminating analysis of how changes in the legal profession are symptomatic of the shift to a "new economy". Trubek et al. (1994) show how this development is replicated on the supranational plane.

4 Atiyah has more recently fully acknowledged the extent of the changes. See Atiyah (1995: 27-34).

5 Corporatization is but a paler version of privatization and is sometimes used as a stage on the way to full privatization. Ownership remains in the hands of the state, but the operation of former public enterprises is subjected to commercial principle. In New Zealand, for instance, this has led to a significant erosion of the social responsibilities of corporatized public enterprises (Chen, 1995: 112).

6 Even though its Service First successor has broadened the stakeholders to whom providers are accountable, and has increased "second generation rights of political participation", and so marks a shift away from "its avowedly consumerist and market ideology", there remain significant limits on the new model of citizenship from the perspective of "social rights" (Scott, 1999: 602-603).

7 As Majone notes (1990: 2), in Europe regulation has generally been conducted not by use of the United States model of specialized, single purpose agencies, but by "traditional ministries or inter-ministerial committees".

8 The expression "new private law" comes from a special 1996 issue of the *Denver University Law Review* (Volume 73(4)) of the same title, where some of the themes in this section were addressed.

9 For instance, in the European context Wedderburn draws a clear distinction between the British and Irish systems based on freedom of contract with some supplementary protective measures, and the Continental systems where collective provision and the principle of compensation for inherent inequality are paramount (1994: 27-33).

10 As Mooney notes at pp 1133-1134, many researchers have reached similar conclusions, both in contract law in other jurisdictions and other areas of law. Farnsworth (1990: 223-224), for example, concludes his survey of contract law by suggesting that "[t]he 1970s were undeniably the decade of the consumer in contract law ... During the 1980s, the pendulum swung in the opposite direction". Atiyah identifies a similar process at work, but offers a very different evaluative assessment, in his overview of the drift of recent change in contract law in the United Kingdom (1995: 27-34).

11 See generally, chapter 4, pp 105-118.

12 Cited in Rose-Ackerman (1990: 517 at 520).

13 The same process occurs in the context of privatization as noted above.

14 The Commission is now known as the Australian Consumer and Competition Commission. The change is significant, representing the growing focus on competition in the regulatory framework.

15 It is important to qualify this general point with the observation that contemporary "contracting" states are expanding investments in retributive institutions, which are premised on greater direct state involvement in criminal justice, and increasing levels of state expenditure so that this particular development represents a "major exception" to the contracting state (Braithwaite, 2000: 227).

16 A similar process has recently been introduced to the United Kingdom's welfare regime, as part of the wider appearance of "contractual governance": see Vincent-Jones (2000: 342-349).

17 Blankenburg (1995: 176; 1999: 442) demonstrates the considerable differences in European practices, in particular by focusing on how in the civil law jurisdictions the more inquisitorial role of the judge implies a more managerial and interventionist practice of ensuring the timely resolution of disputes.

18 Nader sees the turning point as the Roscoe Pound Conference: "Perspectives on Justice in the Future" held at St Paul, Minnesota in 1976, where Chief Justice Burger advocated a change in policy toward access to justice (1988: 273-275). The timing significantly coincides with a wider disenchantment with the policies of the welfare state.

19 Very similar sentiments have been expressed more recently in the United Kingdom with the former Lord Chancellor, Lord MacKay, and the Master of the Rolls (as he then was), Lord Woolf, in support of alternative dispute resolution mechanisms. See generally, Genn (1999a; 2000).

20 I am using the term "hybrid" in a broader way than it is used in the alternative dispute resolution literature, where it refers to mixed patterns within the alternative resolution spectrum, such as fact-based mediation or concilio-arbitration. See generally, Astor and Chinkin (1992: ch 7).

21 This is not to assert that modern law in some way rendered irrelevant other forms of regulation, or that there has not been a large measure of legal pluralism in evidence surrounding and underpinning modern, formal legal systems. Rather, as I emphasized in chapter 3 the point here is merely that modernity is marked by a unique blend of formal and informal law: the centre develops a more significant role, coming to define and control the peripheral forms of informal law.

[22] This term was coined by Santos (1987) to describe a general process of interplay between different legal orders, rather than to capture the particular, historically specific, interrelationship between the courts and alternative dispute resolution described here.

[23] Cited in Parker (1999: 39).

[24] Blankenburg (1995: 181-182) makes the important point that there are very great differences in legal aid regimes between common law and civil law jurisdictions. He suggests that the less adversarial civil law model may explain to some degree the reduced need for legal aid for representation in court. Nonetheless, reductions in funding and eligibility appear to be a feature across the board (Regan and Fleming, 1994).

[25] Albrow (1996: 77-80) rejects the use of postmodernity to describe "the global age", but only by reference to those works that I labelled in chapter 2 as postmodernist. Theories of postmodernization, by contrast, place global developments as central to their concerns.

[26] These abbreviations stand for International Marine Organization (IMO), International Civil Aviation Organization (ICAO), Food and Agriculture Organization (FAO), World Trade Organization/World Intellectual Property Organization (WTO/WIPO), Group of 10 principal creditor nations of the IMF (G-10), and the Economic Commission for Europe (ECE). They represent only a small fraction of the organizations examined by Braithwaite and Drahos (2000).

[27] Primarily, they have been the International Covenant for Civil and Political Rights (ICCPR) and the International Covenant for Economic, Social and Cultural Rights (ICESCR), both of which came into force in 1976.

[28] For a recent example, see *Toonen v Australia* UN Doc. ICCPR/C/50/D488/1992 (8 April, 1994). The finding that the State of Tasmania's criminalization of male homosexuality had infringed Article 17 led to the enactment of the *Human Rights (Sexual Conduct) Act 1994* (Cth).

[29] Though a right to self-determination is contained in these instruments, the UN Human Rights Committee has not accepted that collective rights can be asserted under the ICCPR (Nielsen and Martin, 1998: 99).

[30] For instance, in the United Kingdom, Lord Scarman gave an early expression of the new mood over two decades ago when he concluded that irrespective of whether a treaty has been expressly incorporated into domestic law, the Courts "will interpret statutory language and apply common law principles, wherever possible, so as to reach a conclusion consistent with our international obligations": *Ahmad v Inner London Education Authority* [1978] QB 36 at 48.

[31] The remainder of this section draws heavily from Slaughter (2000).

[32] Since the book was written, the United Kingdom Parliament has enacted the *Human Rights Act* 1998. This development can also be interpreted as evidence of the increasing legitimacy of the judicial interpretive practice.

6 Critique and Reform

> Journalist at the Dublin Motor Show: "Taoiseach [Prime Minister, Mr Charles Haughey], what do you think of the Audi 400?"
> Mr Haughey: "I really can't bring myself to believe that they're *all* guilty."

> Left-wing and right-wing critics, having lost their ideologies, vacillate between apocalypse and intrigue. The next step may well be more desperate and more radical claims combined with pre-adaptive resignation (Luhmann, 1986: 111).

Introduction

The empirical overview of the extent to which contemporary legal systems have been *postmodernized* provides a context for raising questions about the general nature of postmodern theorizing, and its relevance for law. This chapter will examine the extent to which this body of critical work assists in providing the heuristic and evaluative tools necessary to address both the nature of modern law in general as well as the recent changes in legal systems and doctrine surveyed above. The first section of this chapter addresses some of the general theoretical problems associated with the most influential forms of postmodern*ist* theory outlined in chapter 2. The second part will focus on the work of various legal theorists who have made use of some of postmodernism's insights as a critical resource to examine modern law and legal institutions.

A recurrent difficulty confronting any examination of the uses of postmodernism in the context of legal theory is a pervasive reluctance in much of the literature to define the concept with any degree of particularity, or to acknowledge the vast array of meanings it has acquired.[1] Nonetheless it is possible to detect a number of themes that recur throughout this body of work that give it a certain coherence. Only a small sample of theorists from an already vast and expanding body of literature will be examined here. My general argument is that while this genre of theorizing has offered some partial and innovative insights into law, its overall contribution is largely unconvincing and unhelpful. The weaknesses are evident at the levels of the analytical, sociological and normative study of law and legal institutions.

In particular, at the analytical and sociological levels, postmodern accounts offer at best partial accounts of law and legal systems. And in its uncompromising rejection of some of the fundamental elements and achievements of modern law, postmodernism's message is too dystopian and negative to offer a meaningful program for making legal institutions contribute to, and be part of, a better world. By contrast, the notions of postmodernization and postmodernity stressed so far operate at odds with postmodernist prescriptions: not only do they provide concepts for the large-scale analysis of recent social and legal change, but they are theoretically open to evaluating the extent to which those changes have advanced or impeded justice with a view to legal reform.

In addition to positing some general criticisms of both general and legal postmodernist theory, a subsidiary focus of this chapter will be on the question of how useful this body of theory might be in light of the radically changed sociological and historical context of recent legal developments identified in the previous chapter.

Postmodernist Sensibilities and Legal Understanding

From dozens of current meanings of the term, it is possible to distil some core elements of the "postmodern". They are the three powerful "negations" (Hebdige, 1988: 187-203). One of these negations rejects totalizing approaches to explaining the social world. A second oppositional stance emphasizes the need to be against utopian thinking, or large narratives of emancipation or freedom, in both their prescriptive and descriptive manifestations. Third, postmodernism takes a stand against science, objectivity and reason. Because it is unnecessary to hold all of these notions to be a postmodernist, a wide array of theories marches under its banner. The discussion below will critically examine these themes as they appear in different forms in the writings of the leading theorists whose work was surveyed in chapter 2. In their various ways, the most influential postmodern theorists, Michel Foucault, Jacques Derrida, and Jean-François Lyotard, advance elaborate theoretical assaults on totality, utopia and science. Their work will be examined separately with particular reference to the question as to the adequacy of their formulations for understanding law.

Foucault: From the Disciplines to Governmentality

As we have seen in chapter 2, the breadth of Foucault's writings makes a simple classification of his work difficult. Nonetheless, there are three themes in his writing that exhibit some of the key weaknesses of postmodern theory. The first is his critique of totalization in social inquiry;

second is the normative deficiency in his accounts of social phenomena; and finally, these weaknesses persist both in his and others' later work on governmentality.

Foucault's position arguably provides the most sustained and influential theoretical assault on totalizing approaches to the understanding of society in general and law in particular. His technique of genealogy advises against the tendency to see singular events or processes as part of much larger narratives; and his elaborate thesis about power locates it within the practices of specific institutions in relation to their subjects rather than defining it more widely as a property held by a state or class. He sees plural and dispersed disciplinary practices as the most significant mechanisms of domination in modern societies. It follows that "the attempt to think in terms of a totality has in fact proved a hindrance to research" (1980: 81). This methodological injunction is reflected directly in his analysis of law. He contends that the examination of domination in society can be conducted in two essentially incompatible ways, by a focus on law or on the disciplines. Because law operates very differently to the disciplines, to understand modern societies requires attention not to the macro-level legal concepts of sovereignty, law and rights, but to the detailed study of "the manifold forms of domination that can be exercised within society; ... not the uniform edifice of sovereignty, but the multiple forms of subjugation that have a place and function within the social organism" (1980: 96).

It is clear that for Foucault, either/or terms, and only either/or terms, describe the available strategies of analysis. Power should be investigated in its manifestations at the local level *rather than* by reference to the laws that superficially govern its exercise. Accordingly, "the analysis in question should not concern itself with the regulated and legitimate forms of power in their central locations ... On the contrary, it should be concerned with power at its extremities, in its ultimate destinations ...". Furthermore, "right should be viewed ... not in terms of legitimacy to be established, but in terms of the methods of subjugation that it instigates" (1980: 96); and attention should be directed "not towards the juridical edifice of sovereignty ... but towards domination and the material operators of power" (1980: 102). The reason for posing the choice in such stark terms lies in the nature of modern society: power is typically to be found in the extremities, not at the centre; and law masks rather than determines how such power unfolds.

An emphasis on the way power works in the "capillaries" of the social body, in contrast – to pursue the physiological metaphor – to a somewhat Hobbesian focus on its head, undoubtedly offers many important methodological lessons for understanding the law in action. The routine practices by means of which institutions allocate resources, administer, manage and categorize people within their control, can often yield richer and more illuminating insights into how power is wielded than an examination of the formal legal allocation of authority, as a mindset fixated on sovereignty might prefer. Such a research strategy evokes the legal realists' message about the importance of measuring how far the law in action could deviate from the law "in the books"; but it goes much further. It promises a deeper analysis of how institutions both "produce" truth in their quotidian practices, and in doing so how they also subjugate those with whom they deal, as even the most cursory examination of prisons and asylums would demonstrate. Nonetheless, for all the gains, this striking tilt towards the local raises at least as many problems as it resolves.

First, it is notable how the nominalist impulse to understand society exclusively by reference to its constituent disciplinary elements appears to be contradicted by an ultimately "total" historical picture of society and law. For Foucault, not only is modern society distinctive by virtue of its disciplines; it is also a disciplinary *society*, a "carceral archipelago", or even a "*society of normalization*" (1980: 107; italics in original). These are hardly "local" claims; on the contrary, they purport to portray the essential character of an entire social formation. Likewise, to describe the emergence of modern law in terms of its sovereign aloofness from the day-to-day practices of institutional normalization is to offer a quite totalizing picture of *its* social function. A different, but equally large transhistorical periodization is provided in Foucault's later study of "governmentality", to be discussed below. In this account, states move in large historical leaps from being states of justice/societies of law to administrative states/societies of regulation, and finally appear as governmental states (1991: 104). On closer examination, therefore, Foucault's move against totality involves a contradiction: it looks more like a rejection of certain types of totalizing analysis than totalization *per se*.

From the opposite perspective, it is possible to turn the nominalist charge back on Foucault's own studies: they arguably do not go far enough to expose the way power operates in the wide diversity of modern institutions. Foucault concludes that the prison, the asylum, and even institutions like schools, are marked more by the affinities they share than the differences that separate them. In similar fashion and to similar degrees they manifest the techniques of domination, bio-politics, and the making and moulding of subjects by routine exercises of power, reaching even into the soul to do so. But this emphasis on the local readily raises the question of infinite regress: why should prisons in general be held to share some essential features to allow their disciplinary practices to be treated as homogenous? Perhaps instead one should start to examine particular prisons that might have their own, singular, qualitatively different mechanisms for subjugation. One possible explanation for the reductionism in this characterization of the modalities of operation of such institutions is that they are locations for the exercise of the most egregious forms of domination in modern societies. They tend to be what Goffman (1961) describes as "total institutions" which systematically subject persons over whom they hold sway to regimes that *de-individualize* them, but do so because the subjects are in general neither free to leave, nor able to enlist internal mechanisms for accountability. Their subjects are therefore *legally* without "voice" or "exit" rights (Hirschman, 1970).

To generate from such disciplinary institutions a general image of the social formation seriously misrepresents the spectrum of institutions typical of modernity where large numbers of institutions do not operate in this way at all; the disciplines are therefore "the exception rather than the rule within the main institutional sectors of modern societies" (Giddens, 1984: 154). Against this image, a fundamental distinction surely needs to be drawn between institutions where subjects exercise at least some measure of agency in their dealings with them, and those to which they are forcibly consigned. One of the central institutions in contemporary societies – the market – typically operates not by discipline but by the articulation of preferences, which may be more or less autonomously generated. To be sure, the professional practice of marketing involves its own mechanisms for inducing consumption that may involve some of the strategies of the disciplines in relation to their subjects. And of course markets regularly operate coercively due to inequalities of power, scarcity and unfair competition. But they do so in a wholly different way to institutions within which subjects are constrained without their consent.

Such institutions, unlike prisons for example, must operate in an environment where their subjects have significant *legal rights* to go elsewhere. Foucault's focus on disciplinary power is largely indifferent to these other features of modern liberal societies so that the generalization from a small number of disciplinary instances to society as a whole offers a thoroughly inadequate picture of its general nature. In the context of law, it follows that a perspective that may have insightful analyses for the study of crime and related practices, offers few concepts for the understanding of the legal framework of constitutions, markets or property.

Not only does Foucault's scheme fail to identify essential differences between institutions within a particular social space, but it also assumes their continuity throughout the time-span of modernity. Disciplinary power is the dominant and ever-present form of modern subjugation. This conclusion is also overstated, because it ignores the ebb and flow of institutions and their ascendancies over time. Changes in the mechanisms of social control that are peculiar to postmodernity provide an example of the varying historical significance of "liberty and discipline" (Wagner, 1994). Where, as in contemporary advanced societies, social relations have been dramatically transformed by the pervasiveness of signs, images and simulations, and in consequence processes of signification become sociologically dominant, power needs to be understood not simply by reference to discipline. Despite his characteristic exaggeration, Jean Baudrillard's (1987) dismissal of Foucault's work as of no relevance to understanding a heavily mediatized world represents a forceful critique in this context. Moreover, as we have seen in the previous chapter, postmodernity is also characterized by the proliferation of social structures where subjects are free to exit, as reflected in the ever-expanding marketization of social relations. Discipline performs no decisive, or at least exclusive, function in this context. It certainly cannot operate as *the* organizing principle of contemporary societies; rather, it is one of many, and largely reserved for the weakest and most disadvantaged, the "non-consumers" who cannot participate in regular and regulated market activity. In its stead, seduction becomes the increasingly dominant mechanism of social control (Bauman, 1992: 97-98; 1997).

The tendency of selective totalization is also evident in Foucault's theoretical understanding of modern law, and appears in two forms. First, as we have seen above, law is connected simply, and reductively, to sovereignty. Foucault links this model of law to the premodern context of the "juridical monarchy" which visibly, and spectacularly, coerced subjects into obedience. In contrast, disciplinary power operates in a different way from sovereign command in the form of law, and it lies beyond the reach of such coercive rules. It functions in a productive way by normalizing subjects. Normalization describes the techniques deployed in institutions to secure compliance in the form of official scrutiny of minor patterns of behaviour, the establishment of routines and systematic surveillance. Not only does this description afford law a weak social role, remaining largely ineffective in the face of disciplinary power, but it also identifies its dependency on the disciplines. As Foucault concludes: "[t]he general juridical form ... was supported by these tiny, everyday, physical mechanisms" (1977a: 222). To be sure, at many points in his work the centrality of the state is noted, but these statements do not assume significant theoretical meaning in his analysis.

To assume that law functions simply by its ineffectiveness in the face of the disciplines is both an oversimplification of the broad band of legal rules and ignores the effectiveness of legal institutions (Hunt, 1992: 8). Any examination of the wider range of institutions that law both constitutes and regulates reveals a more complicated picture. In the form of facilitative, or "secondary" rules, laws operate in a very different fashion to sovereign commands by delegating powers to individuals or organizations to perform certain acts (Hart, 1961). The wide spectrum of civil laws governing economic and social activity typically operate in this way by affording subjects powers, immunities and privileges that operate in widely divergent ways (Hohfeld, 1919). As the entire Austin/Hart jurisprudential debate demonstrates, a central problem for theoretical understandings of law is how to characterize the many differences between the range of legal rules within the structure of modern law, most of which do not simply prohibit or proscribe (Moles, 1987). And legal rules in the form of "purposive programs" characteristic of welfare state regulation referred to in chapter 4 routinely operate in a very different way again. Furthermore, from the historical perspective outlined in the previous chapter, the growing significance of the contemporary *hybridization* of legal and non-legal rules offers considerable evidence against this description of law. Foucault's model of law likens it too much to the criminal code to offer a sufficiently accurate analysis either of the various types of law or law in general.

Nor is this deficiency remedied by Foucault's analysis of the "juridical liberties", the second element of the legal sphere in his scheme. In contrast to coercive rules, they confer rights, and are "egalitarian in principle"; the disciplines, on the other hand, operate by means of normalization and are "inegalitarian" (1977a: 222). But these superficially valuable "egalitarian" features of the legal orders of modern societies fail to provide any effective protection or security for the subjects for whom they are intended according to Foucault's argument. Instead, he sees these rights purely as complicit in the spread of disciplinary power: law, or "right", "transmits and puts in motion relations that are not relations of sovereignty, but of domination" (1980: 96). Legal rights and the discourse that surrounds them therefore function only to mask a more sinister reality. In a theoretical move that is strikingly evocative of the Marxist analysis that he is otherwise keen to rebut, modern law operates as a smokescreen for domination.

Yet in societies where law functions as an institutional impediment on the exercise of certain sorts of power, and where states conduct their affairs constitutionally, that is, where what is commonly described as the rule of law prevails, disciplinary power is typically compromised, if not actually limited, directly authorized or prohibited. It follows that law is essential to understanding how power unfolds in such contexts, not in the sense of being the exclusive mechanism of social control, but a contingently significant or even a dominant one. Foucault's analyses of power are rich and revelatory, but the manifestations of power he identifies, at least in liberal states, routinely though not exclusively operate by means of a linkage with, and dependency on, the official legal apparatus and state processes. Many of the powers of officials in the case of prisons, asylums and schools, including their techniques of normalization and immunities, derive from legal sources; and their exercise is influenced by the structure of legal rules, and their manner of enforcement. As Habermas concludes:

> [as] soon as he passes from the Classical to the modern age, Foucault pays no attention whatsoever to penal *law* and to the *law* governing penal process. Otherwise he would have to submit to the unmistakable gains in liberality and legal security, and the expansion of civil-rights guarantees even in this area, to an exact interpretation in terms of the theory of power (1987a: 290; emphasis in original).

Any satisfactory account of law must seek to examine how the legal system interacts with its various environments. Certainly, such an account would reveal the highly provisional nature of legal control. Laws and legal frameworks, *like disciplinary mechanisms*, should not be expected to work in a uniform manner.

Law is better seen as integral to the practices of institutions and it connects up in varying ways with their local practices. It routinely operates in a more or less successful manner in its attempts to steer or compel practices in particular domains. This capacity is one that needs to be tested empirically rather than theoretically dismissed *a priori* as Foucault's approach does. Different social spheres are juridified to varying degrees, and the extent to which they are may vary over time and place. Foucault's rigid notions of power and law close off this possibility. They afford no meaningful tools to differentiate descriptively "modern" regimes that exhibit such profoundly variant power structures as parliamentary democracy with comparatively robust civil societies and legal systems at one end of the spectrum, and totalitarian states with meaningless mechanisms for accountability and elaborate, entrenched practices of repression at the other.

Foucault's contrast between his position and that of Hobbes pits a discipline-centred model of society against one derived from a notion of sovereign power located in the monarch or state. In doing so it seriously oversimplifies the available analytical options. Certainly, an understanding of power relations in society on the presumption that the centre commands, and the peripheries follow, is both descriptively and normatively unenlightening. But to see power predominantly at the margins is no less flawed. In Michael Walzer's assessment:

> Hobbes gives us an importantly wrong account of political sovereignty; rhetorically inflated and drained of moral distinctions, it nevertheless captures something of the reality of the modern state. Foucault gives us an importantly wrong account of local discipline; rhetorically inflated and drained of moral distinctions, it nevertheless captures something of the reality of modern society (1986: 53).

Part of the "rhetorical inflation" in Foucault's scheme lies in the claim that power is *only* productive; but in reality it can *also* be repressive, all-too-intentional, -conspiratorial and -centralized. The partiality of this account of power is directly traceable to the methodological limits imposed upon it. In general, social phenomena can be viewed from three theoretical perspectives. One type of inquiry examines social phenomena by reference to how they function internally and how they achieve their aims. Another approach looks at their external effects, such as how they impact on individuals, how subjects come to be under their sway, and are treated by them. Finally, they may be considered from the wider, or "total", perspective of their location within society as a whole, by the roles assigned to them, and the limits placed on their operations by other institutions or larger processes. In shorthand, these accounts are from "within", from "below", and from "above" (Offe, 1985: 221). The first type of approach (from "within") tends to downplay questions of critique because of its methodological predisposition to identify the internal functions and programs of institutions, whereas accounts from "above" and "below" are more susceptible to normative considerations. Each of these partial accounts requires supplementation from the others to provide a complete picture of an institution, or a social formation.

The methodology at the heart of Foucault's work is overwhelmingly directed to provide an account from "within". It produces powerful, compelling and richly-textured images of (some) institutions from the inside; but it offers very little about how they work from below, and consistent with the repudiation of totalizing forms of sociological analysis, bluntly rejects the usefulness of providing an account from "above". The ensuing, constricted view evident in his detailed examination of how prisons, asylums, and to a lesser extent, factories and schools, secure compliance is reflected in a narrow account of their practices, and a disregard of their relation to larger processes. This weakness is complemented by a steadfast, anti-utopian refusal, "drained of moral distinctions", to offer a critical or normative assessment of their treatment of their subjects or their wider social functions.

The Foucauldian subject provides a good demonstration of the strengths and weaknesses of this perspective. He or she is not a bearer of rights or "juridical liberties", as a Hobbesian, Marxist or liberal might (in typically *modern* fashion) put it; but is instead the subject of disciplinary power, inescapably within its embrace, beneath "the gaze" of officialdom. A bleak amoral determinism makes both descriptive and prescriptive talk of freedom irrelevant, particularly as expressed in the discourse of rights that is considered merely to occlude the effectivity of the disciplines. There is no "outside" of power in this vision; in consequence, the notion of emancipation is misconceived. But such a one-sided and simplistic view of the subject too readily collapses the idea of subjectivity into subjugation (Dews, 1987: 160). It replicates the either/or mode of analysis of law noted above, and gives rise to analogous problems of analytical oversimplification. By contrast, an acknowledgement that the modern legal subject has concrete rights would raise questions about law's possible effectiveness, and would therefore muddy the distinction between sovereignty and disciplinary power that Foucault wishes to maintain. Such an examination (from "below") would necessarily pose the question of a subject's agency; it would factor law into the analysis and assess the consequences for subjects of the enhancement or curtailment of their legal rights. A perspective from "above" would look for the impact of other institutions (such as law and politics) on the manner of exercise of disciplinary power, for example by means of the authority conferred on other bodies, and the liberties granted to subjects. Beyond the confines of total institutions, legal rights, such as those to participate in decision-making and to move from one institutional context to another, would also need to be assessed by reference to power.

These questions are central to Max Weber's analysis of modernity (1978 [1921]), and in many respects his concerns track those of Foucault. His work is also disposed to gauge how historically unique institutions, marked by their distinctive internal, instrumental rationality, have been central to the development of modern societies. His studies of some of these institutions, such as bureaucracies and law, are closer to the sovereign centre of society than Foucault's perspective prefers, but the forms of reasoning characteristic of their operations bear striking similarities to Foucault's disciplinary power (Giddens, 1984: 151-153). Within them, a means-ends rationality prevails which facilitates a pattern of coordinated and organized domination. But this is not the end of the matter for Weber, as it appears to be for Foucault. Weber's examination of power and domination focuses in a more multidimensional way on the patterns of legitimation that attend such practices. It directs attention to the ways in which obedience to rules is secured *other than by discipline*, and differentiates power that is legitimated, that is to say, authority, from illegitimate power. In order to do so he deploys a richer hermeneutical framework than Foucault's. His approach embraces the value orientation of social actors alongside the different instrumental rationalities of those in power. Accordingly, the reasons why laws are obeyed are analyzed as *separately* vital to the understanding of law's social effectiveness.

An examination of the range of different forms of compliance inevitably raises questions as to the agency and freedom of subjects, the distinctions between the function and nature of law in different regimes, and the issue of its legitimation. It allows the question of law's efficacy to be posed by reference to the operation of other social spheres, such as the economy. For instance, Weber sees formal rational law, by providing a measure of certainty and calculability, as essential to the emergence of a capitalist economy. For Foucault, by contrast, legitimation and obedience to law, no less than its efficacy and function, fade into the background because of their affinity with explanations of sovereignty. His avoidance of this dimension of social life is directly consistent with his power/knowledge thesis: knowledge claims are always both an effect of, and implicated in, relations of power. But to ignore the role of legitimation, for instance, leads to a seriously narrow analysis of law. A perspective from below might register the extent to which individuals struggle free from such institutions, or subvert their strategies, and how some institutions treat them better than others; indeed, how certain institutions (such as social movements, political parties, a free press, trade unions and the like) are *essential for freedom* (Taylor, 1984: 164-167). And this is the case not despite, *but because of*, their own necessary internal disciplinary mechanisms. Foucault's perspective is methodologically geared to ignore these factors because he characterizes modernity as manifesting not advances in freedom, but rather an intensification of subjection.

The legal rights of subjects would be a key factor in addressing these questions. Such a perspective would attempt to distinguish between the wholly different social processes of domination, socialization and acculturation, and in so doing offer a way of measuring agency, in the place of Foucault's limitlessly plastic subject. Moreover, the insistence in Foucault's conceptual framework of the ubiquity of an all-engrossing power at the heart of all social institutions and discursive practices necessitates not merely a suspension of ethical and political judgement, but its irrelevance: "[t]he categories of meaning, validity and value are to be eliminated not only on the metatheoretical but on the empirical level as well" (Habermas, 1987a: 286). Against this, critical social inquiry requires a complete picture of social institutions; so we need to know why they operate as they do, how they can be reformed, and in whose favour and to what end particular forms of power are employed.

In Foucault's theory, if there is no freedom beyond power, neither is there "truth". His particular stance "against science" asserts that truth itself is also an effect of power. It is always "produced", so that talk of truth in the abstract is meaningless; only "regimes of truth" exist (1980: 131-133). This point is an important rejoinder to the more positivistically inclined, who presume a pre-theoretical access to the "facts". (Of course, this argument fails to challenge rationalist or pragmatist epistemologies that emphasize the inescapably constructed, or "produced", nature of knowledge.) A more valuable theoretical claim is to be found in Foucault's insistence on the politics of truth and the sociology of knowledge, and the myriad ways that organizational and institutional mechanisms create the conditions for the flourishing of certain truths at the expense of others. But Foucault's argument goes too far in its failure to clarify the distinction between epistemic and epistemological relativism. Epistemic relativism is a weak form of relativism, insisting that notions of what counts as truth inescapably differ depending on the social and historical context within which such claims are made. The second, stronger thesis asserts that there is no objective truth that one might establish beyond the effects of power.

The central problem with the latter position is that it appears to be performatively contradicted by the very activity of unmasking that Foucault's work represents (Habermas, 1987: ch 10; Taylor, 1984: 173-180).[2] To identify the all-pervasiveness of regimes of truth directly begs the question of to which regime of truth Foucault's analysis belongs. His argument appears to imply that unlike those subjected to disciplinary power, whose ways of thinking are functionally produced by the very operation of power, *and the nature of which it systematically obscures*, Foucault has somehow eluded its grip. Yet his basic thesis suggests that such an exercise is both sociologically and philosophically impossible. An alternative, more plausible, conclusion to be drawn from theoretical work of this kind is that it provides a more complete picture of the operation of disciplines. But this implicit claim, too, appears to presuppose a notion of objectivity that Foucault wants to deny. Also, given the proscription against objectivity, how is possible to adjudicate between different truth-claims?

This particular version of epistemological relativism has a significant effect on the question of critical analysis: it feeds the refusal to engage in any normative evaluation. In the same way that Foucault's studies obstruct the critique of different disciplinary regimes, the many regimes of truth also escape the critical eye. Law provides a useful theoretical test. The confession beaten out of a suspect is no more or less a produced "truth" than the careful sifting of evidence before an impartial judge and jury. But Foucault appears to offer little or no conceptual material to adjudicate on the morality or justice of these widely divergent "regimes of truth". However, such an exercise is one essential to any adequate ethical or political assessment, and any vision of reform.

A possible solution to some of these various weaknesses is suggested by Foucault's governmentality thesis (1991). "Governmentality" is the process by which power in its myriad manifestations in contemporary societies intersects with the activities of states. Foucault sees states in Western societies from the 16th to the 18th centuries as having undergone a profound transformation. Over this period they developed a repertoire of strategies centred on social scientific techniques of calculation, enumeration and measurement in order to bring entire populations under systematized scrutiny. In consequence, state institutions progressively absorb power relations as part of their responsibilities. They gradually introduce strategies and rationalities of government, not to coerce populations, but to understand them and to enlist them in the practices of governance.

This recognition of the central agencies of governance and their intersection with civil society offers an important supplementary perspective from "above" to Foucault's earlier preference to remove the sovereign from theoretical view. It allows significant historical shifts to be identified, and it displaces discipline as the central organizational feature of modern society. It also fits with a concern in his later work to emphasize the active role played by subjects in the constitution of power (1982). The recent governmentality literature that derives from and elaborates on these ideas adds useful conceptual tools both to identify the way in which institutions are linked to each other in governance, and also to examine historical change. For example, in Donzelot's brilliant analysis, the networks of professional intervention combine with the state to "police" the family (1979), and a series of studies have meticulously charted the manifold shifts away from welfare state strategies in favour of "neo-liberal governance" (Dean, 1999; Rose, 1996; 1999). From this vantage point, the state governs through apparently private institutions; it even "governs through freedom". What appears to be a generalized withdrawal of the state from certain spheres at the present time is better understood according to this literature as a continuance of governance, but by other means.

Despite the incorporation of the active subject and the organs of the state apparatus within this new theoretical framework, the governmentality approach shares many of the methodological assumptions of Foucault's earlier work, and in consequence manifests both its strengths and weaknesses. It remains a form of analysis predominantly from "within". Importantly, it takes the policies and strategies of institutions in a serious way, assuming that these are telling indicators of their nature. But it generally fails to examine them from "below" and is therefore unduly inclined to ignore the ways in which these institutional tactics are subverted or modified in practice. Also, the theme of "governing through freedom" tends to confuse agency with "freedom"; as a result, it downplays both the normative and descriptive question of the empowerment of subjects in the context of particular governmental tactics (Garland, 1997: 198-202). It follows that in spite of its promise to extend beyond the disciplines to institutions such as markets, it lacks the conceptual vocabulary to analyze their distinctive dynamics. A pervasive normative deficit follows: the question as to how the very different forms of governance rank on a moral scale never appears. Another tendency in this work is to conflate the operation of very different instances of governmentality, so that institutions of civil society and the state are seen as part of the same process.

The emphasis on the continuities between the organs of state and the structures of civil society in the governmentality literature is a clear theoretical advance. But insofar as it treats institutions that have the backing of the state in law in the same manner as those that do not, it misses many important factors that distinguish them. As Garland concludes, "To be demarcated in public law as a state agency is to be afforded special access to legal, economic and military resources, *as well as a special form of authority* and a network of supporting organizations" (1997: 195; emphasis added). Moreover, this designation may involve the possibility of being subject to legal obligations and responsibilities to other state agencies. This failure evidences a general theme of marginalization of law no less marked than in Foucault's analysis of the disciplines.

In Foucault's embryonic sketch of the concept of governmentality, law is expressly described as "not what is important" for understanding the historical reconfiguration of states in the modern era (1991: 95). As with the disciplines, law's shared pedigree with sovereignty renders it sociologically superfluous, and Foucault returns to deploy an either/or choice to contrast it with government: "with government it is a question not of imposing law on men, but of disposing things"; and "the instruments of government, instead of being laws, now come to be a range of multiform tactics". The rationality of sovereignty and law with its "knowledge of divine and human laws, of justice and equality", is opposed to government "as the knowledge of things, of the objectives that can and should be attained, and the disposition of things required to reach them" (1991: 96). Later work in this genre expands on the theme. It either ignores law as having particular significance, or unproblematically assumes it to be among the many strategic mechanisms of governance. Such a view of law certainly captures one element of modern law, namely its instrumentalism. It is much less suited, however, to expose the way in which law may significantly inhibit processes of governance. In a similar way to the account of the disciplines, the use of governmentality as an umbrella concept glosses over important and sociologically crucial distinctions between the very different arms of governmental institutions.

It is important to examine how processes of governance are often thwarted by law. In societies where the legal system is relatively autonomous from other organs of the state apparatus, governmentality must operate in a different way from the manner in which it might do business in totalitarian or other states. Certain types of governance are precluded by given constitutional frameworks that administrations cannot simply sidestep. As an example of legal change from the previous chapter shows, crucial factors in determining whether privatization and deregulation strategies could be advanced in Europe were the relevant operative constitutional arrangements (Prosser and Moran, 1994). For example, the Conservative government in the United Kingdom was able to proceed at a far greater speed than governments in other European countries because of the feeble constitutional obstacles it faced in comparison with other European states. The judicial arm of the state may also impede governance, or direct it in ways markedly at odds with strictly "governmental" tactics. For instance, recent decisions of the Australian High Court recognizing native title have had a profound effect on the status of indigenous people and their power to negotiate with other antagonistic groups and an oppositional government. The origin of these decisions lies not in a "problematization of governance" as much of the governmentality literature supposes to be the essence of legal rules, but of political and legal debate about the morality and legality of decisions that stripped indigenous people of entitlements, the balance of political and social forces that influenced the result, and the extent to which a relatively autonomous legal discourse often works against governmental rationalities.

Taking law as more than simply part of the governmental apparatus would require examination of its different institutional features and what real effects they produce on a range of governmental practices. Of course, to suggest that legal decisions of this order do not display the general features of "governmental" rationalities is not to argue simplistically in favour of a complete autonomy for legal discourse. But law is not satisfactorily understood if it is seen simply to conform to general, instrumental "problematizations" of governance. To treat law in this way reflects an unwillingness to push the proclaimed "nominalism" of governmentality to its logical conclusion. In consequence, important legal and political distinctions such as the separation of powers which are crucial to understanding the differing forms of governance, with their separate, incommensurable rationalities and institutional forms, are largely skated over or ignored in a pervasive "expulsion of law" (Hunt, 1992).

Even where law is subjected to specific examination, the standard methodological presuppositions of governmentality tend to impede the provision of a complete picture of its nature. For instance, Rose and Valverde, in an attempt to meet the criticisms of what they call Foucault's "unhelpful" analysis of law – because it oversimplifies by likening it to sovereign command – argue that another theme is also evident in his work, namely that of *law* as "governmentalized" (1998: 542-543). They acknowledge the weaknesses of Foucault's approach to law and discipline, and offer a helpful re-orientation toward law as an institution with its own distinctive dynamics. They proceed to discuss specific legislative schemes that have supported totalitarian power, and identify the "political rights" that attend the emergence of "rule-of-law states in the 19th century" (1998: 544). Having made this concession, they then "approach the role of law as an historian of the present and the perspective of government", but curiously and inexplicably, by means of "leaving aside the general issues of political rights". To engage in such an exercise involves examination of the strategies directed to the conduct of persons. They see these strategies as different from law, claiming that they operate not by "juridical rule" but by "the norm". Following Ewald, the norm refers to images of "normal" social categories – "the normal family, normal conduct, normal business practice" (1998: 544). Also, they repudiate claims about the unity of law as "fiction", a "creation of legal discipline, of legal textbooks, of jurisprudence itself" and suggest turning away "from the canonical texts and the privileged sites of legal reason". Instead, they recommend examining "the meticulous and detailed work of regulatory apparatuses ... of the law of property and trust, of inheritance and slander ... of all the places where ... laws, rules and standards shape of ways of going on" (1998: 545-546).

While the re-insertion of law into the analysis of governance is a clear theoretical advance, the new binary opposition between law and governmentality adduced to replace the earlier model of law and the disciplines only serves to produce a similar set of problems. First, it is difficult to see how or why political rights should be methodologically sidelined in the context of government and its panoply of regulatory strategies. On the contrary, they may, and routinely do, play a vital role in the manner and efficacy of governmental operations. Second, far from being at odds with the norm, notions of *norm*-ality are persistently deployed in legislative schemes. From standard business practice to images of normal behaviour in different contexts, particularly in the contemporary deregulatory environment where priority is given to local, context-specific rules and practices, legal rules are routinely parasitic on pre-established social norms. Moreover, once incorporated into law these norms can claim a special effectiveness because they can be invoked to summon state institutions for enforcement, as Garland notes above. Third, to reject the unity of law is not particularly original; it is the stock-in-trade of all contextual approaches to law and even in traditional positivist jurisprudence represents more an ideal to be pursued rather than an achieved reality. The implication that this theoretical assumption in some way typifies legal analysis is to caricature it.

Fourth, to suppose that displacing "canonical texts and the privileged sites of legal reason" might illuminate specific areas of legal doctrine such as "property and trust" is to dismiss *a priori* the social effectivity of those domains of formal law. For example, any sophisticated contextual analysis of trusts law would need to take seriously these "canonical texts", that is, the technical and doctrinal dimensions of law in order to assess their social effects given that many social actors, from lawyers to their clients who use them as guides for action (eg Chesterman, 1979). Finally, Rose and Valverde's call to look at the spatial contexts of law, such as the power of landlords of shopping malls, local authorities and transport police, too readily ignores the significance of general legal rules in their day-to-day operation. Studies of these contexts would be seriously handicapped by an analysis that omitted to examine, for instance, the enormous power conferred on landlords, their agents and legal advisers by both general and detailed rules of property law. This reluctance to incorporate law into governmentality is further evidenced in a more recent study where the phenomenon of "the shadow of law" is examined without consideration of the robust institutional apparatus of legal systems and legal rules without which there can be no shadow (Rose, 1999: 155-156).

As with Foucault's earlier work, studies of governmentality generally display no clear attempt to grapple with the normative questions that the various practices of governance provoke. In general, governmentality appears no less "drained of moral distinctions" than those earlier studies. In its quest to expunge traditional sociological forms of analysis, this approach tends to displace perspectives from "below" or "above". Analyses appear to avoid examining the extent of success of these rationalities and strategies for government. The governmentality theorists generally fail to see unsuccessful governance, the frustration of public policy by the operation of other social factors, or the ungovernability of certain spheres (Garland, 1997: 200-202). The failure to see governmental failure appears to be a side-effect of the genre's focus on the "conduct of conduct". Also, issues of which regimes are more just, more effective, or more oppressive are sidelined in a form of analysis with an almost positivistic feel to it. This tendency to overlook normative considerations translates directly into a reluctance to address political questions (O'Malley et al., 1997). The political programs of different parties, and contingent political alliances within civil society, have profound impacts on the kind of governance and legislative programs that emerge, and their chances of success. Equally, the political terrain is commonly marked by, and influenced by, symbolic and other rationalities that clash with the instrumental rationality that is held to underpin governmentality (Garland, 1997: 201).

Yet it would be a mistake to dismiss too readily Foucault's work as unhelpful in light of these difficulties. Of all the postmodern theorists his argument represents the most distinctively sociological contribution to understanding law by means of its resolute focus on the practices of social control. Also, as Alan Hunt notes, the popularity of Foucault's work may lie in part in its resonance with recent penetrating critiques of the welfare state that have highlighted the practices of domination that lurk beneath the rights talk that sustains them (1992: 25). One way in which Foucault's work might be retrieved would be if his valuable emphasis on the "capillary" manifestations of power is tied to an analysis of legal forms (Hunt, 1992: 30-38) to provide a corrective to a variety of "legalist" approaches to law that place too much faith, descriptively and prescriptively, in formal law and the official mechanisms of justice within the legal system. They are for that reason less sensitive to the mechanisms by which law operates on the ground and often ignore the routinized practices and procedures that are no less significant in terms of their impact on subjects than the formal legal rules. Foucault's reorientation of the research to this domain opens up the possibility of more effectively addressing particular questions of injustice, and urges against premature claims that because a society has the trappings of the rule of law, its institutions conduct business lawfully. There is no reason to believe that his approach cannot work co-operatively with more traditional forms of macro-sociological analysis and normative critique (Garland, 1997: 204-205).

A tentative, albeit fitful, example of such integration is evident in Rose's recent work which examines contemporary contractualism and citizenship in terms not dissimilar to the concept of postmodernization referred to in chapter 2 (1999: chs 4-5); and his critique of recent schools' policy in the United Kingdom parallels Habermas' suggestions for reform in the same area (1999: 193; Habermas, 1986: 218-220). A more developed and convincing analysis of law in relation to governmentality is presented in Hogg and Carrington's (2001) study of the regimes governing the relations between the state and indigenous peoples. Perhaps Foucault himself foreshadowed a way forward in his (unelaborated and undeveloped) suggestion that rather than seeing historical development in terms of three stages of sovereign power, the rise of the disciplines, and the appearance of governmentality, "in reality one has a triangle, sovereignty, discipline, government ..." (1991: 102). Theorizing in this way would make law less marginal to social analysis and so bring governmentality into a fruitful engagement with certain sociological approaches to law, and various theories of regulation.

Derrida: Deconstruction and the "Force of Law"

Two general ideas from the vast corpus of Jacques Derrida's work appear to offer fruitful insights into the nature and function of law. First, the central focus of the poststructuralist technique of deconstruction on the elusive nature of any determinate linguistic meaning directly bears on the practice of law in the field of interpretation. The second question deconstruction poses for legal analysis arises from the (rather less visible) ethical and political messages that are implicit in its method. In addition, Derrida has more recently come to address the legal domain directly, by developing a thesis about how deconstruction might inform notions of law and justice. These different aspects of his theory will be treated separately.

As we have seen in chapter 2, the technique of deconstruction challenges the notion of fully present, objective meaning and therefore has potentially much to reveal about day-to-day legal activity. A Derridean perspective on judicial interpretation might note how meaning is forever deferred, and how signifiers are connected like links in a chain always anticipating or deferring to others. They both contain "traces" of other concepts, and endlessly require "supplementation" from other concepts. In consequence, meaning is indeterminate or "undecidable". These ideas challenge those forms of legal analysis that place too much emphasis on the constraints that are supposed to inhere in legal language and acts of interpretation. Legal interpretation is concerned to identify the meanings of privileged texts, such as statutes, regulations and the judgments of courts. It also confers primacy on the sources of meaning, with methods of statutory interpretation and techniques of case analysis acting as constraints on interpretive freedom. Deconstruction, by contrast, with its assault on the "metaphysics of presence" emphasizes "intertextuality": texts inescapably refer to other texts, so that meaning cannot be closed or determinate within any particular text. It follows that the claimed autonomy or closure of legal discourse is illusory. Derridean concepts therefore squarely challenge the central tenet of traditional legal discourse.

But as many commentators have suggested, deconstruction, with its heavily negative orientation, encounters serious difficulties in light of the social reality of successful communication. If meaning is so elusive, it is hard to explain how the structures and conventions that govern social life retain their robust effectiveness. A pervasive undecidability of meaning would undermine the largely successful processes of communication by which language conveys agreed and certain meanings. Derridean analyses of language can only retain plausibility as a highly abstract philosophical exercise. Even if it is accepted that *from a philosophical perspective* a greater measure of interpretive uncertainty infects texts than is commonly assumed, how is the *sociological* reality of successful communication to be explained? When one looks to the contexts where meaning is in practice negotiated and agreed upon, or secured by the powerful, and the social processes that lead words and concepts to have a core of settled meaning both in law and in other social spheres, one can see how this theory of language fudges a crucial distinction. It runs together the undeniable notion that the linkage between signifiers creates infinite possibilities in theory for the pluralization of meaning, and that they therefore have no essential fixity in that sense, with the very different notion that meanings manifest that same level of indeterminacy in practice. Deconstruction can only maintain such a position because it is a theory "[w]ith no commitment to exploration of social realities at all" (Anderson, 1983: 53). As Peter Dews concludes,

> empirical knowledge can claim no autonomous authority, but is rather ceaselessly dissolved into the endless reflexive movement of *différance*.

> Any orientation towards truth, that of empirical science no less than that of philosophy, betrays a submission to the metaphysics of presence ... (1987: 37).

Paradoxically, it follows that for all its proclaimed undoing of the Western philosophical tradition, deconstruction purports to sustain the pre-eminent status of philosophy as a branch of knowledge, for it is ceaseless theoretical reflection rather than empirical investigation that is held to yield worldly insights. A more significant problem for deconstruction is posed by an examination of the social structures that ensure that agreement about meaning is not only possible, but is so consistently and repeatedly achieved. Wittgenstein's later work, which identifies linguistic meaning as irreducibly social, provides an insightful philosophical perspective on this question (1958). In this theory of "ordinary language" linguistic meaning is better seen by reference to "forms of life", rather than by focusing on the inherent, essential interconnectedness of signifiers, the related instability of dualisms in language, and the conceptual frameworks from which they originate, as Derrida's deconstruction insists. Forms of life are those rules for normal usage, like the rules of a game, which need to be learnt in order to participate in any language. Linguistic meaning is not forever deferred, but embedded in social practices, in "forms of life", where participants have learned how to use those words in ordinary parlance, and for whom the meaning is clear, mostly determinate, and unmistakably "present".

Legal language works in a similar way. Provisions in statutes, judgments in cases, and terms in regulations, commonly have determinate, unambiguous meanings even if penumbrae of uncertainty necessarily surround their application in some cases. Core meanings are those where substantial social, cultural and professional agreement can be secured to determine meaning, while in other contexts penumbrae spell disagreement. The advantage of this approach is that it poses the empirical question of how meaning is secured in practice. Equally, it engages in an exercise that Derrida's work so determinedly avoids: connecting philosophical inquiries with empirical social analysis. The conventions and practices of everyday life do in fact produce levels of certainty and "decidability" of meaning that seems unthinkable within the deconstructionist creed.

This general point is no less relevant to the practice of law. Legal meaning could, theoretically, always be otherwise; another meaning could be conceivably wrung out of any particular statutory provision. Yet in the face of the endless interpretive possibilities that texts invariably provide, practical communicative consensus seems to happen with striking regularity. Ultimately, Wittgenstein's ordinary language philosophy runs into its own insurmountable sociological difficulties, analogous with those faced by deconstruction, because it ignores the referents of signification.[3]

Referents are those elements of an external world that stubbornly resist the linguistic categories that purport to describe and explain them. But at least the approach recognizes the irreducibly social and empirical nature of language and the construction of meaning.

Unlike Foucault's analyses of the disciplines or governmentality which eschew a normative stance, Derrida's deconstruction does have a discernible, if only implicit and imprecise, ethico-political perspective. Deconstruction's exposure of the illegitimate subordination embedded in the hierarchies and dualisms of Western reason, furthered by the institutional policing of these linguistic formulae, offers the hand of allegiance to the other, the marginalized, the excluded. It supports the rescue and re-valorization of these discredited others. Such a position resonates with the identity politics that have emerged over the last three decades or so to celebrate difference. But this promising conceptual move stalls, given its refusal to offer any larger normative claims, consistent with broader postmodern anti-utopianism. The politics of alterity appear to be devoid of any more positive, normative notions with which to affirm otherness. It steadfastly avoids the difficult ethical and political questions about whether illiberal others would need to be resisted to allow otherness in general to flourish, and about what sort of political and legal arrangements might need to be in place to foster it. While deconstruction remains at the level of attempting to undo the promised stability of both normative and descriptive philosophical claims, it will always remain aloof from the contingent, provisional and practical formulations required in specific political contexts. As Thomas McCarthy concludes, "deconstruction can hardly give voice to the excluded other. The wholesale character of its critique of logocentrism deprives it of any language in which to do so" (1991: 107-108).

Derrida has frequently sought to counter such allegations of anti-utopianism. In relation to law, he has done so by supplying a theory of justice, and a specific institutional focus, in his celebrated paper, "Force of Law: The 'Mystical Foundation of Authority'" (1990). In answer to those many critics of deconstruction who have claimed that its negativity is an obstacle to any coherent ethico-political stance, Derrida insists that "deconstruction is justice" (1990: 945). More specifically, the content of this theory of justice takes the form of an imperative "to do justice to the other". The argument also shifts focus from the purely theoretical at least *in the direction of* the empirical by examining the interrelationship between justice and the practice of law. Yet it would be a mistake to see this discourse on justice and law as a break with his earlier work. As Derrida is at pains to emphasize, his discussion of justice is no more than making explicit latent themes in his former philosophical studies.

In his analysis of justice, Derrida identifies a general blockage, or "aporia", that haunts it in its relation to the practice of law. This aporia is the "difficult and unstable distinction between justice and *droit*", between incalculable justice and the calculable "exercise of justice as law or right..." (1990: 959). The general aporia is manifested in three specific forms. The first aporia can be detected in the practice of judging. It lies in the "epokhe [suspension] of the rule" (1990: 961). Derrida appears to have in mind here the creative act of judicial interpretation where rules are not applied mechanically, but require a deliberative weighing up of the rule so as to "reinvent it in the reaffirmation and the new and free confirmation of its principle" (1990: 961). "The ghost of the undecidable" represents the second aporia. As Derrida notes, the undecidable is "a theme often associated with deconstruction" and expresses the idea of a choice between "two contradictory and very determinate rules" in conjunction with a sense of the impossibility of the avoidance of choice: "A decision that didn't go through the ordeal of the undecidable would not be a free decision, it would only be the programmable application of unfolding of a calculable process. It might be legal; it would not be just" (1990: 963). The third aporia is "the urgency that obstructs the horizon of knowledge". The feature of law identified in this requirement is that a "just decision is always required immediately, 'right away'" (1990: 967). Justice, by contrast, has no "horizon of expectation". In a typically rhetorical word-play, Derrida concludes that "Justice remains, is yet, to come, *à venir*, it has an, it is *à-venir*, the very measure of events irreducibly to come. It will always have it, this *à-venir*, and always has" (1990: 969).

In this novel formulation Derrida identifies some of the distinctive and intractable features of the relationship between justice and the practice of legal interpretation. The question of *applying* rules in both easy and hard cases cannot be explained by simpler positivistic accounts of the rules as determining a particular outcome: an active process of interpretation is necessary to reach judgment in every case. Moreover, legal rules are always already incomplete: no rule can ever be so clear as to yield a "right" or uncontroversial answer for all imaginable fact situations. But to the extent that Derrida's point emphasizes the creative, non-calculative role of legal judgment, it is a commonplace in traditional legal theory. It hardly offers a significant advance on more conventional accounts of the judicial role and its relationship to justice.

Nonetheless Derrida does go well beyond traditional analyses of this aporia when he elaborates on the problems faced by courts in the application of rules. He suggests that to transcend rigid "calculation" involves "madness" or "violence" in decision-making "since it always marks the interruption of the juridico- or ethico- or politico-cognitive deliberation that precedes it, that must precede it" (1990: 967). In presenting the alternatives in terms of either a rigid calculation that slavishly follows rules or an untrammelled discretion that does them violence, this dualism imposes a crude limit on the available hermeneutic options, ignoring those various techniques of construction, the pull of policy, and the influence of community standards and the exercise of an educated judgment, practices that jointly and severally conduce to particular interpretations. Also, if an all-too-rational "calculation" on the one hand, and an irrational "violence" on the other, are the only choices that pertain to the decision-maker, it becomes impossible from the perspective of deconstruction to seek to measure the relative merits, ethical and otherwise, of the various other interpretive strategies available to those who play an adjudicative role.

An assessment of these strategies sociologically and politically, rather than from the purely philosophical, deconstructive standpoint, would identify the empirical and normative complexities of the activity of judging. Whether the judge looks to a wider principle to be found within the legal system that points to a right answer, to public policy, or to the legal rule that provides the most efficient solution, such interpretive options are necessarily imbued with their own practical rationalities, that is, intrinsic notions of justice and fairness, rather than "violence" or "madness". The deliberative process of weighing their respective merits may be in some way at odds with an unpresentable justice, but it must be essential to delivering justice *in the present*. The stark dualism Derrida sets up between calculable law and incalculable justice fails to distinguish the very different notions of assessing the justice of law or laws on the one hand, and *doing justice* according to law on the other. Legal decisions cannot avoid being either just or unjust, regardless of the specific content of a theory of justice by which they may be assessed.

Derrida begins to acknowledge this conclusion in his claim that a decision needs to be the subject of deliberation (it should "go through the ordeal of the undecidable") in order for it to be "just"– though the notion that just decisions can be meaningfully identified without, at the very least, an implicit, calculable concept of justice is perplexing. How can the capacity to characterize decisions as just derive from anything other than a background theory of justice? It appears that Derrida has a theory of justice that comes in through the back door. Despite his express rejection of such an exercise (1990: 965), it appears to operate as a transcendental notion lurking at the fringes of his analysis, a type of Kantian "regulative ideal" that sits uneasily with deconstruction's opposition to the metaphysics of presence. Perhaps the elusiveness of Derrida's theory of justice is traceable to this very dilemma (Litowitz, 1997: 98-103). To explore in depth the possible connections between just applications of rules and an abstract concept of justice would offend the clear division he seeks to draw between law and justice, so is not pursued. Derrida prefers instead to emphasize the *impossibility* of reconciling law and justice so that "justice as the experience of absolute alterity is unpresentable" (1990: 971).

This formulation of the relationship between justice and law in the context of judicial activity represents an evasion not only of the complex ethico-political questions posed by the available range of interpretive strategies, but ultimately of any operational concept of justice. To articulate a theory of justice requires a conceptual separation of is and ought, the ideal and the actual, of laws as they should be and those as they are. And to *do* justice is a practical activity that in the legal context, far from being lost at the moment of decision, can only be *satisfied* at that point. Justice positively requires that judges reach decisions, choose between one rule and another, enforce the tenant's rights against the landlord, exclude the violent husband from the home, compel the employer to re-employ the unfairly dismissed worker. *Not acting* in such circumstances would wreak injustice. Derrida's argument powerfully captures the unavoidable incapacity of legal decision-making to do justice to both sides of a legal argument: after all, the "other" is the losing party. But by expressly severing his idea of justice from the practical requirements of doing justice through law, Derrida's analysis displays the generally evasive anti-institutionalism of a deconstruction.

A different criticism relates to the methodological assumptions of deconstruction, which contribute directly to this dilemma. Deconstruction rules out any sociological or political analysis of either law in general, or the practice of judging in particular, as inadequate from its vantage point. For Derrida, deconstruction can expose a reality far deeper than the mere "critique" offered by traditional political and social theory. Critique attempts to expose merely the social, political and economic forces that deploy law to their several ends. By contrast, Derrida's deconstructive approach examines "a more intrinsic structure, one that a critique of juridical ideology should never overlook" (1990: 941). Accordingly, the specific values and visions of the good that theories of justice propose, and the extent to which legal systems reflect them – essential elements of critique – are sidelined, in favour of deconstruction's proclaimed more penetrating analysis. Deconstruction claims to offer something better: it looks to the more fundamental, intrinsic structure of law rather than identifying the sorts of values that actual legal systems manifest, the ideals that they might aspire to, or indeed the results they achieve. Moreover, law's inner essence lies not in its present characteristics and functions, but is to be seen at the very moment of its institution. Derrida finds that the essential force of law comes from its ultimate foundation that lies beyond law; it is to be found in violence, a "violence without ground" (1990: 943). The performative act of founding a legal order cannot itself be authorized by another law. The first constitution of any nation is the expression of a new political community establishing a legal framework for future relations by some extra-legal act.

The claim that the ultimate foundation of law lies beyond positive law is a common enough one in legal theory, where law and legal validity are seen to be ultimately reducible to non-legal phenomena. But Derrida's extra-legal foundation is distinctive in that it is "violence", rather than, say, the "habit of obedience" for John Austin or the *Grundnorm* of Hans Kelsen, that holds the key to understanding law. He finds in such violence the essential rather than merely contingent feature of law. But this image of law as shot through with violence is no less simplistic than Derrida's account of judging, and has the effect of levelling all distinctions, empirical, ethical and political, between different legal orders. The emphasis on violent origins ignores the important sociological differences between a revolutionary upheaval that may originally have instituted a new legal system, and the necessary conditions for the present functioning of that system. For instance, the essence of law in a totalitarian state is radically distinct from the legal order that originates in a violent overthrow of a tyrannical and oppressive regime by a popular movement, and is responsive to citizens' demands in its subsequent development. The continued efficacy of legal regimes commonly depends not on force or foundational violence, but on legitimation, that is, the acceptance by the bulk of a population that laws should be adhered to because they meet some basic standards of justice, that they have been enacted by democratically elected legislatures, and that they conform to community standards.

To be sure, all laws need to be en-*forced* if they are to be effective, and in the pervasive tendency to see law as an exclusively interpretive endeavour, this aspect of its nature is too readily overlooked. For all their juridical labour, judges ultimately "deal in pain and death" (Cover, 1986: 1601), and Derrida makes an important point by emphasizing this dimension of the routine practice of law. But it goes too far to see in this feature law's very essence. It disables any attempt to distinguish between legal and non-legal exercises of power, violence and force, and it affords no tools to differentiate the legal orders of totalitarian regimes from those of states where law operates with a measure of autonomy from other institutions. Derrida's account also faces difficulties in accounting for those legal systems established without violence, but by popular consensus. For instance, how could it make sense of the emerging transnational human rights jurisprudence, as noted in the previous chapter, which cannot be traced to any such violent founding act? And how could it explain cases where a weakened and discredited regime is removed from office by a newly emergent consensus, as shown in recent post-communist states?

Derrida provides an answer to these objections, at least with respect to non-violent revolutions, in his analysis of the overthrow of apartheid. He insists that like all new constitutions, the South African post-apartheid regime is dependent on the violence of the former in the sense that the new state derives its inheritance from the violence perpetrated in the founding of the apartheid state. The new political community "was only able to be established, in any case to be identified, by beginning with a minority violence" (1987: 21). The post-apartheid state appeals to the "entire nation" and in so doing cannot but recall a nation "of geographic and demographic delimitation effected, in large measure, by white colonization" (1987: 20).

This perceptive insight is no less relevant to most states after decolonization than it is to post-apartheid South Africa, as Derrida emphasizes; but it fails to resolve the general problems of his theory of law. It obstructs a direct and unqualified moral assessment of the legitimacy of the legal infrastructure of the new state. Instead, the implication of this argument is that the earlier violence somehow taints the later constitution, so that any praise of the latter can only be offered obliquely. So, Derrida concedes that the apartheid state was different in that *its* founding violence "could not have itself forgotten, as in the case of states founded on a genocide or a quasi-extermination" (1987: 18). In other states, such as constitutional democracies, a collective amnesia obscures the ineradicable violence that is the real essence of law. As to the detailed reasons why this difference arises, Derrida does not examine. A direct consequence of such an analysis is that

> it suggests that violence cannot fail to be implicated in any possible legal institution in any possible society, thereby insinuating ... that it would be folly to aspire to eliminate it (Fraser, 1991: 1325).

It follows that for deconstruction, law, which is defined so broadly as to apply to any legal system, cannot be criticized for the violence carried out in its name. This absence of a critical edge is consistent with the central tenet of deconstruction that analysis should be conducted at a philosophical rather than at the more superficial level of sociological, political or cultural theory where "critique" thrives. But for all his rejection of the tradition of Western metaphysics, Derrida ends up painting a very "metaphysical" picture of law where deconstruction reveals the inner reality of law which mere "critique" cannot reach (Fraser, 1991). In this respect, Derrida's account of law – "drained of moral distinctions" – cannot get to meaningful political assessment. Where all law is tarred with same violent brush, deconstruction is methodologically prevented from drawing distinction between just and unjust regimes. Within this theoretical framework it is impossible to rank legal regimes by reference to a criterion of justice. Like

Foucault, a profound reluctance to take seriously the concrete, sociological processes of law disables Derrida's analysis.

The difficulties in Derrida's account of law are reflected in his article "in admiration" of Nelson Mandela (1987). Despite his recognition of the remarkable contribution Mandela has made to the struggle to eliminate apartheid in South Africa, and how this contribution was expressed in his commitment to the rule of law, "a man of the law" (1987: 26), Derrida cannot bring himself to applaud him simply because he stands for this particular, invaluable principle of justice. Rather, he applauds Mandela's genius in exposing the contradictions inherent in the apartheid regime's use of legal forms. This is a commendable position, but Derrida cannot go one step further to conclude that what Mandela is an advocate for, in terms of substantive political and ethical ideals, is a model of a legal system that takes seriously its ideology of fairness, due process and equality of treatment, and that these principles represent a vital and essential ingredient for the achievement of a just society. Instead, Mandela's primary strength lies in his identification of the slips, the incoherence, the self-contradiction of the oppressors' logocentric speech, very much in the manner that a deconstructionist would be inclined to do.

Derrida reiterates the theme that violence lies at the heart of law, rather than measuring how the two regimes rank in terms of justice. The deconstructive approach precludes him from concluding that the post-apartheid state is a more just one than its hideous predecessor. Such an exercise would be to slide back into a critique of "juridical ideology" that deconstruction, with its concern for "a more intrinsic structure", rejects. Against this approach, a more insightful and fruitful strategy for understanding legal regimes would be a political one, which examined the contingent rather than necessary relationship between law and certain "forms of *masked, structural* violence" (Fraser, 1991: 1325; italics in original). This would allow a direct analysis of the ways in which legal systems can alternatively restrain, be indifferent to, or even facilitate and foster, official violence.

Ultimately, Derrida seems to want to have it both ways. He would like to be on the side of the politically progressive, while at the same time eschewing the vocabularies of critique that give expression to their aims, and by means of which advances in the direction of a just society are commonly achieved. So, despite displaying evasiveness about the substantive normative content of his theory of justice, he finally insists that although "justice exceeds law and calculation [this fact] should not serve as an alibi for staying out of juridico-political battles"; and that "incalculable justice *requires* us to calculate" (1990: 971). Deconstruction therefore issues an ultimate call, despite itself, to engage in the pursuit of a better world by reference to the requirements of justice.

But coming as it does at the end of an extended analysis emphasizing the unattainable and ineffable nature of justice, this is a very tame call to arms, too little and too late, to participate in an activity already neutered not merely by the privileging of deconstruction over critique, but by a profound, almost presupposed notion that they could not co-exist. This appears to be so given that it remains unclear upon what basis those "juridico-political battles" could be fought given that justice "exceeds" them. Curiously, this belated affirmation of the "classical emancipatory ideal" (1990: 972-973) seems to endorse much of the logocentric legacy of Western moral and political philosophy, with its theories of justice, *and critique*, in their advocacy of the alignment of laws with justice in ways that Derrida's work generally rejects. Perhaps, like Foucault, this move, though seemingly in contradiction with his specific rejection of a notion of justice as a regulative idea, represents the prospect of a late, reluctant, and as yet unrealized, rapprochement between postmodern theorizing and some central themes of modern western philosophy.

Lyotard: From Postindustrialism to Small Narratives (Petits Reçits) and Differends

In Jean-François Lyotard's work the three postmodern negations are principally expressed in his rejection of "grand narratives" and his writings on justice. In a celebrated statement capturing the programmatic nature of his work, he concludes: "Let us wage a war on totality; let us be witnesses to the unpresentable; let us activate the differences and save the honour of the name" (1984: 82). As we have seen in chapter 2, grand narratives refer to political philosophies such as "the emancipation of the rational or working subject", "the dialectics of spirit", or "the creation of wealth" (1984: xxiii). The repudiation of grand narratives has both prescriptive and descriptive dimensions. On the one hand, it assails the large descriptive categories typical of modern historical and sociological explanation and therefore echoes Foucault's rejection of total approaches to sociological inquiry. In addition, it is resolutely anti-utopian. Both dimensions of his work have significant potential relevance for understanding law.

Prescriptively, Lyotard warns against totalizing perspectives on society; but not for the specific reason that Foucault does, namely for their failure to yield useful research. Rather, he eschews metanarratives because they lead to a "terroristic" mentality that by use of notions of universality crush difference and dissent. For him, theoretical totalization and political totalitarianism are inexorably intertwined. His references to Auschwitz and the experience of communist regimes suggest an undeniable linkage between totalitarian practices and the large narratives of progress that underpinned them. But Lyotard draws an exaggerated conclusion from these events, moving too readily from the plausible thesis that certain types of theories offered uncritical explanations of, and even nourished, regimes of grotesque violence, to the questionable notion that all theories that attempt to offer large-scale images and critiques of social structure or development lead to similar results.

The levelling of all "modern" theorizing is evident in his conclusion that Auschwitz, Budapest 1956, and Czechoslovakia 1968 "refute speculative doctrine [and] dialectical materialism" in the same way that the Parisian rioting of May 1968 "refutes the doctrine of parliamentary liberalism" (1988: 179-180). Yet for all the ugly official violence and excesses of the latter, it belittles the horrors wrought by totalitarian regimes to equate these events so readily. In a common postmodernist move, every specific manifestation of modernity is subjected to the same exclusively negative, dismissive gesture. Modern ideas of reason, justice and truth are equally implicated in metanarrative discourse, so that "all utopias come wrapped in barbed wire" (Hebdige, 1988: 196).

Part of the problem with Lyotard's thesis is the vague and ill-defined nature of the concept of the metanarrative. By clustering together all large-scale political ideologies, his criticisms become blunt instruments that strike at targets of very different orders of culpability and merit. For instance, the metanarrative of emancipation that "parliamentary liberalism" expresses occupies a very different place on the scale of moral distinction to those other, wholly distinct, "terroristic" regimes of Nazism and Stalinism. Lyotard's concept of the metanarrative also grossly oversimplifies the many ways in which the broad normative claims of political theory and the large descriptive concepts of sociological analysis may operate. It demonstrates a grave loss of historical perspective and affords the discipline of philosophy too large a social role in its central thesis that "Terror did not begin with the citizens' committees of the French Revolution... No, it is not Pol Pot or Stalin, but Kant and Hegel who lie at its origin" (Benhabib, 1984: 116).

Lyotard's rejection of uniquely modern political philosophies because they are metanarratives supports his advocacy of "narratives" and his cognate theory of justice in *Just Gaming* (Lyotard and Thébaud, 1985) and *The Differend* (1988). Narratives are those non-scientific discourses typical of pre-modern societies, Lyotard's favourite example being the narratives of the Cashinahua Indians of the Amazon basin. Unlike grand narratives, the Indians' stories do not purport to derive their legitimacy from some master-discourse like philosophy or science. Grounded in their traditions and the practice of naming the narrator and audience, the Cashinahua narratives, like all narratives, are self-legitimating. When Lyotard develops this notion into a theory of justice, he concludes that judgment must be conducted "without criteria". He argues against the universalization of prescriptives in favour of playing by the rules of specific language games in particular contexts. No general theory of justice emerges, except in the claim that justice should always be context-dependent, provisional and revisable. Against Habermas' theory of communicative rationality with its claims of an immanent orientation to consensus within language, Lyotard advocates dissensus and the multiplication of incommensurable language games. Only these can operate as guarantees against metalanguages with their intolerance for difference and otherness. The predominant aspiration in this position reflects the Derrida's arguments in its affinity with a politics of recognition.

Despite a recurrent emphasis on the political, little guidance for any substantive politics or ethics, and by implication for any strategies for legal reform, emerges from Lyotard's work. A stance in favour of suppressed discourses and the call for experimentation within them suggests support for a politics of difference or recognition; but in doing so it could be argued that it hardly goes further than a principled liberalism of tolerance or "neo-liberal interest group pluralism" (Benhabib, 1984: 119). If the various language games deployed in the entire range of social contexts are given the same cognitive and ethical value, there can be no vantage point from which to offer a critique of one, or a preference for any one over the other. Given that statements within a particular language are held to have no validity except by reference to its internal rules, they cannot be judged from outside. Lyotard sees even scientific language as operating in the same way as others, with no particular claim to pre-eminence or privileged access to truth.

The general difficulty with this valorization of multiplicity is its complete indifference to ethical or political judgment. Lyotard appears oblivious to the ways in which narratives or language games can systematically obscure, distort and oppress. He assumes that they grow organically within the social structure with the result that "All we can do is gaze in wonderment at the diversity of discursive species" (1984: 26). The sociological deficit in this approach is no less striking than the normative one. If Lyotard had taken a participant's perspective rather than that of the anthropologist he might have concluded that inescapable choices need to be made by social actors when confronted by narratives, languages and regimes of phrases. Language games are not simply "incommensurable", but struggle for dominance in any existing discursive context; and routinely some dominate and oppress others. But he rules out the possibility of forming consensus, that is, the political process of persuasion and mobilization, to overthrow oppressive "regimes of phrases". Of the many problems with this argument, one of the more serious is the denial of language as a practical activity. So, Seyla Benhabib concludes that

> modes of thought cannot harmoniously co-exist in one epistemic space, that their very presence next to each other poses moral as well as cognitive problems, ... that the question of validity inevitably confronts us, and that we cannot extricate ourselves from an answer by gazing in wonderment at the plurality of language games and life-forms (1984: 125).

This image of justice is also problematic in its disregard of the way in which traditional narratives may exclude and alienate. So in one account of the Cashinahua narrative Lyotard notes without critical comment that only men are allowed to tell stories (1992: 43). The concept of self-legitimation functions to expunge any critical distance or assessment of these practices. It shrouds the important message of respecting traditional knowledge and custom with excessive idealization. Lyotard offers no grounds on which to decide on some bases rather than others: "If you asked me why I am on that side [of politics], I think that I would answer that I do not have an answer to the question 'why'" (1985: 69). When all narratives have equal claim to respect why not prefer the racist or sexist, or indeed those that demand that other narratives should be repressed within the social space where they have become dominant, as many *petit reçits* routinely do? Lyotard fails to examine the types of structural forces that lead to the dominance of certain narratives, and the multiform ways in which they oppress where they are not freely chosen. Moreover, his fundamentally liberal political philosophy goes very much against the grain of his repudiation of the many modern, repressive metanarratives of which liberalism is one ("the emancipation of the rational subject").

It is difficult to see what positive prescriptions this theory might offer law. Which of the available multitudinous values should a legal system embody? How is it possible to express institutionally the pluralism that Lyotard recommends? Should it proscribe certain types of behaviour that narratives recommend? What sort of constitutional structures, if any, would be in place to protect such dissensus? Does the "artificial reason" of the law qualify as a self-legitimating narrative? Lyotard offers little to suggest answers to these questions. As Litowitz argues, "Strangely, Lyotard devotes hundreds of pages to discussions of justice and law, but he never actually discloses the *arrangement* he thinks is most defensible" (1997: 132; my italics). For instance, he raises the problem of a conceptual dispute in a discussion about his notion of the "differend". The differend is in the nature of an element from one language that defies translation into another: it is "the unstable state and instance of language wherein something that must be able to be put into phrases cannot yet be" (1988: 13). His practical examples include indigenous peoples and wage-labourers in capitalist societies whose claims are not translatable into the language of existing rights.

It comes as a surprise to find that Lyotard's solution is not to advocate that these complainants should have enhanced legal rights to redress their legitimate grievances; rather he recommends that in such a case judgment should not proceed "as in the case of litigation" (1988: ix), but be suspended so as to avoid wronging conflicting parties. So, in any conflict, Lyotard recommends an indefinite suspension of judgment. In a manner similar to Derrida's notion of the undecidable, he rejects the ethical exercise of deliberation and practical reasoning in favour of assertions about the impossibility of the just decision. This elaborate defence of abstentionism may have its supporters; but it represents an unsatisfactory evasion of important ethical and political questions. In the context of law, what advice can it offer the judge, or the legislator? Apparently, only that judgment should not be reached. Under such a scheme a language game that might excuse the multinational corporation's environmental degradation in the name of economic growth should merely be allowed to co-exist alongside the injured local community's complaints in the name of a legally unresolved dissensus.

Lyotard's notion of justice raises problems when set alongside the vision of the good represented by the (very modern) idea of human rights. Human rights discourse places universality firmly at the centre of its normative framework: rights apply to all regardless of tradition or affiliation. In the form of international covenants, they represent, from an historical perspective, uniquely broad levels of political *consensus*; and they express an ethical metalanguage, with an institutional framework for carrying them into effect in the face of oppositional discourses. As such, they appear to have all of the qualities that Lyotard's theory disparages. But as we have seen in the previous chapter, central objectives of human rights include limiting governmental power, fostering open and accountable political processes, and enhancing the autonomy of individuals and groups. These are the minimal institutional requirements for the justice of which Lyotard speaks, yet they appear inconsistent with much of his argument. A glimmer of concern for the institutional dimension appears in an article where he discusses human rights (1993). He affirms the right to freedom of speech on the basis that it is the key to guaranteeing respect for human otherness, and that it is "perhaps the most fundamental human right", and commends the work of Amnesty International for working to support it. He notes how the "minimal" condition of legal protection of the capacity to speak requires support from a "civilization" that confers on all the "authority to speak" (1993: 141). But Lyotard fails to pursue the important question of how and to what extent legal frameworks and cultural values depend on each other and what institutional preconditions are necessary for the "respect for the Other" (1993: 147) to be secured.

Though Lyotard's primary project is the development of an elaborate theory of knowledge and language as the basis for theory of justice, he also writes about the "postmodern condition" and so necessarily addresses descriptive sociological questions. As we have seen in chapter 2, he offers an albeit sketchy sociological analysis of contemporary society to explain the emergence of this new knowledge by reference to wider structural change. The postmodern condition is both a matter of changed forms and functions of knowledge, and a transformed set of structural conditions within which that knowledge develops. In addition to his prescriptive claims about the undesirability of metanarratives, Lyotard also concludes that *empirically* the metanarrative has declined. This claim is a serious oversimplification. Certainly the horrors of the twentieth century have worked to utterly discredit communist and fascist ideologies, but the same cannot be said for parliamentary liberalism that, far from being rendered illegitimate by events such as May 1968, as Lyotard claims, has become an ever more entrenched and widespread feature of the global political landscape. Indeed if the verb "refute" has any relevance in this context it is by reference to the way in which parliamentary liberalism refutes the "incredulity towards metanarratives" thesis that Lyotard proposes. Over the last couple of decades liberalism both as a political philosophy and a theory advocating the central role of markets in economic justice has become as dominant a "modern" metanarrative as any of those that Lyotard identifies. A no less significant sociological development to "refute" the Lyotardian thesis is the spread of human rights discourse that has become established globally to become as much a *grand reçit* as any other, and is replete with modern notions of universality and freedom.

Lyotard's sociological excursus clearly puts him in breach of his own proscription against large-scale theorizing. An account about the emergence of the "postmodern condition" represents a very large historical narrative about how modern societies based on industrial production have been overtaken by postindustrial societies where what he describes as a pervasive "performativity" characterizes legitimate knowledge. Insofar as the analysis purports to reveal the inner nature of the macro-historical category of "postmodern condition" it is anything but a *petit reçit*. As with Foucault, the repudiation of totalizing approaches to sociological inquiry appears to apply only to *other types* of totalizing discourse. Moreover, Lyotard's own metanarrative ultimately represents an uncritical adoption of theories of postindustrialism (Best and Kellner, 1991: 171). As we have seen in chapter 2, postindustrialism is but one element in the changed structural and cultural features of contemporary advanced capitalist societies. By contrast, the theorists of postmodernization offer a far more convincing and complex understanding of contemporary societies.

Despite the weaknesses, Lyotard's work offers some useful sociological insights. As we have seen in the previous chapter, his notion of "performativity" sheds light on aspects of an emerging rationality of legal discourse no less evident than in other social spheres. Also, his valorization of narratives lends theoretical support to novel perspectives on law such as critical race theory, sexuality and the law, law and literature and "narrative" approaches to law (Litowitz, 1997: 133). Likewise, his emphasis on the temporary nature of contemporary social relations, as expressed in increasingly contractual relationships, captures a distinctive feature of recent social and legal change. And it is important to acknowledge the germ of truth in Lyotard's assault on metanarratives. There is much to agree with in a weak postmodern thesis that theories on the grand scale *may* indeed obscure more than they reveal *and* contain tendencies towards intellectual hubris, which in turn may lend support to political regimes that seek to repress and remove dissent. This is neither an exclusively postmodern, nor a particularly novel, methodological prescription in social theory. It was famously articulated in C. Wright Mills' critique of grand theory (1959), and finds articulate expression in ethnomethodological and phenomenological approaches. The choice ought not to be posed as a simple one between either large- or small-scale theorizing, but how to mark the several limitations of each.

A more instructive approach would be to distinguish between different uses and types of metanarrative. A metanarrative may operate as a descriptive category, mapping out broad shifts in social structure and consciousness across time. However, such a map may be misused. Where the concepts that capture these broad shifts are deployed too systematically and too universally, or where they oversimplify the messy and often unsystematic empirical reality under investigation without regard to local practices, or to "narratives" that may offer significant counter-evidence, they obscure more than they explain. To suggest that the broader concepts are unacceptable as Lyotard does – and this point is no less relevant to Foucault's rejection of totalization – confuses an important recommendation of sociological caution with an unhelpful proscription against any kind of sociological generalization.

Metanarratives may also be prescriptive or normative, and Lyotard makes an important point in emphasizing how they too may be open to abuse. A political or moral philosophy that operates with only one dominant normative principle such as freedom or solidarity, and advocates that all political efforts should be directed to achieving it, will tend to ignore other important values and priorities. In the place of Lyotard's blanket rejection of metanarratives, a better option is to examine how large and small concepts, both prescriptive and descriptive, combine to offer a richer picture of the social world, and the place of law in it.

Legal Postmodernism

Many of the themes noted above have appeared in legal scholarship over the last couple of decades, introduced by theorists who wish to offer deeper insights into law by means of postmodernist ideas. The writing in this genre has displayed each of three "negations" noted at the commencement of this chapter (of utopia, of totality, and of science). In consequence, despite a wide and spreading influence, it manifests comparable and related weaknesses.[4] The negation of utopian solutions is reflected in legal scholarship in an antipathy toward large prescriptive approaches to law and legal institutions. As above, the term "utopia" in this context refers to those grand, modern political and ethical principles, associated with the Enlightenment, which guide both critique and reform. The anti-utopian tendency in postmodernist legal scholarship is evident in a general shift away from large prescriptive claims about law.

A closely related move is the avoidance of prescriptions about present, existing legal doctrines and institutions where those prescriptions are derived from the large modern principles. This is not to argue that these theoretical positions refuse a normative stance. On the contrary, in their systematic rejection of the utopian schemes advanced by modern philosophy they are necessarily and unmistakably normative. But this particular radical rejection of all things modern, a radicalism after the metanarrative, is a predominantly *negative* stance toward law and legal institutions if it contains neither an express nor an implied program for reform. As we shall see, even where specific prescriptions are advanced they frequently reflect problems typical of the normative positions identified in the theories above.

A repudiation of totality appears in the form of a pervasive rejection of any macro-sociological understanding of law in relation to wider social structures or historical processes, and is reflected in tendencies to focus on more marginal dimensions of the legal domain. The third postmodernist negation, namely the stance against science, appears in the notions that legal truth is illusory; law has no ultimate foundation; legal meanings are purely conventional and contingent; and that this is not so much a matter for regret, but a necessary and inescapable condition. Given the diversity of this body of literature, I will offer in this section a critical overview of some of its central themes as exemplified in the work of a selection of the more influential theorists.

The path-breaking and imaginative scholarship of Costas Douzinas, Peter Goodrich and their various collaborators (1991; 1994; 1995; 2000) is an example of an elaboration of such themes. The general trajectory of their argument starts with Douzinas and Warrington's claim that "jurisprudence goes postmodern in order to retain and redraw its old commitment to plural and open forms of reason(s) and communities" (1991: 27). In Derridean fashion this central, "radical" project is proclaimed to share "much common ground with the radical aspirations of late twentieth-century oppositional politics", and to involve attacking mainstream jurisprudential "logonomocentrism" (1991: 28). This and many other affirmations display solidarity with a politics of recognition; and consistent with the postmodernism outlined above the radicalism is not informed by the Enlightenment values of truth, justice and freedom. Nor is there any emphasis on a politics of redistribution. Accordingly, the authors subject Marx, Dworkin and Gadamer to sustained critique. For a positive focus, and one indicative of a clear preference for non-totalizing accounts of law, the authors provide ingenious and iconoclastic assaults on various (marginal) forms of legal activity – the fate of a rejected law review article, an ecclesiastical dispute about aesthetics, a report of the Bar Council on the quality of justice (1991: chs 10-12). Though it is valuable that aspects of legal life beyond the mainstream are subjected to scholarly scrutiny, and with a micro- rather than macro-perspective, it remains unclear how this jurisprudential position qualifies as radical in the wider political sense, as does the project of what, in *being* oppositional, it specifically entails in terms of law and legal institutions, other than simply being against them.

Later attempts to remedy the normative indeterminacy of this approach appear in the deployment of ethics and aesthetics to provide some programmatic ideas. For Douzinas, Goodrich and Hachamovitch, an examination of the "emotional" foundations of law, when combined with a philosophical rejection of moral critique – "Legality does not belong to the moral but to the aesthetic order" (1994: 26-28) – provide the critical framework for evaluating law and legal institutions. Similarly, Douzinas and Warrington propose, "to articulate a theory of ethical action upon which a practice of justice can be built which itself would not reproduce the totalizing tendencies that deconstruction so correctly challenged" (1995: 17). The theory of ethical action they favour is to be found in the "fundamental consideration of the other" (1995: 18). But having identified the law as "an institution that has largely failed to achieve minimal standards of justice in its operation" (1995: 132), the authors' postmodernism fails to register any more developed analysis of the sources and consequences of this pervasive failure, or substantive legal reforms that might assist in reversing it.

Some indication of the empirical evidence that might qualify as establishing failure is suggested by Douzinas, Goodrich and Hachamovitch in a reference to, among other things, the "flagrant miscarriages of justice [that] are perhaps its most manifest contemporary feature" (1994: 16). A later text bearing the title of *Justice Miscarried* (Douzinas and Warrington, 1995) implies that such fundamental manifestations of the failure of law might be taken seriously, if only as examples of the general argument. So it is perplexing to find only a passing reference in the books (1995: ch 1) to any actual cases involving miscarriages of justice, and none to the inadequate institution mechanisms that facilitate them. Nor is it clear why these matters are irrelevant to the authors' concerns with alterity. It seems a particularly striking omission given that both books were written in the United Kingdom in the 1990s, where the "contemporary feature" referred to was the revelation of the miscarriages of justice involving a number of men and women jailed for terrorist crimes they did not commit. But instead of an analysis of how a legal system does not merely offer feeble resistance to injustices of this nature, but is readily enlisted in perpetrating them, the authors propose a general "ethics and aesthetics" of law as their divining rod for justice. Accordingly, analyses of the tragedy of Sophocles' Antigone (1994: ch 6; 1995: ch 2), rather than those of the Birmingham 6 or the Guildford 4 become a central focus.

Without question, Antigone expresses a powerful political message of revolt in the face of brutal and oppressive regimes. But it is unclear what light it sheds on liberal democracies subject to constitutional restraints that might obstruct, contain and possibly prevent the types of behaviour displayed by the tyrant Creon in that play. More specifically, the play has little to say on the subject of miscarriages of justice, which might be considered a useful testing ground for an "aesthetics and ethics" of law, because they are not so much instances of an irreconcilable conflict between a legal and moral norm as confronted Antigone (to obey the law of Creon, as opposed to the norm of family piety), but about the corruption of (modern) procedural justice in the application of otherwise legitimate laws prohibiting murder. It is difficult to extrapolate from the authors' proposed ethics and aesthetics of law any helpful guidance in resolving the injustices in these cases. In contrast, political campaigns that have sought redress for miscarriages of justice – examples, perhaps, of the "late twentieth-century oppositional politics" – have tended, for good reasons, to take a very different "critical" and "political" tack. They do not assert, in typically Derridean style, that all law is necessarily indeterminate or undecidable. Nor do they claim that there is no such thing as a right answer, or that justice is only in the future. Still less do they suggest that justice is marked by "incalculability" (Douzinas and Warrington, 1995: 184). On the contrary, in their pursuit of a very calculable justice, they variously claim at least that: particular laws have been twisted beyond any commonly accepted meaning and expectation; the wrong law has been applied; evidence (of facts) has been concealed, or fabricated; or that appellate courts have failed in their duty to scrutinize properly the conduct of trials.

Such arguments implicitly, and valuably, affirm rather than reject many of the important elements of justice embodied in modern law. They include the independence and impartiality of the judiciary, *rights to* equality of treatment of suspects, and fair assessment of evidence with rights of appeal. These principles require that judges should not act as apologists for corrupt police and prison officers. Furthermore, critiques in this vein rely intensely on moral rather than aesthetic judgment, in a manner akin to Lon Fuller's *Morality of Law* (1969) where law is expected to live up to its proclaimed ideals rather than abandon them as misguided or "impossible" attempts at justice. A typical element in such campaigns is the demand that subjects should be treated in "modern" fashion as abstract individuals, not as "foreign" or "terrorist" or whatever other differences define their various subjectivities. Respect for the other often requires institutional, and therefore, legal, *disregard* for difference.

In contrast, the proposal of a politically uncritical engagement with "the emotional conditions for the possibility of law" (Douzinas, Goodrich and Hachamovitch, 1994: 28), when combined with a philosophical devaluation of moral critique in favour of aesthetic assessment, fatally obstructs an examination of the all-too-emotionally-driven suspension of liberties and rights that are common factors in miscarriages of justice. The autonomy of legal discourse and the independence of its institutional practices from political, populist, "emotional" demands provide important points of resistance to precisely these pressures. This is not to argue that the rule of law exhausts justice, or to ignore the fact that claims that the rule of law exists in a particular society can operate to close off criticism of the routine practices of legal systems that may breed injustice. Rather, it is to suggest that the rule of law, *systematically and institutionally entrenched*, is an essential part of a system of justice. Nor does this assessment imply that aesthetic approaches to law are essentially unhelpful, whether or not postmodern concepts are deployed. It is only where the aesthetic is expected to substitute for the political or the ethical in these analyses, and where no limits are imposed on the aesthetic approach, that it obscures more than it enlightens.

Ironically, the authors' powerful criticism that the "increasing divergence between theory and practice, however, indicated that Marxism ... sorely lacked a theorization of the political" (Douzinas and Warrington, 1991: 115), can be turned back on the bulk of this work. For all the references to "the political", it displays a striking absence of any consideration of the practice of politics or the workings of political institutions. So, in the discussion of Antigone, the authors are largely unconcerned with the play's powerful political implications, relegating this dimension of the play to a footnote (1994: 223). Instead, their central focus is on the play's universal *ethical* call to revolt. To be sure, the question of civil disobedience and revolt against the law needs to be a central focus for jurisprudential study; and the authors to their credit make a powerful case for inclusion of its relevance for the theoretical study of law. But traditional jurisprudential natural law theories, and even positivist accounts, pose these questions no less centrally. And in a more constructive vein they advance more significant normative content. By contrast, the authors simplistically offer ethics as the relevant critical measure for law without any indication of the circumstances when it would or should trump law. No less significant is the absence of any consideration of how bad laws might be changed, rather than disobeyed, and if so, in what direction.

It is relevant to speculate in this context how would an economy or criminal justice system be structured if indeed laws were to be more rigorously policed by an intense ethics of alterity within a particular community? The imperative to do justice to the other seems a slender reed on which to build the relevant principles and regulatory mechanisms. So, the difficult questions about how they would be institutionalized, how disputes would be resolved and by whom, are effectively ignored in this scheme. Such an ethical position, given its profoundly anti-sociological temper, cannot begin to address theoretically and politically the differently situated "others" in society. Why should the owners of vast wealth and power and the impoverished and homeless be treated in the same way, as the ethics of alterity seems blindly to assume? Should they pay the same taxes, and be entitled to the same measure of state support? Precisely at the point where an ethical perspective becomes important, this body of work tails off into a series of empty gestures.

Being committed to an ethics of alterity, like being in a state of grace, represents a commendable starting point, but what actions such an ethical attitude might entail is the true measure of its value; and this work generally provides no answers to this pressing question. Moreover, an ethical framework that only considers the relationships with other *individuals* is congenitally hampered in offering moral prescriptions for *institutions and groups of others*. Are the police, large corporations, or the security agencies "others" to whom an ethics of alterity should be extended? An ethics of alterity without such refinements implies an oversimplified elision of the public and private spheres which of necessity must be regulated by different principles. Given that law itself, no less than specific legal rules or identifiable legal regimes, appears incapable of delivering justice within this theoretical framework, it makes little sense to enlist it to the regulatory project. It is hardly surprising therefore that such a stance fails to yield any recommendations for substantive legal reform. This is not to suggest that the authors would do better to focus on empirical detail; rather, the problem resides in the fact that this style of iconoclastic theorizing appears to be methodologically geared to prevent such exercises.

The general antipathy to the institutional requirements of a system of justice is reiterated in Douzinas' recent study of human rights (2000).

Human rights, with all their Enlightenment baggage, represent but the latest phase in the unfolding of contingent, unjust modern legality. They are characterized by "[t]he gap between the triumph of human rights ideology and the disaster of their practice" (2000: 12). Douzinas emphasizes, in Lyotardian vein, the historically unique levels of bloodshed over the past couple of centuries. He notes how they have accompanied the emergence of human rights discourse, and the institutional mechanisms structured to implement them. It follows that the general sociological and political function of human rights is to obscure, and thereby be in some way complicit with, oppressive regimes. The argument suggests a causal relationship between a rights discourse and reality, but flowing in the wrong direction: the rights discourse is implicated in the terror.

Nevertheless, Douzinas goes on to argue that it does not follow that every aspect of human rights is objectionable. Human rights discourse is to be extolled when it expresses the sentiments of the oppressed, the marginalized, the other; when human rights-talk assumes this form it becomes "the utopian element behind legal rights" (2000: 245). The problem appears when these sentiments are incorporated into "historicist" narratives of human progress, where they merely serve as ideological ballast, "the legitimating device of some of the most sclerotic regimes and powers". When they receive institutional expression in any form they acquire all the ugliness of modern law: they become "obscured in ever more declarations, treaties and diplomatic lunches" (2000: 380). The gist of this argument is that as felt ideals, or ethics, human rights express important and valuable images of justice, that do "not belong to the abstract human being of the declarations or conventions ..." (2000: 145). But when they assume the form of law, either in international or domestic contexts, they become corrupted.

Douzinas shows some inconsistency in this conclusion. At one point he admits that human rights conventions "are of use to human rights activists, by offering a standard for criticizing their governments" implying surely that their normative force may actually lead to changes in practice and law (2000: 144). But he fails to explore the consequences of such an admission, preferring to see the deployment of such a standard merely as a form of micro-politics of resistance. It is worth speculating as to what the point of such criticism is if it does not translate into political, social and legal change. The governments and the officials responsible for human rights abuses tend to be as unmoved by "criticisms" from human rights activists as they are by the pleas of their victims.

As a practical matter human rights become meaningful, in the sense that they effectively change practices, when human rights-informed criticism translates into institutional transformation. The process is advanced by structures that can restrain governmental power, often assisted by *extraterritorial* political pressure when mobilized with local oppositional groups into political campaigns. The norms of human rights conventions, with their provisions referring to abstract human subjects, in conjunction with the decisions of human rights tribunals, are central to this process. One reason for their normative force is that they have a legitimacy grounded in a past international political consensus about some basic shared human needs and purposes. Only when such criticisms attain the normative force of domestic legislation, and when the judgments of courts, both international and domestic, decree that prisoners be freed, refugees allowed to settle, and indigenous peoples afforded recognition of traditional rights do human rights norms become valuable. As Risse, Ropp and Sikkink (1999) demonstrate in a detailed empirical study of the entrenchment of human rights in formerly authoritarian regimes, only structural embedding of human rights in the form of domestic legislation, typically the result of political pressure from diverse alliances of NGOs and other governments, secures meaningful protection for citizens. But Douzinas ignores the positive, empirical gains that the entrenchment of human rights has achieved.

This oversight is reflected in Douzinas' extended discussion of legal subjectivity. He glosses over the ways in which human rights confer a genuine further layer of legal entitlement upon individual citizens that may empower them against governments; instead, "the legal element of rights returns us to subjection, external determination and constraint" (2000: 226). Also, because the analysis focuses predominantly on the individual subject of modern law and human rights it ignores the important gains in legal subjectivity acquired by groups such as NGOs and indigenous peoples in international forums. It is a curious recognition of otherness that would withhold legal protection from those others within the framework of international human rights.

Because human rights abuses have been perpetrated in unimaginable numbers and forms over the last century is no reason, as Douzinas insists, to withdraw support for the incorporation of human rights into domestic law, any more than high rates of rape suggest that laws outlawing sexual violence should be repealed. The argument is sociologically simplistic because it fails to take into account the distinction between the existence and efficacy of rules, and largely ignores empirical research into the effects of human rights. As a number of studies referred to in the previous chapter suggest, the deepening of human rights discourse *within nations* can offer and has already offered very real advances in the rights of citizens, and importantly, non-citizens.[5] It is just when they lack a firm institutional basis that a real gap between the ideology and the practice emerges. The weakness in Douzinas' argument largely resides in the failure to take seriously the question of the institutional conditions for securing human rights. In this respect it typifies a recurrent aporia in postmodernist accounts of law.

Of course, the extension of human rights norms is no simple solution to the goal of spreading justice on a global scale. As Douzinas powerfully argues, the Enlightenment model of justice – individualist, universal, liberal – appears uncongenial to other types of rights, such as social rights. Also, the reconciliation of the norms of traditional cultures and societies, often expressed in national laws, remains a difficult problem in the development of supranational human rights. There are no uncomplicated answers to the question of priority where the important value of cultural specificity clashes with the universalism of human rights. But this is no argument to abandon the project altogether, and to assume that as institutionalized norms, with their essential, professional corps of officials, they obstruct rather than advance the goals they espouse. Douzinas' position has all the hallmarks of what Stanley Fish sees in the anti-professional stance: "at the moment that a left-wing intellectual turns anti-professional, he has become a right-wing intellectual in disguise" (1989: 231). In contrast to the micro-politics of resistance that appears as the only noble option in this account, a more satisfactory political strategy is the development of critiques of existing legal systems that foster particular injustices, and collective action to advance concrete political and legal reforms as institutional bulwarks to resist their recurrence.

The postmodern negation of science appears in legal postmodernism in the form of the "contingency" or "undecidability" seen to lie at the heart of law. Law is held to lack a secure, identifiable foundation from which the truth of its pronouncements might be established. It follows that the notion of law's predictability and its autonomy from other spheres is illusory. In a clear evocation of an earlier theme within the Critical Legal Studies (CLS) movement, the contingencies of law are seen to be evident in its incapacity to establish certain, determinate, true meanings. In contrast to its official ideology, law is defined by "its errors, its weaknesses, its shifts of position, its subordination to policy" (Douzinas, Goodrich and Hachamovitch, 1994: 16). This argument recurs in much of the wider postmodern literature on law. For Anthony Carty "postmodernism marks the reintroduction of ontology into law, not as a solution to the question of the foundation of law, but as a firm assertion that law has no foundation" (1990: 6), while Margaret Davies emphasizes "the gaps, logical incoherence, and acts of theoretical force, which are integral to the ideology of the law" (1996: 64). Within these lines of critique the negative dimension of deconstructionist accounts comes to the fore, with its tendency to emphasize the "un-ness" of things, with their incapacity to conceal traces of the "other" within the formal identity of law. As Drucilla Cornell formulates it, "the Law of Law is only 'present' in its absolute absence. The 'never have been' of an unrecoverable past is understood as the lack of origin 'presentable' *only* as absence" (1992: 93).

As was noted above in relation to Derrida's work, the notion of the uncertain identity of law grounded in the inescapable imprecision of language, and the idea that the origins of law are always outside law, and therefore are non-legal, are familiar and recurrent themes in traditional jurisprudential inquiry. In the case of rules, according to traditional accounts they are always seen to exhibit a measure of indeterminacy at the margins. But in postmodern analyses, as with the Critical Legal Studies (CLS) movement that preceded them, a more ambitious claim is made: every dimension of law is of this order. But in general little evidence is offered to substantiate such a broad conclusion other than the discussion of a small number of cases. These case analyses do reveal important aspects of deconstructive techniques and expose how legal reasoning often comes to rely on other forms of rationality to sustain its claims. For example, Goodrich provides an insightful examination of nervous shock cases in the law of negligence by means of identifying various rhetorical tropes deployed by judges in their reasoning: far from being simple applications of legal principle, the judgments are shot through with arguments that have their origin in non-legal discourses (1994: ch 4). Likewise, Douzinas and Warrington (1995) provide compelling accounts of how notions of otherness can drive processes of judicial interpretation so as to render legal rules inadequate mechanisms for the expression of a meaningful ethic of alterity within the law. These are undoubtedly novel and valuable angles of analysis of judicial reasoning, but they hardly sustain the more radical claims the authors make about law's undecidability for the reason that they ignore the effectiveness of interpretive principles and professional understandings that impose clear limits on judicial freedom. It follows that

> Deconstruction within the law – which ... usually amounts in practice to quite ordinary efforts at undermining a particular line of reasoning – is inadequate in large part because it fails to account for interpretive norms and criteria. In law and elsewhere, texts have reasonably fixed meanings because of shared interpretive principles (Sunstein, 1989: 463).

The difficulties of the deconstructive stance as a description of legal reasoning are compounded by its normative deficiencies. Despite the political and moral critique of the outcome of particular cases, there is nonetheless a level of political and moral abstentionism about what normative principles or interpretive norms ought to govern judicial decision-making. Rather, a form of subversion is the game: ideologies are suspect, claims to objectivity are shown to be specious, truth is illusory. In certain contexts, this type of critique can undermine certain patterns of authority; but in its reluctance to suggest what might be put in its place, it is politically suspect. It pulls the rug from under any critique of judicial bias, conflict of interest, or corruption. And if all meaning is elastic, what sense does it make to have faith in the capacity of laws to regulate or punish unjust and exploitative practices? As Terry Eagleton concludes:

> [i]t is unwise to assume that ambiguity, indeterminacy, undecidability are always subversive strikes against an arrogantly monological certitude; on the contrary, they are the stock-in-trade of many a judicial inquiry and official investigation (1990: 379-380).

A more philosophical elaboration of postmodernist ideas in the legal sphere appears in Margaret Davies' *Delimiting the Law* (1996). Building on her insightful and highly original earlier work, Davies is concerned to interrogate the boundary-rider project of traditional legal theory by means of which it seeks to identify what distinguishes law from non-law. She finds, particularly in the positivism of Austin, Kelsen and Hart, flawed attempts to assert law's autonomy from other social spheres such as politics and morality. The shared fault of each of these theorists lies in their concealment of the non-legal origins from which law emerges. Their positivism overlooks the violence inherent in those origins, presuming that law is self-contained, located within clearly definable and readily discernible limits. In deconstructive vein, she finds law's "undecidability" to reside in the fact that its foundation can never be entirely legal, so that it is always legal and non-legal at the same time in an "unresolvable contradiction" (1996: 80). In a searching and perceptive analysis of the weak points in the works of the leading proponents of legal positivism, Davies demonstrates the insuperable difficulties that they have in attempting to purge law completely of non-legal elements. Austin's sovereign command, Hart's rule of recognition, and Kelsen's *Grundnorm* all fail to overcome this contradictory element of law.

As Davies insists, the express purpose behind her own exercise in deconstruction is political: "the overtly political nature of this enquiry arises when we start to think about how the concept of law can be reformulated ... in order to further our political goals" (1996: 38). But for all the commendable promise of political engagement, it is very difficult to see how any political program can be launched from this platform given that the analysis is pitched overwhelmingly at identifying how *all* law and legal systems are seen to suffer from the same problem of contradiction. Though she castigates traditional legal theory for perpetrating "the myths of [law's] purity, closure, and fixity: the blind insistence that 'proper' law is separate from the other sorts of norms which order society" (1996: 39), Davies appears unable to move to a fully reformulated concept of law to do so. Partly because she sides with Derrida in the conclusion that all law is based on a covert foundational violence that resurfaces in the repeated decisions made in the daily routines of legal practice, it becomes impossible to articulate the "*significant political* differences" that she wishes to expose within law (1996: 37; italics in original). Across the entire range of possible legal orders, Davies assumes that law exhibits the same deficiencies; there are no concepts in her scheme that offer the means for making the desired political discriminations.

At base, the normative deficit in this approach is compounded by the sociological one, as is typical of postmodern theory in general. Though Davies expresses at various points a powerful and incisive feminist critique of certain aspects of (modern) law, she seems unwilling or unable, from the vantage point of deconstruction, to develop a positive jurisprudential position that might give expression to the politics that inform her critical examination of law. In her bold theoretical move of uncovering the impurity and permeability of law in general, she ends up replicating the very weakness of the traditional jurisprudence she decries: by essentializing law across time and place, but with a negative rather than positive valuation, she forecloses the possibility of identifying how particular reforms within existing legal systems might point the way forward. Instead of a genuinely political analysis of law that might hold out viable means for achieving justice through law, she advances a purely transcendental, metaphysical critique of law from which no such politics can be deduced.

The "exhaustion of utopian energies" (Habermas, 1989) is also evident, but assumes a different form, in Peter Fitzpatrick's accounts of the emergence and development of modern law (1992; 2001). Though his is not expressly a postmodernist approach to law, it lies squarely within the genre by virtue of his extended deployment of the theoretical resources provided by this body of work. In an impressively elaborated body of writing, Fitzpatrick offers an eloquent and probing exegesis of the "mythological", racist and oppressive dimensions of modern law. On this account, the glare of Enlightenment reason is dimmed by the colonialism and racism that have been the continuous historical practice of Western law. Following Derrida, Western law, far from treating subjects as abstract and free, and based on reason and science as it pretends, is a "white mythology" (1992: x; 32). From its inception it has identified otherness only to crush it in favour of capitalist development. Its claims to universality function to hide the Western particularism at the heart of its project of domination. In a meticulous development of Foucault's account of subjectivity and governmentality, Fitzpatrick argues that modern liberal legality dominates by its connection with administration: "law, even in its own apparent expansion, seems to serve increasingly as an agent, accessory and support in the advance of scientific administration" (1992: 154). Far from restraining power, the rule of law is implicated in the domination of administration. Legal subjects in modernity fall into a habit of obedience as a result of the constrictive institutional pressures toward self-discipline.

The examples offered by Fitzpatrick to elucidate his argument are those of judicial review of administrative action in cases of national security and prisons. Even though he identifies a recent "judicial assertiveness" in administrative law that appears to restrain bureaucratic arbitrariness, it ultimately either defers to authorities in important instances, or overturns so infinitesimal a number of decisions that its influence is negligible. Its net effect therefore is to "confirm" administration (1992: 163). This analysis of the way law intersects with disciplinary mechanisms represents an advance on Foucault's marginalization of law, but it nonetheless suffers from similar weaknesses. Because it identifies law's function in a wholly reductionist manner, it is blind to the gains that access to law may have not only for prisoners but citizens at large. Moreover, Fitzpatrick's account affords administration far too dominant a role in the understanding of modern societies. These societies are hardly exhausted by their bureaucratic structures, especially in their most recent forms where shrinking states hive off former functions to the private sector. No less "drained of moral distinctions" than the theories above, the argument reiterates the theme that modern law has no lasting or desirable achievements in any of its historical or sociological manifestations. As is evident from his examples, *all* modern law is cast in this mould.

Fitzpatrick's particular anti-utopianism is further reflected in an incapacity to find any progressive potential even in *alternatives to law*. So, his account of the spreading influence of "popular justice" in the form of the Community Boards of San Francisco sees it as a "supposed retreat" from modern legality; on the contrary it represents "an extension of formal regulation" (1992: 169). In Derridean style, the dualism of formalism/informalism reveals, when subjected to a deconstructive reading, a striking interconnection, "a mythic mutuality" which guarantees "the integrity of law depends on the popular justice it opposes" (1992: 180).

The critical thinker who is of a mind to consider how our modern law might be rendered more just is warned off such an exercise by this work. To place faith in the (mythic) forms of modern legality such as tighter judicial review of administrative action is just as misguided as, for instance, a preference for community-based informal forums where otherwise marginalized non-legal norms can be reasserted: all models extend "formal regulation". To be sure, alternative dispute resolution presents certain ethical dilemmas, some of which Fitzpatrick alludes to; but shoring up the legitimacy of the formal legal system would seem to be one of the least significant. Its recent ascendancy in most areas of law can at least in part be attributable to some morally positive features, such as its capacity in many instances to deliver more effective justice than the formal courts can. In other words popular political and ethical legitimacy are more plausible factors in the emergence of alternative dispute resolution than the formal system's aim to extend domination. A similarly dystopian message is insinuated in Fitzpatrick's argument about racism insofar as it suggests that modern law in all its manifestations is irremediably tainted by its racist origins, with each historical instance expressing that rigid teleology.

This account of law's historical progression ignores ways in which modern law in many jurisdictions has shed many of those racist characteristics, and what that might mean for his argument. By implication, those changes would appear merely to affirm modern law's essential nature. To be sure, many of Fitzpatrick's points, powerfully made, richly explore the extent to which modern law's specification of the abstract subject is contradicted by its historical practice. But in assuming this is one of its immutable features, it represents a highly essentialist, metaphysical image of law rather than politically charged examination of its nature. It is therefore incapable of delivering any specific political or moral guidance for reform.[6] In the context of racism, a direct consequence of the approach is an implication that campaigns to make law colour-blind have little point, being incapable of changing this fundamental condition. Such an analysis seems to express exactly what Luhmann had in mind in his sombre prediction that former critical approaches to law might give way to "more radical claims combined with pre-adaptive resignation" (1986: 111).

Like Douzinas, Fitzpatrick has more recently brought the same deconstructive, rather than critical, tools to bear on supranational law. His main target is the legal framework of the European Union (Bergeron and Fitzpatrick, 1998; Fitzpatrick, 2001). Though he acknowledges how the Union has worked to advance effectively a form of legal pluralism, it is a repugnant one for the reason that

> [t]he EU and its law do all this, however, not in a supposedly postmodernist responsiveness to and regard for each such thing in its quivering specificity but in its monadic orientation towards their own determinative work, their own particular *telos* (2001: 143; italics in original).

The EU replicates all-too-systematically the "modernist mission of state formation" and in its development, "nationalism is heightened rather than diminished" (2001: 142, 145). This general argument is unconvincing: if legal pluralism has been advanced, it necessarily entails some degree of fragmentation of power and national sovereignty (MacCormick, 1993; 1997). By contrast, within Fitzpatrick's theoretical framework, it becomes impossible to consider any gains that might inform a political or moral stance in relation to this emergent legal system, or indeed to imagine what type of evidence might be adduced to refute the argument. Every change, however apparently at odds with the general characteristics of the object in view, is seen to represent its more solid instantiation. Thus the process of globalization and its legal dimensions are seen to conform to the general pattern of development. They are "more crudely colonial than the project of law and development", and being "more and more effected in the name of the global or human rights or of the world community ... they still manifest the most blatant discriminations and sustain an operative *imperium*" (2001: 214; 217; italics in original). In a manner reminiscent of many types of Marxist analysis that saw each unfolding stage of capitalist development as yet another, or even more, pernicious form of class oppression, in this model each reconfiguration of nation entrenches rather than unsettles the hold of nationalist state-building and imperialism.

Importantly, in this respect the argument represents a break with one postmodernist theme: it is a totalizing narrative *par excellence*. Law absorbs and accumulates both oppositional forces and allies alike to retain its social pre-eminence. This reductive sociological image, like other forms of legal change Fitzpatrick examines, glosses over the manifold and uneven losses and gains consequent on the consolidation of the EU and its legal institutions, as well as the phenomenon of globalization generally. The moral questions as to whether the changes in the rights of prisoners or immigrants in the United Kingdom are more or less just because of the influence of the ECHR, or whether the WTO should provide standing to parties other than states, are rendered irrelevant by this analysis. The result is a message of hopelessness in the face of a monolithic, deterministic and all-embracing legal modernity, which Fitzpatrick at one point, in an unusually frank disclosure, appears to acknowledge: "Utopian alternatives to the administered world prove to be modes of further implicating us in it" (1992: 178). This lugubrious picture looks unconvincing when set against, for instance, Braithwaite and Drahos' (2000) detailed empirical study of global business regulation, which reveals a far more complicated story, where regular, if limited, opportunities for reform appear in favour of consumers and weaker parties against large corporations.

An elaborated and more explicit anti-utopian stance is to be found in Pierre Schlag's work in which many of the theoretical ideas outlined above circulate. A primary target of Schlag's position is the "normativity" that permeates both traditional and critical forms of academic legal studies and scholarship. Critiques of law in general or of particular aspects of legal practice are irrelevant at best, undesirable at worst. Given that judges do not read law reviews, critiques of doctrine are ineffectual, and normative arguments against certain legal forms and practices are impotent in face of the daily operations of bureaucratic legal institutions. It follows that those who would measure law by some external standard such as justice, ethics or the public interest are "normative and nowhere to go" (1990).

Schlag suggests that normative legal thought should not only be abandoned because it is ineffectual. Its function of nourishing the official ideology of law makes it not so much useless but pernicious: it merely offers support for the self-perpetuating network of bureaucratic practices and institutions incapable of realizing the ideals supposed to guide it. Schlag makes an important point in emphasizing the legitimating role that normative legal thought plays, as opposed to the purely external relationship to legal practice it commonly assumes. Rule of law arguments permeate the official language of the law, and cloak its pervasive deficiencies (1996: 53-55). All too often acts of injustice perpetrated by and through the legal system are dismissed on the grounds that because the legal system is underpinned by rule of law values, any criticism of its operations is an expression of bad faith. For Schlag, a better pastime than normative legal theory would be, to borrow Lyotard's phrase, merely to "gaze in wonderment" at the language game of legal practice rather than seek to engage in the political exercise of persuading judges, lawyers, legislators or bureaucrats to abandon those practices that impede rather than advance justice. There are also clear resonances here of Foucault's work. Not only does Schlag reject a normative approach to understanding social and legal phenomena; he also sees law not as an autonomous institution with its distinctive normative vocabulary, but merely another form of power in whose grip subjects, from practising lawyers to legal academics, are inescapably caught. It is a large bureaucratic edifice that lawyers may never change, but can only manipulate.

This image of the possible sphere of influence of normative legal scholarship is remarkably constricted. Legal academics' journal articles may well remain unread by judges (particularly if one is arguing against taking any normative position); but law reviews are only one platform in a vast array of discursive domains where normative perspectives on law flourish. Critiques of the operation of particular laws may appear in submissions to government departments, may form part of public inquiries, may find their way into newspaper columns and the election campaigns of political parties. Normative legal theory connects with other critical stances toward the law expressed by all social actors. It forms part of the core of political activity throughout the public and private sphere. As the example of feminism has demonstrated over the last few decades, vigorous normative critiques of law, at the very many levels of legal practice and politics, and which have included academic participation, have secured significant, if unfinished, gains. Moreover, normative legal theory bears directly on *legislation*, which is curiously invisible in Schlag's image of law. An examination of any area of legal reform, from the abolition of slavery to the introduction of anti-discrimination and health and safety laws demonstrates how normative legal theory lies at the very heart of progressive social and legal change. Ironically, in the image of the judge reading the professor's law review article as the paradigm case of normative legal exchange, this analysis places the judge in just as central a position in the legal landscape as does the traditional legal formalism that it otherwise castigates.

Schlag's position raises many of the problems that surround the general postmodern "oppositionism" detailed above. He never addresses the issue as to what should replace the thoroughly corrupted edifice of modern law, which is especially troubling given that the critique of its manifold features implies that its subjects would be better off without it. For all its self-distancing from the CLS movement, Schlag's argument echoes many of its themes, as does legal postmodernism in general. It too was committed to disparaging piecemeal reform of present legal systems. A direct consequence of that approach to law is silence in the face of specific, and unwelcome, directions of legal change, such as the waves of deregulation in the US in the 1980s (Rose-Ackerman, 1990: 517). Schlag's position appears to have taken up the project of political and legal abstentionism where CLS left off, and it converges with political conservatism in rejecting any progressive reformist agenda. But it can also be seen as an even more deficient theoretical move: at the very least CLS held out the prospect of a more just legal order than that offered by legal formalism. By contrast, Schlag's thesis, having identified the repugnance of modern law, implies that it is our inescapable fate to be caught in its embrace, because of the unavoidable futility of our efforts to transform it.

Schlag's irreverent survey of mainstream positions in jurisprudence deals some telling blows to the uncritical complacency evident in some of this work. He advances a set of important criticisms of its incapacity to reflect on its ideological role, and how it feeds into the professional self-image of participants in the legal system. But the problem with proposing that we should not be normative about law is that Schlag cannot avoid offering his own, very normative attitude towards it. Not only does a theoretical "mind your own business", directed to legal scholars working in the academy, become the order of the day; but also, at a deeper level the approach is highly normative in its uniformly negative position toward legal institutions. Because law is variously described as an institution that "kicks people around", "a game of power and manipulation", and a location for the operation of "favour banks" for clients (1996: 51), it has very little to commend it. Legal practice offends the principle of "a government of laws, not men" as much as it represents its embodiment. Such unfavourable descriptions necessarily entail the prescription that we should not lend support to the enterprise of law; on the contrary, we should be "Against the Law" (Schlag, 1996; ix; Campos, Schlag and Smith, 1996).

Schlag therefore appears to be engaged in a performative contradiction: we should not be opposed to specific features in the legal landscape so as to recommend changes in the law; but it is perfectly acceptable to assail the institution as a whole. The central (implicit) normative message is akin to what Habermas describes as the "cryptonormativism" at the heart of Foucault's work: beneath a theoretical stance that steadfastly eschews critique lurks an all-too-normative refusal (Habermas, 1987a: 276-286). In the face of the many, apparently immutable, deficiencies of modern American law in its entirety, and by implication all modern legal systems which can be described as founded on the rule of law, what could one possibly be but in opposition to it? Why this normative stance is superior to arguing that the law would do better if it held fast to its rule of law rhetoric is not explored. Instead, Schlag prefers the more comfortable option of withdrawing from express normativity altogether. It allows him to evade the important (normative) question as to what alternative structure or structures would be preferable to the defective institution of modern law.

In general, the evidence that is adduced to reach such grand, negative sociological conclusions about modern law is strikingly slender and one-sided. Popular cultural understandings of law take priority over broad sociological studies. In one account, an episode of the television series *LA Law* figures more prominently than, say, Max Weber in providing an insight into the way in which law routinely functions (1996: 29-99). It demonstrates that legal players may manipulate the system to achieve success for their clients, but such success could never be described as justice. Not only are the mechanisms by which legal change comes about unthinkable within this lugubrious framework, but such changes could never alter the underlying oppressive nature of modern law. Because it sees nothing of value in any particular legal system, the analysis renders irrelevant any normative distinctions between different legal systems across time and space.

The "utopian" idea that normative theory should in any way inform or influence legal practice receives its most eloquent and uncompromising expression in the work of Stanley Fish. Fish emphasizes a postmodern "readerly" rather than "writerly" approach to textual interpretation (see Hassan, 1985) with a specific focus on the ways in which the interpretive horizon of the professional community with the power and responsibility to make interpretations is decisive in establishing truth. Though he deploys a very different theoretical vocabulary, and focuses on very different subject matters, like Foucault, Fish sees truth as inescapably and exclusively located and produced *within* "interpretive communities". Any notion that one might come up with a more insightful, or a more truthful perspective on a particular social activity from the outside is merely to judge by reference to the standards of a different interpretive community, which is no less partial in its assessments than its object of focus. It follows that normative theories from outside about professional activities such as law are quite impotent in the face of their normal operations. Liberal accounts such as Dworkin's, or radical perspectives such as CLS, express a futile "theory hope" in their aim of influencing law by presenting an alternative, external vision (1989: chs 4-5, 15, 17). As expressions of the practice of a different interpretive community, namely that of the community of theorists, they may have effects internal to that community; but they cannot claim any validity in another community which has different and incommensurable standards of truth.

In his privileging of the epistemological, normative and sociological dimensions of the "local" interpretive community, Fish succeeds in a succinct and elegant set of theoretical steps to combine the three postmodern negations of totality, science and utopia. In keeping with the many pre-postmodern relativisms before him, he asserts that interpretations in the manner of language games go "all the way down", so that to give epistemological priority to any one over others makes no sense. He draws no distinction between the natural and the social world, so to the member of the Flat Earth Society who maintains that the expression "the sun rises" is literally true one can only point to Galileo or Copernicus to identify other, but no more or less plausible, astronomical interpretations. It follows from this argument that of the infinite number of ways that the image of a runaway truck hurtling towards an unsuspecting pedestrian might be interpreted, as long as interpretations originated from the perspective of a particular interpretive community they would be able to claim the mantle of validity and truth; but also, for that very reason no one interpretation would have more explanatory power than others. Against this, surely some interpretations, especially those that predicted serious injury in the event of standing still, would be more accurate, more *truthful* than others? Fish's argument may be more credible because of his focus on the human practices of interpretation rather than the natural sciences, but notions of truth, or explanatory adequacy, are no less relevant in this context.

Fish argues that normative judgment as to whether certain practices or interpretations are good or right, that is, as standards that transcend a particular discipline, is no less relative and subjective than descriptive claims are. Accordingly, there is no way to judge other than from *within* one's interpretive community that any one normative judgment is any better than another. This does not mean that we cannot or should not judge communities who have what we consider to be morally repugnant views and practices. In this regard, Fish has no problem directing his acerbic and witty critical gaze onto any number of left and right political positions. It is merely that because we cannot get universal agreement on what are the best values, there can be no way of judging between them (1989: 226-231). But in requiring that values attain universal agreement to qualify as objective measures of conduct and institutions, Fish seems to make excessive requirements for their validity. Against this approach it is important to differentiate politically and morally between different interpretive communities, or in Foucault's analogous terms, "regimes of truth". A more satisfactory account would require not merely some sociological understanding of their *real* effects on the subjects over whom they hold sway, but also an *evaluative stance* on them. As Martha Nussbaum argues, to jettison such beliefs, and the commitments that they provoke, quite apart from leading to a life "flat and lacking in wonder", will obstruct

> a type of information that is crucial to good ethical and also legal reasoning; to respond with the pain of compassion at the sight of another person's suffering is to understand the importance of that suffering in a way no uncommitted person could possibly do. Without the information given by such emotions few difficult issues concerning poverty, or damages, or privacy, or mitigation, could be well addressed (1994: 737-738).

Such an exercise is totally at odds with the claim that interpretation goes all the way down. On the contrary, it involves attempting to identify which values better help to understand the world in which we live. The point is neatly illustrated by Isaiah Berlin's famous example from Nazi Germany. One could describe the effect of the rise of Nazism in pre-war Germany as alternatively producing: population decline; an increase in the mortality rate; the killing of millions of people; or the systematic massacre of millions of people. Each of these statements would be true, even, or particularly, in the objective sense rejected by Fish. But only the last description would adequately explain the genocidal nature of that particular regime. It is precisely the value-laden nature of that specific description that helps it to do so.[7] It follows that both values and facts conjoin to provide more adequate, more truthful descriptions of the social world.

By contrast, Fish's notoriously vague notion of interpretive communities avoids such sociological and ethical discriminations. Having abandoned any notion of objectivity, communities are taken as given; and there is no sense in which their practices may be more or less repressive, democratic or responsive by any sociological or critical measure. His perspective operates without judgment to embrace communities governed by fear and threats of violence as well as those whose deliberations and shared meanings are consensual and democratic. It follows that this position proudly gives up on the practice of determining and assessing the different reasons that people have for behaving as they do. This is not to deny the power that interpretive communities have over meanings, as all of us within our various interpretive communities well know. Indeed, Fish makes a particularly persuasive argument emphasizing the essentially political process whereby meanings come to be fixed, rather than discovered "out there", and the hermeneutically suspect nature of attempts to identify literal meaning from creative interpretation, core from penumbral meanings, meanings embedded in texts and those injected into them, and so on (Fish, 1993).

But the assault on these dichotomies merely displaces to another level important distinctions between different types of interpretive practices that members of communities routinely engage in. Even if Fish is right in his conclusion that literal meanings are no less located in the practices of interpretive communities than active interpretation, the question still remains as to the consequences that flow from the distinction as defined in his terms. Should judges defer to such deeply ingrained community meanings, while there might be grounds for considering other matters (policy, principle, institutional practice, distributive justice) in those cases of penumbral meaning where no such community agreement about meaning is discernible? Fish provides no answer to such important questions because for him all competing interpretive accounts are political, and no transcendent measure exists for determining whether one might be better than another.

The sociological weakness of this approach is evident in Fish's account of change within communities. Even where he acknowledges that interpretive communities routinely change their practices, and that such change may be stimulated by upheavals that occur outside the community, it is nonetheless the case that the community is the "engine of change" rather being the "object of change" (1989: ch 7). For instance, he concludes that a revolution in literary theory that may induce changes in literary work, and a political revolution that might withdraw funding entirely for literature departments, would be "in principle" no different in impact on the interpretive community of literary critics. The reason for assimilating the two processes is because "both would vary with the extent to which the profession or part of the profession did or did not consider the phenomenon as, at some level, a literary one" (1989: 149-150). Certainly social change must include the perspectives of those members of communities upon whom change bears; but this is only a part of the story. Where one institution dominates or destroys another, where some institutions lead and some follow are important questions that the study of interpretive communities should embrace. In the case of law, we need to know, for instance, whether law has a measure of autonomy from the political sphere rather than be subservient to it, whether a process of juridification hinders rather than assists other institutions to flourish, and whether law contributes to justice or frustrates it.

As with other anti-totalizing approaches to law, Fish's conclusion that society is made of a potentially infinite number of interpretive communities with their own internal criteria for truth ends up being a far more ambitious claim than it first pretends. Despite its appearance of an account of how interpretive communities operate internally, and how they deal with external stimuli, the assertion necessarily amounts to the kind of meta-interpretive argument that this theory rejects. In the manner of a systems theorist, Fish ultimately offers a total image of society, as composed of hermetically sealed interpretive communities. Moreover, this account is advanced not merely as an interpretation from within the community of theorists, but as a more adequate description of a social world beyond interpretation, a world that puts up more resistance to some interpretations of it than others, and one that often carries on independently of how it is described. In this respect, it runs into the difficulties of all forms of relativism, namely how to escape the self-contradiction of positing that all truths are relative, while implying that that very claim is not.

Conclusion

The postmodernist theorizing overviewed here has a very patchy record in terms of its capacity to offer insights into the nature of law. To be sure, this style of conceptual approach has offered some advances: for instance, the emphasis on small-scale analysis has generated many unconventional and insightful studies into aspects of law ignored by earlier scholarship, such as studies of law and the senses (Bently and Flynn, 1996), or narratives of law (Bellow and Minow, 1996). Moreover, the wider influence of this work lies in its affinity with those critical approaches to law that emphasize and express a politics of identity, and expose the many ways in which legal rules and institutions erect barriers to recognition of cultural, sexual and political difference. Likewise, this politics of recognition represents an important supplement to the politics of redistribution institutionalized in the welfare state.

To the extent that postmodernist approaches have informed sensitive critiques of overly simplistic descriptive and prescriptive master narratives in the field of law, their influence has been equally positive. This is no less true of critical perspectives, so that in the field of feminism for example, the anti-metanarrative approach (eg Smart, 1991; 1993; Frug, 1992) has provided valuable theoretical challenges to essentialist positions by urging a reconnection with the messy empirical reality that totalizing critique blithely ignores. From this perspective, law is valuably seen as a complex domain requiring progressive political engagement in the pursuit of a more just world.[8] Nonetheless, it is important to recognize how far postmodernism, in this respect, expresses some very traditional concerns about grand theory in the social sciences (eg Mills 1959). Also, the "alterity" cherished by much postmodernist and poststructuralist work receives support in some traditional liberal accounts of law, such as Hart's (1963) defence of tolerance for sexual difference and Dworkin's advocacy of a legal order that secures equal concern and respect for citizens (1986).

As Nancy Fraser (1997) suggests, a politics of recognition represents a seriously regressive development if it displaces the politics of redistribution that underpinned the project of solidarity and equality typical of welfare states. Oppression is just as prevalent in the economic as in the cultural sphere; and strong institutions, legal and otherwise, are needed to reverse it. The various postmodern formulations of alterity, deconstruction, *petits reçits*, the "ethics and aesthetics" of law, in their various ways generally represent enfeebled attempts to express a justice that would address material *inequality*. An example of the limited contribution that the postmodern store of critical concepts can offer questions of economic justice is reflected in Drucilla Cornell's recent book on the question of employees' rights (2000). Her earlier theoretical work on justice (1991; 1992), which was heavily influenced by Derrida, provides negligible theoretical support in this endeavour; rather, she turns to the prototypically modern Hegel for some relevant normative and analytical concepts to advance arguments in favour of a fast-disappearing pillar of industrial justice: that employees never be dismissed at will, but only for just cause.

At a fundamental level, postmodern theory suffers from a conflation of two very different orders of inquiry in law. The first might be considered conceptual or philosophical, by means of which some essential, immutable elements of legality might be identified. A second approach would take the conceptual model and see the extent to which it matches the various real sociological and historical forms. As we have seen, from Foucault and Derrida to their legal epigones, for all the attempts to elude essentializing, totalizing analysis, postmodernist approaches tend to replicate a type of transhistorical totalization because the predominant focus of this work in relation to law is on its timeless and immutable features, where the primary perspective is metaphysical rather than political.

When such analyses purport to make a sociological, political or historical point in the same analysis they run into serious difficulties. In particular, the sociological, normative and analytical deficits evident in this line of theory provide little or no tools to address the changes examined in the previous chapter. Not only are these theories indifferent or hostile to notions of human rights, as we have seen, but in general they offer little guidance on the ethical aspects of other developments. To questions such as: should greater freedom of contract prevail in workplace relations, or legal aid budgets be cut, or the legal structures of privatization afford greater or less consumer sovereignty, these theories have nothing to say, and with their own good reasons: law is irremediably tainted, across the time span and spaces of modernity. Against the epistemological relativism, the ethical thinness, and the related loss of faith in law and legal institutions typical both of general and of legal postmodernism, it remains politically and ethically important to affirm commitment to a style of sociological inquiry in law that emphasizes truth and justice, and seeks to identify the appropriate role for law in achieving them. As Stanley Cohen puts it:

> To say that people want justice and legality is to agree that of course the discourse of legality draws its legitimacy from a widely held, if inchoate, sense of the ideal ... The problem of skeptical, postmodernist thought is not so much that it is 'unrealistic' but that its slogans ... are so intellectually naive. For most of the world, the old truths of racism, naked injustice, mass starvation and brutal physical oppression still apply (1993: 201, 207).

The question as to how legal analysis might come to play a progressive role in addressing such problems, particularly in light of the recent changes identified in the previous chapter, will form the conclusion of this study.

Notes

1. This point does not apply to a number of general, insightful overviews of this general body of scholarship. For instance, Margaret Davies (1994; 1996) develops an innovative integration of poststructuralism, deconstruction and postmodernism by reference to the work of Derrida, Foucault and Lyotard. Ultimately, she adopts a Derridean theory of legal interpretation and an ethics of alterity. I discuss her theory below at pp 249-251. In another comprehensive study (Feldman, 2000), postmodernism appears as a narrower enterprise, namely, the cluster of pessimistic sensibilities and attitudes towards rationality and progress triggered by the Holocaust, their expression in the work of Foucault and Derrida, and how ultimately they are reflected in legal scholarship. Helen Stacy (2001) offers an extensive, critical and original analysis of some of the leading postmodernist theorists. However, none of these works focus on postmodernity as I have defined it in chapter 2.
2. Derrida makes a similar point: (1976: 31-63).
3. I have explored some of these problems in relation to law in Edgeworth (1986).
4. A number of detailed anthologies have already provided critical analyses of this literature: Stacy (2001); Feldman (2000); Minda (1995); Patterson (1994).
5. See pp 187-190 above.
6. For an elaboration of this critical analysis of Derrida's work, see Fraser (1991).
7. This argument links values to facts to provide true sociological accounts in a way that Nussbaum would find too objectivist. It is developed in Bhaskar (1979: 75-83).
8. For a sophisticated and valuable argument favouring selective deployment of some elements of a postmodern approach in social policy debates, with clear implications for legal reform, see Hillyard and Watson (1996).

7 What Next?

> The prefix 'post' suggests living in interstitial time (Bell, 1973: 37).

> The radical privatization of human fate goes along and apace with the radical deregulation of industry and finances ... privatization, consumer choice – and the criminalization of those unable to choose (Bauman, 1997: 44).

Introduction

Any account of the changed nature of contemporary law necessarily contains implications both for the conduct of future legal scholarship and for the reform of law and legal institutions. In particular, the emergent legal landscape raises the question as to whether the traditional conceptual frameworks and vocabularies of legal theory are capable of adequately addressing recent developments. Theoretical studies in law can be divided into the analytical, the sociological and the normative. Analytical jurisprudence focuses on the essential characteristics or unity of law. Sociological perspectives examine law as a social institution, identifying how it impacts on, relates to, and is influenced by, other sectors of society. Finally, normative approaches to law explore how questions of justice, ethics and morality bear critically on law and legal institutions. Moreover, normative inquiry is most directly relevant to the question of reform of particular laws and legal systems. Each of these approaches appear to be challenged by the new constellation.

To examine the dominant styles of conceptual inquiry in law from this perspective does not in any way entail predicting the future direction of legal change. If the convulsive changes of the last couple of decades have any lesson, it is to warn against prognoses about what different forms law might assume in the near future on the basis of the present evidence. And more recent "post 9/11" developments, with their own profound dynamics, on law and elsewhere, should caution against any kind of confident proclamations about the end of history. Indeed, it seems highly inadvisable now to engage in the kind of legal futurology expressed at the high point of the welfare state where conclusions about the inevitable direction of legal progress seemed to be supported by empirical fact. Perhaps the critique of this type of teleological understanding of social and legal change has been the most useful theoretical contribution postmodernism has made. Instead, the following discussion will raise separately issues posed for some of the various branches of legal theorizing by recent developments, and possible directions of reform. It is not, nor is intended to be, an in-depth exploration, but raises in a brief and speculative manner, some suggestive lines of inquiry.

Re-imagining Analytical Jurisprudence

The process of legal postmodernization is a confronting one for traditional analytical jurisprudence, and suggests the need to revise its investigation of the nature of law in contemporary societies. Legal theories within the analytical tradition have generally been designed to comprehend the nature of law and the legal systems of *modern* nation states. The formal law of modern societies has routinely been identified by means of theoretical tools that primarily evoke the notion of sovereignty. In the early legal positivism of Thomas Hobbes and John Austin, no less than those of Hans Kelsen and H.L.A. Hart, a central concern is the identification of a hierarchy of rules originating in a *single*, foundational source. This general philosophical project dovetailed neatly with the political objective of nation states to establish a singular, unambiguous and exclusive source of legal authority. The image that theorists have provided, and the reality they were concerned to analyze, is one of an essentially monocentric legal order. This general perspective is no less relevant to distinctly anti-positivistic legal philosophies, such as Ronald Dworkin's, who in like manner seeks to examine the fabric of unitary legal orders. But contemporary developments have forced this central notion to run into serious difficulties.

The growing spread and effectiveness of supranational law in domestic contexts squarely challenges the conceptual reference points of this body of work. It seems to be out of step with recent changes. For example, a positivistic focus on the formal law of the European Union, would attempt to identify variously the relevant sovereign, basic norm, or rule of recognition that represented the foundation of this system of law. The central questions in this jurisprudential inquiry would be: Has the European Parliament become the new sovereign power, or do the member nation states retain sovereignty? In Austinian terms, does the European Parliament function as a collective delegate of the sovereign parliaments, or is it a "political superior" to them? Or again, to which entity is "the habit of obedience" shown? Austin's positivism, consonant with the imperialistic ambitions of the more powerful of the 19th century nation states, asserted that international law was not law but at most "positive morality". It looks largely unsatisfactory for the purpose of understanding the increasing spread and enforceability of supranational norms. From a Hartian perspective, the class of rules to which the rule of recognition applies would become the object of focus. Would international human rights qualify as a member of this class of rules? When such questions are posed, these conceptual frameworks appear unwieldy and unsuited to comprehend the complexities of contemporary legal systems. The growing domestic force of supranational norms suggests that established perspectives on laws that emanate beyond the borders of the nation state need to be substantially recast. The present polycentric legal landscape appears to evade these unifying conceptual schemes.

Problems of this nature have been explored in depth by Neil MacCormick (1993; 1997). MacCormick's particular focus is on the legal systems of the member states of the European Union, but his arguments are also relevant to other states given the global reach of the institutions of transnational governance. Because we have moved historically beyond the sovereign state, MacCormick concludes that any jurisprudential scheme grounded in a unitary notion of sovereignty must be revised. With the original appearance of the European Community, MacCormick argues that both external sovereignty (the absence of any power beyond the state to impose law upon it) and internal sovereignty (the exclusive power to make domestic law) have been radically transformed. The member states' sovereignty has been divided internally where Community law overrides it. Externally, their sovereignty has been restrained by virtue of the legal powers exercisable by the Union's institutions over member states. The transformations of sovereignty do not only limit its scope; the magnitude of the Union as a collection of states also provides them with enhanced, collective independence of action.

This is not to argue that general jurisprudence ceases to be relevant in this new landscape; rather, its central concepts need to be adjusted to the new conditions. Indeed, the changes classed as evidence of the general process of globalization may underscore and confer added importance on this type of traditional general jurisprudence. As any consideration of the interplay between globalization and legal theory might suggest, concepts such as "right", "sanction" and "rule" are particularly apposite to examine aspects of the new legal order (Twining, 2000: 255). The nature of the norms emanating from bodies such as the World Trade Organization (WTO), the United Nations Human Rights Committee (UNHRC), and the International Labor Organization (ILO) can be richly illuminated by the deployment of these conceptual tools. The legal status of the emergent international *lex mercatoria* and the status in domestic law of multilateral treaties is no less in need of such conceptual elaboration.

Jurisprudential understandings of judicial reasoning are equally put into question by recent developments and they face parallel challenges in explaining shifts in the interpretive norms governing judicial behaviour. Modern analyses of legal interpretation have emphasized the distinctively "artificial reason" of law marked by its exclusive identification of the legal norms specific to nations by reference to some positivist master-test. Where theories have recognized the limits of law, and examined alternative hermeneutic strategies for judges in hard cases, they have confined their attention to norms available within a particular sovereign state. Even anti-positivist accounts have exhibited a similar tendency. So, Ronald Dworkin concludes that "interpretive theories are by their nature addressed to a particular legal culture, generally the culture to which their authors belong" (1986: 102). The "principles" he identifies as guiding judges in cases where the legal rules fail to yield a clear answer emerge solely from the political history of a particular community. But increasingly norms in the nature of "principles" suffuse international conventions and treaties, and the opinions of international tribunals. In this novel environment, this theory faces the task of examining the extent to which these changes threaten or affirm the original argument (Twining, 2000: 63-65). Contemporary developments may also furnish evidence to give new life to this philosophical understanding of law. General principles appear to be a common feature of the transnational legal regime of business regulation, offering greater flexibility for economic actors (Braithwaite and Drahos, 2000: ch 26). A principle-based theory of law may therefore be particularly suited to understanding how it functions at the present time.

Dworkin's emphasis on community as the source of these principles is confronted by similar challenges. His theory must now come to terms with a novel pattern of overlapping and interpenetrating communities bound by various regional, ethnic and racial ties, shared politics of gender and sexuality, with commonalities of interests that straddle the boundaries of nation states. At the present time, Dworkin's model judge faces the truly Herculean task of deciding whether to factor supranational norms into domestic interpretive practices to reach an appropriate "right answer" in hard cases (1977; 1986). In particular, do human rights norms which are, as Habermas (2001: 108) argues, "legal norms with an exclusively moral content" qualify in Dworkin's scheme as special examples of "principles" of law so as to exercise transnational, normative gravitational force in cases where legal rules do not yield a clear answer? Likewise, Hart's (1961: ch 6) recommendation that public policy supplement legal rules when they are unclear needs to be revised in light of the emergent contemporary practices where human rights norms, and the legal developments in other states assume, with moral justification, greater normative weight. Related changes affect the sphere of statutory interpretation. Traditional interpretive norms such as municipal legislative purpose, implicitly referenced to the intention of the national legislature, are being progressively supplemented by international human rights norms so as to prompt a reconsideration of these descriptive and prescriptive approaches to judicial behaviour.

If the changes at the supranational level pose acute theoretical difficulties for traditional analytical jurisprudence, so too do the transformations "downwards" that parallel the contraction of the welfare state. As we have seen, one manifestation of the emergence of the contracting state is the progressive transfer of responsibility for the resolution of legal disputes away from the formal legal system to deal with problems of overload. States are increasingly deploying diversionary strategies, turning to civil society to provide justice by means of reconfiguring access to justice strategies. An example of the process is the harnessing of various forms of alternative dispute resolution to court procedures. With a widening continuum of adjudicatory practices, the traditional lines of demarcation of the legal from the non-legal start to blur. These new institutional mechanisms offer further challenges for definitions of law. In analytical jurisprudence, the concept of law might need to be expanded to embrace these emergent, hybridized normative forms. It might be questionable as to whether disputes resolved by court-annexed mediation, compulsory or otherwise, would be legal by any traditional jurisprudential master-test. In consequence, any analytical approach to law would need to address the interpenetration of other normative codes into the formal legal code. To understand the nature of this "interlegality" (Santos, 1987) requires an analysis of, among other factors, the relative dominance of the different codes.

A further dimension of this process where both norms originating from supranational sources and those with local origins assume greater significance within the formal legal system and the official discourse of law, and where each contributes to the reconfiguration of the formal structures of the law of sovereign states, is the appearance of an historically unique form of legal pluralism. A process of "glocalization" (Robertson, 1992: 173-174) of law is as much in train as is its globalization, evidenced by the present, historically unique ways in which supranational, national and local laws are combined. The growing recognition of indigenous law by some states provides a good example of this novel and widespread development. Contemporary legal frameworks of indigenous law within national legal systems owe as much to international human rights law as they do to traditional customary norms. Moreover, the progressive development of this body of law entails subtle re-alignment of these separate normative orders. And such changes are not confined to the law governing indigenous peoples; more traditional regions of law are subject to similar pressures. So, in the case of criminal law, the appearance of the International Criminal Court has been paralleled by increasing moves toward community-based forms of correction. It follows that a relativist approach to legal forms needs to be the methodological touchstone for contemporary legal theorizing given the difficulties of generalizing about the nature of law across jurisdictions and cultures because of the diversity of normative forms in the new environment. This approach is already established in the field of legal pluralism, where a dominant focus is concerned more with the interaction between official and unofficial forms of ordering, rather than focus on the effect of law on society, or vice versa (Merry, 1988: 873). But even this approach may now need to be revised in light of a blurring of the distinction between official and unofficial forms of normative order.

Recent developments pose new questions for "particular jurisprudence" no less significant than for general jurisprudential inquiry. Particular jurisprudence relates to "general aspects of a single legal system or order or its constituent phenomena" (Twining, 2000: 13). It includes the theoretical examination of specific domains of legal doctrine. The many changes that have occurred over the last three decades prompt a revision of conceptual approaches to doctrinal categories. The domains of contract, property and citizenship examined above clearly reflect wider social change. For instance, the concept of property, which at the height of the welfare state was encumbered with greatly increased social obligations could be seen as displaying not so much a right of exclusion but a right of access (Macpherson, 1973), needs updating in light of progressive waves of privatization and marketization over the last couple of decades. There is much evidence to suggest that the meaning of property is best defined once more by predominant, and ascendant, rights to exclude and alienate, at the expense of rights of public access, and that in this respect it evokes many features of the early modern concept of property. But to identify such a "neo-liberal" model is insufficient; it also needs to take account of the unfolding transnational distribution of rights in both the sphere of tangible and intellectual property (see Braithwaite and Drahos, 2000). To the extent that these general developments at the level of legal systems and legal doctrines have occurred in many jurisdictions at roughly the same time, the degree and pace of change suggests new agendas and wider horizons for the comparative study of legal institutions (Twining, 2000: ch 7).

Understanding Law Sociologically

Contemporary change has also transformed the co-ordinates by reference to which sociology has traditionally operated. Douglas Kellner concludes in an overview of the problems facing the social sciences that at the present time, some of the fundamental social trends and future potentialities of our era

> require at least dramatic revision and updating of previous social theories (whether Marxian, Weberian, structural-functionalist, neo-conservative or whatever). While I do not believe that we should jettison all the grand theories of the past we certainly have to be careful in applying previous paradigms to contemporary conditions (1988: 267).

This argument is directly relevant to the problems posed for legal sociology at the present time. Max Weber's typology of the different forms of law and legitimation in traditional and modern societies provides a useful litmus test. For Weber, a distinguishing feature of modernity lies in the appearance of rational-legal authority (Weber, 1978 [1921]). He concluded that the comparative certainty yielded by this system of law was an essential element for the development of capitalist economies. It is now reasonable to inquire as to how relevant this analysis is to analyzing the legal architecture of contemporary societies. As we have seen in chapter 5, this principle appears to be rejected in the pervasive popular embrace of delegalization both within and beyond contemporary legal systems. Inglehart's broad empirical study of changing social values offers some explanation of this trend (1997). As evidence of what he described as a global appearance of "postmodernization", he found a widespread dissipation of support for rational-legal authority in advanced societies over a twenty-four year period commencing in 1970. This shift is reflected in a widespread "debureaucratization" of institutions (Crook et al., 1992: ch 6) of which the growth of informalism in law is a clear example. The consequential growth of hybridized and polycentric legal structures requires a pluralistic approach in the sociological examination of law, no less than in analytical inquiries.

The recent embrace of capitalist economic forms by Asian nations also appears to undermine the Weberian linkage between the rise of capitalism and the appearance of formal legal rationality. The rules that govern this new order are often not easily described as formal-rational. In the case of emergent Asian capitalism, for instance, the relevant governing norms are more informal, particularistic and private in nature than in public, positive and abstract (Jones, 1994). Equally, the rules and structural framework of *lex mercatoria* and international commercial arbitration that play such an important role in the governance of international trade rely more on legitimation through reflexivity of the legal regime (Banakar, 1998) than on the legal-rational legitimation that Weber found to be central in his studies of the legal orders of developed capitalist societies. Far from the convergence of legal orders implicit in

Weber's legal modernization thesis, patterns of *both* convergence and divergence of legalities mark the current global landscape where increasing numbers of states adopt capitalist economic models (Gessner et al., 2001: 1-36).

The entrenched assimilation of society and the nation state within sociology also needs to be reconsidered for the purposes of analyzing law. Traditionally, legal sociology and law and society studies have not devoted serious attention to questions beyond the nation state when examining the social workings or origins of law. Indeed, they have tended to be no less territorially bounded than doctrinal analyses of law in their organizing assumptions. As has been noted in chapter 4, the many theories of the law in the welfare state are no less deficient in this respect: despite their emphasis on social context of law, they were not geared to consider factors beyond the territorial boundaries of nations. To understand the complexity of contemporary law, effective socio-legal scholarship must develop a sociology of globalization (Gessner and Budak, 1995). In a later study (Gessner et al., 2001), the authors identify the novelty and complexity of contemporary global business regulation, but note the sparseness of the empirical study of the operation of these emergent legal structures. The immense, political, economic and sociological importance of these novel social forces demands a revision of socio-legal research priorities.

Although it is still in an embryonic state, a sociology of the interplay between supranational and national law is beginning to appear. John Braithwaite and Peter Drahos' (2000) work on international business regulation provides some guidance for such research. In a broad-ranging examination of the interplay between global and local systems, they analyze how regulatory laws are made, reformulated and reformed by global institutions, and the alliances by means of which legal change comes about. Their studies revealed that, far from being monolithic, institutions of global governance display a somewhat chaotic and contradictory pattern of regulation. In this environment many opportunities are available for alliances and they tend to undermine any unitary notion of the domination of multinational capitalism. The authors identify how the process of enrolling the support of powerful actors (state and non-state) can work to the advantage of weaker groups such as consumers in cases where commercial interests or national interests are in conflict. Also, the nature of the legal instruments that figure prominently in the unfolding regimes of transnational of governance are distinctive. As noted above, Braithwaite and Drahos found that broad "principles" were commonly deployed in preference to clearly defined legal rules. How these principles function in practice is as important sociologically as is the analytical study of their nature as noted above.

One important methodological strategy they deploy is to examine the ways in which "webs of influence" are decisive in the formulation of regulations that have global scope. Where institutions are more malleable in a rapidly changing world, the links and networks that connect them become just as relevant to understand how they operate as their internal structures (see also, Gessner et al., 2001: 1-36; Picciotto, 1996-97; Snyder, 1999). For instance, this form of analysis demonstrates that in order to understand why certain rules come to be global standards that later appear in domestic legislation throughout the world, it is necessary to look not merely at international law-making institutions such as the International Maritime Organization, but also at the personnel who chair key committees, the groups or corporations that have access to them, the economic interests they tend to reflect, the alliances between governments and multinational corporations and so on.

Where supranational legal norms increasingly intrude into domains formerly monopolized by sovereign national law, a methodology which emphasizes the networks that connect these forms of normative regulation to local institutions and practices is more likely to yield insights into how contemporary law operates and changes. As Robert Post notes, the operation of these various "newly minted international institutions" (2001: 335), staffed by cosmopolitan legal professionals from diverse backgrounds and traditions, gives rise to the question as to their capacity to achieve and maintain the standards of the rule of law. He concludes that law and society scholarship might come into renewed prominence by addressing these developments.

A related strategy for trying to analyze contemporary legal change is by reference to the ways in which domestic interest groups operate beyond the sovereign state. To do this, a transnational conflict model, rather than an orientation to the activities of states, is needed (Benvenisti, 1999). Sectarian domestic interests can influence supranational law to suit their ends, and in ways that may contribute to a widening of inequalities of power and resources domestically. Moreover, governments are also combining to develop networks of governance beyond the formal institutional structures of international law. By doing so, they can outmanoeuvre unwelcome domestic constituencies and reward others. This "Real New World Order" (Slaughter, 2001) is evidence of a novel framework of political power; it also poses acute problems of democratic accountability given that the practice of executive agreements may circumvent normal domestic legislative processes. Any consideration of the disproportionate power exercised by some social actors raises the more general issue for sociological studies in law of how recent changes impact on the disadvantaged. Postmodernity is marked by novel patterns of inequality. Research into the extent to which the emergent pluralistic legal frameworks ameliorate or contribute to the plight of the disadvantaged is essential to this question.

The notion of webs, linkages and networks of influence is equally important for examining the ways in which the processes of law work within states. This is a very different methodological principle from the postmodernist focus on micro-politics, or the local contexts of law. Where formal and informal institutions of dispute processing are linked in historically unprecedented ways, any understanding of how law operates, how effective it may be at constraining power, and how successful it is at delivering justice requires greater attention not just to the institutions, but to the mechanisms by which they are interconnected. These networks may be more or less co-operative, functional, or open. And the ways in which they are connected, or whether they are connected at all, may have a more decisive bearing on whether justice is delivered than the separate capacities of each.

A final consideration relevant to the sociological understanding of contemporary law relates to the historical temporalization emphasized in this study. It pertains to the survival of the term "postmodern". How long is it possible for us to be "post"? After the critiques of the last chapter there might be a strong argument that it is time to abandon this perspective altogether. John Frow (1991) has already written an eloquent epitaph. Of course, a great flood of expressly postmodernist later writing would appear to have undermined this diagnosis, and there seems to be no prospect of this particular well drying up, even, or especially, in relation to law (eg Feldman, 2000; Stacy, 2001). But, at least from the sociological and historical dimension of the concept of postmodernization emphasized here, there must come a time when the notion of being "post" has to yield to an idea with essentially positive rather than negative connotations. In Daniel Bell's words, the use of "the prefix *post-* indicates living in interstitial time" (1973: 37). Usage of the term "post-war" in the last century is an analogy. Where a former war casts long shadows over the societies that endured them, their "post-ness" became their most noteworthy and essential feature. Eventually, institutions, experiences, and lives come to be conducted more by reference to contemporary or even future, rather than retrospective, reference points and landmarks. In the case of the Second World War, for instance, the influence of which had begun to run its course by the mid-1960s, the term "post-war" came to be replaced by more positive notions such as the "affluent" or "permissive" society.

The same argument applies to "postmodernization". Over time it will come to be overshadowed by periodizing concepts that emphasize more prospective features of historical uniqueness. In a telling shift, the foremost theorist of postmodernity, Zygmunt Bauman, has moved on from using the epithet postmodern to describe the contemporary social world as "liquid modernity" (2000). Nonetheless, even in this work he continues to deploy the same methodological tools, and offers a similar analysis and conclusion about present social change to the kind evident in his earlier works, and so demonstrates their continued usefulness. Even if the epithet comes to be abandoned, I would argue that it will continue to be important as an historical and sociological marker, not unlike the way the epithet "post-war" is still relevant in the explanation of earlier historical periods. But as yet, I am convinced by Frederic Jameson, who has expressed his frustration about the looseness of the term, but *faute de mieux* has felt compelled to use it:

> I occasionally get just as tired of the slogan 'postmodern' as anyone else, but when I am tempted to regret my complicity with it, to deplore its misuses and its notoriety, and to conclude with some reluctance that it raises more problems than it solves, I find myself pausing to wonder whether any other concept can dramatize the issues in quite so effective and economical a fashion (1991: 418).

Even if postmodernization is seen merely as a rearrangement of some of the major components of the deep structures of social and legal modernization, and is destined to be overhauled by a framework with different features, it may nonetheless even from a future perspective serve the useful purpose of revealing the "interstitial" nature of this most recent phase of social and legal change.

Normative Legal Theory

Normative legal theory is confronted by special challenges in light of the new paradigm. The normative framework that emerged with the welfare state needs to be recast in a markedly transformed environment. The key concerns of that earlier discourse centred on the extent to which welfare state reforms impacted on the rule of law, the effectiveness of policies of redistribution of power and resources as expressed in legal doctrines, and the responsiveness of legal structures to citizens' needs. The communitarian and egalitarian values that prompted particular reform strategies in the welfare state suggest different reforms in the contemporary legal landscape. For instance, how might the concern with ameliorating the rights of the disadvantaged be redressed in this new context? A simple resort to old notions of the heavily bureaucratized welfare state settlement would hardly represent an advance. Accordingly, those who are committed to progressive reform need to "work themselves free of the seductive pleasures of moral superiority about the venality of the market and false nostalgia about the vanished compassion of the old civic contract" (Ignatieff, 1989: 72). Proposals for the re-nationalization of utilities or the return to command and control regulation are not effective responses to the need for regulatory reform in the present. In this light, it is worth revisiting some of the normative theories that were characteristic of debate about law in the welfare state.

In particular, Nonet and Selznick's notion of "responsive law" contains valuable normative concepts with which to assess our reconfigured legality. We have already seen in chapter 4 how it offered both a framework for the analysis of the changing structure and content of the law in the welfare state, and also recommendations for reform. Despite its datedness as a descriptive account of contemporary developments, the notion of responsive law continues to provide useful guidance to the question about how legal institutions could be reformed in the presently changed historical context. Its demands that law become "postbureaucratic", that it be more accessible to citizens, that it facilitate better the purposes it intends to promote, while retaining a recognition of, and an allegiance to, the benefits of formal, autonomous law, suggests a rich and powerful prescriptive approach to law. It enshrines the vital principle that the practices of law (in the adjudicative, legislative, administrative dimensions) should respect the concerns of, and respond to the criticisms of, those most affected by its operations. Many features of the new landscape need reform if law is to be responsive by these criteria.

One important element of responsive law – the notion that legal institutions reserve a place for recognition of the "public interest" – which, as we have seen in chapter 5, has been fragmented by recent market-driven reforms, needs to be revived in relation to the array of domestic institutions that have replaced the regulatory structures of the welfare state, as well as to those supranational law-making bodies which, as presently organized, are too inaccessible to citizens. Privatized institutions should therefore be subject to a wide array of accountability mechanisms beyond the new contractual framework of obligations to citizens. Public interest requirements include transparency of their operations, adequate citizen and employee representation on boards, and enhanced labour rights. The fact of privatization has been empirically shown to erect no intrinsic barriers to the fulfilment of such duties (eg Prosser, 1999). Also, wherever services are delivered to the public on behalf of the state, regulatory structures ought routinely to make space for input from citizens affected by their activities not merely in relation to complaints, but in respect of selection of service providers and the framing of standards of service (see Vincent-Jones, 1998).

Recent shifts towards informalism within legal systems also raise significant policy questions about how effective they are in delivering justice. Do they represent, as some suggest, an erosion of the strengths of formal law, or do they advance levels of participation in the legal system, thereby serving the interests of all participants? The answer to this question surely depends on the type of informal justice on offer. Informal law is an important mechanism for extending access to justice to all, *but only* if it embraces many of the ideals that form the core principles of formal, that is to say, if the "morality of law" (Fuller, 1969) is extended to the procedural framework of informal justice. One way in which this process might be usefully furthered is by the adoption of a "fifth wave" of access to justice to supplement the welfare state's earlier four (Parker, 1999: ch 8). This wave might take the form of a legal requirement that all large organizations in society incorporate mechanisms for justice delivery as part of their structures of governance. Localized industry- and institution-based dispute resolution forums would then become a feature of all sites of significant social power. In this way, justice would be less monopolized by law and lawyers, citizens would be more involved in the delivery of justice, and insofar as this wave would be backed up and overseen by formal law, the strengths of both systems could work together, rather than against one another (Parker, 1999: 199-200).

The idea of responsive law is no less relevant to the increasingly important structures of supranational law. In order to further responsiveness at this level, a greater level of accessibility is a pressing need for those affected by their decisions because of the growing power and influence these bodies have over the lives of citizens. For instance, rules of standing need to be revised to include alliances of citizens from civil society wider than states and corporations. An important reform would be for the WTO to allow advocacy by NGOs on behalf of consumers, labour and the environmentalist groups (Arup, 2000). Moreover, transparency would be assisted if WTO dispute settlement proceedings were open to the public (Petersmann, 2001). In this way, a measure of proceduralization would be established by providing deliberative space for emergent interests from civil society to have some influence on their decisions. These objectives might be further advanced in the direction of a "proceduralist paradigm" (Habermas, 1996) by reforms such as the extension of standing rights to individuals or organizations to petition the International Court of Justice, and that citizens be afforded representation in a second chamber at the United Nations (Held, 1995).

The impetus that the spread of global law has given to the comparative study of legal institutions (Twining, 2000) extends to the normative assessment of law. Because globalization exposes nations to influences beyond their borders, they are forced to develop and critically assess their laws in a wider context. From the normative viewpoint of responsive law, this development could make the search for justice in a particular social sphere an exercise of seeing more readily how other nations have established legal institutions more responsive to citizens' demands. They might stimulate analyses of how a similar body of global law is refracted through the very different lenses of highly differentiated national legal cultures. This perspective might lead to a more vigorous search for "best practice" models of justice from different jurisdictions which face similar social and economic problems, in a manner that is now a commonplace in the discourse of business management.

As the welfare state retreats, the vulnerabilities of those less able to compete in the market are increased. Elaborate inequalities of wealth, power, income and opportunity are a distinctive feature of contemporary societies, and they constitute one further point of departure from the legal and social arrangements typical of the welfare state. This problem must be a focus of a progressive politics of law. In addition to the idea of responsive law, a legal politics of redistribution needs to be nurtured for the reason that from a domestic perspective, recent transformations have generally not worked to assist the disadvantaged to anything like the same degree as they have favoured corporate interests. This general trend reflects a dramatic change in the welfare state's Keynesian compromise between private property rights and public, civil rights in favour of the former. Enhancing social rights at the domestic level is an essential element of any strategy to further equality.

Changes at the supranational level have been no less inegalitarian. Where too many elements of existing global law chiefly serve the interests of the most privileged interests in the global economy (Scheuerman, 2001: 117), the establishment of a public interest dimension in the new legal landscape is as pressing as it is in the domestic context. Emerging networks of influence display alliances between similar groups from within different nations that co-operate to gain advantage of domestic rivals. According to one study, the better-organized domestic groups such as producers, employers and service suppliers combine in supranational alliances to exploit those who are less organized, such as consumers, employees and citizens in positions of environmental vulnerability (Benvenisti, 1999: 169). The results of such alliances commonly lead to "tragedies of the global commons", as where multinational corporations ally with local politicians to advance their respective short-term interests at the expense of a long-term public interest. Also, a decline in voter power is evident in the process of treaty negotiation and ratification, with little in the way of institutional oversight mechanisms to infuse a public interest element to protect weaker groups. Furthermore, increasingly footloose global capital threatens further welfare state safety nets by imposing pressure on national legislators to reduce standards of protection for the weak in the market, the workplace and the environment (Benvenisti, 1999: 196-201).

Another way of buttressing the shrinking bundle of social rights component of domestic citizenship is by means of an expansion of human rights principles. A deepening of human rights jurisprudence in relation to economic, political and social rights within both international and domestic law might reverse the present tilt in favour of civil (contractual and private property) rights, with their entrenched indifference to questions of inequality. In the same way that the welfare state represented the constitutionalization of the domestic economy in the sense of bringing a measure of equality of citizenship into its operations, human rights have the potential to infuse similar principles into the global domain. A helpful starting point for reform would be to integrate human rights principles into the GATT/WTO system. As Petersmann argues, international economic law has for too long operated without attention to human rights. The dominant UN human rights instruments largely neglect human rights, and human rights considerations have failed to influence traditional interpretations of GATT and WTO law (2001: 38). In the European context, an egalitarian redistribution of rights might require a thoroughgoing social dimension in "a more closely regulated labour market, co-operative training programmes, and a concept of regional citizenship, socially rather than economically determined" (Ward, 1996: 159).

Traditional philosophical resources may be increasingly insufficient for the purposes of theorizing these issues, or for the evaluation and critique of existing law. For example, John Rawls' (1971) powerful philosophical defence of an egalitarian society is based on the preferences of a notional citizen within a particular society to guide the establishment of just institutions. Yet how might this argument illuminate the requirements for a more egalitarian global order are far from clear (Twining, 2000: 69-75). Importantly, given that the institutional arrangements within nation states are increasingly influenced by supranational forces, Rawls' theory needs to embrace a global focus to provide a framework for an adequate contemporary theory of justice (Pogge, 1989).

As we have seen, the revival of notions of community has been a positive feature in recent legal developments; not only the global, but also the local has assumed greater normative significance in debates about justice. And a revived social democratic message would take more seriously than the more bureaucratic welfare state reforms ever did the importance of the local, valuing the social contexts within which norms develop. But it would temper the postmodernist discourse of difference, and politics of recognition, with a politics of redistribution (Fraser, 1997).

It would withhold recognition of communitarian practices that are exploitative or degrading. So, for Selznick,

> The communitarian persuasion does not entail a flight from reason into the warm, unreflective embrace of particularity and historicity ... [It] is wholly compatible with recognizing the moral worth of particularity and historicity ... [A] genuinely empirical critical morality will readily recognize, without idealizing, the tacit knowledge in custom and social practice (Selznick, 1998: 27-28).

In the pursuit of this "genuinely empirical critical morality", socio-legal studies scholarship may rise to the challenge if it brings together normative and descriptive accounts in a mutually productive fashion. This will entail re-asserting the utopian impulse, not in the sense of maintaining that a better world is the necessary end-point of contemporary trends, or that perfection is attainable. Rather, it is to claim that tangible advances in justice are prefigured in certain domains within present legal systems, and that they might be readily extended. As Nicola Lacey insists:

> Our Utopianism and our rhetoric ... must indeed by audacious, albeit not naive about their own political implications. They must resist an indulgence in the fantasy of a direct legal institutionalization which contradicts some of the deepest premises on which they are themselves based ... [but] the idea that there are ethical arguments which bear on law and its reform, and indeed that law could be less unjust than it is, remains central to progressive legal scholarship (1996: 150).

In this endeavour, the reform and transformation of our legal systems is a central task. In an age of growing global and local inequalities, rights of access to justice, equal treatment before the law, and redistribution of power and wealth by the operation of legal rules must remain central concerns for those concerned to strive for more just legal institutions. This means that rights and rights-talk will continue to be of central importance to the creation and reform of mechanisms to improve the delivery of justice (Bartholomew and Hunt: 1991). A reconfigured responsiveness in law offers a way forward, but only if legal systems in their present polycentric forms respond at all levels to the needs and interests of the many, rather than the few.

Bibliography

Ackerman, B. (1997), "The Rise of World Constitutionalism", 83 *Virginia Law Review* 771-97.

Adams, J. and Brownsword, R. (1987), *Understanding Contract Law*, Fontana, London.

Adler, P. (1995), "The Future of Alternative Dispute Resolution: Reflections on ADR as a Social Movement" in S. Merry and N. Milner eds., *The Possibility of Popular Justice: A Case Study of Community Mediation in the United States*, University of Michigan Press, Ann Arbor, 67-88.

Albrow, M. (1996), *The Global Age: State and Society Beyond Modernity*, Polity, Cambridge.

Alston, P. and Chiam, M., eds. (1995), *Treaty-Making and Australia: Globalization versus Sovereignty?*, Federation Press, Sydney.

Amis, M. (1995), *The Information*, Flamingo, London.

Anderson, B. (1983), *Imagined Communities: Reflections on the Origin and Spread of Nationalism*, Verso, London.

Anderson, P. (1983), *In The Tracks of Historical Materialism*, Verso, London.

Anderson, S. and Cavanagh, J. (1996), *The Top 200: The Rise of Global Corporate Power*, Institute for Policy Studies, Washington.

Aronson, M. (1997), "An Administrative Lawyer's Perspective on Outsourcing and Privatization", in M. Taggart ed., *The Province of Administrative Law*, Hart, Oxford, 40-70.

Arthurs, H. (1985), *Beyond the Law: Legal Pluralism in Nineteenth Century England*, University of Toronto Press, Toronto.

Arthurs, H. and Kreklewich, R. (1996), "Law, Legal Institutions, and the Legal Profession in the New Economy", 34 *Osgoode Hall Law Journal* 1-60.

Arup, C. (2000), *The New World Trade Organization Agreements: Globalizing Law Through Services and Intellectual Property*, Cambridge University Press, Cambridge.

Astor, H. and Chinkin, C. (1992), *Dispute Resolution in Australia*, Butterworths, Sydney.

Atiyah, P. (1979), *The Rise and Fall of Freedom of Contract*, Clarendon, Oxford.

Atiyah, P. (1995), *An Introduction to the Law of Contract*, 5th ed., Clarendon, Oxford.

Attanasio, J. (1995), "Rapporteur's Overview and Conclusions: Of Sovereignty, Globalization and Courts", *New York University Journal of International Law and Politics*, 1-33.

Aubert, V. (1986), "The Rule of Law and the Promotional Function of Law in the Welfare State" in G. Teubner ed., *Dilemmas of Law in the Welfare State*, Walter de Gruyter, Berlin, 28-39.

Austin, J. (1954 (orig. 1832)), *The Province of Jurisprudence Determined*, Weidenfeld and Nicolson, London.

Ayres, I. and Braithwaite, J. (1992), *Responsive Regulation*, Oxford University Press, Oxford.

Baglioni, G. (1990), "Industrial Relations in the 1980s" in G. Baglioni and C. Crouch eds., *European Industrial Relations: The Challenge of Flexibility*, Sage, London, 1-41.

Bainbridge, S. (2002), "Employee Involvement Postcollective Bargaining", in R. Kagan, M. Krygier and K. Winston eds., *Legality and Community: On the Intellectual Legacy of Philip Selznick*, Rowman and Littlefield, Lanham, Md., 203-18.

Banakar, R. (1998), "Reflexive Legitimacy in International Arbitration", in V. Gessner and A. Budak eds., *Emerging Legal Certainty: Empirical Studies on the Globalization of Law*, Ashgate, Aldershot, 347-98.

Barron, A. (1993), "The Illusions of the 'I': Citizenship and the Politics of Identity", in A. Norrie ed., *Closure or Critique: New Directions in Legal Theory*, Edinburgh University Press, Edinburgh, 80-100.

Barron, A. and Scott, C. (1992), "The Citizen's Charter Programme", 55 *Modern Law Review* 526-46.

Barsh, R. (1994), "Indigenous Peoples in the 1990s: From Object to Subject of International Law?", 7 *Harvard Human Rights Journal* 33-86.

Bartholomew, A. and Hunt, A. (1991), "What's Wrong with Rights?", 9 *Law and Inequality* 1-58.

Baudrillard, J. (1987), *Forget Foucault*, Semiotext(e), New York.

Bauman, Z. (1987), *Legislators and Interpreters: On Modernity, Post-Modernity and Intellectuals*, Polity, Cambridge.

Bauman, Z. (1988a), "Is there a Postmodern Sociology?", 5 *Theory, Culture and Society* 217-38.

Bauman, Z. (1988b), "Sociology and Postmodernity", 36 *Sociological Review* 790-813.

Bauman, Z. (1991), *Modernity and Ambivalence*, Polity, Cambridge.

Bauman, Z. (1992), *Intimations of Postmodernity*, Routledge, London.

Bauman, Z. (1993), *Postmodern Ethics*, Blackwell, Oxford.

Bauman, Z. (1996), "Morality in the Age of Contingency" in P. Heelas, S. Lash and P. Morris eds., *Detraditionalization: Critical Reflections on Authority and Identity*, Blackwell, Oxford, 49-58.

Bauman, Z. (1997), *Postmodernity and its Discontents*, Polity, Cambridge.

Bauman, Z. (2000), *Liquid Modernity*, Polity, Cambridge.

Baylis, J. and Smith, S., eds. (1997), *The Globalization of World Politics: An Introduction to International Relations*, Oxford.University Press, New York.

Beck, U. (1992), *Risk Society: Towards a New Modernity*, Sage, London.

Becker, M. (1996), "Problems with the Privatization of Heterosexuality", 73 *Denver University Law Review*, 1169-84.

Bell, D. (1973), *The Coming of Postindustrial Society*, Basic Books, New York.

Bell, D. (1980), *The Winding Passage: Essays and Sociological Journeys: 1960-1980*, ABT Books, Cambridge, Mass.

Bellow, G. and Minow, M., eds. (1996), *Law Stories*, University of Michigan Press, Ann Arbor.

Benhabib, S. (1984), "Epistemologies of Postmodernism: A Rejoinder to Jean-François Lyotard", 33 *New German Critique* 103-26.

Ben-Israel, R. (1997), "From Collective to Individual Justice: Changing Employment Relations in Israel", in J. Bellace and M. Rood eds., *Labor Law at the Crossroads: Changing Employment Relations*, Kluwer, The Hague, 27-34.

Bently, L. and Flynn, L., eds. (1996), *Law and the Senses: Sensational Jurisprudence*, Pluto, London.

Benvenisti, E. (1999), "Exit and Voice in the Age of Globalization", 98 *Michigan Law Review* 167-213.

Bergeron, J. and Fitzpatrick, P. (1998), *Europe's Other: European Law Between Modernity and Postmodernity*, Ashgate, Aldershot.

Berman, H. (1983), *Law and Revolution: The Formation of the Western Legal Tradition*, Harvard University Press, Cambridge, Mass.

Berman, M. (1982), *All That Is Solid Melts Into Air: The Experience of Modernity*, Simon and Schuster, New York.

Best, S. and Kellner, D. (1991), *Postmodern Theory: Critical Interrogations*, Macmillan, London.

Bhaskar, R. (1979), *The Possibility of Naturalism*, Harvester, Brighton.

Blagg, H. (1997), "A Just Measure of Shame? Aboriginal and Youth Conferencing in Australia", 37 *British Journal of Criminology* 481-501.

Blankenburg, E. (1984), "The Poverty of Evolutionism: A Critique of Teubner's Case for 'Reflexive Law'", 18 *Law and Society Review* 273-89.

Blankenburg, E. (1994), "The Infrastructure for Avoiding Civil Litigation: Comparing Cultures of Legal Behaviour in the Netherlands and West Germany" 28 *Law and Society Review* 789-808.

Blankenburg, E. (1995), "Access to Justice and Alternatives to Courts: European Procedural Justice Compared", 14 *Civil Justice Quarterly* 176-89.

Blankenburg, E. (1999), "Civil Justice: Access, Cost, and Expedition. The Netherlands" in A. Zuckerman ed., *Civil Justice in Crisis: Comparative Perspectives of Civil Procedure*, Oxford University Press, Oxford, 442-63.

Bloch, M. (1961), *Feudal Society*, Routledge and Kegan Paul, London.

Bodin, J. (1955 (orig. 1576)), *The Six Books of a Commonwealth*, Blackwell, Oxford.

Boston, J., ed. (1995), *The State Under Contract*, Bridget Williams Books, Wellington.

Bowles, S. and Gintis, H. (1986), *Democracy and Capitalism: Property, Community and the Contradictions of Modern Social Thought*, Routledge, London.

Bradbrook, A. (1998), "Residential Tenancies: The Second Stage of Reforms", 20 *Sydney Law Review* 402-34.

Bradgate, R., Graham, C. and Howells, G. (1994), "Regulating Fairness and Promoting Welfarism in Contract: An Institutional Perspective" in R. Brownsword, G. Howells, and T. Wilhelmsson eds., *Welfarism in Contract Law*, Dartmouth, Aldershot, 158-87.

Braithwaite, J. (2000), "The New Regulatory State and the Transformation of Criminology", 40 *British Journal of Criminology* 222-38.

Braithwaite, J. (2002), *Restorative Justice and Responsive Regulation*, Oxford University Press, Oxford.

Braithwaite, J. and Drahos, P. (2000), *Global Business Regulation*, Cambridge University Press, Melbourne.

Breyer, S. (1990), "Regulation and Deregulation in the United States: Airlines, Telecommunications and Antitrust" in G. Majone ed., *De-regulation or Re-regulation? Regulatory Reform in Europe and the United States*, Pinter, London, 7-58.

Brownsword, R. (2000), *Contract Law: Themes for the Twenty-First Century*, Butterworths, London.

Buckley, F., ed. (1999), *The Fall and Rise of Freedom of Contract*, Duke University Press, Durham, North Carolina.

Buergenthal, T. (1997), "Modern Constitutions and Human Rights Treaties", 36 *Columbia Journal of International Law* 211-23.

Callinicos, A. (1989), *Against Postmodernism: A Marxist Critique*, Polity, Cambridge.

Campbell, D. and Vincent-Jones, P., eds. (1996), *Contract and Economic Organization: Socio-Legal Initiatives*, Dartmouth, Aldershot.

Campos, P., Schlag, P. and Smith, S. (1996), *Against the Law*, Duke University Press, Durham, North Carolina.

Cappelletti, M., ed. (1981), *Access to Justice and the Welfare State*, Alphen, Sijthoff.

Cappelletti, M. (1993), "Alternative Dispute Resolution Processes within the World-wide Access to Justice Movement", 56 *Modern Law Review* 282-96.
Cappelletti, M. and Garth, B., eds. (1978), *Access to Justice, Vol. 1*, Giuffre, Milan.
Carney, T. and Ramia, G. (1999), "From Citizenship to Contractualism: the Transition from Unemployment Benefits to Employment Services in Australia", 6 *Australian Journal of Administrative Law* 117-39.
Carty A., ed. (1990), *Postmodern Law: Enlightenment, Revolution and the Death of Man*, Edinburgh University Press, Edinburgh.
Cawson, A. (1982), *Corporatism and Welfare*, Heinemann, London.
Cawson, A. (1986), *Corporatism and Political Theory*, Basil Blackwell, Oxford.
Cerny, P. (1990), *The Changing Architecture of Politics: Structure, Agency and the Future of the State*, Sage, London.
Cesarani, D. and Fulbrook, M., eds. (1996), *Citizenship, Nationality and Migration in Europe*, Routledge, London.
Chen, M. (1995), "The Reconfiguration of the State and the Appropriate Scope of Judicial Review" in J. Boston ed., *The State Under Contract*, Bridget Williams Books, Wellington, 112-23.
Chesterman, M. (1979), *Charities, Trusts and Social Welfare*, Weidenfeld and Nicolson, London.
Chinkin, C. (1993), *Third Parties in International Law*, Clarendon, Oxford.
Choudhry, S. (1999), "Globalization in Search of Justificiation: Toward a Theory of Comparative Constitutional Interpretation", 74 *Indiana Law Journal* 819-97.
Cohen, S. (1993), "Intellectual Skepticism and Radical Commitment: The Case of Radical Criminology", 13 *Studies in Law, Politics and Society* 187-209.
Coke, E. (1642), *Second Part of the Institutes of the Law of England*, Flesher, London.
Cornell, D. (1991), *Beyond Accommodation: Ethical Feminism, Deconstruction and the Law*, Routledge, New York.
Cornell, D. (1992), *The Philosophy of the Limit*, Routledge, New York.
Cornell, D. (2000), *Just Cause: Freedom, Identity and Rights*, Rowman and Littlefield, Lanham, Md.
Cotterrell, R. (1989), *The Politics of Jurisprudence: a Critical Introduction to Legal Philosophy*, Butterworths, London.
Cotterrell, R. (1995), *Law's Community: Legal Theory in Sociological Perspective*, Clarendon, Oxford.
Cover, R. (1986), "Violence and the Word", 95 *Yale Law Journal* 1601-29.
Cox, R. (1998), "The Consequences of Welfare Reform: How Conceptions of Social Rights are Changing" 27 *Journal of Social Policy* 1-16.
Cranston, R. (1985), *Legal Foundations of the Welfare State*, Weidenfeld and Nicolson, London.
Creighton, B. (1997), "The Role of the State in Regulating Employment Relations: an Australian Perspective", 2 *Flinders Journal of Law Reform* 103-29.
Crook, S., Pakulski, J. and Waters, M. (1992), *Postmodernization: Change in Advanced Society*, Sage, London.
Cunningham, A. (1994), "The European Convention on Human Rights, Customary International Law and the Constitution", 43 *International and Comparative Law Quarterly* 537-67.
Dana, D. (2000), "The New 'Contractarian' Paradigm in Environmental Regulation", 2000 *University of Illinois Law Review* 35-59.
Davies, M. (1994), *Asking the Law Question*, Law Book Company, Sydney.

Davies, M. (1996), *Delimiting the Law: 'Postmodernism' and the Politics of Law*, Pluto, London.

Dean, M. (1999), *Governmentality: Power and Rule in Modern Society*, Sage, London.

Derrida, J. (1976), *Of Grammatology*, Johns Hopkins University Press, Baltimore.

Derrida, J. (1978), *Writing and Difference*, University of Chicago Press, Chicago.

Derrida, J. (1982), *Margins of Philosophy*, University of Chicago Press, Chicago.

Derrida, J. (1987), "Laws of Reflection: Nelson Mandela, in Admiration" in J. Derrida and M. Tlili eds. *For Nelson Mandela*, Seaver Books, New York, 13-42.

Derrida, J. (1990), "The Force of Law: 'The Mystical Foundations of Authority'", 11 *Cardozo Law Review* 919-1046.

Dewar, J. (2000), "Family Law and Its Discontents", 14 *International Journal of Law, Policy and the Family* 59-85.

Dewar, J., Giddings, J. and Parker, S. (1999), "The Impact of Legal Aid Changes on the Practice of Family Law", 13 *Australian Journal of Family Law* 33-51.

Dews, P. (1984), "Foucault's Theory of Subjectivity", 144 *New Left Review* 72-95.

Dews, P. (1987), *Logics of Disintegration: Post-Structuralist Thought and the Claims of Critical Theory*, Verso, London.

Dezalay, Y. (1990), "The *Big Bang* and the Law: The Internationalization and Restructuration of the Legal Field", 7 *Theory, Culture and Society* 279-93.

Dezalay, Y. (1994), "The Forum Should Fit the Fuss: The Economics and Politics of Negotiated Justice", in M. Cain and C. Harrington eds., *Lawyers in a Postmodern World: Translation and Transgression*, Open University Press, Buckingham, 155-82.

Dezalay, Y. and Garth, B. (1996), *Dealing in Virtue: International Commercial Arbitration and the Construction of a Transnational Legal Order*, University of Chicago Press, Chicago.

Diller, M. (2000), "The Revolution in Welfare Administration: Rules, Discretion, and Entrepreneurial Government", 75 *New York University Law Review* 1121-20.

Donnison, D. (1984), "The Progressive Potential of Privatization", in J. LeGrand and P. Robinson eds., *Privatisation and the Welfare State*, Allen and Unwin, London, 41-57.

Donzelot, J. (1979), *The Policing of Families*, Pantheon, New York.

Douzinas, C. (2000), *The End of Human Rights: Critical Legal Thought at the Turn of the Century*, Hart, Oxford.

Douzinas, C. and Warrington, R. (1991), *Postmodern Jurisprudence: The Law of Text in the Texts of Law*, Routledge, London and New York.

Douzinas, C., Goodrich, P. and Hachamovitch Y., eds. (1994), *Politics, Postmodernity and Critical Legal Studies: The Legality of the Contingent*, Routledge, London.

Douzinas, C. and Warrington, R. (1995), *Justice Miscarried: Ethics and Aesthetics in Law*, Harvester, Hemel Hempstead.

Dworkin, R. (1977), *Taking Rights Seriously*, Duckworth, London.

Dworkin, R. (1986), *Law's Empire*, Harvard University Press, Cambridge, Mass.

Duxbury, N. (1986), "Look Back in Unger: A Review of Roberto Unger's *Law in Modern Society*", 49 *Modern Law Review* 658-79.

Eagleton, T. (1983), *Literary Theory: An Introduction*, Blackwell, Oxford.

Eagleton, T. (1990), *The Ideology of the Aesthetic*, Blackwell, Oxford.

Eagleton, T. (1996), *The Illusions of Postmodernism*, Blackwell, Oxford.

Edgeworth, B. (1986), "Legal Positivism and the Philosophy of Language: A Critique of H.L.A. Hart's 'Descriptive Sociology'" 6 *Legal Studies* 115-39.

Effron, J. (1988), "The Contractualization of the Law of Leaseholds: Pitfalls and Opportunities", 14 *Monash University Law Review* 83-113.

Ehrenreich, N. (1996), "The Progressive Potential in Privatization", 73 *University of Denver Law Review* 1235-52.

Ertman, M. (1996), "Contractual Purgatory for Sexual Marginorities: Not Heaven but Not Hell Either" 73 *Denver Law Journal* 1107-68.

Esping-Andersen, G. (1990), *The Three Worlds of Welfare Capitalism*, Polity, Massachusetts.

Evans, E. (1978), *Social Policy 1830-1914: Individualism, Collectivism and the Origins of the Welfare State*, Routledge and Kegan Paul, London and Boston.

Ewald, F. (1986), "A Concept of Social Law", in G. Teubner ed., *Dilemmas of Law in the Welfare State*, de Gruyter, Berlin, 40-75.

Ewald, F. (1987), "Justice, Equality, Judgement: On 'Social Justice'", in G. Teubner ed., *Juridification of Social Spheres: A Comparative Analysis in the Areas of Labour, Corporate, Antitrust, and Social Welfare Law*, de Gruyter, Berlin, 91-110.

Farnsworth, E. (1990), "Developments in Contract Law During the 1980s: The Top Ten", 41 *Case Western Reserve Law Review* 203-230.

Featherstone, M., and Lash, S. (1995), "Globalization, Modernity and the Spatialization of Social Theory: An Introduction", in M. Featherstone, S. Lash and R. Robertson eds., *Global Modernities*, Sage, London, 1-24.

Feldman, S. (2000), *American Legal Thought from Premodernism to Postmodernism: An Intellectual Voyage*, Oxford University Press, New York.

Fiedler, L. (1971), *The Collected Essays of Leslie Fiedler*, Vol. 2, Stein and Day, New York.

Fish, S. (1989), *Doing What Comes Naturally: Interpretation and Theory in Literature and the Law*, Duke University Press, Durham, North Carolina.

Fish, S. (1993), "The Law Wishes to Have a Formal Existence", in A. Norrie ed., *Closure or Critique: New Directions in Legal Theory*, Edinburgh University Press, Edinburgh, 157-74.

Fiss, O. (1979), "The Supreme Court 1978 Term. Foreword: The Forms of Justice", 93 *Harvard Law Review* 1-58.

Fiss, O. (1984), "Comment: Against Settlement", 93 *Yale Law Journal* 1073-1090.

Fitzpatrick, P. (1992), *The Mythology of Modern Law*, Routledge, London.

Fitzpatrick, P. (2001), *Modernism and the Grounds of Law*, Cambridge University Press, Cambridge.

Flora, P. and Alber, J. (1981), "Modernization, Democratization, and the Development of Welfare States in Western Europe" in P. Flora and A. Heidenheimer eds., *The Development of Welfare States in Europe and America*, Transaction Books, New Brunswick, 37-80.

Flora, P. and Heidenheimer A. (1981), "Introduction" and "The Historical Core and Changing Boundaries of the Welfare State", in P. Flora and A. Heidenheimer eds., *The Development of Welfare States in Europe and America*, Transaction Books, New Brunswick, 1-34.

Fn'Pierre, P. and Work, L. (1992-93), "On the Growth and Development of Dispute Resolution", 81 *Kentucky Law Journal* 959-75.

Forrest, R. and Murie, A. (1988), *Selling the Welfare State: The Privatization of Public Housing*, Routledge, London.

Foucault, M. (1967), *Madness and Civilization: A History of Insanity in the Age of Reason*, Tavistock, London.

Foucault, M. (1973a), *The Birth of the Clinic: An Archaeology of Medical Perception*, Tavistock, London.

Foucault, M. (1973b), *The Order of Things: An Archaeology of the Human Sciences*, Vintage Books, New York.

Foucault, M. (1977a), *Discipline and Punish: The Birth of the Prison*, Pantheon Books, New York.

Foucault, M. (1977b), *The Archaeology of Knowledge*, Tavistock, London.

Foucault, M. (1980a), *Power/Knowledge*, C. Gordon ed., Pantheon, New York.

Foucault, M. (1982), "The Subject and Power" in H. Dreyfus and P. Rabinow eds, *Michel Foucault*, Chicago University Press, Chicago, 208-26.

Foucault, M. (1990), *The History of Sexuality: Vol 1*, Penguin, London.

Foucault, M. (1991), "Governmentality", in G. Burchell, C. Gordon, and P. Miller eds., *The Foucault Effect: Studies in Governmentality*, University of Chicago Press, Chicago, 87-104.

Fraser, N. (1991), "The Force of Law: Metaphysical or Political?" 13 *Cardozo Law Review* 1325-31.

Fraser, N. (1997), *Justice Interruptus: Critical Reflections on the "Postsocialist" Condition*, Routledge, New York.

Fraser, N. and Nicholson, L. (1988), "Social Criticism Without Philosophy: An Encounter Between Feminism and Postmodernism" in A. Ross ed., *Universal Abandon?: The Politics of Postmodernism*, University of Minnesota Press, Minneapolis, 83-104.

Freeman, J. (2000a), "Private Parties, Public Functions and the New Administrative Law", 52 *Administrative Law Review* 813-58.

Freeman, J. (2000b), "The Contracting State", 28 *Florida State University Law Review* 155-214.

Freeman, M., ed. (1994), *Lloyd's Introduction to Jurisprudence*, 6th ed., Sweet and Maxwell, London.

Friedman, L. (1965), *Contract Law in America*, University of Wisconsin Press, Madison.

Friedman, L. (1985), *Total Justice*, Russell Sage Foundation, New York.

Friedman, L. (1986), "Legal Culture and the Welfare State" in G. Teubner ed., *Dilemmas of Law in the Welfare State*, Walter de Gruyter, Berlin, 13-27.

Friedman, L. (1996), "Borders: On the Emerging Sociology of Transnational Law", 32 *Stanford Journal of International Law* 65-90.

Friedmann, W. (1959), *Law in a Changing Society*, Stevens, London.

Friedmann, W. (1971), *The State and the Rule of Law in a Mixed Economy*, Stevens, London.

Frow, J. (1991), *What Was Postmodernism?*, Local Consumption Publications, Sydney.

Frug, M. (1992), *Postmodern Legal Feminism*, Routledge, New York.

Fuller, L. (1969), *The Morality of Law*, 2nd ed., Yale University Press, New Haven.

Gagné, G. (1992), "Les transformations du droit dans la problématique de la transition à la postmodernité", 33 *Les Cahiers de Droit* 701-33.

Galanter, M. (1966), "The Modernization of Law", in M. Weiner ed., *Modernization*, Basic Books, New York, 153-65.

Galanter, M. (1985), "A Settlement Judge, Not a Trial Judge: Judicial Mediation in the United States", 12 *Journal of Law and Society* 1-18.

Galanter, M. (1986), "The Day After the Litigation Explosion", 46 *Maryland Law Review* 3-39.

Galanter, M. (1992), "Law Abounding", 55 *Modern Law Review* 1-24.

Garland, D. (1997), "'Governmentality' and the Problem of Crime: Foucault, Criminology, Sociology", 1 *Theoretical Criminology*, 173-214.

Garth, B. (1992), "Privatization and the New Market for Disputes", *Studies in Law, Politics and Society* 367-91.

Gellner, E. (1985), *Relativism and the Social Sciences*, Cambridge University Press, Cambridge.

Genn, H. (1993), "Tribunals and Informal Justice", 56 *Modern Law Review* 393-411.

Genn, H. (1999a), *Mediation in Action: Resolving Court Disputes Without Trial*, Calouste Gulbenkian Foundation, London.

Genn, H. (1999b), *Paths to Justice: What People Do and Think About Going to Law*, Hart, Oxford.

Gessner, V., Appelbaum, R. and Felstiner, W. (2001), "Introduction", in R. Appelbaum, V. Gessner and W. Felstiner eds., *Rules and Networks: The Legal Culture of Global Business Transactions*, Hart, Oxford, 1-36.

Giddens, A. (1984), *The Constitution of Society*, Polity, Cambridge.

Giddens, A. (1990), *The Consequences of Modernity*, Stanford University Press, Stanford.

Gilmore, G. (1974), *The Death of Contract*, Ohio State University Press, Columbus.

Glendon, M. (1981), *The New Family and the New Property*, Butterworths, Toronto.

Goffman, E. (1961), *Asylums*, Penguin, Harmondsworth.

Goldthorpe, J., Bechhofer, F. and Platt J. (1968), *The Affluent Worker: Industrial Attitudes and Behaviour*, Cambridge University Press, Cambridge.

Goriely, T. (1995), "The Governments's Legal Aid Reforms" in A. Zuckerman and R. Cranston eds., *Reform of Civil Procedure: Essays on Access to Justice*, Clarendon, Oxford, 351-69.

Goodrich, P. (1994), "*Jani Anglorum*: Signs, Symptoms, Slips and Interpretation" in C. Douzinas, P. Goodrich and Y. Hachamovitch eds., *Politics, Postmodernity and Critical Legal Studies: The Legality of the Contingent*, Routledge, London, 107-44.

Gorz, A. (1985), *Farewell to the Working Class*, Pluto, London.

Grabosky, P. and Braithwaite, J. (1986), *Of Manners Gentle: Enforcement Strategies of Australian Business Regulatory* Agencies, Oxford University Press, Melbourne.

Graham, C. (2000), *Regulating Public Utilities: A Constitutional Approach*, Hart, Oxford.

Graham, C. and Prosser, T. (1991), *Privatizing Public Enterprises: Constitutions, The State and Regulation in Comparative Perspective*, Oxford University Press, Oxford.

Gray, K. (1979), "Lease or Licence to Evade the Rent Act?", 38 *Cambridge Law Journal* 38-44.

Habermas, J. (1976), *Legitimation Crisis*, Beacon Press, Boston.

Habermas, J. (1981), *The Theory of Communicative Action, Vol 1: Reason and the Rationalization of Society*, Beacon, Boston.

Habermas, J. (1986), "Law as Medium and Law as Institution", in G. Teubner ed., *Dilemmas of Law in the Welfare State*, Walter de Gruyter, Berlin, 203-20.

Habermas, J. (1987a), *The Philosophical Discourse of Modernity*, Polity, Cambridge.

Habermas, J. (1987b), *The Theory of Communicative Action, Vol 2: System and Lifeworld: The Decline of Functionalist Reason*, Beacon, Boston.

Habermas, J. (1989), "The New Obscurity: The Crisis of the Welfare State and the Exhaustion of Utopian Energies" in J. Habermas ed., *The New Conservatism*, MIT Press, Cambridge, Mass., 48-70.

Habermas, J. (1996), *Between Facts and Norms*, MIT Press, Cambridge, Mass.

Habermas, J. (2001), "The Postnational Constellation and the Future of Democracy", in J. Habermas, *The Postnational Constellation: Political Essays*, Polity Press, Cambridge, 58-112.

Hall, S. (1980), "Reformism and the Legislation of Consent" in *Permissiveness and Control: The Fate of the Sixties Legislation*, National Deviancy Conference ed., Macmillan, London, 1-43.

Hancher, L. and Moran, M. (1989), "Organizing Regulatory Space", in L. Hancher and M. Moran eds., *Capitalism, Culture and Economic Regulation*, Clarendon Press, Oxford, 271-99.

Hanf, K. (1994), "The Political Economy of Ecological Modernization: Creating a Regulated Market for Environmental Quality" in M. Moran and T. Prosser eds., *Privatization and Regulatory Change in Europe*, Open University Press, Buckingham, United Kingdom, 127-44.

Harden, I. (1992), *The Contracting State*, Open University Press, Buckingham.

Harland, D. (1997), "The United Nations Guidelines for Consumer Protection: Their Impact in the First Decade" in I. Ramsay ed., *Consumer Law in the Global Economy: National and International Dimensions*, Ashgate, Aldershot, 1-14.

Hart, H. (1961), *The Concept of Law*, Clarendon Press, Oxford.

Hart, H. (1963), *Law, Liberty and Morality*, Oxford University Press, Oxford.

Harvey, D. (1989), *The Condition of Postmodernity*, Blackwell, Oxford.

Hassan, I. (1971), *The Dismemberment of Orpheus: Toward a Postmodern Literature*, University of Wisconsin Press, Madison.

Hassan, I. (1985), "The Culture of Postmodernism", 2 *Theory, Culture and Society* 119-32.

Hayek, F. (1982), *Law, Legislation and Liberty*, Routledge, London.

Hebdige, D. (1988), *Hiding in the Light: On Images and Things*, Routledge, London.

Heelas, P. (1996), "On Things not Being Worse, and the Ethic of Humanity" in P. Heelas, S. Lash and P. Morris eds., *Detraditionalization: Critical Reflections on Authority and Identity*, Blackwell, Oxford, 200-22.

Held, D. (1995), *Democracy and the Global Order: From the Modern State to Cosmopolitan Governance*, Polity, Cambridge.

Heller, A. and Feher, F. (1988), *The Postmodern Political Condition*, Polity, Cambridge.

Hicks, S. (1995), "Sources of Law: Towards a New Middle Ages of Law", 5 *European Journal of Law, Philosophy and Computer Science* 13-18.

Hillyard, P. and Watson, S. (1996), "Postmodern Social Policy: A Contradiction in Terms?", 25 *Journal of Social Policy* 321-46.

Hirschman, A. (1970), *Exit, Voice, and Loyalty: Responses to Decline in Firms, Organizations, and States*, Harvard University Press, Cambridge, Mass.

Hirst, P. and Thompson, G. (1996), *Globalization in Question*, Polity, Cambridge.

Hobbes, T. (1968), *Leviathan*, C. Macpherson ed., Penguin, Harmondsworth.

Hobe, S. (1997), "Global Challenges to Statehood: The Increasingly Important Role of Nongovernmental Organizations", 5 *Global Legal Studies Journal* 191-209.

Hogg, R. and Carrington, K. (2001), "Governing Rural Australia: Land, Space and Race", in G. Wickham and G. Pavlich eds. *Rethinking Law, Society and Governance: Foucault's Bequest*, Routledge, London, 43-60.

Hohfeld, W. (1919), *Fundamental Legal Conceptions*, Yale University Press, New Haven.

Howse, R., Prichard, J. and Trebilcock, M. (1990), "Smaller or Smarter Government?", 40 *University of Toronto Law Journal* 498-541.

Hunt, A. (1990), "The Big Fear: Law Confronts Postmodernism" 35 *McGill Law Journal* 507-40.

Hunt, A. (1992), "Foucault's Expulsion of Law: Towards a Retrieval" 17 *Law and Social Inquiry* 1-38.

Hunt, M. (1997), *Using Human Rights Law in English Courts*, Hart Publishing, Oxford.

Huyssens, A. (1984), "Mapping the Postmodern", 33 *New German Critique* 5-52.

Ignatieff, M. (1989), "Citizenship and Moral Narcissism", 60 *Political Quarterly* 63-74.

Inglehart, R. (1977), *The Silent Revolution: Changing Values and Political Styles among Western Publics*, Princeton University Press, Princeton.

Inglehart, R. (1997), *Modernization and Postmodernization: Cultural, Political and Economic Change in 43 Societies*, Princeton University Press, Princeton.

Jackson, P. and Price, C. (1994), *Privatization and Deregulation: A Review of the Issues*, Longman, London.

James, C. (1963), *Beyond a Boundary*, Stanley Paul, London.

Jameson, F. (1984), "Postmodernism, or the Cultural Logic of Late Capitalism", 146 *New Left Review* 53-93.

Jameson, F. (1991), *Postmodernism, or, the Cultural Logic of Late Capitalism*, Duke University Press, Durham, NC.

Jencks, C. (1977), *The Language of Postmodern Architecture*, Academy, London.

Jones, C. (1994), "Capitalism, Globalization and the Rule of Law: An Alternative Trajectory of Legal Change in China", 3 *Social and Legal Studies* 195-222.

Kagan, R. (2001), "Introduction", in P. Nonet and P. Selznick, *Law and Society in Transition: Toward Responsive Law*, 2nd ed., Harper and Row, New York, i-xxvi.

Kagan, R., Krygier, M. and Winston, K., eds. (2002), *Legality and Community: On the Intellectual Legacy of Philip Selznick*, Rowman and Littlefield, Lanham, Md.

Kamenka, E., Brown, R. and Erh-Soon Tay, A., eds. (1978), *Law and Society: The Crisis in Legal Ideals*, Edward Arnold, London.

Keith, K. (1995), "A New Zealand Perspective on Globalization" in P. Alston and M. Chiam eds., *Treaty-Making and Australia: Globalization versus Sovereignty?*, Federation Press, Sydney, 283-91.

Kellner, D. (1988), "Postmodernism as Social Theory: Some Challenges and Problems", 5 *Theory, Culture and Society* 239-69.

Kelsen, H. (1967), *The Pure Theory of Law*, University of California Press, Berkeley.

Kemeny, J. (1995), *From Public Housing to the Social Market: Rental Policy Strategies in Comparative Perspective*, Routledge, London.

Kenny, M. (1999), "The Way We Live Now", *Irish Independent*, October 3.

Kinley, D. (1998), "The Legal Dimension of Human Rights" in D. Kinley ed., *Human Rights in Australian Law*, Federation Press, Leichhardt, New South Wales, 2-25.

Kirby, M. (1995), "The Role of International Standards in Australian Courts", in P. Alston and M. Chiam eds., *Treaty-Making and Australia: Globalization versus Sovereignty?*, Federation Press, Sydney, 81-92.

Kosonen, P. (1995), "European Welfare State Models: Converging Trends", 25 *International Journal of Sociology* 81-110.

Krygier, M. and Czarnota, A., eds. (1999), *The Rule of Law After Communism: Problems and Prospects in East-Central Europe*, Ashgate, Aldershot.

Kuhn, T. (1962), *The Structure of Scientific Revolutions*, University of Chicago Press, Chicago.

Lacey, N. (1996), "Normative Reconstruction in Socio-Legal Theory", 5 *Social and Legal Studies* 131-57.

Ladeur, K. (1995), *Postmoderne Rechtstheorie: Selbstreferenz, Selbstorganisation, Prozeduralisierung*, 2nd ed., Duncker and Humblot, Berlin.

Ladeur, K. (1997), "Postmodern Constitutional Theory: A Prospect for the Self-Organising Society", 60 *Modern Law Review* 617-629.

Lasch, C. (1977), *Culture of Narcissism: American Life in an Age of Declining Expectations*, Abacus, London.

Lash, S. (1990), *Sociology of Postmodernism*, Routledge, London.

Lash, S. and Urry, J. (1987), *The End of Organized Capitalism*, Polity, Cambridge.

Lash, S. and Urry, J. (1994), *Economies of Signs and Space*, Sage, London.

Latour, B. (1994), *We Have Never Been Modern*, Harvard University Press, Cambridge, Mass.

Laux, J. and Molot, M. (1988), *State Capitalism: Public Enterprises in Canada*, Cornell University Press, Ithaca.

Leaman, J. (1994), "Privatization and Regulatory Reform in Germany" in M. Moran and T. Prosser eds., *Privatization and Regulatory Change in Europe*, Open University Press, Buckingham.

Levi-Strauss, C. (1968), *Structural Anthropology*, Weidenfeld and Nicolson, London.

Litowitz, D. (1997), *Postmodern Philosophy and Law*, University Press of Kansas, Kansas.

Lodge, D. (1985), *Small World: An Academic Romance*, Penguin, London.

Lowi, T. (1987), "The Welfare State, The New Regulation, and The Rule of Law" in A. Hutchinson and P. Monahan eds., *The Rule of Law: Ideal or Ideology*, Carswell, Toronto, 17-58.

Luban, D. (1995), "Settlements and Erosion of the Public Realm", 83 *Georgetown Law Journal* 2619-2662.

Luhmann, N. (1985), *A Sociological Theory of Law*, Routledge, London.

Luhmann, N. (1986), "The Self-Reproduction of Law and its Limits" in G. Teubner ed., *Dilemmas of Law in the Welfare State*, de Gruyter, Berlin, 111-27.

Lyotard, J-F. (1984), *The Postmodern Condition: A Report on Knowledge*, Manchester University Press, Manchester.

Lyotard, J-F. (1988), *The Differend*, Minneapolis, University of Minnesota Press.

Lyotard, J-F. (1992), *The Postmodern Explained to Children: Correspondence 1982-1985*, J. Pefanis and M. Thomas eds., Power, Sydney.

Lyotard, J-F. (1993), "The Other's Rights", in *On Human Rights: The Oxford Amnesty Lectures*, S. Shute and S. Hurley eds., Basic Books, New York, 135-47.

Lyotard, J-F. and Thébaud, J-L. (1985), *Just Gaming*, University of Minnesota Press, Minneapolis.

McBarnet, D. (1981), *Conviction: Law, State and the Construction of Justice*, Macmillan, London.

McCarthy, T. (1991), *Ideals and Illusions: On Reconstruction, Deconstruction in Contemporary Critical Theory*, MIT Press, Cambridge, Mass.

MacCormick, N. (1993), "Beyond the Sovereign State", 56 *Modern Law Review* 1-18.

MacCormick, N. (1997), "Democracy, Subsidiarity and Citizenship in the 'European Commonwealth'", 16 *Law and Philosophy* 331-56.

MacDermott, T. (1998), "Labour Law and Human Rights", in D. Kinley ed., *Human Rights in Australian Law*, Federation Press, Leichhardt, New South Wales, 194-220.

McHale, B. (1987), *Postmodernist Fiction*, Methuen, London.

McLean, J. (1996), "Contracting in the Corporatised and Privatised Environment", 7 *Public Law Review* 223-232.

Macpherson, C. (1973), "A Political Theory of Property" in C. Macpherson, *Democratic Theory: Essays in Retrieval*, Clarendon, Oxford, 120-40.

McPherson, K. (1999), "Public Governance Through Private Contract: A State Audit Perspective", 3 *Flinders Journal of Law Reform* 9-32.

Maine, H. (1917 (orig. 1861)), *Ancient Law*, Dent, London.

Majone, G., ed. (1990), *Deregulation or Reregulation? Regulatory Reform in Europe and the United States*, Pinter, London.

Malbon, J. (1998), "The Regulatory Tightrope" in M. Hossain and J. Malbon eds., *Who Benefits from Privatization?*, Routledge, London, 9-33.

Man, T. (1997), "National Legal Restructuring in Accordance with International Norms: GATT/WTO and China's Foreign Trade Reform", 4 *Indiana Journal of Global Legal Studies* 471-508.

Marshall, T. (1963), *Sociology at the Crossroads*, Heinemann, London.

Mathews, J. (1989), *Tools of Change*, Pluto, Sydney.

Matsuda, M. (1997), "Were You There? Witnessing Welfare Retreat", 31 *University of San Francisco Law Review* 779-88.

Meek, C. (1998), "Privatization Doesn't Necessarily Equal Competition" in M. Hossain and J. Malbon eds., *Who Benefits from Privatization?*, Routledge, London, 100-18.

Merrills, J. (1993), *The Development of International Law by the European Court of Human Rights*, 2nd ed., Manchester University Press, Manchester.

Merry, S. (1979), "Going to Court: Strategies of Dispute Management in an American Urban Neighbourhood", 13 *Law and Society Review* 891-925.

Merry, S. (1988), "Legal Pluralism", 22 *law and Society Review* 869.

Merry, S. (1990), "The Discourses of Mediation and the Power of Naming"., 2 *Yale Journal of Law and the Humanities* 1-36.

Mills, C. (1959), *The Sociological Imagination*, Oxford University Press, New York.

Minda, G. (1995), *Postmodern Legal Movements*, New York University Press, New York.

Mishra, R. (1984), *The Welfare State in Crisis*, Wheatsheaf, Brighton.

Mnookin, R. and Kornhauser, L. (1979), "Bargaining in the Shadow of the Law: The Case of Divorce", 88 *Yale Law Journal* 950-97.

Moles, R. (1987), *Definition and Rule in Jurisrudence: A Reassessment of H.L.A Hart and the Positivist Tradition*, Blackwell, Oxford.

Mooney, R. (1995), "The New Conceptualism in Contract Law", 74 *Oregon Law Review* 1131-1207.

Moran, M. and Prosser, T. (1994), *Privatization and Regulatory Change in Europe*, Open University Press, Buckingham.

Morrison, W. (1997), *Jurisprudence: From the Greeks to Postmodernism*, Cavendish, London.

Nader, L. (1988), "The ADR Explosion - The Implication of Rhetoric in Legal Reform", 8 *Windsor Yearbook of Access to Justice* 269-91.

Newman, J. (1990), *The Postmodern Church*, Four Courts Press, Dublin.

Nice, J. (1996), "The New Private Law: An Introduction", 73 *Denver Law Journal* 993-99.

Nielsen, J. and Martin, G. (1998), "Indigenous Australian People and Human Rights" in D. Kinley ed., *Human Rights in Australian Law*, Federation Press, Leichhardt, New South Wales, 92-119.

Nolan, D. (1997), "The (Limited and Shrinking) Role of the State in the Regulation of Employment Relations: Private Resolution of Statutory Disputes in the USA", 2 *Flinders Journal of Law Reform* 147-76.

Nonet, P. and Selznick, P. (1978), *Law and Society in Transition: Toward Responsive Law*, Harper and Row, New York.

Nussbaum, M. (1994) "Skepticism about Practical Reason in Literature and the Law"107 *Harvard Law Review* 714-44.

Offe, C. (1985), *Disorganized Capitalism*, Polity, Cambridge.

Offe, C. (1987a), "The Utopia of the Zero-Option: Modernity and Modernization as Normative Political Criteria", 7 *Praxis International* 1-24.

Offe, C. (1987b), "Democracy Against the Welfare State", 15 *Political Theory* 501-37.

O'Malley, P. (1992), "Risk, Power and Crime Prevention", 21 *Economy and Society* 257-75.

O'Malley, P., Weir, L. and Shearing, C. (1997), "Governmentality, Criticism, Politics", 26 *Economy and Society* 501-17.

Osborne, D. and Gaebler, T. (1992), *Reinventing Government*, Addison-Wesley, New York.

Otto, D. (1996), "Nongovernmental Organisations in the United Nations System: The Emerging Role of International Civil Society", 18 *Human Rights Quarterly* 107-141.

Parker, C. (1999), *Just Lawyers: Regulation and Access to Justice*, Oxford University Press, Oxford.

Parsons, T. (1977), *The Evolution of Societies*, Toby, J., ed., Prentice Hall, New Jersey.

Parsons, T. (1977-78), "Reviw: Roberto Unger's *Law in Modern Society, Law and Society Review*, 145-49.

Partington, M. (1987), "The Juridification of Social Welfare in Britain" in G. Teubner ed., *Juridification of Social Spheres*, de Gruyter, Berlin, 419-38.

Paterson, A. (1996), "Professionalism and the Legal Services Market", 3 *International Journal of the Legal Profession* 137-68.

Patterson, D., ed. (1994), *Postmodernism and Law*, Dartmouth, Aldershot.

Peller, G. (1996), "Public Imperialism and Private Resistance: Progressive Possibilities of the New Private Law", 73 *Denver University Law Review* 1001-09.

Petersen, H. and Zahle, H., eds. (1995), *Legal Polycentricity: Consequences of Pluralism in Law*, Dartmouth, Aldershot.

Petersmann, E-U. (2001), "Human Rights and International Economic Law in the 21st Century", *Journal of International Economic Law* 3-39.

Pfennigstorf, W. (1975), "Legal Expenses Insurance", 23 *American Journal of Comparative Law* 451-489.

Picciotto, S. (1992), *International Business Taxation: A Study in the Internationalization of Business Regulation*, Weidenfeld and Nicolson, London.

Picciotto, S. (1996-97), "Networks in International Economic Integration: Fragmented States and the Dilemmas of Neo-Liberalism", 17 *Northwestern Journal of Law and Business* 1014-56.

Pierce, R. (1996), "The Due Process Counterrevolution of the 1990s?", 96 *Columbia Law Review* 1973-99.

Pierson, C. (1991), *Beyond the Welfare State*, Polity, Cambridge.

Piore, M. and Sabel, C. (1984), *The Second Industrial Divide*, Basic Books, New York.

Pogge, T. (1989), *Realizing Rawls*, Cornell University Press, Ithaca.

Pogge, T. (2001), "The Influence of the Global Order on the Prospects for Genuine Democracy in the Developing Countries", 14 *Ratio Juris* 326-43.

Polanyi, K. (1944), *The Great Transformation*, Rinehart, New York.

Pollert, A. (1988), "The Flexible Firm: Fixation or Fact?", 2 (3) *Work, Employment and Society* 281-316.

Post, R. (1992), "Postmodern Temptations: Review of F. Jameson, (1991), *Postmodernism, or, the Cultural Logic of Late Capitalism*, Duke University Press, Durham, North Carolina", 4 *Yale Journal of Law and the Humanities* 391-98.

Post, R. (2001), "The Challenge of Globalization to American Public Law Scholarship", 2 *Theoretical Inquiries in Law* 323-36.

Preuss, U. (1986), "The Concept of Rights and the Welfare State", in G. Teubner ed., *Dilemmas of Law in the Welfare State*, de Gruyter, Berlin, 151-72.

Prosser, T. (1986), *Nationalised Industries and Public Control*, Oxford University Press, Oxford.

Prosser, T. (1994), "Privatization, Regulation and Public Services", *Juridical Review* 3-17.

Prosser, T. (1999), "Theorising Utility Regulation" 62 *Modern Law Review* 196-217.

Prosser, T. and Moran, M. (1994), *Privatization and Regulatory Change in Europe*, Open University Press, Buckingham.

Quigley, W. (1998), "Backwards into the Future: How Welfare Changes in the Millennium Resemble English Poor Law of the Middle Ages", *Stanford Law and Policy Review* 101-13.

Rawls, J. (1971), *A Theory of Justice*, Harvard University Press, Cambridge, Mass.

Redding, P. (1986), "Habermas, Lyotard, Wittgenstein: Philosophy at the Limits of Modernity, 14 *Thesis Eleven* 9-25.

Regan, F. and Fleming, D. (1994), "International Perspectives on Legal Aid", 19 *Alternative Law Journal* 183-85.

Regan, F., Paterson, A., Goriely, T. and Fleming, D (1999), *The Transformation of Legal Aid: Comparative and Historical Studies*, Oxford University Press, Oxford.

Reich, C. (1964), "The New Property", 73 *Yale Law Journal* 733-87.

Reich, N. (1992), "Diverse Approaches to Consumer Protection Philosophy", 14 *Journal of Consumer Policy* 257-92.

Reznik, J. (1982), "Managerial Judges", 96 *Harvard Law Review* 376-448.

Rhodes, R. (1994), "The Hollowing Out of the State", 65 *Political Quarterly* 138-51.

Richardson, I. (1995), "Rights Jurisprudence - Justice for All?" in P. Joseph ed., *Essays on the Constitution*, Brooker's, Wellington, 61-83.

Rickman, N. and Gray, A. (1995), "The Role of Legal Expenses Insurance in Securing Access to the Market for Legal Services" in A. Zuckerman and R. Cranston eds., *Reform of Civil Procedure: Essays on 'Access to Justice'*, Clarendon Press, Oxford, 305-25.

Risse, T. and Ropp, S. (1999), "Conclusion" in T. Risse, S. Ropp, and K. Sikkink eds., *The Power of Human Rights: International Norms and Domestic Change*, Cambridge University Press, Cambridge, 260-78.

Risse, T., Ropp, S. and Sikkink, K., eds. (1999), *The Power of Human Rights: International Norms and Domestic Change*, Cambridge University Press, Cambridge.

Robertson, M. (1998), "Is ADR Part of a Movement Towards Consumer-Oriented Services in Australia?", 1 *The ADR Bulletin* 1-6.

Robertson, R. (1992), *Globalization: Social Theory and Global Culture*, Sage, London.

Robertson, R. (1995), "Glocalization: Time-Space and Homogeneity-Heterogeneity" in M. Featherstone, S. Lash and R. Robertson eds., *Global Modernities*, Sage, London, 25-44.

Rood, M. (1994), "Labour Law in the 21st Century", in Lord Wedderburn, M. Rood, G. Lyon-Caen, W. Däubler and P. Van der Heijden (1994), *Labour Law in the Post-Industrial Era: Essays in Honour of Hugo Sinzheimer*, Dartmouth, Aldershot, 83-92.

Rose, N. (1996), *Inventing Ourselves: Psychology, Personhood, and Power*, Cambridge University Press, Cambridge.

Rose, N. (1999), *Powers of Freedom: Reframing Political Thought*, Cambridge University Press.

Rose, N. and Valverde, M. (1998), "Governed by Law" 7 *Socio-Legal Studies* 541-51.

Rose-Ackerman, S. (1990), "Defending the State: A Skeptical Look at 'Regulatory Reform' in the Eighties", 61 *University of Colorado Law Review* 517-35.

Ross, A., ed. (1988), *Universal Abandon: The Politics of Postmodernism*, University of Minnesota Press, Minneapolis.

Ruggie, J. (1993), "Territoriality and Beyond: Problematizing Modernity in International Relations", 47 *International Organization* 139-74.

Ryan, M. (1982), *Marxism and Deconstruction*, Johns Hopkins University Press, Baltimore.

Sackville, R. (1975), *Law and Poverty in Australia: Report No 2*, Commission of Inquiry into Poverty, AGPS, Canberra.

Salisbury, R. (1979), "Why No Corporatism in America?" in P. Schmitter and G. Lehmbruch eds., *Trends Toward Corporatist Inter-Mediation*, Sage, London, 213-30.

Sandberg, D. (1994), "The Pirate Privateers", *New Internationalist* 14-15.

Sander, F., Allen, W. and Hensler, D. (1996) "Judicial (Mis)Use of ADR?", 27 *University of Toledo Law Journal* 885-920.

Santos, B. (1987), "Law: A Map of Misreading. Toward a Postmodern Conception of Law", 14 *Journal of Law and Society* 279-302.

Santos, B. (1995), *Toward a New Common Sense: Law, Science and Politics in the Paradigmatic Transition*, Routledge, New York.

Sassen, S. (1996), *Losing Control?: Sovereignty in an Age of Globalization*, Columbia University Press, New York.

Sassen, S. (1998), *Globalization and Its Discontents*, Columbia University Press, New York.

Saunders, C. (1995), "Articles of Faith or Lucky Breaks?" 17 *Sydney Law Review* 150-76.

Saussure, F. (1966), *Course in General Linguistics*, Philosophy Library, New York.

Schachter, O. (1997), "The Decline of the Nation State and its Implications for International Law", 36 *Columbia Journal of Transnational Law* 7-23.

Scheuerman, W. (1999), "Globalization and the Rule of Law", 6 *Constellations* 3-25.

Scheuerman, W. (2001), "Global law in Our High Speed Economy", in R. Appelbaum, V. Gessner and W. Felstiner eds., *Rules and Networks: The Legal Culture of Global Business Transactions*, Hart, Oxford, 103-21.

Schlag, P. (1990), "Normative and Nowhere to Go", 43 *Stanford Law Review* 167-91.

Schlag, P. (1996), "Normativity and the Politics of Form" in P. Campos, P. Schlag and S. Smith, *Against the Law*, Duke University Press, Durham, NC, 29-99.

Schmitter, P. (1974), "Still the Century of Corporatism?", 36 *Review of Politics* 85-131.

Schmitter, P. and Lehmbruch, G., eds. (1979), *Trends Towards Corporatist Inter-Mediation*, Sage, London.

Scott, C. (1999), "Regulation Inside Government: Rebadging the Citizen's Charter", *Public Law* 595-603.

Selznick, P. (1969), *Law, Society and Industrial Justice*, Transaction Books, New York.

Selznick, P. (1998), "The Communitarian Persuasion" in E. Christodoulidis ed., *Communitarianism and Citizenship*, Ashgate, Aldershot, 15-29.

Sennett, R. (1978), *The Fall of Public Man*, Vintage Books, New York.

Shames, M. (1998), "Preserving Consumer Protection and Education in a Deregulated Electric Services World: Challenges for the Postmodern Regulator" in M. Hossain and J. Malbon eds., *Who Benefits from Privatization?*, Routledge, London, 119-56.

Shklar, J. (1964), *Legalism: An Essay on Law, Morality and Politics*, Harvard University Press, Cambridge, Mass.

Silbey, S. and Sarat, A. (1989), "Dispute Processing in Law and Legal Scholarship: From Institutional Critique to the Reconstruction of the Juridical Subject", 66 *Denver Law Review* 437-98.

Simitis, S. (1994), "The Rediscovery of the Individual in Labour Law" in R. Ragowski and G. Teubner eds., *Reflexive Labour Law: Studies in Industrial Relations and Employment Regulation*, Kluwer, Deventer, 183-205.

Slaughter, A-M. (1997), "The Real New World Order", 76 *Foreign Affairs* 183-98.

Slaughter, A-M. (2000), "Judicial Globalization", 40 *Virginia Journal of International Law* 1103-24.

Smart, B. (1992), *Modern Conditions, Postmodern Controversies*, Routledge, London.

Smart, B. (1993), *Postmodernity*, Routledge, London.

Smart, C. (1991), "Feminist Jurisprudence", in P. Fitzpatrick ed., *Dangerous Supplements*, Pluto, London, 133-58.

Smart, C. (1993), "Proscription, Prescription and the Desire for Certainty?: Feminist Theory in the Field of Law", 13 *Studies in Law, Politics and Society* 37-54.

Smith A. and Webster F., eds. (1997), *The Postmodern University?: Contested Visions of Higher Education in Society*, Open University Press, Buckingham.

Smith, R. (1996), "Legal Aid on an Ebbing Tide", 23 *Journal of Law and Society* 570-79.

Snyder, F. (1999), "Governing Economic Globalization: Global Legal Pluralism and European Law", 5 *European Law Review* 334-74.

Solum, L. (1993), "Alternative Court Structures in the Future of the Californian Judiciary: 2020 Vision", 66 *Southern California Law Review* 2121-82.

Sontag, S. (1966), *Against Interpretation*, Dell, New York.

Stacy, H. (2001), *Postmodernism and Law*, Ashgate, Aldershot.

Starkey, D. (1995), "Diana plays Beauty to the Post-modern Beast", *The Australian*, 22 November.

Starr, P. (1988), "The Meaning of Privatization", 6 *Yale Law and Policy Review* 6-41.

Steiner, H. (1987), *Moral Argument and Social Vision in the Courts*, University of Wisconsin Press, Madison.

Steiner, H. (1991), "The Youth of Rights", 104 *Harvard Law Review* 917-35.

Steiner, H. and Alston, P. (2000), *Human Rights in Context: Law, Politics, Morals*, 2nd ed., Oxford University Press, Oxford.

Steiner, P. (1983), "The Legalization of American Society: Economic Regulation", 81 *Michigan Law Review* 1285-1306.

Stone, K. (1996), "Mandatory Arbitration of Individual Employment Rights: The Yellow Dog Contract of the 1990s", 73 *Denver University Law Review* 1017-50.

Strang, H., and Braithwaite, J., eds. (2001), *Restorative Justice and Civil Society*, Cambridge University Press, Port Melbourne.

Strange, S. (1996), *Retreat of the State*, Cambridge University Press, Cambridge.

Streeck, W. (1996), "Neo-Voluntarism: A New European Social Policy Regime?" in G. Marks et al, *Governance in the European Union*, Sage, London, 64-94.

Sunstein, C. (1989), "Interpreting Statutes in the Regulatory State", 103 *Harvard Law Review* 405-508.

Sunstein, C. (1990), *After the Rights Revolution*, Harvard University Press, Cambridge.

Swann, D. (1988), *The Retreat of the State: De-Regulation and Privatization in the United Kingdom and United States*, Harvester, London.

Taggart, M. (1991), "Corporatization, Privatization and Public Law", 2 *Public Law Review* 77-108.

Taggart, M. (1997), "The Province of Administrative Law Determined?" in M. Taggart ed., *The Province of Administrative Law*, Hart, Oxford, 1-20.

Taylor, B. (1988), *Modernism, Postmodernism, Realism*, Winchester School of Art Press, Hampshire.

Taylor, C. (1984), "Foucault on Freedom and Truth", 12 *Political Theory* 152-83.

Taylor, C. and Gutman, A., eds. (1992), *Multiculturalism and "The Politics of Recognition"*, Princeton University Press, Princeton.

Teubner, G. (1983), "Substantive and Reflexive Elements in Modern Law", 17 *Law and Society Review* 239-85.

Teubner, G. (1984), "After Legal Instrumentalism: Strategic Models of Post-regulatory Law", 12 *International Journal of the Sociology of Law* 375-400.

Teubner, G., ed. (1986), *Dilemmas of Law in the Welfare State*, de Gruyter, Berlin.

Teubner, G., ed. (1987), *Juridification of Social Spheres*, de Gruyter, Berlin.

Teubner, G., ed. (1988), *Autopoietic Law: A New Approach to Law and Society*, de Gruyter, Berlin.
Teubner, G. (1993), *Law as an Autopoietic System*, Blackwell, Oxford.
Teubner, G., ed. (1997), *Global Bukowina: Lex Mercatoria*, Ashgate, Aldershot.
Therborn, G. (1987), "Welfare States and Capitalist Markets", 30 *Acta Sociologica* 237-54.
Touraine, A. (1985), "An Introduction to the Study of New Social Movements", 52 *Social Research* 749-87.
Touraine, A. (1989), "Is Sociology Still the Study of Society?", 23 *Thesis Eleven* 5-34.
Toynbee, A. (1963), *A Study of History, Vol. VIII*, Oxford University Press, Oxford.
Trubek, D., Dezalay, Y., Buchanan, R. and Davis, J. (1994), "Global Restructuring and the Law: Studies in the Internationalization of Legal Fields and the Creation of Transnational Arenas", 44 *Case Western Reserve Law Review* 407-99.
Twining, W. (2000), *Globalization and Legal Theory*, Butterworths, London.
Umbreit, M. (1994), *Victim Meets Offender: The Impact of Restorative Justice and Mediation*, Criminal Justice Press, New York.
Unger, R. (1976), *Law in Modern Society*, Free Press, New York.
Unger, R. (1987), *Social Theory: Its Situation and Its Task*, Cambridge University Press, New York.
United Nations (1985), *General Assembly, Consumer Protection*, Res. No. 39/248, 9 April.
Vincent-Jones, P. (1998), "Responsive Law and Governance in Public Services Provision: A Future for the Local Contracting State", 61 *Modern Law Review* 362-81.
Vincent-Jones, P. (2000), "Contractual Governance: Insitutional and Organizational Analysis", 20 *Oxford Journal of Legal Studies* 317-51.
Waaldijk, K. (2000), "Civil Developments: Patterns of Reform in the Legal Position of Same-Sex Partners in Europe", 17 *Revue Canadienne de Droit Familial* 62-88.
Wagner, P. (1994), *A Sociology of Modernity: Freedom and Discipline*, Routledge, London.
Wald, P. (1997), "ADR and the Courts: An Update", 46 *Duke Law Journal* 1445-73.
Walker, G. (1988), *The Rule of Law: Foundation of Constitutional Democracy*, Melbourne University Press, Melbourne.
Walzer, M. (1986), "The Politics of Michel Foucault", in D. Hoy ed., *Foucault: A Critical Reader*, Blackwell, Oxford, 51-68
Ward, I. (1996), *A Critical Introduction to European Law*, Butterworths, London.
Weber, M. (1978 (orig. 1921)), *Economy and Society*, University of California Press, Berkeley.
Wedderburn, Lord, Rood, M., Lyon-Caen, G., Däubler, W. and Van der Heijden, P. (1994), *Labour Law in the Post-Industrial Era: Essays in Honour of Hugo Sinzheimer*, Dartmouth, Aldershot.
Weiler, J. (2000), "Cain and Abel - Convergence and Divergence in International Trade Law" in J. Weiler ed., *The EU, the WTO and the NAFTA: Towards a Common Law of International Trade*, Oxford University Press, Oxford.
Wiener, J. (1999), *Globalization and the Harmonization of Law*, Pinter, London.
Wilhelmsson, T. (1994), "The Philosophy of Welfarism and its Emergence in the Modern Scandinavian Contract Law" in R. Brownsword, G. Howells and T. Wilhelmsson eds, *Welfarism in Contract Law*, Dartmouth, Aldershot, 63-96.
Wilhelmsson, T. (1995), "Legal Integration as the Disintegration of National Law" in H. Petersen, and H. Zahle eds., *Legal Polycentricity*, Dartmouth, Aldershot, 127-47.
Williams, R. (1976), *Keywords*, Fontana, London.

Willke, H. (1986), "Three Types of Legal Structure: The Conditional, the Purposive and the Relational Program", in G. Teubner ed., *Dilemmas of Law in the Welfare State*, de Gruyter, Berlin, 280-98.

Wilson, M. (1997), "The Role of the State in the Regulation of Employment Relations: The New Zealand Experience", 2 *Flinders Journal of Law Reform* 131-46.

Wittgenstein, L. (1958), *Philosophical Investigations*, Blackwell, Oxford.

Woodman, G. (1991), "The Alternative Law of Alternative Dispute Resolution", 32 *Les Cahiers de Droit* 3-31.

Woolf, Lord (1999), "Preface" in H. Genn, *Mediation in Action: Resolving Court Disputes Without Trial*, Calouste Gulbenkian Foundation, London.

Wyvekyns, A. and Faget, J., eds. (2001), *La Justice de Proximité en Europe: Pratiques et Enjeux*, Éditions Érès, Ramonville Saint-Agne.

Yeatman, A. (1995), "Interpreting Contemporary Contractualism" in J. Boston ed., *The State Under Contract*, Bridget Williams Books, Wellington.

Zander, M. (2000), *The State of Justice*, Sweet and Maxwell, London.

Zehr, H. (1990), *Changing Lenses: A New Focus on Criminal Justice*, Herald, Scottsdale, Pa.

Zuckerman, A., ed. (1999), *Civil Justice in Crisis: Comparative Pespectives of Civil Procedure*, Oxford University Press, Oxford.

Index

abstentionism, 237, 255
access to justice
postmodernization, 134, 147, 161, 164–7, 171–6, 204n.16
welfare state, 82, **94–96**
Adams, J., 83
administrative law, 81, 84–5, 92, 96, 140, 142, 250–1
aesthetic postmodernism, 18, 22–3, 44, 241–3, 261
Alston, P., 177
alterity, 226, 229, 244, 260–1, 262n.1
alternative dispute resolution (ADR), 96, 160–73, 175, 204n.17, 204n.18, 204n.20, 251–2, 267
anti-discrimination laws, 83, 150, 153
Aronson, M., 138, 140, 142
artificial reason, 70, 93, 94, 100, 103, 164, 186, 236
Atiyah, P., 83-4, 87, 137, 143, 150, 204n10
autonomy of law. *See* legal autonomy
autopoiesis, 13, 164
decline of welfare state, **117–23**

Banakar, R., 191–2, 269
Barron, A., 62n.5, 141
Bartholomew, A., 278
Bauman, Z., 3, 7, 9, 10, 13, 35, 47, 48–51, 60, 63n.10, 69. 70. 78, 99, 105, 106, 118, 143, 151, 159, 211, 263, 272
Benhabib, S., 234–6
Blankenburg, E., 66, 166, 174, 175, 204n.17, 205n.24
Braithwaite, J., 111, 152–5, 170, 178, 180, 181, 185, 194, 198, 201, 204n.14, 205n.25, 253, 266, 268, 270–1
Brownsword, R., 83, 181
Buckley, F., 143, 149
bureaucratic societies, 21–2, 53, 72, 75, 78, 91, 108, 113, 116

Campbell, D., 140
capitalist disorganization, 10, 53, 61, 119
postmodernity and, **39–47,** 58, 138, 148, 200
Cappelletti, M., 95, 96, 160–3, 166, 170, 204n.23
Carney, T., 156–9
Carrington, K., 223
Chesterman, M., 221
Chinkin, C., 161–5, 178, 204n.20
citizenship, 137, 141, 159, 174, 184, 192–7, 203n.5, 223. *See also* social citizenship
paradigms of law, 200
civil rights, 72–4, 81, 83, 89, 195–7, 211–12
class
composition, 13
economic reorganization and, 40, 59, 79
late modernity and postmodernity compared, 61
postmodernization, 119, 159
welfare state, 74–5, 79, 90, 104, 113
cognitive mapping, **18–63**, 62n.2
collectivism, 88, 146–8, 159, 185, 194, 196, 203n.8, 205n.28
command and control, 140, **152–5**, 200
common law jurisdictions, 186, 188, 204n.22, 205n.29
communications, 107, 113, 178–9, 196, 224, 235
communism, 128, 230, 233–4. *See also* post-communist states
communitarianism, 107, 179
community, 23, 52, 59, 138, 155, 161, 164–5, 169, 170, 178, 184, 189, 230–1, 251, 256–60, 266

competition policy, 136–8, 160, 172–3, 178, 204n.13
complexity, 124, 126, 163, 187, 200, 201
conditional program, 123
conditionalization of welfare provision, 156-9
constitutional principles, 85, 86, 123, 168, 185–6, 188, 197, 210, 212, 219–20, 230–1
 cross-fertilization, 188
consumer law, 83, 114, 118, 119, 136–40, 149, 154, 173, 181, 200, 203n.9
contracting state, 3, 13–15, 17n.1, 54, 57, 61, 125, 143–4, 178, 200, 204n.14
contracts
 legal postmodernization, 146–52, 156, 201, 203n.9, 223, 239
 welfare rights, **155–60**
contractual freedom, 82–4, 93–4, 100, 109, 110, 136, 143, 149, 192, 203n.8
contractualization, 145, 147, 149–51, 156 *See also* welfare rights
co-regulation, 154, 181, 200
Cornell, D., 247, 261
corporatism, 40–2, 54, 61, 63n.8, 103–4, 131n.1, 195
 welfare state, 89, 137, 147–8
corporatization, 138, 203n.4
Cotterrell, R., 97, 189
criminal law, 150, 155, 170, 174, 185, 204n.14, 210, 212
Critical Legal Studies (CLS) movement, 255, 257
critical theory, 119, 129, 206, 212, 214, 217, 239
Crook, S., 10, 13, 35, 52–4, 56–8, 61, 79, 155, 176
cultural theorizing, 16, 30, 23–39, 49–51, 113, 115, 129, 224, 229, 231, 234, 239–41
 postmodernism, 18, **19–34**, 203
customary law, 102, 120, 125, 200
Czarnota, A., 198

Davies, M., 4, 247, 249–50, 262n.1
decentralization, 13, 152, 155, 200
deconstruction, 17n.4, 27–9, **223–233**
 legal postmodernism, 252, 261, 262n.1
de-differentiation, 53, 61, 164, 200
dematerialization, 139, 145, 148–9, 200
democratic state, 213, 230
Derrida, J., 26–9, 223–233
diversionary strategies, 160–1, 170, 172, 175
Douzinas, C, 240–8
Drahos, P., 178, 180–1, 185, 194, 198, 201, 205n.25, 253, 266, 268, 270–1
Dworkin, R., 163, 167, 189, 198, 241, 257, 261, 264, 266

Eagleton, T., 6, 26, 28, 249
Enlightenment, 20–4, 29, 51, 68, 87, 241, 247
environmental regulation, 153, 212
epistemology, 216–17, 257, 261
equality and inequality
 Foucault, 219
 legal postmodernism, 261
 legal postmodernization, 133–4, 166–7, 184, 192, 196
 Lyotard, 236
 welfare state, 44, 52, 56–7, 82–3, 90, 94–5, 100–3, 109, 112, 114
ethics, 47–8, 51, 115, 184
 Derrida, 226, 228–9
 Foucault, 216, 217
 legal postmodernism, 241, 244, 251–2, 258, 261
 Lyotard, 235, 237
European welfare states, 76–7
evolutionary approaches, 66, 108, 111, 20, 124, 120, 124, 202
Ewald, F., 60, 111–2, 169, 184, 221

Faget, J., 169
fairness, 140, 142, 145, 149, 228, 242–3
family law, 86–8, 113–14, 150–1, 169, 201
Feldman, S., 17, 262, 272
Fish, S., 247, 256–60
Fitzpatrick, P., 250–3
Foucault, M., 29–34, 65, 207–223
Fraser, N., 16, 66, 94, 231-2, 235, 261–2

freedom, 19–20, 29–32, 34, 50,–2, 112, 113–14, 141, 151–2, 188, 193, 196 *See also* utopia
freedom of contract. *See* contractual freedom
Freeman, J., 17, 57, 135, 142–4
Friedman, L., 64, 74, 78, 81, 91, 96, 106, 150, 165, 176
Friedmann, W., 77, 89, 100–02, 108–10, 135, 142–3, 202
Frug, M., 260
functional differentiation, 67, 79, 108, 118, 119, 125, 200 *See also* organized differentiation
functionalism, 53

Galanter, M., 71, 92, 95, 162, 164, 167, 171
Garland, D., 168, 218–22
Genn, H., 161–6, 174, 204n.17
Giddens, A., 8, 17, 47, 60, 79, 210, 215
Glendon, A., 87–8, 94–5, 148, 150–1
globalization
  legal postmodernism, 12–13, 253
  legal postmodernization, 177, 180, 183, 186–8, 192, 196
  markets, 116, 119
  postmodernity, 9, 41–4, 47–8, 55
  rule of law, **197–9**, 202
  welfare state, 77, 98, 105
globalized legal hermeneutics, **185–90**
glocalization, 201, 267
Goodrich, P., 240–3, 248
governance, 64, 67, 88–9, 218–20, 222
governmentality, 66, 217–23, 250
Graham, C., 135, 137–8, 140–1, 144, 201
Gray, K., 96, 150, 174

Habermas, J., 235
  crisis of capitalism, 49
  on Foucault, 212–13, 216, 217
  legal paradigms, 1–2, 16, 66, 96, 132n.12, 200
  legal postmodernism, 256
  legal postmodernization, 73, 158, 160, 200, 266
  periodization, 72–3, 97n.3
  on postmodernism, 4, 52, 62
  on welfare state, 65, 112–116, 117, 120–1, 131n.4, 132n.12, 144, 155, 176
Hancher, L., 178
Harden, I., 17n.1, 57, 140–3
harmonization of rules, 110, 119, 180–1
Hart, H., 87–8, 184, 189, 211–12, 261, 264–5
Harvey, D., 2, 10, 13, 35, 44–7, 50, 53, 60–2, 94, 189
Hayek, F., 78, 101, 123
Hebdige, D., 4, 6, 18, 38, 207, 234
hermeneutics, 215, 228, 259 *See also* globalized legal hermeneutics
Hillyard, P., 262
Hogg, R., 223
human rights, **182–5**, 265–7, 276,
Hunt, A., 17, 211, 220, 222, 278

identity politics, 150, 260
indigenous rights, 151, 171, 184–5, 194, 220, 236, 246
individualism, 52, 58, 67, 71, 83, 87–8, 97, 146–9, 193, 195
industrialization, 67, 78, 106
informal justice, 96, 109, 111, 114, 127, **160–72, 190–2,** 198, 204n.19, 251. *See also* alternative dispute resolution; justice of proximity; legal subjects; privatization of justice
Inglehart, R., 13, 35, 58, 107, 116, 166, 168

Jencks, C., 21–3, 62, 63
juridification
  colonisation of lifeworld, **112–16**
  decline of welfare state, **116–130**
  social spheres, 82, 91
  waves of, 73, 155, 160, 172
jurisprudence, 221, 230, 240–1, 255, 264–8
justice
  Derridean deconstruction, 226–233, 251–2, 259–62
  legal postmodernism, 241–4
  Lyotard on, 37, 234–8
  official mechanisms of, 223

paradigms of law, 200
pyramid, 162
states of, 209
justice of proximity, **169–72**

Keynesian strategies, 41, 42, 44, 47, 89, 181
Kinley, D., 183, 186
Kirby, M., 199
knowledge, 22, 24, 27, 29–39, 49, 50–1, 67, 71, 78, 82, 216, 219, 224–5, 227, 236, 238
Krygier, M., 131, 198

Lacey, N., 278
Ladeur, K., 128–9
laissez-faire polity, 76, 102, 149
language, 24–9, 36–8, 224–6, 235–8, 254
Lash, S., 10, 35, 39–47, 49, 61, 62n.1, 63n.8, 63n.9, 78, 101, 119, 170
late legal modernization (in welfare state), **80–96**, 124
late modernity, 3, 60–2, 65, 78, 124, 200
law. *See also* modern law; reflexive law
approaches to, 240
Derridean deconstruction, 223, 226–33
Foucault's analysis, 208–23
Lyotard and, 236–9
paradigmatic transition, 56, 60, **128–30**
postmodern perspectives on, 2, 10
structural, systemic and doctrinal change in, 2, 7
legal aid, 95–6, 166, 173, **174–6**, 204n.22
legal autonomy, 70–2, 80, 100, 103, 108, 109, 127, 163–5, 172, 179, 188, 191–2, 197–8, 230, 243, 254, 259
legal-bureaucratic model of welfare provision, 157
legal change, **1–17**, 65–7, 69–72, 80–4, 86–7, 94–5, 102, 128–30, 136, 255–6
global, 117, 119, 126–8, 130
legal postmodernism, 253, 255
postmodernity and, **9–10**, 20, 35, 43–4, 47, 58, 104, 107, 120
postmodernization, 134, 136, 138, 167, 201, 206–7, 245
welfare state, 80–2, 90, 100–2, 109–11
legal modernization. *See* late legal modernization
legal paradigms, 16, 111, 114–16, 128–30, 153–4, 170, 178, 200
legal pluralism, 14, 74, 96, 117, 122, 127, 165, 171, 200, 202, 204n.19
postmodern, 235, 248
legal positivism, 200, 216, 221, 244, 264–6
legal postmodernism, 16, **240–60**
absence of the social, **10–12**
legal postmodernization, 59, 96, **133–205**. *See also* contracts; legal aid; privatization; welfare rights
legal professions, 70–1, 108, 161, 164, 172–3, 188, 203n.3, 256
legal realism, 97, 200, 209
legal reform, 161–3, 167–9, 172–3, 175
legal postmodernism, 250, 252–3, 255
legal postmodernization, 134, 146, 152, 156, 160, 172–5, 180–2
legal sociology, **12–15**, 82, 93–4, 97, 98, 106–7, 268–73
legal subjects, 73, 83, 94, 101, 103, 111–12, 137, 167, 170, 176–7, 192–4, 197, 214–15, 243, 250–2
from rights-bearing to interests-bearing, **167–9**
legal postmodernism, 246
paradigms of law, 200
legal systems, 68–9, 89, 93, 110–11, 121, 160, 163, 173, 213, 219, 222, 229–32, 242–3, 254
legal postmodernism, 255–6
overload, 161
paradigms, 154, 200
legal temporality, 148, 158, 170, 189–90, 195, 200
legitimacy, 168, 171, 183, 191, 205n.31, 231, 234, 246, 252, 261–2
legitimation, 117, 119, 208, 215–6, 230, 236, 254
lex mercatoria, 14, 126–7, 130, 177, 190–2, 198

liberalism, 5, 19, 33, 71, 142, 150, 173, 197, 200, 234, 238, 260. *See also* neo-liberalism
legal postmodernism, 235, 238
lifeworld, juridification and colonization of, **112–16,** 131n.4
logocentrism, 226, 232–3
logonomocentrism, 241
Luhmann, N., 66, 70, 73, 82, 132n.12, 185, 206, 252
Lyotard, J-F., 5–6, 16, 23–4, 35–9, 65, 107, 123, 168, 233–9

MacCormick, N., 15, 106, 176–9, 193, 265
Macpherson, C., 150
Majone, G., 81, 97n.2, 203n.6
Malbon. J., 136–7
managerialism, 114, 163, 200, 204n.15
mapping. *See* cognitive mapping
marginalization of law, 219, 223, 251
market orientation
law of welfare state, 104, 115, 119
legal postmodernization, 136, 142, 147–8, 153–5, 158–9, 175, 181–2, 185, 191, 198, 200, 202, 203n.5
Marshall, T., 71–3, 81, 86, 91, 95, 141, 159, 174, 192, 196, 200
Martin, G., 185, 205n.28
Marxism, 32–4, 45, 212, 214, 241, 243, 253
materialization of formal law, 84, 114, 118, 149–50
metanarratives, 36–8, 233–4, 236, 238–9
Mills, C., 4, 17, 19–20, 23–4, 29, 239
miscarriages of justice, 241–3
mixed economy, and rule of law, **100–2**
modern, 3–4, 6, 12, 16, 21–3, 64–5, 125, 210, 233–4, 238, 261
modern age, 19, 29–32, 50, 129, 213
modern institutions, 209, 210, 215
modern law, 3, **68-75**, 109, 111, 112, 132n.13, 160, 164–8, 171, 176, 185, 189, 192–4, 201, 207, 209, 211–12, 215, 219, 251, 255–6
and legal postmodernism, 242–3, 245, 246, 250
paradigm, 200, 204n.19
reconfiguration of spatial and temporal co-ordinates, 73, 82, **91–4**
welfare state and, **64–97**
modern societies, 3, 6, 9, 31, 67-8, 99, 106–9, 112, 119, 132n.13, 208–10, 212–15, 218, 238, 251
modern sociology, 13–14
modernism, 6–7, 15, 20, 22, 240
modernity. *See also* late modernity
and Foucault, 210, 216
legal and social change, 1–2, 5–7, 8, 13, 253
legal postmodernity, 159, 165, 200, 252
and postmodernity, 20, 29–30, 32, 34, 49, 52, 54–5
welfare state, 64–5, 79, 92, 94, 96, 108, 124
modernization, 52, 53, 58, 61, 67–8, 72, 77–80, 88–9, 96, 101, 107–8. *See also* late legal modernization; *See under* welfare state
definition, 6–7
Moles, R., 212
monocentric tendencies, 69, 78, 80, 91, 95, 107, 110, 176, 200
Mooney, R., 83, 149, 203n.1, 204n.10
Moran, M., 135, 152–3, 178, 219
multinational corporations (MNCs), 54, 127, 134, 177, 193, 196, 198–9

Nader, L., 161, 167, 170, 204n.16
nation state, 9, 48, 50, 53–5, 59, 67–9, 73–4, 78, 106, 108, 264
consolidation, 91–2
decline, 3, 10, 12, 14–15, 99, 122, 126–8, 136
law, 69, 91, 169, 200
legal postmodernism, 252–3, 246–7, 251
postmodernization, 176–7, 180, 183, 192–4, 196
nationalization
postmodernization, 137–8, 144
welfare state, 77–9, 84, 92, 101, 200
natural law, 125, 190, 200, 244

neo-evolutionist theories, 12–15, 116–7, 127
neo-liberalism, 62, 115–6, 121, 136, 139, 151, 182, 218, 235
new contract, 144, 150
new property, 85–7, 94, 144, 150
new regulatory state, 155
NGOs. *See* non-government organizations
Nielsen, J., 185, 205n.28
Nonet, P., 13, 66, 93, 97, 108–11, 115, 117, 120, 131n.6, 143–4, 148, 169, 186, 189, 274–6
non-government organizations, 54, 177, 180, 182–3, 193–4, 246
Nussbaum, M., 258, 262n.8

occupational bonding, 148
Offe, C., 39, 43, 49, 52, 63n.10, 72, 78, 81, 119, 123, 162, 169, 176
O'Malley, P., 155, 222
organized capitalism, 35, 39–40, 61–2, 88–9, 101, 114–15, 119, 158
organized differentiation, 79, 124–5, 200
outsourcing, 43, 45, 61, 140, 142

Pakulski, J., 10, 13, 35, 52–4, 57–8, 176
paradigms of law, 17n.1, 111, 114–16, **128–30**, 153–4, 170, 178, 200. *See also* postmodern legal paradigm
Parker, C., 95–6, 116, 161, 172–3, 205n.21, 275
participation
  in international forums, 177, 193–4
  in labour market, 156, 159
  in legal system, 109, 140, 170, 176–8, 192–4, 196–7
performativity, 168, 169, 238–9
permeable domestic law, **176–199**
Picciotto, S., 198, 271
Pierson, C., 57, 64, 76–7, 156
pluralism, 51, 74, 96, 127, 148, 165, 194, 195, 235–6, 241, 252. *See also* legal pluralism
politics of recognition, 59, 61, 105, 235, 241, 260
politics of redistribution. *See* redistribution
polycentricity, 107, 126, 176, 185, 200
positive law, 72, 74, 80, 82, 104, 125, 185–6
positivism, 5, 127, 200, 221, 222, 227. *See also* legal positivism
Post, R., 11–12, 14, 201, 271
post-communist states, 1, 188, 230
post-Fordist production, 13, 35, 41, 45, 110, 119, 128, 146, 148, 157, 166
postliberal society, 13–14, 98, 103, 106–7, 143
  responsive law, **108–12**
  rule of law, 101, **102–8**
postmaterialist values, 58, 107, 116
postmodern, 1–4, 6–7, 11, 18–19, 35, 62, 65, 115, 121, 238
postmodern legal paradigm, 14–15, 115, 125, 153–4, 200
postmodern legal theory, 128, **240–62**
postmodern societies, 101, 119, 168, 170
postmodern theory, **8–9**, **60**
  meaning of concept, 5, **6–8**, 9–12, 18, 207, 233
  origins as historical and cultural category, **19–23**
  poststructuralism as, 28–31, 34, 63n.6
  problems of, **15–17**
  sensibilities and legal understanding, **207–39**
  sensibilities and societies, **35–59**
postmodernity. *See also* capitalist disorganization
  capitalist disorganization, 39, 44, 46
  late modernity compared, 61
  legal postmodernism, 223, 246–7, 260–1, 263
  legal postmodernization, 125–6, 130, 143, 132n.13, 165, 264
  legal sociology, 13, 16–17
  meaning of concept, **6–8**, 19, 35, 38
  poststructuralism and, 33–4
  problem of meaning, **4–6**
  sociology, 47–60, 63n.10
  welfare state, 65–6, 107–8, 125
postmodernization, 16, 52–3, 58–62, 63, 96, 98, 107, 116, 119, 146, 151, 155, 167, 200, 204n.24, 207, 234, 251 *See also* paradigms of

law; reflexive law; relational programs
decline of welfare state, **116–30,** 12, 18–19, 35
meaning of concept, **6–8**, 10, 12, 18–19, 35
postnational constellation, 62, 116, 202
poststructuralism, 8, 36, 60, 62n.5, 63n.6, 127, 223, 260, 262n.1
post-welfare state, 1, 13, 98
legal paradigm, 8, 15, 116, 132n.12
premodernity, 107, 169, 200, 211, 234
private law
deregulation, 134, 139, **145–60,** 173
legal postmodernism, 244
postmodernization, 143, 145, 150, 182, 191, 201
reform in welfare state, **82–8**, 89, 92, 94, 103–4, 109
private property. *See* property law
privatization, 54, 56–7, 101, **134–45**, 165, 181, 200, 203n.2, 203n 4, 204n.12, 218–19
privatization of justice, 137–40, 158, 161, 165–6, 169–70
procedural justice, 81, 103–4, 114–18, 147, 149
proceduralization, 128, 132n8
property law, 81, 85–6, 89, 94, 100, 109, 110, 114, 135, 150, 182, 196. *See also* new property
Prosser, T., 89, 135, 137–9, 144, 219
proximity. *See* justice of proximity
public interest, 135, 137, 141–5, 198, 254
public interest law, 95, 104, 136, 143, 161, 168
public interest state, 85, 142–3, 186
public ownership, 135–7, 203n.4
public/private distinction, 71, 84, 87–8, 90, 95, 101, 103–4, 131n.4, 141
purposive program, 123–4, 132n.12, 168, 190, 212

redistribution
legal postmodernism, 241
paradigms of law, 200
politics of, 89, 95, 260
postmodern societies, 104
postmodernization, 137–8, 147, 192, 195–6
welfare state, 79, 90, 92, 103, 114, 137, 276
reflexive law, 13, 14, **117–23**, 148, 192
reform. *See* legal reform
regulation
international, 179, 180–2, 185, 194, 196, 198
modern law, 204n.19
postmodernization, 134–9, 143, 149, 152–5, 178, 201, 203n.6
welfare state, 100–1, 109–13, 212
regulatory law, 98–101, 105, 113, 118–21, 131n.1
Reich, C., 56, 65, 85–6, 135, 144, 149–50, 157
relational programs, **123–6**
relativism, 8, 12, 37, 51, 217, 257, 260–1
responsive law
postliberal society, **108–12**, 115, 117, 168–9
postmodernization, 144–5, 155, 173, 199, 274–6
restorative justice, 155, 170
rights, 84–6, 71–4, 81, 89–93, 112, 114, 136-8, 141, 144, 146, 148–50, 154, 157, 159, 167, 182–5, 192, 196, 237, 242. *See also* human rights; welfare rights
Foucault on, 210, 212–15, 222,
legal postmodernism, 244–7, 261
Lyotard, 237
rights-bearing legal subjects, **167–9**
Rose, N., 220–2
Rose-Ackerman, S., 153–4, 204n.12, 251
rule of law, 243
globalization, 188, **197–9**
legal postmodernism, 250–1, 254, 256
mixed economy, **100–2**
postliberal society, 98, **102–7**
postmodernization, 166, 168, 171

Santos, B., 14, 17, 54, 65, 128–30, 165, 177, 185, 195, 201, 205n.20, 267
Schlag, P., 253–6

science, 28–30, 36–8, 68, 70, 207, 216
legal postmodernism, 240, 250
Lyotard on, 234
Scott, C., 141, 203
secularization of law, 68, 88, 126
self-regulation, 81, 121, 154
Selznick, P., 13, 66, 93, 97, 104, 108–11, 117, 120, 131n.6, 143–4, 148, 169, 186, 189, 273–6, 278
Slaughter, A-M., 181, 183, 186, 188–9, 195, 198, 205n.30, 272
Smart, B., 18, 24, 108
Smart, C., 260
social change, **1–17**, 18, 39, 49, 51–2, 56–60, 62
social citizenship, 86–91, 95, 141, 144, 159, 174, 184, 195, 196, 200, 203n.5
social-democratic consensus, 97
social law, 98, 104, 107, 111, 137, 169, 171, 184, 191, 195, 200, 211–13, 221–2, 239
welfare state, 91–2, 97
sovereignty, 14–15, 55–6, 61, 67, 69–70, 74, 80, 91–3, 106, 140, 176–7, 182–6, 192–7, 200. *See also* human rights
sharing and pooling, **177–82**
Starr, P., 71, 139, 142, 145, 203n.2
Stacy, H., 17, 262, 272
stratificatory differentiation, 125, 200
structuralism, **24–6**, 27–9, 32–3, 37
subjects, 33, 209–15, 218, 223, 243, 250–2. *See also* legal subjects
substantive justice, 81, 103, 104, 107, 112, 141, 145, 149, 192, 200
substantive legal rationality, 117–18, 200
supranational citizenship, 193, 202, 247, 252

Taggart, M., 135, 138, 140, 142–3
Teubner, G., 12–14, 81, 82, 91, 98, 117–23, 126–7, 148, 162, 164, 192
time/space compression (welfare state), **79–80,** 94
totality
rejection of, 207–9, 214, 233, 238, 240–1
transnational law, 105, 126–7, 130, 178, 191, 230
truth, 209, 216–7, 225, 234, 240
legal postmodernism, 256–8, 260
Twining, W., 264, 266, 274–7

Unger, R., 13, 60, 70, 98, 102–8, 131n.1, 143, 190, 199, 202, 207
universal legal rights, 86, 90, 135, 136, 150, 159, 237, 247
Urry, J., 10, 35, 39–47, 61, 63n.8, 63n.9, 78, 101, 119, 170
utopia, rejection of, 207, 214, 226, 233, 240, 251, 253

Valverde, M., 220–1
Vincent-Jones, P., 140, 144, 204

Warrington, R., 241–3, 248
Waters, M., 10, 13, 35, 52–4, 57–8, 176
Watson, S., 262
Weber, M., 10, 21–2, 102, 165, 198, 215, 256, 2
welfare rights, 134, 156–8, 175–6, 195
contracting, **155–60**
welfare state, 40, 42–5, 51–7, 62, 75-7, 135, 137, 141, 144–5, 148–51, 156–9,
decline of, 2, 10, 12, **116–32**, 204n.16, 218, 260
law, 13–14, **80-97**, **99–116**, 135, 137, 140–50, 158, 171, 175–6, 182, 184, 190–2, 200–1
legal paradigms, 200
modern law and, **64–97**
modernization and, **77–80**
state apparatus, 64, **69–70,** 77, 82
structural change and law, 66–7, **80–2**
supranational developments, 173, 176–99
Willke, H., 66, 123–6, 128, 131
Wittgenstein, 36–7, 225

Zuckerman, A., 161, 163